Praise for *Adam Smith in Beijing*

"In this deeply learned, sharply argued, and fascinating book Giovanni Arrighi shows that the mandate of capitalist heaven is shifting to China, more generally to East Asia, but Americans won't like it. . . . Meanwhile Professor Arrighi offers a truly insightful analysis of the thought of a great political economist: Adam Smith. This is by far the best book to date in the rapidly growing literature on 'China's rise'."
Bruce Cumings, Professor in History and the College, University of Chicago

"Proceeding from a bracing re-reading of Smith and Marx, through a reconsideration of the 'Great Divergence' of East and West, to a blistering deconstruction of the Project for a New American Century, Arrighi dismisses neo-liberal interpretations of China's economic 'miracle' and credits instead China's own robust market economy tradition. In the process, he leads us on a breathtaking tour of the history of world capitalism over the past three hundred years, and suggests where we may be headed in the future."
William T. Rowe, Professor of Chinese History, Johns Hopkins University

"In this wonderfully provocative and wide-ranging book, Arrighi offers a fresh and challenging interpretation of China's economic ascent."
Gillian Hart, Professor of Geography, Berkeley, University of California

"The convincing power of Arrighi's argument lies in his choice to conceive geopolitics as the endless process of construction of political cultures associating class conflicts and collective commonwealth in different specific ways."
Samir Amin, Director of the Third World Forum

"An original, brilliant, always powerfully challenging analysis."
Wang Hui, Professor of Chinese Language and Literature at Tsinghua University, Beijing

"In the vast landscape of literature on China rising, Giovanni Arrighi's *Adam Smith in Beijing* stands out as a beacon of bold creativity and as pursuing a sustained trailblazing argument."
Göran Therborn, Professor of Social and Political Sciences, University of Cambridge

"With its iconoclastic vision, analytical rigor, and vast information, this book easily dwarfs the rest of the rapidly expanding literature on the subject . . . Arrighi's book is unquestionably a masterpiece on the evolution of the world capitalist system and the contemporary international relations."
Heterodox Economics

ADAM SMITH IN BEIJING

Lineages of the Twenty-First Century

GIOVANNI ARRIGHI

VERSO

London • New York

First published by Verso 2007
© Giovanni Arrighi 2007

This paperback edition first published by Verso 2008
© Giovanni Arrighi 2008

The moral rights of the author have been asserted

1 3 5 7 9 10 8 6 4 2

Verso
UK: 6 Meard Street, London W1F 0EG
USA: 20 Jay Street, Suite 1010, Brooklyn, NY 11201
www.versobooks.com

Verso is the imprint of New Left Books
ISBN 978-1-84467-298-1

British Library Cataloguing in Publication Data
A catalogue record for this book is available from the British Library

Library of Congress Cataloging-in-Publication Data
A catalog record for this book is available from the Library of Congress

Typeset in Sabon by Hewer Text UK Ltd, Edinburgh

Printed and bound in Great Britain by
Marston Book Services Ltd, Oxfordshire

To Andre Gunder Frank (1929–2005)

CONTENTS

LIST OF FIGURES

PREFACE AND ACKNOWLEDGMENTS

This book is a sequel and elaboration of two earlier works, *The Long Twentieth Century* and *Chaos and Governance in the Modern World System.*[1] It focuses on two developments that, more than any other, are shaping world politics, economy, and society. One is the rise and demise of the neo-conservative Project for a New American Century; the other is the emergence of China as the leader of the East Asian economic renaissance. Due attention will be paid to the many state and non-state actors that have contributed to these two developments, but the main focus of the analysis will be on the US and Chinese states as the key actors of the unfolding global transformation.

Friends, students, and colleagues who have read and commented on the manuscript before the final round of revisions have given unusually discrepant assessments of its components. Chapters that some readers enjoyed most, others enjoyed least. Chapters and sections that some readers thought central to the argument of the book, others found superfluous. Discrepancies in readers' reactions are normal but not to the extent that I have experienced with this book. I think that the anomaly can be traced to the double purpose of the book—hinted at in its title—and to the different methods deployed in its pursuit.

The purpose of the book is as much to offer an interpretation of the ongoing shift of the epicenter of the global political economy from North America to East Asia in light of Adam Smith's theory of economic development, as it is to offer an interpretation of *The Wealth of Nations* in light of that shift. This double purpose is pursued throughout the book, but some parts rely more heavily on

1 Giovanni Arrighi, *The Long Twentieth Century: Money, Power and the Origins of our Times* (London, Verso, 1994) and Giovanni Arrighi and Beverly J. Silver, *Chaos and Governance in the Modern World System* (Minneapolis, MN, University of Minnesota Press, 1999).

theoretical arguments, others on historical analyses, and yet others on the discussion of contemporary phenomena. Inevitably, readers with little patience for theory, or for the analysis of distant and unfamiliar pasts, or for history still in the making, may be tempted to skip sections or even entire chapters. Aware of this possibility, I have done my best to ensure that readers who do so can still get the gist of at least one of the two overall arguments of the book—the one concerning the relocation of the epicenter of the global political economy to East Asia, and the one concerning *The Wealth of Nations*. All I ask in exchange is that the book be judged as a *whole* and not just in its discrete parts.

This book has long been in the making, and long is the list of my intellectual debts. Without the assistance of many East Asian collaborators, I would have had no access to key texts in Chinese and Japanese, some of which appear in the bibliography. Ikeda Satoshi, Hui Po-keung, Lu Aiguo, Shih Miin-wen, Hung Ho-fung, and Zhang Lu all helped in this respect. In addition, Ikeda introduced me to the Japanese literature on the China-centered tribute trade system; Hui taught me to read Braudel from an East Asian perspective; Hung guided my forays into the social dynamic of late imperial China; and Lu Aiguo has reined in my excessive optimism about the nature of China's recent achievements.

An earlier and shorter version of Part II was published as "The Social and Political Economy of Global Turbulence," in *New Left Review*, II/20 (2003), pp. 5–71. Like a portion of Chapter 1, it engages critically with the work of Robert Brenner. It is part of an ongoing attempt on my part to convince Brenner to take historical sociology more seriously than economics. I am thankful to Bob for the intellectual stimulation provided by his work and for taking my criticisms in stride.

An earlier version of Part III was published as "Hegemony Unraveling-I," in *New Left Review*, II/32 (2005), pp. 23–80, and "Hegemony Unraveling-II," in *New Left Review*, II/33 (2005), pp. 83–116. The two articles have been thoroughly restructured and rewritten but many of the ideas in Chapter 8 still originate in a seminar that David Harvey and I jointly taught at Johns Hopkins University. I am grateful to David and the participants in the seminar for helping me recast key contentions of *The Long Twentieth Century* and *Chaos and Governance* in a tighter and more solid analytical framework.

Portions of Chapters 1, 11, and 12 draw from a paper co-authored with Hui Po-keung, Hung Ho-fung, and Mark Selden published as "Historical Capitalism, East and West," in *The Resurgence of East*

Asia. 500, 150 and 50 Year Perspectives, edited by G. Arrighi, T. Hamashita, and M. Selden (London: Routledge, 2003) and from a sole-authored paper published as "States, Markets and Capitalism, East and West," in *Worlds of Capitalism. Institutions, Economic Performance, and Governance in the Era of Globalization*, edited by M. Miller (London, Routledge, 2005). I have already mentioned my intellectual debts to Hui and Hung. In addition, I must thank Mark Selden for his generous guidance of my attempts to grasp the East Asian experience as well as for comments on Chapter 1.

Benjamin Brewer, Andre Gunder Frank, Antonina Gentile, Greta Krippner, Thomas Ehrlich Reifer, Steve Sherman, Arthur Stinchcombe, Sugihara Kaoru, Charles Tilly, and Susan Watkins made helpful comments on papers and articles that were later incorporated in the book. Astra Bonini and Daniel Pasciuti helped in producing the figures and Dan also did bibliographical research on specific issues. Baris Cetin Eren contributed to keeping the material of Chapter 7 up to date, while Ravi Palat and Kevan Harris incessantly bombarded me with evidence for and against my arguments of which I have made abundant use. Kevan also read the entire manuscript offering valuable substantive and editorial suggestions. Patrick Loy provided me with some excellent quotes, and James Galbraith gave me useful hints concerning both Adam Smith and contemporary China. Comments by Joel Andreas, Nicole Aschoff, Georgi Derluguian, Amy Holmes, Richard Lachman, Vladimir Popov, Benjamin Scully, and Zhan Shaohua were most helpful in the final round of revisions.

Perry Anderson and Beverly Silver have acted as usual as my primary advisors. Their respective roles of "good cop" (Perry) and "bad cop" (Beverly) have been equally crucial in the realization of this work. I am most grateful to both for their intellectual guidance and moral support.

This book is dedicated to the memory of my good friend Andre Gunder Frank. In the thirty-six years since we met in Paris in 1969 until his death we struggled together and against one another to get to the root causes of global inequities. We had many disputes, but we were traveling the same road and in the end we discovered that we were headed pretty much in the same direction. I know—because he said so—that he disagreed with much of my critique of Bob Brenner; but I think that he would have recognized the lasting influence of his thought on the overall arguments of this book.

March 2007

INTRODUCTION

"When the twentieth century opened," wrote Geoffrey Barraclough in the mid 1960s, "European power in Asia and Africa stood at its zenith; no nation, it seemed, could withstand the superiority of European arms and commerce. Sixty years later only the vestiges of European domination remained. . . . Never before in the whole of human history had so revolutionary a reversal occurred with such rapidity." The change in the position of the peoples of Asia and Africa "was the surest sign of the advent of a new era." Barraclough had few doubts that when the history of the first half of the twentieth century—which for most historians was still dominated by European wars and problems—came to be written in a longer perspective, "no single theme will prove to be of greater importance than the revolt against the west."[1] The contention of this book is that, when the history of the *second* half of the twentieth century will be written in such a longer perspective, the chances are that no single theme will prove to be of greater significance than the economic renaissance of East Asia. The revolt against the West created the political conditions for the social and economic empowerment of the peoples of the non-Western world. The economic renaissance of East Asia is the first and clearest sign that such an empowerment has begun.

We speak of renaissance because—in Gilbert Rozman's words— "East Asia is a great region of the past, having been in the forefront of world development for at least two thousand years, until the sixteenth, seventeenth, or even the eighteenth century, after which it suffered a relatively brief but deeply felt eclipse."[2] The renaissance has occurred through a snowballing process of connected economic "miracles" in a succession of East Asian states, starting in Japan in the 1950s and 1960s,

---

1 Geoffrey Barraclough, *An Introduction to Contemporary History* (Harmondsworth, Penguin, 1967), pp. 153–4.

2 Gilbert Rozman, *The East Asian Region: Confucian Heritage and its Modern Adaptation* (Princeton, NJ, Princeton University Press, 1991), p. 6.

rolling on in South Korea, Taiwan, Hong Kong, Singapore, Malaysia, and Thailand in the 1970s and 1980s, and culminating in the 1990s and early 2000s in the emergence of China as the world's most dynamic center of economic and commercial expansion. According to Terutomo Ozawa—who first introduced the notion of a snowballing process to describe the East Asian ascent—"the Chinese miracle, though still in its inchoate phase, will be no doubt . . . the *most* dramatic in terms of its impact on the rest of the world . . . especially on neighboring countries."[3] In a similar vein, Martin Wolf has proclaimed that

> Should [Asia's rise] proceed as it has over the last few decades, it will bring the two centuries of global domination by Europe and, subsequently, its giant North American offshoot to an end. Japan was but the harbinger of an Asian future. The country has proved too small and inward-looking to transform the world. What follows it—China, above all—will prove neither. . . . Europe was the past, the US is the present and a China-dominated Asia the future of the global economy. That future seems bound to come. The big questions are how soon and how smoothly it does so.[4]

The Asian future envisaged by Wolf may not be as inevitable as he implies. But even if he is only in part right, the East Asian renaissance suggests that Adam Smith's prediction of an eventual equalization of power between the conquering West and the conquered non-West might finally come true. Like Karl Marx after him, Smith saw a major turning point in world history in the European "discoveries" of America and of a passage to the East Indies by the Cape of Good Hope. He was, nonetheless, far less sanguine than Marx about the ultimate benefits for humanity of these events.

> Their consequences have already been great; but, in the short period of between two and three centuries which has elapsed since these discoveries were made, it is impossible that the whole extent of their consequences can have been seen. What benefits, or what misfortunes to mankind may hereafter result from these events, no

---

3 Terutomo Ozawa, "Pax Americana-Led Macro-Clustering and Flying-Geese-Style Catch-Up in East Asia: Mechanisms of Regionalized Endogenous Growth," *Journal of Asian Economics*, 13 (2003), p. 700, emphasis in the original. The "snowballing" metaphor was first introduced in Terutomo Ozawa, "Foreign Direct Investment and Structural Transformation: Japan as a Recycler of Market and Industry," *Business and the Contemporary World*, 5, 2 (1993), pp. 30–1.

4 "Asia Is Awakening," *Financial Times*, September 22, 2003.

human wisdom can foresee. By uniting, in some measure, the most distant parts of the world, by enabling them to relieve one another's wants, to increase one another's enjoyments, and to encourage one another's industry, their general tendency would seem to be beneficial. To the natives, however, both of the East and West Indies, all the commercial benefits which can have resulted from these events have been sunk and lost in the dreadful misfortunes which they have occasioned. . . . At the particular time when these discoveries were made, the *superiority of force* happened to be so great on the side of the Europeans, that they were enabled to commit with impunity every sort of injustice in those remote countries. Hereafter, perhaps, the natives of those countries may grow stronger, or those of Europe may grow weaker, and the inhabitants of all the different quarters of the world may arrive at that equality of courage and force which, by inspiring mutual fear, can alone overawe the injustice of independent nations into some sort of respect for the rights of one another.[5]

Far from the natives of Europe growing weaker and those of non-European countries growing stronger, for almost two centuries after the publication of *The Wealth of Nations* the "superiority of force" on the side of the Europeans and their offsprings in North America and elsewhere grew further, and so did their capacity "to commit with impunity every sort of injustice" in the non-European world. Indeed, when Smith was writing, East Asia's "eclipse" had hardly begun. On the contrary, the remarkable peace, prosperity, and demographic growth that China experienced for much of the eighteenth century was a source of inspiration for leading figures of the European Enlightenment. Leibniz, Voltaire, and Quesnay, among others, "looked to China for moral instruction, guidance in institutional development, and supporting evidence for their advocacy of causes as varied as benevolent absolutism, meritocracy, and an agriculturally based national economy."[6] The most striking contrast with European states was the Chinese empire's size and population. In Quesnay's characterization, the Chinese empire was "what all

---

5 Adam Smith, *An Inquiry into the Nature and Causes of the Wealth of Nations*, 2 vols (London, Methuen, 1961), vol. II, p. 141, emphasis added.

6 Michael Adas, *Machines as Measure of Men: Science, Technology and Ideologies of Western Dominance* (Ithaca, NY, Cornell University Press, 1989), p. 79; see also Ho-fung Hung, "Orientalist Knowledge and Social Theories: China and European Conceptions of East–West Differences from 1600 to 1900," *Sociological Theory*, 21, 3 (2003).

Europe would be if the latter were united under a single sovereign"—
a characterization that was echoed in Smith's remark that the extent
of China's "home market" was "not much inferior to the market of
all the different countries of Europe put together."[7]

Over the next half century, a great leap forward in European military
power undermined this positive image of China. European merchants
and adventurers had long emphasized the military vulnerability of an
empire ruled by a scholar-gentry class, while complaining bitterly about
the bureaucratic and cultural handicaps they met in trading with China.
These indictments and complaints fostered a fundamentally negative
view of China as a bureaucratically oppressive and militarily weak
empire. By 1836, three years before Britain launched the first Opium
War against China (1839–42), the author of an anonymous essay
published in Canton ominously declared that "there is, probably, at
the present no more infallible a criterion of the civilization and advancement of societies than the proficiency which each has attained in
'the murderous art,' the perfection and variety of their implements for
mutual destruction, and the skill with which they have learned to use
them." He then went on to dismiss the Chinese imperial navy as a
"monstrous burlesque," to argue that antiquated cannon and unruly
armies made China "powerless on land," and to view these weaknesses
as symptoms of a fundamental deficiency of Chinese society as a whole.
In reporting these views, Michael Adas adds that the growing importance of military prowess "in shaping European assessments of the
overall merit of non-Western peoples boded ill for the Chinese, who had
fallen far behind the aggressive 'barbarians' at their southern gates."[8]

In the century following the defeat of China in the first Opium
War, the eclipse of East Asia turned into what Ken Pomeranz has
called the "Great Divergence."[9] The political and economic fortunes
of two world regions up until then characterized by similar living
standards diverged sharply, Europe ascending rapidly to the zenith of
its power and East Asia descending just as rapidly to its nadir. By the
end of the Second World War, China had become the world's poorest
country; Japan had become a militarily occupied, "semi-sovereign"

---

7 François Quesnay, "From *Despotism in China*," in F. Schurmann and O.
Schell, eds, *Imperial China* (New York, Vintage, 1969), p. 115; Smith, *Wealth of
Nations*, vol. II, p. 202.

8 Adas, *Machines as Measure of Men*, pp. 89–93, 124–5, 185–6. See also
Geoffrey Parker, "Taking Up the Gun," *MHQ: The Quarterly Journal of Military
History*, 1, 4 (1989), pp. 98–9.

9 Kenneth Pomeranz, *The Great Divergence: Europe, China, and the Making of
the Modern World Economy* (Princeton, NJ, Princeton University Press, 2000).

state; and most other countries in the region were either still struggling against colonial rule or were about to be torn asunder by the emerging Cold War divide. In East Asia, as elsewhere, there were few signs of an imminent validation of Smith's contention that the widening and deepening of exchanges in the global economy would act as an equalizer of power between peoples of European and non-European descent. To be sure, the Second World War had given a tremendous impulse to the revolt against the West. Throughout Asia and Africa, old sovereignties were re-established and scores of new ones were created. But decolonization was matched by the formation of the most extensive and potentially destructive apparatus of Western force the world had ever seen.[10]

The situation appeared to be changing in the late 1960s and early 1970s, when the mighty US military apparatus failed to coerce the Vietnamese people into a permanent scission along the Cold War divide. Writing for the bicentenary of the publication of *The Wealth of Nations*, and shortly after the United States had decided to withdraw from Vietnam, Paolo Sylos-Labini wondered whether the time had finally come when—as Smith had envisaged—"the inhabitants of all the different quarters of the world . . . arrive at that equality of courage and force which, by inspiring mutual fear, can alone overawe the injustice of independent nations into some sort of respect for the rights of one another."[11] The economic conjuncture also seemed to favor the countries that had come to constitute the Third World.[12] Their natural

---

10 The far-flung network of quasi-permanent overseas military bases put in place by the US during and after the Second World War was, in Stephen Krasner's words, "without historical precedent; no state had previously based its own troops on the sovereign territory of other states in such extensive numbers for so long a peacetime period" (Stephen Krasner, "A Trade Strategy for the United States," *Ethics and International Affairs*, 2 [1988], p. 21).

11 Paolo Sylos-Labini, "Competition: The Product Markets," in T. Wilson and A.S. Skinner, eds, *The Market and the State: Essays in Honor of Adam Smith* (Oxford, Clarendon Press, 1976), pp. 230–2.

12 The emergence of a "Third World" in the 1950s was a joint product of the revolt against the West and of the Cold War world order. While the historical non-West came to be grouped almost entirely in the Third World, the historical West split into three distinct components. Its more prosperous components (North America, Western Europe, and Australia) joined by Japan, came to constitute the First World. One of its less prosperous components (the USSR and Eastern Europe) came to constitute the Second World, and another (Latin America) joined the non-West to constitute the Third World. With the end of the Cold War and the disappearance of the Second World, the expressions First and Third World became anachronistic and were replaced by the expressions global North and South, respectively. In this book, we shall use the old or new designations depending on the context.

resources were in great demand, and so were their abundant and cheap labor supplies. Capital flows from First to Third (and Second) World countries experienced a major expansion; the rapid industrialization of Third World countries was undermining the previous concentration of manufacturing activities in First (and Second) World countries; and Third World countries had united across ideological divides to demand a New International Economic Order.

In revisiting Sylos-Labini's reflections eighteen years later, I noted that any hope (or fear) of an imminent equalization of the opportunities of the peoples of the world to benefit from the ongoing process of world economic integration had been premature. In the 1980s, a US-driven escalation of competition in world financial markets had suddenly dried up the supply of funds to Third and Second World countries and provoked a major contraction of world demand for their products. Terms of trade had swung back in favor of the First World as fast and sharply as they had swung against it in the 1970s. Disoriented and disorganized by the increasing turbulence of the global economy, and hard-pressed by a new escalation of the armament race, the Soviet empire had disintegrated. Instead of having two superpowers to play against one another, Third World countries now had to compete with former Second World countries in gaining access to the markets and resources of the First World. At the same time, the United States and its European allies seized the opportunity created by the collapse of the USSR to claim with some success a global "monopoly" of the legitimate use of violence, fostering the belief that their superiority of force was not just greater than ever but for all practical purposes unchallengeable.[13]

I nonetheless also noted that the backlash had not re-established power relations to their pre–1970 condition. For the waning of Soviet power had been accompanied by the waxing of what Bruce Cumings dubbed the "capitalist archipelago" of East Asia.[14] Japan was by far the biggest among the "islands" of this archipelago. The most important among the other islands were the city-states of Singapore and Hong Kong, the garrison state of Taiwan, and the half-national state of South Korea. None of these states were powerful by conventional standards. While Hong Kong was not even a sovereign state, the three bigger states—Japan, South Korea, and Taiwan—

---

13 Giovanni Arrighi, *The Long Twentieth Century: Money, Power and the Origins of our Times* (London, Verso, 1994), pp. 21–2.

14 Bruce Cumings, "The Political Economy of the Pacific Rim," in R.A. Palat, ed., *Pacific-Asia and the Future of the World System* (Westport, CT, Greenwood Press, 1993), pp. 25–6.

were wholly dependent on the United States not just for military protection but also for much of their energy and food supplies, as well as for the profitable disposal of their manufactures. And yet, the collective economic power of the archipelago as new "workshop" and "cash box" of the world was forcing the traditional centers of capitalist power—Western Europe and North America—to restructure and reorganize their own industries, their own economies, and their own ways of life.[15]

A bifurcation of this kind between military and economic power, I argued, had no precedent in the annals of capitalist history and could develop in three quite different directions. The United States and its European allies might have attempted to use their military superiority to extract a "protection payment" from the emerging capitalist centers of East Asia. If the attempt succeeded, the first truly global empire in world history might have come into existence. If no such attempt was made, or, if made, did not succeed, over time East Asia might have become the center of a world-market society of the kind envisaged by Adam Smith. But it was also possible that the bifurcation would result in endless worldwide chaos. As I put it then paraphrasing Joseph Schumpeter, before humanity chokes (or basks) in the dungeon (or paradise) of a Western-centered global empire or of an East Asian-centered world-market society, "it might well burn up in the horrors (or glories) of the escalating violence that has accompanied the liquidation of the Cold War world order."[16]

Trends and events of the thirteen years since this was written have changed radically the probability that each of these outcomes will actually materialize. Worldwide violence has escalated further and, as will be argued in Part III, the Bush administration's embrace of the Project for a New American Century in response to the events of September 11, 2001 was, in key respects, an attempt to bring into existence the first truly global empire in world history. The abysmal failure of the Project on the Iraqi testing ground has not eliminated but nonetheless greatly reduced the chances that a Western-centered global empire will ever materialize. The chances of endless worldwide chaos have probably increased. At the same time, the probability that we will witness the formation of an East Asian-centered world-market society has also increased. The brighter prospects of this outcome are in part due to the disastrous implications for US world

---

15 Arrighi, *The Long Twentieth Century*, p. 22.

16 Ibid., pp. 354–6, paraphrasing Joseph Schumpeter, *Capitalism, Socialism, and Democracy* (London, George Allen & Unwin, 1954), p. 163.

power of the Iraqi adventure. For the most part, however, they are due to China's spectacular economic advance since the early 1990s.

The implications of China's ascent are momentous. China is not a vassal of the United States, like Japan or Taiwan, nor is it a mere city-state like Hong Kong and Singapore. Although the reach of its military power pales in comparison with that of the United States, and the growth of its manufacturing industries still depend on exports to the US market, the dependence of US wealth and power on the import of cheap Chinese commodities and on Chinese purchases of US Treasury bonds is just as great, if not greater. More important, China has increasingly replaced the United States as the main driving force of commercial and economic expansion in East Asia and beyond.

The overall thesis put forward in this book is that the failure of the Project for a New American Century and the success of Chinese economic development, taken jointly, have made the realization of Smith's vision of a world-market society based on greater equality among the world's civilizations more likely than it ever was in the almost two and a half centuries since the publication of *The Wealth of Nations*. The book is divided into four parts, one primarily theoretical and three primarily empirical.

The chapters of Part I lay down the theoretical underpinnings of the investigation. I begin by surveying the recent discovery of the significance of Adam Smith's theory of economic development for an understanding of Pomeranz's "Great Divergence." I then reconstruct Smith's theory and compare it with Marx's and Schumpeter's theories of capitalist development. My main contentions in Part I are, first, that Smith was neither an advocate nor a theorist of capitalist development and, second, that his theory of markets as instruments of rule is especially relevant to an understanding of non-capitalist market economies, such as China was prior to its subordinate incorporation in the globalizing European system of states, and might well become again in the twenty-first century under totally different domestic and world-historical conditions.

The chapters of Part II use the expanded Smithian perspective developed in Part I to track the global turbulence that preceded and set the stage for the US embrace of the Project for a New American Century and China's economic ascent. I trace the origins of the turbulence to an over-accumulation of capital in a global context shaped by the revolt against the West and other revolutionary upheavals of the first half of the twentieth century. The result was a first deep crisis of US hegemony in the late 1960s and 1970s—what I shall call the "signal crisis" of US hegemony. The United States responded to this crisis in the 1980s by aggressively competing for capital in global financial markets and with a major escalation of the armament race with the USSR. Although the response succeeded in reviving the political and economic fortunes of the United States beyond the rosiest expectations of its promoters, it also had the unintended consequences of aggravating the turbulence of the global political economy and of making the national wealth and power of the United States ever more dependent on the savings, capital, and credit of foreign investors and governments.

Part III analyzes the Bush administration's adoption of the Project for a New American Century as a response to these unintended consequences of previous US policies. After analyzing the debacle of the Project, I recast its adoption and failure in the expanded Smithian perspective developed in Part I and elaborated in Part II. It will be argued that the Iraqi adventure definitively confirmed the earlier verdict of the Vietnam War—that is, that the Western superiority of force has reached its limits and shows strong tendencies towards implosion. Moreover, the Vietnam and Iraq verdicts appear to complement one another. While defeat in Vietnam induced the United States to bring China back into world politics to contain the political damages of military defeat, the outcome of the Iraqi debacle may well be the emergence of China as the true winner of the US War on Terror.

Part IV deals specifically with the dynamics of China's ascent. After pointing out the difficulties that the United States faces in its attempts to put the genie of Chinese economic expansion back in the bottle of US domination, I emphasize how attempts to foresee China's future behavior vis-à-vis the United States, its neighbors, and the world at large on the basis of the past experience of the Western system of states are fundamentally flawed. For one thing, the global expansion of the Western system has transformed its mode of operation, making much of its past experience irrelevant to an understanding of present transformations. More important, as the relevance of the historical legacy of the Western system of states has decreased, the relevance of the earlier China-centered system has increased. Insofar as we can tell, the new Asian age, if there is going to be one, will be the bearer of a fundamental hybridization of the two legacies.

The concluding epilogue sums up the reasons why US attempts to roll back the empowerment of the global South have backfired. They have precipitated what I shall call the "terminal crisis" of US hegemony, and have created conditions for the establishment of the kind of commonwealth of civilization that Smith envisaged more favorable than ever before. The emergence of such a commonwealth is far from certain. Western domination may be reproduced in more subtle ways than in the past and, above all, a long period of escalating violence and endless worldwide chaos remains a possibility. What world order, or disorder, will eventually materialize largely depends on the capacity of the more populous Southern states, first and foremost China and India, to open up for themselves and the world a socially more equitable and ecologically more sustainable developmental path than the one that has made the fortunes of the West.

Part I

ADAM SMITH AND
THE NEW ASIAN AGE

1

MARX IN DETROIT, SMITH IN BEIJING

"The Chinese modernization effort of recent years," wrote John K. Fairbank on the eve of the 1989 Tiananmen crackdown, "is on so titanic a scale that it is hard to grasp."

> Can China switch from a command economy to a free market in goods, capital, people, and even ideas? If so, can Party dictatorship survive? A period of railway and city building, typical of the nineteenth century, coincides with a flowering of postindustrial electronic technology. Issues of the Renaissance and the Enlightenment in the West compete with a reappraisal of China's own values. Change is headlong; China's develop-ment is stretched thin. Wang Yang-ming's unity of theory and practice, so admired since the sixteenth century, is hard to find. No wonder Deng Xiaoping's reforms confuse us as well as people in China.[1]

The success of the reforms was completely unexpected. "No economist"—notes Thomas Rawski—"anticipated China's im-mense dynamism."[2] Even Paul Krugman got it wrong. As the East Asian economic expansion was entering its Chinese phase, he drew a parallel between East Asian reliance on heavy investment and big shifts of labor from farms into factories and the similar reliance of Warsaw Pact nations in the 1950s. "From the perspective of the year 2010," he concluded, "current projections of Asian supremacy extrapolated from recent trends may well look almost as silly as 1960s-vintage forecasts of Soviet industrial supremacy did from the perspective of the

---

1 John K. Fairbank, "Keeping Up with the New China," *New York Review*, March 16, 1989, p. 17.

2 Thomas G. Rawski, "Reforming China's Economy: What Have We Learned?" *The China Journal*, 41 (1999), p. 139.

Brezhnev years."[3] Worse still, at a 1996 conference in Taipei a "well-known American economist" told the audience that Russia, rather than China, "got the reform path about right"—a view echoed the following year by *The Economist*'s contention that China's economic transformation and its growth could not be maintained if gradual reform was not given up in favor of a Chinese variant of shock therapy.[4]

Although during the East Asian crisis of 1997–98 Chinese economic growth slowed, China avoided the catastrophic experience of countries that followed *The Economist*'s advice. Indeed, in light of China's insulation from the worst effects of the crisis, Joseph Stiglitz reversed *The Economist*'s contention, arguing that the Chinese success was due precisely to *not* having given up gradualism in favor of the shock therapies advocated by the so-called Washington Consensus. Unlike Russia, he claimed, China "never confused ends [the welfare of the population] with means [privatization and trade liberalization]."

> It recognized that if it was to maintain social stability, it had to avoid massive unemployment. Job creation had to go in tandem with restructuring. When China liberalized, it did so gradually and in ways that ensured that resources that were displaced were redeployed to more efficient uses, not left in fruitless unemployment.[5]

As the US new-economy bubble burst in 2001, and Chinese economic growth emerged as the main driving force of recovery in East Asia and beyond, earlier projections of a coming new Asian age no longer looked as silly as they did to Krugman ten years earlier. But the very purpose and social consequences of the spectacular Chinese economic ascent came under severe scrutiny both in China and abroad. Few

---

3 Paul Krugman, "The Myth of Asia's Miracle," *Foreign Affairs*, 73, 6 (1994), p. 78. For a more balanced comparative assessment of Soviet economic growth, see V. Popov, "Life Cycle of the Centrally Planned Economy: Why Soviet Growth Rates Peaked in the 1950s" available at http://www.nes.ru/%7Evpopov/documents/Soviet%20Growth-Boston.pdf.

4 Rawski, "Reforming China's Economy," p. 140; "The death of gradualism," China Survey, *The Economist*, March 8, 1997.

5 Joseph Stiglitz, *Globalization and its Discontents* (New York, Norton, 2002), pp. 125–6. Two years later, Joshua Cooper Ramo, a member of the Council on Foreign Relations in the US and of the Foreign Policy Center in Britain, suggested that it was now possible to speak of an emerging "Beijing Consensus." See Joseph Cooper Ramo, *The Beijing Consensus: Notes on the New Physics of Chinese Power* (London, Foreign Affairs Policy Centre, 2004).

outside the Chinese Communist Party—and, for all we know, even inside it—seemed to take seriously Deng's claim that the purpose of the reforms was the creation of a *socialist* market economy. Two years after Deng reiterated the slogan "To get rich is glorious," Elisabeth Wright reported in *The Times* (London) that "Money has replaced Marxism as China's god." Once released from prison, even Tiananmen pro-democracy activists tended "to take the commercial road . . . often joining forces with the offspring of the party elite." After a period of decline, membership in the Communist Party started to grow steadily, not out of ideological conviction but out of political and commercial expediency. "Not for nothing," she added, "is China's present system called 'Market Leninism'."[6]

The socially corrosive effects of moneymaking soon came under attack. In a book first published in Hong Kong in 1997, and republished in Beijing the following year, where it became a bestseller, Fudan University-trained He Qinglian contended that the main results of Deng's reforms were huge inequality, generalized corruption, and the erosion of the moral basis of society. In her view, rather than production of new wealth, what occurred in the 1990s was "plunder"— that is, the transfer of state property to power-holders and their hangers-on and the transfer by state banks of the personal savings of ordinary citizens to state enterprises. The only thing that had trickled down to ordinary people was cynicism and the collapse of ethics. In reporting He's views, Liu Binyan and Perry Link concurred with her assessment that such a system was self-destructive and therefore unsustainable.[7]

Western Marxists eagerly seized upon indictments of this kind to dismiss the idea that any kind of socialism, market or otherwise, still existed in China. Thus, in introducing Martin Hart-Landsberg's and Paul Burkett's book-length article on "China and Socialism," the editors of *Monthly Review* claimed that

> once a post revolutionary country starts down the path of capitalist development, especially when trying to attain very rapid growth— one step leads to another until the harmful and destructive characteristics of the capitalist system finally reemerge. Rather

---

6 E. Wright, "To Be Rich Is Glorious," *World Press Review*, 41, 7 (1994), pp. 10–11. The slogan "To get rich is glorious" was first launched in 1982, but its impact gained momentum only after 1992, when during a tour of China's southern provinces Deng called for everyone in the country to go into business and get rich "even more boldly" and "even faster" than in the 1980s. See Liu Binyan and Perry Link, "A Great Leap Backward," *New York Review*, October 8, 1998.

7 Liu and Link, "A Great Leap Backward," p. 23.

than promising a new world of "market socialism," what distinguishes China today is the speed with which it has erased past egalitarian achievements and created gross inequalities and human and ecological destruction. . . . There is no market road to socialism if that means setting aside the most pressing human needs and the promise of human equality.[8]

Although no one denies the inroads of capitalist tendencies in the wake of Deng's reforms, their nature, extent, and consequences remain controversial even among Marxists. Samir Amin, for one, thinks that socialism in China has so far neither won nor lost. "As long as the principle of equal access to land is recognized and is effectively implemented," he claims, "it is not too late for social action to successfully influence an as yet uncertain evolution."

The revolution and the plunge into modernity have transformed the people of China more than any other in the Third World today. The Chinese popular classes have confidence in themselves. . . . They are largely free from submissive attitudes. . . . Social struggles are a daily occurrence, number in the thousands, are often violent and do not always result in failure.[9]

Recent developments support Amin's assessment of the extent and effectiveness of popular struggles in China. Faced with rising inequality and unrest in the countryside, in February 2006 the Chinese government announced major initiatives under the banner of a "new socialist countryside" to expand health, education, and welfare benefits for farmers, while further postponing the privatization of land property. "The central government has changed direction to focus on uneven development," explained Wen Tiejun of Renmin University. "The economic gap is creating social conflict, and social conflict has become a more and more serious problem." A month later, for the first time in a decade, the National People's Congress was consumed with an ideological debate over socialism and capitalism that many assumed had been made moot by China's long streak of rapid economic growth. Reliance on market mechanisms was not

---

8 Harry Magdoff and John Bellamy Foster, "China and Socialism: Market Reform and Class Struggle. Editors' Foreword," *Monthly Review*, 56, 3 (2004), p. 6. Although there are dissenting voices, this has become the predominant view among Western leftists.

9 Samir Amin, "China, Market Socialism, and U.S. Hegemony," *Review*, 28, 3 (2005), pp. 274–5.

in question; but glaring disparities between rich and poor, rampant corruption, labor abuses, and land seizures were. "If you establish a market economy in a place like China, where the rule of law is imperfect," commented Liu Guoguang of the Chinese Academy of Social Sciences, "if you do not emphasize the socialist spirit of fairness and social responsibility, then the market economy you establish is going to be an elitist market economy."[10]

What is an *elitist* market economy"? Is it the same as a *capitalist* market economy? What else can a market economy be? Is not a *socialist* market economy an oxymoron, as it is widely believed left, right, and center? And if it is not an oxymoron, what is it, and under what conditions can it be expected to materialize? Seeking to bridge the chasm between official discourse in Beijing—emphasizing "socialism with Chinese characteristics"—and the reality of unbridled capitalism in which party officials are eager partners, in 2005 the Communist Party launched a campaign among political leaders and senior academics to modernize and deploy Marxism in confronting what Communist Party leader, Hu Jintao, called "changes, contradictions and problems in all fields." The campaign involves new translations of Marxist literature, the updating of texts on Marxism for secondary-school and university students, and research on how Marxism can be redefined to inform China's policies even as private enterprise increasingly becomes the basis of its economy.[11]

Whatever the results of the campaign, the confusion that surrounds Deng's reforms is symptomatic of widespread misconceptions about the relationship between market economy, capitalism, and economic development. The misconceptions are as much theoretical as they are practical. It is entirely possible, indeed likely, that they will be resolved in practice before they are resolved in theory. But this is no excuse for not seeking their theoretical resolution ahead of their practical resolution, which is what we shall try to do in this book.

Neo-Smithian Marxism

Developments in the ideological realm are unreliable indicators of social realities. They may signal as much the absence as the presence

---

10 J. Yardley, "China Unveils Plan to Aid Farmers, but Avoids Land Issue," *New York Times*, February 23, 2006. J. Kahn, "A Sharp Debate Erupts in China Over Ideologies," *New York Times*, March 12, 2006.

11 E. Cody, "China Confronts Contradictions between Marxism and Markets," *Washington Post*, December 5, 2005.

of the realities they purport to represent. Thus, in an essay entitled
"Marx in Detroit" published at the height of the revival of Marxist
influences in the wake of 1968, the Marxist philosopher Mario Tronti
dismissed the idea that the formation of social-democratic and
communist parties of Marxist inspiration made Europe the epicenter
of class struggle.[12] The true epicenter, he claimed, had been the
United States, where Marxist influences had been minimal but workers had been most successful in forcing capital to restructure itself to
accommodate their demands for higher wages. In Europe Marx lived
on ideologically, but it was in the United States that labor–capital
relations were "objectively Marxian."

> For at least half a century, up to the post-Second World War period,
> Marx could be read [in the United States] in the reality of the
> struggles and of the responses provoked by the demands of the
> struggles. This does not mean that Marx's books provide us with an
> interpretation of American labor struggles. Rather, it means that
> these struggles provide us with a key for an accurate interpretation of
> Marx's most advanced texts. . . . *Capital* and the *Grundrisse*.[13]

Tronti's contention was an expression of the crisis of identity that
Marxism experienced at a time of renewed influence in the capitalist
West. Ever since its founding as a theory of capitalist development
and a doctrine of socialist transformation, Marxism had seen its
influence migrating relentlessly from the centers to ever more peripheral locations of world capitalism. By the late 1960s, the epicenters
of its diffusion had become poor Third World countries such as
China, Vietnam, Cuba, and Portugal's African colonies—countries
whose social realities had little, if anything, in common with those
theorized in *Capital* and the *Grundrisse*. It was at this time that under
the joint impact of US difficulties in Vietnam and student rebellions,
Marxism migrated back to the First World. But when Western
radicals started reading *Capital*, they had a hard time recognizing
its relevance to their political concerns. As David Harvey recalls,

> In the early 1970s it was hard to find the direct relevance of
> Volume I of *Capital* to the political issues that dominated the

---

12 This was actually the title of a section of the postscript to the second edition
of his book *Operai e capitale* (Turin: Einaudi, 1971), pp. 267–311, but it might just as
well have been the title of the entire postscript.

13 Ibid., pp. 269, 300, 303–4.

day. We needed Lenin to get from Marx to an understanding of the imperialist war that so unnerved us in Vietnam. . . . And it frequently entailed an act of faith in the whole history of the Marxist movement (or in some charismatic figure like Mao or Castro) to believe in the inner connection between Marx's *Capital* and all that we were interested in. This is not to say there was nothing in the text to fascinate and delight—the extraordinary insights that came from consideration of the commodity fetish, the wonderful sense of how class struggle had altered the world from the pristine forms of capital accumulation that Marx described. . . . But the plain fact was that *Capital* did not have that much direct relevance to daily life.[14]

There can be little doubt that a huge gulf separated Marx's theory of capital from the Marxism of Fidel Castro, Amilcar Cabral, Ho Chi Minh, or Mao Zedong, and that this gulf could be bridged only through an act of faith in the unity of Marxist history. But it is not altogether true that in the late 1960s and early 1970s Marx's theory of capital did not have some direct relevance to daily life in the First World. This was a time of intensifying class conflict in Europe and elsewhere and Tronti was not alone in thinking that these struggles, like the earlier ones in the United States, threw new light on Marx's *Capital*.[15] It was in this context that a growing number of Western Marxists on both sides of the Atlantic rediscovered the labor process and class conflict in the workplace that had figured so prominently in Volume I of *Capital*. Until the 1960s, no Marxist theorist of any prominence had followed Marx's invitation to "take leave for a time of [the] noisy sphere [of the market], where everything takes place on the surface and in view of all men, and follow [the possessor of money and the possessor of labor-power] into the hidden abodes of production," where, he promised, "[w]e shall at last force the secret of

14 David Harvey, *Spaces of Hope* (Berkeley, CA, University of California Press, 2000), pp. 6–7.

15 On the intellectual and political tendency of *operaismo* (workerism) pioneered by Tronti, see Steve Wright, *Storming Heaven: Class Composition and Class Struggle in Italian Autonomist Marxism* (London, Pluto, 2002) and "Children of a Lesser Marxism," *Historical Materialism*, 12, 1 (2004). Partly inspired by Tronti's disciple Antonio Negri, Michel Aglietta, *A Theory of Capitalist Regulation: The US Experience* (London, New Left Books, 1979) and other representatives of the French Regulation school put the organization of the labor process that had emerged out of workers' struggles and capitalist responses to those struggles in the US automobile industry (Fordism) at the center of their conceptualization of twentieth-century capitalism.

profit-making."[16] Deserted by Marxists, the hidden abodes of production had been the preserve of US industrial sociology and labor history, which inspired Tronti's discovery of Marx in Detroit. But, in the 1970s, Marxists at long last rediscovered the labor process as the contested terrain of managerial prerogatives and workers' resistance to exploitation.[17]

Instead of forcing the secret of profit-making, as Marx had promised, the rediscovery deepened the cleavage between Marxists concerned primarily with Third World emancipation from the legacy of colonial imperialism and Marxists concerned primarily with working-class emancipation. The problem was that *Capital* did provide key insights into class conflict; but Marx's presuppositions concerning the development of capitalism on a world scale did not stand up to empirical scrutiny.

Marx's presuppositions bear a close resemblance to the "flat world" thesis that Thomas Friedman has been peddling in recent years. After reading (or rereading) the *Communist Manifesto*, Friedman confesses to be "in awe at how incisively Marx detailed the forces that were flattening the world during the rise of the Industrial Revolution, and how much he foreshadowed the way these same forces would keep flattening the world right up to the present."[18] He then goes on to quote the famous passages in which Marx and Engels contended that the need of constantly expanding markets drives the bourgeoisie to establish connections "over the whole surface of the globe"; to replace old-established national industries with industries "that no longer work up indigenous raw material, but raw material drawn from the remotest zones; industries whose products are consumed, not only at home, but in every quarter of the globe."

---

16 Karl Marx, *Capital*, vol. I (Moscow, Foreign Languages House, 1959), p. 176.

17 In the United States, the Marxist rediscovery of the labor process was pioneered by Harry Braverman's *Labor and Monopoly Capital: The Degradation of Work in the Twentieth Century* (New York, Monthly Review Press, 1974), radical political economists of the social structure of accumulation school, and Michael Burawoy's industrial ethnography. See, among others, Richard Edwards, *Contested Terrain* (New York, Basic Books, 1979), David Gordon, Richard Edwards, and Michael Reich, *Segmented Work, Divided Workers: The Historical Transformation of Labor in the United States* (New York, Cambridge University Press, 1982), and Michael Burawoy, *Manufacturing Consent: Changes in the Labor Process under Monopoly Capitalism* (Chicago, University of Chicago Press, 1982). It reached its apogee with the widespread adoption of *Capital* as one of the classics of sociological theory in many US universities.

18 Thomas L. Friedman, *The World Is Flat: A Brief History of the Twenty-First Century* (New York, Farrar, Straus & Giroux, 2005), pp. 201–4.

As a result, "the old local and national seclusion and self-sufficiency" give way to "intercourse in every direction, universal inter-dependence of nations"—a universal interdependence that brings in its train generalized capitalist development.

> The bourgeoisie, by the rapid development of all instruments of production, by the immensely facilitated means of communication, draws all, even the most barbarian nations into civilization. The cheap prices of commodities are the heavy artillery with which it batters down all Chinese walls. . . . It compels all nations, on pain of extinction, to adopt the bourgeois mode of production; it compels them to introduce what it calls civilization into their midst, i.e., to become bourgeois themselves. In one word, it creates a world after its own image.[19]

As Harvey noted long before Friedman, it is hard to imagine a more compelling description of "globalization" as we know it today than the one Marx and Engels provided 150 years ago.[20] But what Friedman misses, and Marx and Engels did not foresee, is that in the intervening 150 years the increasing interdependence of nations did not "flatten" the world through generalized capitalist development. Whether the present recentering of the global economy on Asia will eventually result in a flatter world of one kind or another is a question that for now we must leave open. What is certain is that, over the past two centuries, the increasing interdependence of the Western and non-Western worlds has been associated not with the convergence hypothesized in the *Communist Manifesto* but with a huge divergence.

At about the same time that Tronti and others were rediscovering Marx in the hidden abodes of Fordist production, Andre Gunder Frank launched the metaphor "development of underdevelopment" to describe and explain this huge divergence. The divergence, he claimed, was nothing but the expression of a process of global capitalist expansion that simultaneously generated development (wealth) in its core locations (Western Europe and later North America and Japan) and underdevelopment (poverty) everywhere else. The process was presented as resting on a series of

---

19 Karl Marx and Frederick Engels, *The Communist Manifesto* (Harmondsworth, Penguin, 1967), pp. 83–4.

20 David Harvey, "Globalization in Question," *Rethinking Marxism*," VIII, 4 (1995).

metropolis–satellite relationships through which the metropolis appropriates economic surplus from its satellites for its own economic development, while the "satellites remain underdeveloped for lack of access to their own surplus and as a consequence of the same polarization and exploitative contradictions which the metropolis *introduces* and *maintains* in the satellite's domestic structure." The mechanisms of surplus appropriation and expropriation varied across space and over time; but the metropolis–satellite or core–periphery structure of the process of capitalist expansion remained in place, continually polarizing rather than equalizing the wealth and poverty of nations.[21]

Frank's conceptualization of the development of underdevelopment has been widely criticized for reducing class relations to an epiphenomenon of core–periphery relations. In one of these critiques, Robert Brenner acknowledged that "the expansion of capitalism through trade and investment did not automatically bring with it the capitalist economic development that the Marx of the *Manifesto* had predicted."

> In the course of the growth of the world market, Chinese Walls to the advance of the productive forces might be erected as well as battered down. When such "development of underdevelopment" occurred, Frank [rightly] pointed out, the "national bourgeoisie" acquired an interest not in . . . development, but in supporting precisely the class system of production and surplus extraction [that] fettered economic advance. . . . As Frank asserted, to expect under these circumstances that capitalist penetration would develop the country was, by and large, wishful thinking.[22]

Brenner nonetheless found Frank's scheme of things fundamentally flawed for treating class "as a derivative phenomenon, arising directly from the needs of profit maximization." More specifically, the problem with Frank's account is that "the demands of the market, of profit, determine the class structure, subject only to the limitations of geography and demography—as if the significance of these factors was not, in turn, to a great extent socio-historically determined, and as if the potential for profit did not itself depend on the class

---

21 Andre Gunder Frank, *Capitalism and Underdevelopment in Latin America* (New York, Monthly Review Press, 1969), pp. 9–15.

22 Robert Brenner, "The Origins of Capitalist Development: A Critique of Neo-Smithian Marxism," *New Left Review*, 1, 104 (1977), pp. 90–1.

structure."[23] For Brenner, in other words, the main reason why the *Manifesto*'s prediction of generalized capitalist development failed to materialize was not the inherently polarizing tendencies of the process of world-market formation, but the inherent incapacity of world-market formation to generate capitalist development unless appropriate pre-existing social conditions were present at the local level.

Brenner listed two conditions as paramount. First, those who organize production must have lost the capacity to reproduce themselves and their established class position outside the market economy. Second, the direct producers must have lost control over the means of production. The first condition is necessary in order to activate and sustain the competition that will force the organizers of production to cut costs so as to maximize profits through specialization and innovations. The second condition, in turn, is necessary in order to activate and sustain the competition that will force the direct producers to sell their labor-power to the organizers of production and to subject themselves to the discipline imposed on them by the latter. These two conditions, claims Brenner, are not automatically created by the global spread of market exchanges in the pursuit of profit. Rather, they are brought into existence by the particular social histories of the countries that are brought under the sway of the world market. The main reason why the *Manifesto*'s prediction of generalized capitalist development failed to materialize, therefore, is that only in some countries did the history of class struggle bring into existence the two necessary conditions of capitalist development.[24]

Brenner contrasts his model of capitalist development—which is a restatement of Marx's theory of capitalist production as sketched in Volume I of *Capital*—with that put forward by Adam Smith in *The Wealth of Nations*. In Smith's model, a nation's wealth is a function of the specialization of productive tasks that ensues from the division of labor among productive units, the degree of which is in turn determined by the extent of the market. In such a model, Brenner argues, the process of economic development is driven by the expansion of the market regardless of whether or not those who organize production have lost the capacity to reproduce their class position outside the market economy and the direct producers have lost

---

23 Ibid., p. 86.

24 Robert Brenner, "World System Theory and the Transition to Capitalism: Historical and Theoretical Perspectives," unpublished English version (1981) of a paper published in Jochen Blaschke, ed., *Perspectiven des Weltsystems* (Frankfurt, Campus Verlag, 1983), pp. 1, 4, 6; Brenner, "Origins of Capitalist Development," pp. 35–6.

control over the means of production. In this respect, Smith's model is
the matrix of a great variety of models of capitalist development,
including Frank's, which Brenner characterizes as exemplars of "Neo-
Smithian Marxism."[25]

The limits and contradictions of this characterization will become
evident as we proceed. For our present purposes, however, it has the
advantage of drawing a distinction between the development of a
market economy and capitalist development proper. Drawn with
specific reference to the origins of capitalist development in Europe,
the distinction is nonetheless compatible with Amin's assessment
that, as long as the principle of equal access to land continues to be
recognized and implemented, it is not too late for social action in
contemporary China to steer evolution in a non-capitalist direction.
For as long as that principle is upheld in practice, Brenner's second
condition of capitalist development (that the direct producers must
have lost control over the means of production) is far from being fully
established. In spite of the spread of market exchanges in the pursuit
of profit, therefore, the nature of development in China is not
necessarily capitalist.

This, of course, does not mean that socialism is alive and well in
Communist China, nor that it is a likely outcome of social action. All
it means is that, even if socialism has already lost out in China,
capitalism, by this definition, has not yet won. The social outcome of
China's titanic modernization effort remains indeterminate, and for
all we know, socialism and capitalism as understood on the basis of
past experience may not be the most useful notions with which to
monitor and comprehend the evolving situation.

Smithian Dynamic and the Great Divergence

The economic resurgence of China—whatever its eventual social outcome—has given rise to a new awareness among a growing group of
scholars that there is a fundamental world-historical difference between
processes of market formation and processes of capitalist development.
Integral to this new awareness has been the discovery (or rediscovery)
that trade and markets were more developed in East Asia in general, and
in China in particular, than in Europe, through the eighteenth century. In
interpreting this greater development, R. Bin Wong has challenged Philip
Huang's argument that, prior to the Industrial Revolution, Europe was

---

25 Brenner, "The Origins of Capitalist Development," pp. 33–41.

growing along an evolutionary trajectory headed towards unlimited economic improvement, while China was growing along an "involutionary" trajectory of "growth without development" characterized by decreasing returns to the increasing number of days worked annually.[26] Against this view, Wong claimed that the European and Chinese trajectories shared important features that "were part of the Smithian dynamics of market-based growth supported by labor intensification in the advanced regions of China and Europe in the centuries preceding the industrial revolution."[27]

As previously noted and further elaborated in Chapter 2, the essence of this dynamic is a process of economic improvement driven by productivity gains attending a widening and deepening division of labor limited only by the extent of the market. As economic improvement raises incomes and effective demand, the extent of the market increases, thereby creating the conditions for new rounds of division of labor and economic improvement. Over time, however, this virtuous circle comes up against the limits imposed on the extent of the market by the spatial scale and institutional setting of the process. When these limits are reached, the process enters a high-level equilibrium trap. It follows that, if Europe and China were experiencing the same Smithian dynamics, the real puzzle is not why China was caught in a high-level equilibrium trap but why Europe escaped such a trap through the Industrial Revolution.

Frank and Pomeranz raised the same issue even more explicitly. Frank pointed out that Smith himself saw China as being ahead of Europe along the same developmental trajectory and did not foresee the European breakthrough.

> Smith . . . was the last major (Western) social theorist to appreciate that Europe was a Johnny-come-lately in the development of

---

26 "In the Euro-American experience, agrarian change in the early modern and modern period was generally accompanied by expansion in both absolute output and output per unit of labor. Therefore it has seemed so important to distinguish what might be termed simple 'growth,' with expanding output, from 'development,' with improved labor productivity. For China, however, the distinction is crucial . . . [because] in the six centuries preceding the Revolution . . . agricultural output expanded, enough to keep pace with dramatic population growth, but chiefly by intensification and involution. Productivity and income per labor day either stagnated, as in intensification, or shrank, as in involution" (Philip C.C. Huang, *The Peasant Family and Rural Development in the Yangzi Delta, 1350–1988* [Stanford, CA, Stanford University Press, 1990], p. 12).

27 R. Bin Wong, *China Transformed: Historical Change and the Limits of European Experience* (Ithaca, NY, Cornell University Press, 1997), pp. 16–23, 30–1.

the wealth of nations: "China is a much richer country than any part of Europe," Smith remarked in 1776. Smith did not anticipate any change in this comparison and showed no awareness that he was writing at the beginning of what has come to be called the "industrial revolution."[28]

Pomeranz, for his part, challenged on empirical grounds the argument that Western Europe grew faster than China because it had the most efficient markets for goods and for factors of production. Even as late as 1789, he argues, "western European land, labor, and product markets . . . were on the whole probably *further* from perfect competition—that is, less likely to be composed of multiple buyers and sellers with opportunities to choose freely among many trading partners—than those in most of China and thus less suited to the growth process envisioned by Adam Smith."[29]

Taken jointly, these contentions bear some resemblance to Tronti's discovery of Marx in Detroit. Just as Tronti had detected a fundamental discrepancy between Europe's ideological embrace of Marxism and the greater factual relevance of US working-class history for an accurate interpretation of Marx's *Capital*, Wong, Frank, and Pomeranz now detected an equally fundamental discrepancy between the Western embrace of the ideology of free markets and the greater factual relevance of late imperial China for an accurate interpretation of Smith's *Wealth of Nations*. To paraphrase Tronti, they discovered Smith in Beijing.

This new discovery, like the earlier one, has more than mere historiographical interest. It raises questions of the greatest theoretical and practical significance. First, if the common Smithian dynamic of the European and Chinese economies cannot account for the massive deployment of mineral sources of energy in transport and industry that propelled the rise of the West to global supremacy, what

---

28 Andre Gunder Frank, *ReOrient: Global Economy in the Asian Age* (Berkeley, CA, University of California Press, 1998), p. 13.

29 Kenneth Pomeranz, *The Great Divergence: Europe, China, and the Making of the Modern World Economy* (Princeton, NJ, Princeton University Press, 2000), p. 17, emphasis in the original. The idea that late imperial China was characterized by a condition of nearly perfect competition was already implicit in Ramon Myers's description of its economy as "reticular" or "web-like." In this description, a reticular economy consisted of small-scale economic organizations contracting with each other in a highly competitive environment and relying almost exclusively on the market to handle transaction costs. Quoted in John Lee, "Trade and Economy in Preindustrial East Asia, *c.* 1500–*c.* 1800: East Asian in the Age of Global Integration," *The Journal of Asian Studies*, 58, 1 (1999), p. 19.

can? Second, why was the British-led globalization of industrial capitalism in the nineteenth century associated with a sharp economic decline of the East Asian region, and especially of its Chinese center, for at least a century (let us say from the first Opium War to the end of the Second World War)? And why was this long decline followed by an even sharper economic resurgence of that same region in the second half of the twentieth century? Is there any connection between the earlier regional and global primacy of the Chinese market economy and its present resurgence? And if there is, how does it help in understanding the nature, causes, and prospective consequences of the resurgence?

Wong, Frank, and Pomeranz focus on the first question and provide different but complementary answers. Following E. Anthony Wrigley, Wong conceives of the British Industrial Revolution as a historical contingency largely unrelated to previous developments. Its main feature was productivity gains based on coal as a new source of heat, and steam as a new source of mechanical energy, that far surpassed what could be achieved under the Smithian dynamic. "Once this fundamental break took place, Europe headed off along a new economic trajectory." But the break itself remains unexplained: "technologies of production," we are told, "do not change according to any simple and direct economic logic." Like "forces of production" in Marxist accounts, they are "the exogenous variable that drives other economic changes."[30]

In contrast to Wong, Frank traces the occurrence in England/Europe and the non-occurrence in China/Asia of the Industrial Revolution to opposite outcomes of the common Smithian dynamic. In Asia in general, and in China in particular, economic expansion created the labor surplus and capital shortage that underlie Smithian high-level equilibrium traps. In Europe, in contrast, economic expansion created a labor shortage and a capital surplus. It was this opposite outcome that, according to Frank, after 1750 led to the Industrial Revolution.[31] The intensive burst of technological innovations that remains exogenous (that is, unexplained) in Wong's reconstruction of the European and Chinese dynamics thus becomes

---

30 Wong, *China Transformed*, pp. 48–52. Cf. E.A. Wrigley, *Continuity, Chance and Change: The Character of the Industrial Revolution in England* (Cambridge, Cambridge University Press, 1988) and "The Limits to Growth: Malthus and the Classical Economists," in M.S. Teitebaum and J.M. Winten, eds, *Population and Resources in Western Intellectual Traditions* (Cambridge, Cambridge University Press, 1989).

31 Frank, *ReOrient*, p. 304.

endogenous in Frank's reconstruction. This endogenous explanation of the Industrial Revolution, however, provides no explanation of why the common Smithian dynamic had opposite effects in the West and in the East.

Pomeranz does provide an explanation by tracing what he calls the Great Divergence to differences in resource endowments and in core–periphery relations—that is, to the fact that the Americas provided core regions of Northwest Europe with a far more abundant supply of primary products and demand for manufactures than East Asian core regions could obtain from their own peripheries. Like Wong, he relies on Wrigley's earlier contention that a rich domestic endowment of cheap fossil fuel was essential to the take-off of the Industrial Revolution in Britain. But in his view, in the absence of American supplies of primary products, it would have been impossible for European technology and investment to develop in labor-saving, land- and energy-gobbling directions, at the very moment when the intensification of resource pressures previously shared by all (core?) regions of the global economy were forcing East Asian development along ever more resource-saving, labor-absorbing paths. This ecological relief

> was predicated not merely on the natural bounty of the New World, but also on ways in which the slave trade and other features of European colonial systems created a new *kind* of periphery, which enabled Europe to exchange an ever growing volume of manufactured exports for an ever growing volume of land-intensive products.[32]

Pomeranz's contentions have prompted Brenner to reiterate his earlier critique of neo-Smithian Marxism with a vengeance. In an article co-authored with Christopher Isett, he takes issue with Pomeranz's equation of developments in the Yangzi delta and in England prior to the Industrial Revolution.

> In the Yangzi delta, the main economic agents possessed direct non-market access to the means of their reproduction. They were therefore shielded from the requirement to allocate their resources in the most productive manner in response to competition. As a result, they were enabled to allocate their resources in ways that, while individually sensible, ran counter to the aggregate require-

---

32 Pomeranz, *The Great Divergence*, p. 20, emphasis in the original; p. 264.

ments of economic development, with the consequence that the region experienced a Malthusian pattern of economic evolution that ultimately issued, in the eighteenth and nineteenth centuries, in demographic-cum-ecological crisis. In England, in contrast to the Yangzi delta, the main economic agents had lost the capacity to secure their economic reproduction either through extra-economic coercion of the direct producers or their possession of the full means of subsistence. They were therefore both free and compelled by competition to allocate their resources so as to maximize their rate of return (the gains from trade). The region experienced, as a result, a Smithian pattern of economic evolution, *or self-sustaining growth*, that brought it, in the eighteenth and nineteenth centuries, to the edge neither of demographic nor ecological crisis, but to the industrial revolution.[33]

As in his earlier critique of neo-Smithian Marxism, Brenner once again emphasizes the dependence of economic agents upon the market as a condition of their mutual competition that force each and every one of them to specialize, invest, and innovate. And, once again, he emphasizes the primacy of the internal social structure of countries and regions over their relations to other countries and regions in the determination of developmental trajectories. Yet Smithian growth—which in the critique of neo-Smithian Marxism was "self-limiting"—in the critique of Pomeranz has somehow become "self-sustaining" and a prelude to the Industrial Revolution. In Brenner's new position, self-limiting growth is not Smithian but Malthusian.

Leaving aside Brenner's characterization of Smithian growth as self-limiting in one critique and self-sustaining in the other critique—a discrepancy which he does not explain—let us note that even Huang (who is as critical as Brenner of Pomeranz's equation of developments in the Yangzi delta and in England prior to the Industrial Revolution) does not think that "a simple Malthusian notion of subsistence crisis driven purely by population pressure" adequately describes tendencies in the Yangzi delta in the eighteenth century. In Huang's view, the impending crisis was driven primarily by commercialization, that is, by an increasing dependence of economic agents upon the market.

---

33 Robent Brenner and Christopher Isett, "England's Divergence from China's Yangzi Delta: Property Relations, Microeconomics, and Patterns of Development," *The Journal of Asian Studies*, 61, 2 (2002), p. 613, emphasis added.

In North China, while commercialization provided opportunities for enrichment to some, it brought impoverishment to many others who took market risks but did not fare well. In the Yangzi delta, involutionary commercialization represented by cotton and silk cultivation enabled the farm economy to absorb more population, but it did not substantially alter the pre-existing context of social inequality. The result of the conjuncture of population pressure with inequality was the formation of an expanding poor peasant class (in absolute numbers even if not necessarily in terms of proportions of the population), ranging from landless agricultural workers to tenant cultivators who also hired out as day-laborers.[34]

Thus, whatever the differences between the European and Chinese developmental trajectories before the Industrial Revolution—and as we shall see, there were plenty—there is broad agreement (including Huang) that the degree of commercialization was not one of them. Wong's, Frank's, and Pomeranz's discovery of Smith in Beijing, therefore, was no mirage. Their explanations of the nineteenth-century divergence of the European and East Asian developmental paths, however, either miss relevant historical aspects of the divergence, or beg a number of questions that they themselves raise.

First, while Britain's endowment of cheap fossil fuels might have some validity as one of the reasons why Britain escaped from the Smithian trap through the Industrial Revolution earlier than the rest of Europe, it cannot explain why China—which was one of the best-endowed countries in the world in terms of coal deposits—did not make a similar escape. More important, feedbacks and spin-offs from the mining, transportation, and utilization of coal, as well as American supplies of primary products, became crucial to the British/European breakthrough later rather than earlier in the nineteenth century, that is, well after the Industrial Revolution was underway. As Patrick O'Brien observes,

> the Great Divergence and the Industrial Revolution form part of a interconnected narrative; and the degree of divergence in labor productivities and real incomes between Europe and China, that had so clearly appeared by 1914, is inconceivable without the

---

34 Philip C.C. Huang, "Development or Involution in Eighteenth-Century Britain and China? A Review of Kenneth Pomeranz's *The Great Divergence: China, Europe, and the Making of the Modern World Economy*," *The Journal of Asian Studies*, 61, 2 (2002), p. 531.

massive supplies of basic foodstuffs and raw materials imported from the Americas and other primary producers. But since those supplies came on stream over the second half of the nineteenth century, questions of what started and what sustained the Industrial Revolution should not be conflated.[35]

Second, as Frank maintains, according to all available evidence (including Adam Smith's own assessment), prior to the Great Divergence wages and demand were higher and capital more abundant in Europe than in Asia, and this difference in all likelihood contributed to making labor-saving, energy-consuming technology economical in the West but not in the East. Nevertheless, Frank provides no explanation of why processes of market formation that were more advanced in the East were associated with higher wages and demand, and more abundant capital, in the West. By his own account, before the Industrial Revolution the only competitive advantage the Europeans had vis-à-vis the East was based on the mining and transportation of American silver, as well as its investment in various trading ventures, including intra-Asian trade. In his view, however, this one competitive advantage enabled the Europeans to hold out in Asia for three centuries but not to gain a commanding position in a global economy that remained centered on Asia, because the flow of American silver benefited Asian economies more than the European. Throughout the eighteenth century, European manufactures in Asia remained uncompetitive and China remained the "ultimate sink" of the world's money.[36] But, if this was the case, why was China affected by a shortage and Europe by a surplus of capital? And why was Europe experiencing greater demand for labor and higher wages than China?

Third, the puzzle of the European escape from a Smithian high-level equilibrium trap through the Industrial Revolution must be dealt with in conjunction with the puzzle of why the globalization of that revolution was associated for about a century with the economic decline, and then with a rapid economic renaissance of the East Asian region. In concluding his critical assessment of Pomeranz's thesis, O'Brien asks:

> *if* the English economy might well (but for coal and its close involvement with the Americas) have gone the way of the Yangzi Delta, then why has even that commercialized and advanced region of the Manchu

---

35 Patrick O'Brien, "Metanarratives in Global Histories of Material Progress," *The International History Review*, 23, 2 (2001), pp. 360, 364, 367.

36 Frank, *ReOrient*, pp. 283, 356–7.

Empire taken such a long time to regain the economic rank and status it held in the world economy in the mid-eighteenth century?[37]

As we shall see, the really interesting and difficult question is not why it has taken so long for the Yangzi delta, China, and East Asia to regain the economic ground they had lost vis-à-vis the West since the mid eighteenth century. Rather, it is how and why China has managed to regain so much ground, so quickly *after* more than a century of political-economic eclipse. Either way, a model of the Great Divergence must tell us something, not just about its origins, but also about its development over time, its limits, and its prospects.

The Persistence of the Smithian Legacy

Kaoru Sugihara has attempted to construct such a comprehensive model. While substantially agreeing with Pomeranz's and Wong's accounts of the origins of the Great Divergence, he departs from them in emphasizing the importance of major differences in the man–land ratio between the core regions of East Asia and those of Western Europe before 1800, as both cause and effect of an unprecedented and unparalleled East Asian Industr*ious* Revolution. From the sixteenth through the eighteenth century—he claims—the development of labor-absorbing institutions and labor-intensive technologies in response to natural resource constraints (especially scarcity of land) enabled East Asian states to experience a major increase in population accompanied, not by a deterioration, but by a modest improvement in the standard of living.[38]

This escape from Malthusian checks was especially remarkable in China, whose population had previously risen several times to a ceiling of 100–150 million only to fall, whereas by 1800 it rose to nearly 400 million. "This was clearly a world demographic landmark"—notes Sugihara—"and its impact on world GDP far outweighed that of post-

---

37 O'Brien, "Metanarratives in Global Histories of Material Progress," p. 367, emphasis in the original.

38 Kaoru Sugihara, "The East Asian Path of Economic Development: A Long-Term Perspective," in G. Arrighi, T. Hamashita, and M. Seldon, eds, *The Resurgence of East Asia: 500, 150 and 50 Year Perspectives* (London and New York, Routledge, 2003), pp. 82, 94, 117 n. 2. The exclusive focus on Sugihara in this section is motivated by the fact that, to my knowledge, he is the only observer who has attempted to construct a comprehensive model of the origins, evolution and limits of the Great Divergence. The objective here is to clarify the hypotheses that will guide our investigation, not to provide a historical account of the divergence, which will be done in the third and fourth parts of the book.

industrial revolution Britain, whose share of world GDP in 1820 was less than 6 percent." The "Chinese miracle," as Sugihara calls this achievement, was replicated on a smaller territorial scale in Japan, where population growth was less explosive than in China but the improvement in standard of living more significant.[39]

The concept of "industrious revolution" (*kinben kakumei*) was in fact originally introduced by Hayami Akira with reference to Tokugawa Japan. In his view, the freeing of the peasantry from servitude in the seventeenth century, the entrenching of family-based farming, an increase in population, and a growing scarcity of farmland had jointly contributed to the emergence of a mode of production that relied heavily on investment in human labor. Although peasants had to work longer and harder, their incomes also increased. They therefore learned to value work and developed a strong work ethic.[40] The concept was later used by Jan de Vries with reference to pre-industrial Europe in the different substantive meaning of a preamble to the Industrial Revolution driven by a growing demand for marketed goods among rural households.[41]

In using the concept with reference to China, Sugihara, like Wong and Pomeranz, conceives of the Industrious Revolution, not as a preamble to the Industrial Revolution, but as a market-based development that had no inherent tendency to generate the capital- and energy-intensive developmental path opened up by Britain and carried to its ultimate destination by the United States. Nevertheless, Sugihara's central claim is that the instrumentalities and outcomes of the East Asian Industrious Revolution established a distinctive technological and institutional path which has played a crucial role in shaping East Asian responses to the challenges and opportunities created by the Western Industrial Revolution. Particularly significant in this respect was the development of a labor-absorbing institutional framework centered on the household (often, though not always, the family) and, to a lesser extent, the village community. Against the traditional view that small-scale production lacks internal forces for economic improvement, Sugihara underscores important advantages of this institutional framework in comparison with the class-based, large-scale production that was becoming dominant in England.

---

39 Ibid., pp. 79, 89–90; Kaoru Sugihara, "The State and the Industrious Revolution in Japan," working paper no. 02/04, Global Economic History Network, Department of Economic History, London School of Economics.

40 Quoted in Lee, "Trade and Economy in Preindustrial East Asia," p. 6.

41 Jan de Vries, "The Industrial Revolution and the Industrious Revolution," *Journal of Economic History*, 54, 2 (1994).

While in England workers were deprived of the opportunity to share in managerial concerns and to develop interpersonal skills needed for flexible specialization, in East Asia

> an ability to perform multiple tasks well, rather than specialization in a particular task, was preferred, and a will to cooperate with other members of the family rather than the furthering of individual talent was encouraged. Above all, it was important for every member of the family to try to fit into the work pattern of the farm, respond flexibly to extra or emergency needs, sympathize with the problems relating to the management of production, and anticipate and prevent potential problems. Managerial skill, with a general background of technical skill, was an ability which was actively sought after at the family level.[42]

Moreover, as long as East Asian peasants observed social codes, the transaction costs of trade were small, and the risk involved in technical innovations was relatively low. Although the East Asian institutional framework left little room for big innovations, or for investment in fixed capital or long-distance trade, it provided excellent opportunities for the development of labor-intensive technologies that made an unmistakable contribution to the improvement of living conditions by keeping all members of the household fully employed. The difference between this kind of development and development along the Western path "was that it mobilized human rather than non-human resources."[43]

According to Sugihara, this disposition to mobilize human rather than non-human resources in the pursuit of economic improvement continued to characterize the East Asian developmental path even when East Asian states sought to incorporate within their economies Western technologies. Thus, by the 1880s, the Japanese government adopted an industrialization strategy based on the recognition that in Japan both land and capital were scarce, while labor was abundant and of relatively good quality. The new strategy accordingly encouraged "active use of the tradition of labor-intensive technology, modernization of traditional industry, and conscious adaptation of Western technology to different conditions of factor endowment." Sugihara calls this hybrid developmental path "labor-intensive industrialization," because "it absorbed and utilized labor more fully

---

42 Sugihara, "The East Asian Path of Economic Development," p. 87.
43 Ibid., pp. 88, 90.

and depended less on the replacement of labor by machinery and capital than the Western path."[44]

In the first half of the twentieth century, labor-intensive industrialization increased the competitiveness of Japanese products vis-à-vis other Asian countries, such as India, which had a long tradition of labor-intensive technology but were prevented by colonial rule from developing in the same direction as Japan. Nevertheless, the fusion of the East Asian and Western developmental paths remained limited through the Second World War. As a result, despite an increase in land productivity, and the growth of labor-intensive industries, East Asia's labor productivity continued to lag behind that of the West, and the region's share of world GDP continued to decrease. It is not clear from Sugihara's account what exactly prevented the fusion of the two paths from materializing more fully than it did in the first half of the twentieth century. He is nonetheless quite explicit on the circumstances that *did* enable the fusion to materialize fully (and bear extraordinary fruit) after the Second World War. A first circumstance was the radical change in the politics of the situation brought about by the establishment of the Cold War regime under US hegemony.

> In contrast to the pre-war situation, Japan was expected to use her economic strength to counter communist penetration in Asia, and was now able to import all necessary raw materials and resources, including oil, from the rest of the world (by contrast, the US ban on oil exports to Japan in 1941 was an immediate cause of the [Pearl Harbor] attack). In the postwar period Japan also enjoyed favorable opportunities to increase exports of manufactured goods to advanced Western countries. This change in international circumstances allowed Japan, and later a number of other Asian countries, to pursue the systematic introduction of capital-intensive and resource-intensive heavy and chemical industries to an economy with relatively cheap and disciplined labor.[45]

A second circumstance that facilitated the fusion of the East Asian and Western developmental paths after the Second World War was the tendency of the United States and the USSR, in competition with each other, to use abundant mineral resources as a basis for forging powerful military-industrial complexes based on large-scale production in the steel, aircraft, armament, space, and petrochemical

---

44 Ibid., pp. 94, 99.
45 Ibid., p. 81.

industries. As a result, the capital and natural resource intensity of the Western developmental path increased further, creating new opportunities for profitable specialization not only in labor-intensive industries but also in the relatively resource-saving sectors of capital-intensive industries. Japan promptly seized these opportunities by shifting from labor-intensive industrialization—a strategy that aimed at combining directly within particular industries or factories imported technologies and cheap labor trained to replace capital—towards the development of interlinked industries and firms with different degrees of labor and capital intensity, while retaining a strong overall bias towards the East Asian tradition of greater utilization of human than of non-human resources.[46]

Finally, the surge of nationalism under the Cold War regime created conditions for fierce competition between relatively low-wage industrializers and higher-income countries.

> As soon as wages in one country rose even fractionally, [that country] had to seek a new industry which would produce a higher quality commodity to survive the competition, creating an effect similar to the "flying geese pattern of economic development." At the same time, successive entrance of new low wage countries ensured the lengthening of the chain of "flying geese." It is this aspect of industrialization, part of the enlargement of the East Asian path, that has been responsible for the increase in East Asia's share in world GDP.[47]

---

46 Ibid., pp. 105–10, 112–14.

47 Ibid., p. 110. The flying-geese pattern of economic development to which Sugihara refers is a "leading sector" model of spatial diffusion of industrial innovations. Originally advanced by Kaname Akamatsu in 1961, it was subsequently developed into several new versions. See Kaname Akamatsu, "A Theory of Unbalanced Growth in the World Economy," *Weltwirtschaftliches Archiv*, 86, 1 (1961); K. Kojima and Terutomo Ozawa, "Toward a Theory of Industrial Restructuring and Dynamic Comparative Advantage," *Hitotsubashi Journal of Economics*, 26, 2 (1985); Bruce Cumings, "The Origins and Development of the Northeast Asian Political Economy: Industrial Sectors, Product Cycles, and Political Consequences," in F.C. Deyo, ed., *The Political Economy of the New Asian Industrialism* (Ithaca, NY, Cornell University Press, 1987); Terutomo Ozawa, "Foreign Direct Investment and Structural Transformation: Japan as a Recycler of Market and Industry," *Business and the Contemporary World*, 5, 2 (1993); K. Kojima, "The 'Flying Geese' Model of Asian Economic Development: Origin, Theoretical Extensions, and Regional Policy Implications," *Journal of Asian Economics*, 11 (2000); Terutomo Ozawa, "Pax Americana-Led Macro-Clustering and Flying-Geese-Style Catch-Up in East Asia: Mechanisms of Regionalized Endogenous Growth," *Journal of Asian Economics*, 13 (2003). One of these versions underlies Ozawa's snowballing process of connected East Asian economic miracles mentioned in the Introduction and discussed in Chapter 11.

The East Asian economic resurgence has thus been due not to a convergence towards the Western capital-intensive, energy-consuming path but to a fusion between that path and the East Asian labor-intensive, energy-saving path. In Sugihara's view, this fusion has crucial implications for the future of world economy and society. The Industrial Revolution that opened up the Western path, he claims, was a "miracle of production" that greatly expanded the productive capacity of a small proportion of world population. The Industrious Revolution that opened up the East Asian path, in contrast, was a "miracle of distribution" that created the possibility of a diffusion of the benefits of the miracle of production to the vast majority of world population through labor-intensive, energy-saving industrialization. Indeed, in view of the environmental destruction associated with the diffusion of industrialization, the miracle of distribution can only continue if "the Western path [converges] with the East Asian path, not the other way round."[48]

Sugihara's thesis can be summed up with reference to Figures 1.1 and 1.2, which show the share of world GDP and the GDP per capita of the leading states of the Western and East Asian developmental paths (Britain and the United States for the first, and China and Japan for the second). As can be seen from Figure 1.2, the Western Industrial Revolution of the late eighteenth and early nineteenth centuries strengthened the ongoing tendency towards the widening of the GDP *per capita* gap in favor of the leading Western states. And yet, as can be seen from Figure 1.1, insofar as the share of world GDP is concerned, the East Asian Industrious Revolution managed to counter the impact of the Western Industrial Revolution through the early nineteenth century, leading to a further widening of the gap in East Asia's favor. From 1820 to 1950, as the East Asian Industrious Revolution attained its limits and the Western Industrial Revolution entered its second, truly revolutionary stage with the application of the new sources of energy to the production of means of production and to long-distance transport (railways and steamships), the share of total world GDP shifted drastically in favor of the Western path. After 1950, as the Western capital- and energy-intensive path attained its own limits and the selective incorporation of Western technologies within the labor-intensive, energy-saving East Asian path bore fruits, the latter began to narrow the GDP per capita gap (Figure 1.2) and even more so the gap in the share of total world GDP (Figure 1.1).[49]

---

48 Sugihara, "The East Asian Path of Economic Development," p. 116.

49 The measurement of GDP in terms of Purchasing Power Parities makes the East Asian GDP per capita and share of world GDP appear significantly greater than they would if current exchange rates had been used. The trends sketched in the text, however, would be the same even if current exchange rate measurements had been used.

Figure 1.1 Combined GDP as a percentage of world GDP: US + UK versus China + Japan

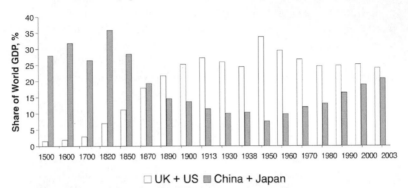

Note: GDP in millions of 1990 International Geary-Khamis Dollars.
Source: based on Angus Maddison, *Contours of the World Economy, 1–2030* AD (New York, Oxford University Press, 2007).

Figure 1.2 Combined GDP per capita: US + UK versus China + Japan (logged)

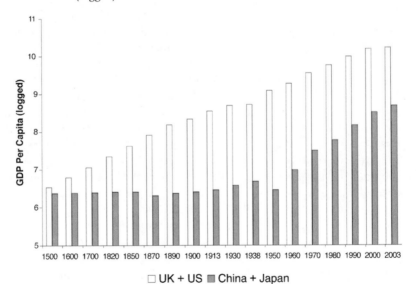

Note: GDP per capita in 1990 International Geary-Khamis Dollars logged.
Source: based on Angus Maddison, *Contours of the World Economy, 1–2030,* AD (New York, Oxford University Press, 2007).

The central argument of this book is a revised and expanded version of this thesis. The revision will begin with a conceptual clarification of the notions of market-based Smithian growth and capitalist development proper. Sugihara's labor-intensive, energy-saving developmental path resembles what Huang calls "involution-ary growth." Like Sugihara, Huang acknowledges that the absorption of sideline non-agricultural work performed by women, children, and the elderly, reduced the operating costs of household production units, giving them a competitive edge over larger capitalist units using hired labor. For Huang, however, the resulting virtual disappearance after the seventeenth century of the larger wage-labor-based farms that previously existed in parts of China does not constitute "devel-opment" or "evolution" along a distinctive East Asian path, as it does for Sugihara, but "growth without development" or "involution."[50] If we identify "evolution" and "development" as the displacement of labor-intensive household production by capital-intensive production in units employing wage labor, as Huang and Brenner do, then this disappearance should indeed be characterized as "involutionary." But if we leave open the possibility that labor-intensive production may play a lasting role in the promotion of economic development, as Sugihara hypothesizes, then such a characterization is unwarranted. This raises the issue of what particular concept of market-based development is most useful to describe and explain the demise and re-emergence of East Asia as a leading region of world economic growth.

Closely related to the above is the issue of what exactly is a market-based Smithian dynamic in comparison with a capitalist dynamic proper. Were the European and East Asian Industrious Revolutions both instances of a Smithian dynamic, as Wong, Pomeranz, Frank, and Sugihara claim? Or were they distinct experiences, the East Asian being headed towards economic stagnation and the European to-wards unlimited economic growth, as Huang and Brenner claim? Moreover, Sugihara suggests that the Western path of capital-inten-sive development had limits of its own. What exactly were these limits in comparison to those of the labor-intensive East Asian path? These are the questions that we address in the next two chapters.

---

50 Huang, "Development or Involution in Eighteenth-Century Britain and China?" pp. 514, 534.

2

THE HISTORICAL SOCIOLOGY
OF ADAM SMITH

If economists have had something to say on the theme of economic development, "this is only because they did not restrict themselves to economic theory, but—and indeed quite superficially as a rule—studied historical sociology or made assumptions about the economic future." By way of illustration, Joseph Schumpeter went on to list the "division of labor, the origins of private-property in land, increasing control over nature, economic freedom, and legal security" as "the most important elements constituting the 'economic sociology' of Adam Smith." All these elements, he added, "clearly relate to the social framework of the economic course of events, not to any immanent spontaneity of the latter."[1]

Schumpeter's claim aimed at distinguishing between the traditional concern of economic theory with movements towards or around an equilibrium and his own concern with economic development understood as a "spontaneous and discontinuous . . . disturbance of equilibrium, which forever alters and displaces the equilibrium state previously existing." The separation of "statics" and "dynamics" did enable economic theorists, most notably J.B. Clark, to see that dynamic elements, such as increases in capital and population or changes in technique and productive organization, disturb static equilibria. These dynamic elements, however, remained exogenous, that is unexplained, in economic theory. In Schumpeter's view, this methodology had some justification in the case of increases in capital and population, but not in the case of changes in technique and productive organization. These originated within the economic process itself and therefore had to be treated as endogenous sources of economic development. This approach paralleled that of Marx according to whom "there is an *internal* economic development

---

1 Joseph Schumpeter, *The Theory of Economic Development* (New York, Oxford University Press, 1961), pp. 59–60 n.

and no mere adaptation of economic life to changing data." As Schumpeter readily conceded, however, his analysis "covers only a small part of [Marx's] ground."[2]

Schumpeter's methodological concerns with the shortcoming of economic theory are closely related to an important distinction between two different kinds of market-based economic development. One kind occurs within a given social framework; it exploits the hidden potential of that framework for economic growth, but it does not alter the framework itself in any fundamental way. Fundamental changes in the social framework capable of increasing or reducing the potential for economic growth may occur. But they originate in processes and actions of a non-economic nature *rather than from within the process of economic growth*. This kind of development corresponds broadly, but by no means exactly, to the notions of Smithian growth, Industrious Revolution, and non-capitalist market-based development that we have repeatedly encountered in Chapter 1.

The second kind of market-based economic development, in contrast, is one that tends to destroy the social framework within which it occurs and to create the conditions (not necessarily realized) for the emergence of new social frameworks with a different growth potential. The social framework can change also for reasons other than the inner dynamic of the economic process. In this case, however, changes originating in processes and actions of a non-economic nature are secondary or subordinated to the changes that originate from within the economic process. This kind of development, which we shall designate as Schumpeterian or Marxian depending on the context, corresponds broadly, but again by no means exactly, to the notions of Industrial Revolution and market-based capitalist development.

The purpose of this chapter is to elucidate the nature of the first kind of economic development as theorized by Smith himself. We shall focus specifically on his conception of the market as an instrument of government; of competition and the division of labor, as mutually interacting conditions of economic expansion within an established social framework; of a "natural" and an "unnatural" developmental path; and of national wealth as a source of national power. Marx's and Schumpeter's critiques of Smith's conception of economic development will be examined in Chapter 3, focusing specifically on the capitalist tendency to overcome barriers to the self-expansion of capital through the "creative" (and not so creative) destruction of the social frameworks on which economic expansion

---

2 Ibid., emphasis in the original.

had previously been based. We shall then use these different conceptions of economic development to reformulate Sugihara's thesis of the continuing significance for world society of the developmental path opened up by the East Asian Industrious Revolution.

The Market as Instrument of Government

Among "the master economists of the past," Smith may well be "one of the most widely referred to and most rarely read."[3] But whether or not this is the case, along with Marx, he is certainly one of the most misunderstood. Three myths in particular surround his legacy: that he was a theorist and advocate of "self-regulating" markets; that he was a theorist and advocate of capitalism as an engine of "endless" economic expansion; and that he was a theorist and advocate of the kind of division of labor that occurred in the pin factory described in the first chapter of *The Wealth of Nations*. In reality, he was none of the above.

As Donald Winch has authoritatively argued, Smith's description of political economy as "a branch of the science of a statesman or legislator" and of his own contribution as a "theory," or set of "general principles," concerning law and government is an accurate characterization of his intentions and achievements.[4] Far from theorizing a self-regulating market that would work best with a minimalist state or with no state at all, *The Wealth of Nations*, no less than the *Theory of Moral Sentiments* and the unpublished *Lectures on Jurisprudence*, pre-

---

3 Robert Heilbroner, "Economic Predictions," *The New Yorker*, July 8, 1991, p. 73. In a personal recollection Frank notes that, as it has often been observed, "the first three (out of the thirty-two) chapters [of *The Wealth of Nations*] . . . is about as far as any ill-advised modern reader is likely to get in the book. (That *is* as far as we got in Frank Knight's course on the history of economic thought at the University of Chicago. . . . Milton Friedman all but abandoned Smith altogether, preferring to replace him by Alfred Marshall . . . [instructing] us to learn from the *footnotes* of Marshall's *Principles of Economics* . . . and to relegate virtually the entire empirically rich text and appendixes to oblivion)" (Andre Gunder Frank, "On the Roots of Development and Underdevelopment in the New World: Smith and Marx vs the Weberians," *International Review of Sociology*, 2nd series, 10, 2–3 (1974), p. 121, emphasis in the original).

4 Donald Winch, *Adam Smith's Politics: An Essay in Historiographic Revision* (Cambridge, Cambridge University Press, 1978). See also Knud Haakonssen, *The Science of a Legislator: The Natural Jurisprudence of David Hume and Adam Smith* (Cambridge, Cambridge University Press, 1981) and Patricia Werhane, *Adam Smith and his Legacy for Modern Capitalism* (New York, Oxford University Press, 1991).

supposed the existence of a strong state that would create and reproduce the conditions for the existence of the market; that would use the market as an effective instrument of government; that would regulate its operation; and that would actively inter- vene to correct or counter its socially or politically undesirable outcomes. Indeed, the purpose of Smith's political economy was as much "to supply the state . . . with a revenue sufficient for the public services," as it was "to provide a plentiful . . . subsistence for the people, or more properly to enable them to provide such a . . . subsistence for themselves."[5] In this endeavor, the spheres in which Smith advised the legislator to intervene were legion, including the provision of protection from internal and external threats to the security of individuals and the state (police and national defense), the administration of justice, the provision of the physical infrastructure needed to facilitate trade and commu- nication, the regulation of money and credit, and the education of the mass of the population to counter the negative effects of the division of labor on its intellectual qualities. In these and other spheres, Smith's advice to the legislator was based on considera- tions that were social and political rather than economic.[6]

The dogmatic belief in the benefits of minimalist governments and self-regulating markets typical of the nineteenth-century "liberal creed," or the equally dogmatic belief in the curative powers of "shock therapies" advocated by the Washington Consensus in the late twentieth century, were completely alien to Smith. Indeed, he would probably have agreed with Karl Polanyi's contention that such beliefs are utopian and unworkable. To expect that complete freedom of trade would be established in Great Britain seemed to him "as absurd as to expect that an Oceana or Utopia should ever be established in it." Nor was such complete freedom ("perfect liberty" as he some- times called it) a necessary condition of economic prosperity. "If a nation could not prosper without the enjoyment of perfect liberty and perfect justice, there is not in the world a nation which could ever have prospered." And although Smith never leaves any doubt that he favored trade liberalization, he was strongly opposed to anything resembling the shock therapies of the 1980s and 1990s. Where large

5 Adam Smith, *An Inquiry into the Nature and Causes of the Wealth of Nations*, 2 vols (London, Methuen, 1961), vol. I, p. 449.

6 Winch, *Adam Smith's Politics*, chs 5, 6, and 7; Haakonssen, *Science of a Legislator*, pp. 93–5, 160ff; Werhane, *Adam Smith and his Legacy*; Jerry Z. Muller, *Adam Smith in his Time and ours: Designing the Decent Society* (New York, Free Press, 1993), pp. 140–8.

sectors of the economy are affected, change "should never be introduced suddenly, but slowly, gradually, and after very long warning."
Special circumspection should be exercised in withdrawing protection
from trades that employ "a great multitude of hands" or trades in
subsistence goods that arouse strong popular feelings. Indeed, in the
latter case, "government must yield to [the people's] prejudices, and,
in order to preserve the public tranquillity, establish that system
which they approve of."[7]

The government's use of the market, in other words, not only had a
social purpose but was subject to powerful social constraints. The
reasons why Smith thought that it was wholly unrealistic to expect
free trade to be fully established in Great Britain, for example, were
strictly social.

> Not only the prejudices of the public, but what is much more
> unconquerable, the private interests of many individuals, irresist-
> ibly oppose it. Were the officers of the army to oppose with the
> same zeal and unanimity any reduction of their forces, with which
> master manufacturers set themselves against every law that is
> likely to increase the number of their rivals in the home market;
> were the former to animate their soldiers, in the same manner as
> the latter enflame their workmen, to attack with violence and
> outrage the proposers of any such regulation; to attempt to reduce
> the army would be as dangerous as it has now become to attempt
> to diminish in any respect the monopoly which our manufacturers
> have obtained against us.[8]

---

7 The substance of the argument and all the quotes from Smith in this
paragraph are taken from Donald Winch, "Science of the Legislator: Adam Smith
and After," *The Economic Journal*, 93 (1983), pp. 504–9. The contention that
Smith would have concurred with Polanyi's indictment of the liberal creed is mine.
Polanyi himself is somewhat ambiguous on Smith's relationship to the liberal
creed. While criticizing Smith for inventing through a misreading of the past the
concept of Economic Man, he nonetheless acknowledged that "wealth was to
[Smith] merely an aspect of the life of the community, to the purposes of which it
remained subordinate . . . There is no intimation in his work that the economic
interests of the capitalists laid down the law to society; no intimation that they
were the secular spokesmen of the divine providence which governed the economic
world as a separate entity. The economic sphere, with him, is not yet subject to
laws of its own that provide us with standards of good and evil" (Karl Polanyi,
The Great Transformation: The Political and Economic Origins of our Time
[Boston, Beacon Press, 1957]).

8 Smith, *Wealth of Nations*, vol. I, pp. 493–4.

Competition and the Falling Rate of Profit

Smith was no more a theorist and advocate of capitalism as an engine of "endless" economic expansion than he was a theorist and advocate of "self-regulating" markets. Contrary to widespread opinion, the idea that over time the accumulation of capital tends to drive down the rate of profit, eventually bringing economic expansion to an end, is not Marx's idea but Smith's. As we shall see in Chapter 3, Marx's own version of the "law" of the tendency of the rate of profit to fall is in fact aimed at demonstrating that Smith's version is overly pessimistic about the long-term potential of capitalist development.

In Smith's version of the "law," the tendency of the rate of profit to fall is the outcome of the increase in competition that inevitably accompanies the accumulation of an increasing mass of capital within established spheres of production and channels of trade.

> As capitals increase in any country, the profits which can be made by employing them necessarily diminish. It becomes gradually more and more difficult to find within the country a profitable method of employing any new capital. There arises in consequence a competition between different capitals, the owner of one endeavoring to get possession of that employment which is occupied by another. . . . [To this end, he] must not only sell what he deals in somewhat cheaper, but in order to get it to sell, he must sometimes too buy it dearer . . . [T]he profits which can be made by the use of a capital are in this manner diminished, as it were, at both ends.[9]

The opening up of new spheres of production and channels of trade can temporarily counter the tendency. But if there is freedom of entry (Smith's "perfect liberty") the tendency inevitably resumes under the impact of renewed competition.

> The establishment of any new manufacture, of any new branch of commerce, or of any new practice in agriculture, is always a

9 Ibid., vol. I, p. 375. A few pages later, Smith makes the same point more succinctly. "The whole capital of the country being augmented, the competition between the different capitals of which it was composed, would naturally be augmented with it. The owners of those particular capitals would be obliged to content themselves with a smaller proportion of the produce of that labor which their respective capitals employed" (ibid., p. 378).

speculation, from which the projector promises himself extraordinary profits. These profits sometimes are very great, and sometimes, more frequently, perhaps are quite otherwise; but in general they bear no regular proportion to those of other old trades in the neighborhood. If the project succeeds, they are commonly at first very high. When the trade or practice becomes thoroughly established and well known, the competition reduces them to the level of other trades.[10]

This general level to which profits are reduced may be high or low depending on whether merchants and manufacturers are in a position to restrict entry into their spheres of operation through private agreements or through governmental regulation. If they are not in a position to do so, profits will fall as low as it is considered "tolerable" in view of the risks involved in the employment of capital in trade and production.[11] But, if they can restrict entry and keep the market undersupplied, profits will be significantly higher than their tolerable level. In the first case, the expansion of trade and production *comes* to an end because of low profits; in the second case, it is *brought* to an end by the inclination of merchants and manufacturers to keep the level of profits as high as possible.[12] Either way, the economic process does not spontaneously generate any tendency to overcome the limits imposed on further economic growth by the fall in the rate of profit.

In advising governments on how to deal with these tendencies, Smith shows none of the capital-friendly dispositions typical of later liberal and neo-liberal ideologies. On the contrary,

> In Smith's conception . . . the fall in the rate of profit was a positive phenomenon *if* it was a reflection of the gradual elimination of monopolistic barriers of various kinds . . . that is, a positive phenomenon provided that it was a reflection of increasing competition and provided that it did not fall to the minimum acceptable level.[13]

---

10 Ibid., p. 128. This view, which was accepted in full by both Ricardo and Marx, clearly anticipates Schumpeter's theory of innovations. Paolo Sylos-Labini, "Competition: The Product Markets," in T. Wilson and A.S. Skinner, eds, *The Market and the State: Essays in Honour of Adam Smith* (Oxford, Clarendon Press, 1976), p. 219.

11 "The lowest ordinary rate of profit must always be something more than what is sufficient to compensate the occasional losses to which every employment of stock is exposed" (Smith, *Wealth of Nations*, vol. I, pp. 107–8).

12 See Sylos-Labini, "Competition," pp. 216–20.

13 Ibid., p. 220, emphasis in the original.

For Smith, in other words, a fundamental task of governments is to ensure that capitalists compete with one another in reducing profits to the bare minimum necessary to compensate for the risks of investing resources in trade and production. This interpretation fits Smith's definition of the contrasting interests of "the three great, original and constituent orders of every civilized society," that is, those who live by rent, those who live by wages, and those who live by profit. The interests of the first two orders (or social classes, as we would call them today), argues Smith, tend to coincide with the general social interest because the real value of both rents and wages tends to rise with the economic expansion and to fall with the economic decline of society. The interests of profit earners, in contrast, may clash with the general social interest, because they always involve a widening of the market and a narrowing of the competition. And while to

> widen the market may frequently be agreeable enough to the interest of the public . . . to narrow the competition must always be against it, and can serve only the dealers, by raising their profits above what they naturally would be, to levy, for their own benefit, an absurd tax upon their fellow citizens.[14]

Worse still, besides clashing with the general interest, profit earners pursue their interests with greater lucidity, power, and determination than the other social classes. The ease and security of the landowners' situation "renders them too often, not only ignorant, but incapable of that application of mind which is necessary in order to foresee and understand the consequences of any public regulation." As for the wage earner, "he is incapable either of comprehending the general social interest, or of understanding its connection with his own." Moreover, in public deliberations "his voice is little heard and less regarded, except upon some particular occasions, when his clamor is animated, set on, and supported by his employers, not for his, but their own particular purposes." Profit earners, in contrast, particularly those who employ the largest capitals, "by their wealth draw to themselves the greatest share of public consideration." Moreover, since "during their whole lives they are engaged in plans and projects, they have . . . a better knowledge of their interest than he [who lives by rent] has of his."[15]

In the pursuit of the general social interest, legislators were thus advised to countervail rather than accommodate capitalist interests

---

14 Smith, *Wealth of Nations*, vol. I, pp. 276, 278.
15 Ibid., pp. 276–8.

and power. Far from being capital-friendly, Smith's advice to the legislator was almost invariably labor-friendly.

> Our merchants and master-manufacturers complain much of the bad effects of high wages in raising the price, and thereby lessening the sale of their goods both at home and abroad. They say nothing concerning the bad effects of high profits. They are silent with regard to the pernicious effects of their own gains. They complain only of those of other people.[16]

In Smith's view, complaints about high wages are especially unwarranted, because the "liberal reward of labor" is both the effect of increasing national wealth and the cause of increasing population and of the industriousness of the common people. "To complain of it, is to lament over the necessary effect and cause of the greater prosperity."[17] Nowhere was the association between high wages and economic progress more clearly in evidence than in the North American colonies.

> Every colonist gets more land than he can possibly cultivate. He has no rent, and scarce any taxes to pay. . . . He has every motive to render as great as possible a produce, which is thus almost entirely his own. . . . He is eager, therefore, to collect laborers from all quarters, and to reward them with the most liberal wages. But those liberal wages, joined with the plenty and cheapness of land, soon make those laborers leave him, in order to become landlords themselves, and to reward, with equal liberality, other laborers, who soon leave them for the same reason that they left their first master. . . . In other countries, rent and profit eat up wages, and the two superior orders of people oppress the inferior one. But in new colonies, the interest of the two superior orders obliges them to treat the inferior one with more generosity and humanity; at least, where that inferior one is not in a state of slavery.[18]

Conditions in a new colony, however, are exceptional, because it "must always for some time be more under-stocked in proportion to

---

16 Ibid., p. 110; also vol. II, p. 113.

17 Ibid., vol. I, pp. 90–1. As Winch notes, there is no hint here of Thomas Malthus's subsequent dwelling on the gloomy prospects posed by diminishing returns in agriculture and mass pauperism, an issue to which we shall return in Chapter 3. See Winch, "Science of the Legislator," pp. 513–14.

18 Smith, *Wealth of Nations*, vol. II, pp. 76–7.

the extent of its territory, and more under-peopled in proportion to the extent of its stock, than the greater part of other countries." Smith contrasts this condition with that of a country "fully peopled in proportion to what either its territory could maintain or its stock employ" and with "as great a quantity of stock . . . employed in every particular branch as the nature and extent of the trade would admit." In such a country, "competition . . . would be as great, and consequently the ordinary profit as low as possible." Smith doubts that any country "has ever yet arrived at this degree of opulence" but mentions two radically different likely candidates: China and Holland.[19]

We shall later return to Smith's comparative analysis of developmental conditions in China, Europe, and North America. For now, let us note that, in this context, Smith compares the North American colonies on the one side, and China and Holland on the other, to illustrate his conception of economic development as a process embedded in, and limited by a particular physical, institutional, and social environment. More specifically, Smith conceives of economic development as the filling-up with people and physical capital ("stock") of a spatial container ("country") that encompasses a given endowment of natural resources and is shaped internally and bounded externally by laws and institutions. When the spatial container is "under-stocked" and "under-peopled," as in the case of the North American colonies, there is great potential for economic growth—a condition or "state" that Smith calls "progressive." When the spatial container is "fully stocked" and "fully peopled," as in the case of China and Holland, in contrast, the potential for economic growth, if any, is not so great—a condition or "state" that Smith calls "stationary" but that in contemporary language would be described as one of economic maturity. The task of the legislator is to endow its domains with laws and institutions that make possible the full realization of the growth potential. Thus China appeared to Smith "to have been long stationary" and to have "probably long ago" "acquired that full complement of riches which the nature of its soil and climate, and its situation with respect to other countries, allowed it to acquire." This complement of riches, however, "may be much inferior to what, with other laws and institutions, the nature of its soil, climate, and situation might admit of."[20]

It is not clear, at least to this reader, to what extent Smith thought that changes in the laws and institutions of a country could overcome

19 Ibid., vol. I, pp. 103–8.
20 Ibid., p. 106.

the limits imposed on economic growth by the country's size and endowment of natural resources. It is nonetheless clear that, as Schumpeter claimed, the process of economic development as understood by Smith has no *inherent* mechanism of overcoming the tendency towards settling in a "stationary state" or getting stuck in a "high-level equilibrium trap"—as Mark Elvin has characterized the stationary state of late imperial China.[21] Nowhere does Smith suggest that the invisible hand of the market acting on its own can get the economy unstuck from such a trap. If anything or anyone can, it is the visible hand of the government through suitable changes in laws and institutions. Closely related to the above, it is also clear that, in bringing about changes in laws and institutions, governments are not just subject to powerful social constraints, as previously noted, but respond also to contradictions of the process of economic development that are primarily social rather than economic.

Division of Labor and the Deterioration of the Intellectual Quality of the Population

The issue of state action in response to the social contradictions of economic development brings us to the third myth that surrounds Smith's legacy: the myth that he was a theorist and advocate of the kind of division of labor described in the opening passages of *The Wealth of Nations*. Schumpeter has famously stated that nobody either before or after Smith ever thought of putting on the division of labor the burden that he did. With Smith "it is practically the only factor in economic progress."[22] While the second statement is an exaggeration, the first is true only with reference to the division of labor *among* independent production units connected by market exchanges (Marx's "social division of labor") rather than the division of labor *within* production units (Marx's "technical division of labor").[23]

In the narrative of *The Wealth of Nations*, these two kinds of division of labor occupy an opposite strategic position than they do in the first volume of Marx's *Capital*. Marx begins his story with the

---

21 Mark Elvin, *The Pattern of the Chinese Past* (Stanford, CA, Stanford University Press, 1973), p. 314, and Chapter 11 below.

22 Joseph Schumpeter, *History of Economic Analysis* (New York, Oxford University Press, 1954), p. 187.

23 Karl Marx, *Capital*, vol. I (Moscow, Foreign Languages Publishing House, 1959), pp. 350–6.

market and the underlying social division of labor but soon invites us to leave the "noisy sphere" of the market and to follow the owner of the means of production and the possessor of labor-power into the "hidden abodes of production" in order to find out "not only how capital produces, but how capital is produced."[24] Smith, in contrast, begins his story by illustrating with the example of a pin factory how the division of labor improves the productive powers of labor. From then on, however, he leaves the hidden abode of production and remains focused on the social division of labor (between town and countryside, or between different economic sectors and activities); on the market exchanges that connect the units specializing in different economic activities; on the competition that promotes further division of labor and specialization among branches of trade and production; and on what governments can do to promote, regulate, and take advantage of the synergy between competition and division of labor. It is only in advocating government action in the education of the masses towards the end of *The Wealth of Nations* that Smith implicitly returns to the technical division of labor. But, instead of emphasizing its positive effects on the productive powers of labor, as he did at the beginning of his story, he now denounces its deleterious effects upon the workforce.

> In the progress of the division of labor, the employment of the far greater part of those who live by labor, that is, of the great body of the people, comes to be confined to a few very simple operations; frequently to one or two. But the understandings of the greater part of men are necessarily formed by their ordinary employments. The man whose life is spent in performing a few simple operations, of which the effects too are, perhaps, always the same, or very nearly the same, has no occasion to exert his understanding, or to exercise his invention in finding out expedients for removing difficulties which never occur. He naturally loses, therefore, the habit of such exertion, and generally becomes as stupid and ignorant as it is possible for a human creature to become. . . . Of the great and extensive interests of his country he is altogether incapable of judging; and unless very particular pains have been taken to render him otherwise, he is equally incapable of defending his country at war. . . . It corrupts even the activity of his body, and renders him incapable of exerting his strength with vigor and perseverance, in any other employment than that to which he has been bred. His

---

24 Ibid., p. 176.

dexterity at his own particular trade seems, in this manner, to be acquired at the expense of his intellectual, social and martial virtues. But in every improved and civilized society this is the state into which the laboring poor, that is, the great body of the people, must necessarily fall, unless government takes some pains to prevent it.[25]

Leaving aside for now the negative effects of the technical division of labor on martial virtues, its negative effects on the capacity to judge the national interest is consistent with Smith's previously noted poor opinion of the wage earner's capacity "either of comprehending the general social interest, or of understanding its connection with his own." However, in claiming that the technical division of labor undermines the wage worker's ability to find out intelligent and creative expedients for removing difficulties in his own jobs, or to effectively perform jobs other than "that to which he has been bred," Smith appears to contradict his earlier contention that the same phenomenon improves the productive powers of labor. E.G. West, for example, finds a "striking inconsistency" between these two contentions, especially in view of the fact that one of the reasons why Smith expects the division of labor to improve the productiveness of labor is that it enhances the inventiveness of workers by directing their whole attention towards discovering easier or readier methods of performing simple operations.[26]

Taking issue with West, Nathan Rosenberg has argued that "although the division of labor has potentially disastrous effects upon the moral and intellectual qualities of the labor force, and although Smith was seriously concerned with these effects, he did not fear that such developments would constitute a serious impediment to continued technological change."[27] In support of this argument, Rosenberg points out that for Smith technological innovations had two sources other than workers' inventiveness: the activities of producers of capital goods and the activities of what Smith called "philosophers" but today we would call scientists.

All the improvements in machinery . . . have by no means been the invention of those who had occasion to use the machines. Many

---

25 Smith, *Wealth of Nations*, vol. II, pp. 302–3.

26 E.G. West, "Adam Smith's Two Views on the Division of Labour," *Economica*, 31, 122 (1964), p. 26.

27 Nathan Rosenberg, "Adam Smith on the Division of Labor: Two Views or One?" *Economica*, 32, 127 (1965), pp. 138–9.

improvements have been made by the ingenuity of the makers of the machines, when to make them became the business of a peculiar trade; and some by that of those who are called philosophers or men of speculation, whose trade is not to do anything, but to observe everything; and who, upon that account, are often capable of combining together the powers of the most distant and dissimilar objects. In the progress of society, philosophy or speculation becomes, like every other employment, the principal or sole trade and occupation of a particular class of citizens. Like every other employment too, it is subdivided into a great number of different branches, each of which affords occupation to a particular tribe or class of philosophers; and this subdivision . . . as in every other business, improves dexterity, and saves time. Each individual becomes more expert in his own particular branch, more work is done upon the whole, and the quantity of science is considerably increased by it.[28]

Rosenberg suggests that, in Smith's scheme of things, the relative importance of these three sources of technological change (direct producers, producers of means of production, and philosophers/ scientists) varies with the progress of the division of labor. In the early stages of this progress, the level of knowledge and understanding of the majority of the population is considerable, and anyone involved in the production process can contribute to the kind of simple innovations that are required to save time and energies and to overcome difficulties. The more the division of labor advances, the lesser the capacity of the majority of the population to contribute to technological change, partly because of the increasing complexity of innovations and partly because of the increasing atrophy of the mind associated with ever more monotonous and uniform work. However, while the modal level of knowledge and understanding shrinks, the extensive specialization in the production of knowledge itself permits higher levels of scientific attainment that generate unique and unprecedented opportunities for technical progress.[29] As Smith himself put it,

Though in a rude society there is a good deal of variety in the occupations of every individual, there is not a great deal in those of the whole society. Every man does or is capable of doing, almost

---

28 Smith, *Wealth of Nations*, vol. I, p. 14.
29 Rosenberg, "Adam Smith on the Division of Labor," pp. 136–7.

every thing which any other man does, or is capable of doing. Every man has a considerable degree of knowledge, ingenuity and invention; but scarce any man has a great degree. The degree, however, which is commonly possessed, is generally sufficient for conducting the whole simple business of society. In a civilized state, on the contrary, though there is little variety in the occupations of the greater part of individuals, there is an almost infinite variety in those of the whole society. These varied occupations present an almost infinite variety of objects to the contemplation of those few, who . . . have leisure and inclination to examine the occupation of other people. The contemplation of so great variety of objects necessarily exercises their minds in endless comparisons and combinations, and renders their understandings, in an extraordinary degree, both acute and comprehensive.[30]

Rosenberg's interpretation of this passage as portraying a shift from direct producers to scientists as the main agency of changes in techniques and productive organization is a valid one, provided that we qualify it in two important respects. First, the shift in question is consistent with Smith's conception of economic development as a process embedded in, and limited by, a particular physical, institutional, and social environment. It simply specifies the mechanisms through which an expansion of the national market due to increasing incomes on the one side, and an increasing division of labor on the other, sustain one another in a virtuous circle of economic growth, as long as the territorial container in which they are both embedded can accommodate an ever increasing mass of capital without driving the rate of profit below the minimum acceptable level. But nowhere does Smith suggest that increasing the division of labor can on its own prevent the economy from getting stuck in a high-level equilibrium trap (his "stationary state") once the container has become "over-stocked" and "over-peopled." As previously noted, only the visible hand of the government can unstick the economy from such a trap through suitable changes in laws and institutions.

Second, despite the use of the pin factory to illustrate the positive effects of specialization on the productive powers of labor, the passage quoted above and its general context make abundantly clear that Smith attributes the greatest positive effects on the productive powers of labor to the emergence of specialized units and branches of production (that is, to an increase in the social division of labor),

---

30 Smith, *Wealth of Nations*, vol. II, p. 304.

rather than to the specialization of work roles within the units themselves (that is, to an increase in the technical division of labor). That is to say, the two developments that for Smith are most important in improving the productive powers of labor are the emergence of a sector specializing in the production of capital goods and the emergence of individuals and organizations specializing in the production of scientific knowledge. While both developments depend on an increasing *size of the market*, unlike the emergence of specialized work roles they do not necessarily depend on an increasing *size of the production units* connected by the market.

Smith's utter skepticism concerning the efficiency and usefulness of big business strongly supports this contention. The skepticism is evident not just from his advice to governments to countervail the power of big business discussed earlier, but also from his negative view of joint-stock companies.

> These companies, though they may, perhaps, have been useful for the first introduction of some branches of commerce, by making, at their own expence, an experiment which the state might not think prudent to make, have in the long-run proved, universally, either burdensome or useless, and have either mismanaged or confined the trade.[31]

Since shareholders "seldom pretend to understand any thing of the business of the company" and "give themselves no trouble about it, but receive contentedly such half yearly or yearly dividend, as the directors think proper to make to them,"

> Negligence and profusion . . . must always prevail, more or less, in the management of the affairs of such a company. It is upon this account that joint-stock companies for foreign trade have . . . very seldom succeeded without an exclusive privilege; and frequently have not succeeded with one. Without an exclusive privilege they have commonly mismanaged the trade. With an exclusive privilege they have both mismanaged and confined it.[32]

Managerial "negligence and profusion" is not the only reason for the poor performance of joint-stock companies. Lack of flexibility in adapting to local conditions is just as important in the case of

---

31 Ibid., p. 255.
32 Ibid., pp. 264–5.

companies operating simultaneously in different national markets without exclusive privileges—companies, that is, that closely resemble today's multinational corporations.

> To buy in one market, in order to sell, with profit, in another, when there are many competitors in both; to watch over, not only the occasional variations in the demand, but the much greater and more frequent variations in the competition, or in the supply which that demand is likely to get from other people, and to suit with dexterity and judgment both the quantity and quality of each assortment of goods to all these circumstances, is a species of warfare of which the operations are continually changing, and which can scarce ever be conducted successfully, without such unremitting exertion of vigilance and attention, as cannot long be expected from the directors of a joint-stock company.[33]

Smith acknowledges that when "all the operations are capable of being reduced to what is called a routine, or to such uniformity of method as admits of little or no variation," a joint-stock company might be able "to carry on successfully, without an exclusive privilege." But he mentions only four activities in which this might be the case: banking, insurance, the construction and maintenance of navigable canals, and the supply of water to a great city. Manufacturing is definitely not one of them.

> The joint-stock companies, which are established for the public-spirited purpose of promoting some particular manufacture, over and above managing their own affairs ill, to the diminution of the general stock of the society, can in other respects scarce ever fail to do more harm than good. Notwithstanding the most upright intentions, the unavoidable partiality of their directors to particular branches of manufacture . . . is a real discouragement to the rest, and necessarily breaks, more or less, that natural proportion which would otherwise establish itself between judicious industry and profit, and which, to the general industry of the country, is of all the encouragements the greatest and the most effectual.[34]

---

33 Ibid., p. 278.
34 Ibid., pp. 279–82.

Alternative Paths to Opulence

The reference in the above passage to a "natural proportion . . . between judicious industry and profit" brings us to a fourth clarification of Smith's conception of economic development. As previously noted, Smith singles out China and Holland as the most likely exemplars of a country "fully peopled in proportion to what either its territory could maintain or its stock employ" and with "as great a quantity of stock . . . employed in every particular branch as the nature and extent of the trade would admit." Nevertheless, Smith also tells us that China and Holland had reached this condition of economic maturity by developing along very different paths.

China is repeatedly mentioned as the exemplar of a country that had followed the path to economic maturity that Smith calls "the natural course of things" or "the natural progress of opulence." In such a "natural" course of things, "the greater part of capital . . . is, first, directed to agriculture, afterwards to manufactures, and last of all to foreign commerce." The extension and improvement of cultivation create a demand for investment in manufactures, and the expansion of agricultural and industrial production, in turn, generates a surplus of goods that can be exchanged abroad for goods of greater value. "Had human institutions . . . never disturbed the natural course of things, the progressive wealth and increase of the towns would, in every political society, be consequential, and in proportion to the improvement and cultivation of the territory or country."[35]

Holland, in contrast, is taken as the most extreme (ideal-typical, in Max Weber's language) exemplar of a country that had followed the European path to economic maturity, which Smith calls "unnatural and retrograde."

> But though [the] natural order of things must have taken place in some degree in every . . . society, it has, in all the modern states of Europe, been, in many respects, entirely inverted. The foreign commerce of some of their cities has introduced all their finer manufactures, or such as were fit for distant trade; and manufactures and foreign commerce together, have given birth to the principal improvements of agriculture. The manners and customs which the nature of their original government introduced,

---

35 Ibid., vol. I, pp. 403–5.

and which remained after that government was greatly altered, necessarily forced them into this unnatural and retrograde order.[36]

Smith's depictions of China are a far cry from the indictments of Montesquieu, Diderot, and Rousseau that eventually gave rise to Marx's infamous notion of an "Asiatic mode of production." They nonetheless are not as full of admiration as the depictions of the Sinophile faction of the European Enlightenment most prominently represented by Leibniz, Voltaire, and Quesnay.[37] The sources of information that inspired the latter were occasionally subjected to ridicule as "drawn up . . . by weak and wondering travellers; frequently by stupid and lying missionaries."[38] More important, China's laws and institutions were called to task for imposing unnecessary limits upon further economic expansion. Thus, after stating that China's "home market" was probably as large as that of all the different countries of Europe put together, and that it had probably expanded as far as its territory, natural resources, and situation with respect to other countries allowed, Smith goes on to say that a "country which neglects . . . foreign commerce, and which admits the vessels of foreign nations into one or two of its ports only, cannot transact the same quantity of business which it might do with different laws and institutions."

A more extensive foreign trade . . . which to this great home market added the foreign market of all the rest of the world; especially if any considerable part of this trade was carried on in Chinese ships; could scarcely fail to increase very much the manufactures of China, and to improve very much the productive powers of its manufacturing industry. By more extensive navigation, the Chinese would naturally learn the art of using and constructing themselves all the different machines made use of in other countries, as well as the other improvements of art and industry which are practiced in all the different parts of the world. Upon their present plan they have little opportunity of improving

---

36 Ibid., pp. 405–6.

37 On the split within the Enlightenment among admirers and denigrators of Qing China, see Michael Adas, *Machines as Measure of Men: Science, Technology and Ideologies of Western Dominance* (Ithaca, NY, Cornell University Press, 1989), pp. 79–93. On Marx's Asiatic mode of production, see Perry Anderson, *Lineages of the Absolute State* (London, New Left Books, 1979), p. 462–549.

38 Smith, *Wealth of Nations*, vol. II, p. 251.

themselves by the example of any other nation; except that of the Japanese.[39]

Leaving aside for now the question of its historical accuracy, this criticism of Chinese laws and institutions does not in any way imply that European laws and institutions were superior to the Chinese, and even less that the "unnatural and retrograde" European path of economic development was superior to the "natural" Chinese path. The criticism simply expresses the opinion that an alleged Chinese neglect of foreign trade prevented the "natural" Chinese path from fully running its course. But nowhere does Smith suggest that China could or should have followed the "unnatural and retrograde" European path. On the contrary, the main thrust of his advice to European statesmen is to steer the course of development in their own countries towards the "natural" path.

Smith justified this advice on several grounds. In part, he justified it in terms of the impact that different kinds of investment could be expected to have on the national market and national wealth. Capitals employed in agriculture and retail trade, he claimed, have the greatest positive impact, because they must reside within the country, being "confined almost to a precise spot, to the farm, and to the shop of the retailer." Capital employed in the wholesale trade, in contrast, "seems to have no fixed or necessary residence anywhere, but may wonder about from place to place, according as it can either buy cheap or sell dear." It nonetheless has a different impact on the national market depending on whether it is employed in the "home trade" (that is, "in purchasing in one part of the same country, and selling in another, the produce of the industry of that country"), or in the "foreign trade of consumption" (that is, "in purchasing foreign goods for home consumption"), or in the "carrying trade" (that is, "in transacting the commerce of foreign countries, or in carrying the surplus produce of one to another"). Capital invested in the home trade has the greatest positive impact, because "an equal capital affords the greatest revenue, and creates the greatest employment to the people of the country." Capital invested in purchasing foreign goods for home consumption has a less immediate and certain positive impact than the home trade, because there is no guarantee that the revenue and employment created abroad by the purchase of foreign goods will eventually generate an equivalent revenue and employment in the economy of the investing country. But the least

---

39 Smith, *Wealth of Nations*, vol. I, p. 106; vol. II, p. 202.

positive impact is that of the capital of a country invested in the carrying trade, because it is "altogether withdrawn from supporting the productive labor of that particular country, to support that of foreign countries."[40]

This first argument in favor of the "natural" developmental path simply states that the best possible way to develop a national market economy is to start with the expansion and improvement of agriculture and domestic trade. This expansion and improvement creates opportunities for the spontaneous development of manufacturing activities in a relationship of mutual support with agricultural activities. Agricultural and industrial growth, in turn, generate a surplus of commodities that is more profitable to sell abroad in exchange for other commodities than to sell them in the home market. As foreign trade further increases the size of the market, new opportunities arise for the emergence of new specialized branches of production and for the accumulation of capital over and above what can be profitably employed "in supplying the consumption, and supporting the productive labor of that particular country." When that happens, "the surplus part of [capital] naturally disgorges itself into the carrying trade, and is employed in performing the same offices to other countries."

> The carrying trade is the natural effect and symptom of great national wealth; but it does not seem to be the natural cause of it. Those statesmen who have been disposed to favor it with particular encouragements, seem to have mistaken the effect and symptom for the cause.[41]

This argument in favor of the "natural" path of economic development is complemented by two other arguments that epitomize Smith's anti-urban bias. As Rosenberg has noted, this bias is a logical consequence of Smith's dual contention that geographic concentration made urban areas the epicenter of restraints upon the competitive process and that the rural population is less subject to the negative effects of the division of labor than the urban population.[42]

> The inhabitants of a town, being collected in one place, can easily combine together. The most insignificant trades carried on in

---

40 Ibid., vol. I, pp. 385, 389–92, 456.
41 Ibid., p. 395.
42 Rosenberg, "Adam Smith on the Division of Labor," p. 138 n.

towns have accordingly . . . been incorporated; and even where
they have never been incorporated, yet the corporation spirit, the
jealousy of strangers, the aversion to take apprentices, or to
communicate the secret of their trade, generally prevail in them,
and often teach them, by voluntary associations and agreements, to
prevent that free competition which they cannot prohibit by bye-
laws. . . . The inhabitants of the country, [in contrast,] dispersed
in distant places cannot easily combine together. They have not
only never been incorporated, but the corporation spirit never
prevailed among them.[43]

This difference in the urban and rural condition, often backed by
legislation, enables "the inhabitants of the towns to raise their prices,
without fearing to be under-sold by the free competition of their
countrymen . . . [and] of foreigners." Although "landlords, farmers,
and laborers of the country" are the ones who eventually pay for these
higher prices, they seldom oppose state-backed urban monopolies,
because "the clamor and sophistry of merchants and manufacturers
easily persuade them that the private interests of a part, and of a
subordinate part of the society, is the general interest of the whole."[44]
Smith repeats here the argument discussed earlier of the capacity of
profit earners to impose on society a class interest that does not
correspond to the general interest. But, in doing so, he draws a
distinction between rural and urban workers that was missing in the
discussion of the class interests of those who live by profit, by rent,
and by wages. For the relation of unequal exchange between town
and country is said to benefit, not just the merchants and manufacturers who are the promoters of its establishment, but urban workers
as well.

It is in this context that Smith asserts that the agricultural worker is
less subject than the industrial worker to the negative effects of the
technical division of labor. Although "generally regarded as the
pattern of stupidity and ignorance," the common agricultural worker
"is seldom defective in [the] judgment and discretion" required to
manage the great variety of instruments with which he works and of
materials upon which he works. "His understanding . . . being
accustomed to consider a greater variety of objects, is generally much
superior to that of the other, whose all attention from morning till
night is commonly occupied in performing one or two very simple

---

43 Smith, *Wealth of Nations*, vol. I, pp. 140–1; see also vol. II, pp. 383–4.
44 Ibid., vol. I, pp. 142–3.

operations." Moreover, the changing conditions of agricultural production "with every change of the weather, as well as with many
other accidents," continually impose demands upon and thereby keep
alive the judgment and discretion of the agricultural worker to a far
greater extent than is the case among urban workers who face
conditions of production "which are always the same or very nearly
the same." Indeed, if given a chance to become small proprietors, the
agricultural workers would be better entrepreneurs than large proprietors.[45]

In the absence of restraints on competition in urban areas, the
superior intelligence and skills of agricultural workers would be
reflected in a higher rank and in higher wages of rural laborers than
of urban workers, as it was said to be the case in countries such as
China that followed the "natural" developmental path. But, in
countries where the "unnatural" path was followed, as in Europe,
the opposite was true. Smith nonetheless notes that, at least in Great
Britain, this "unnatural" state of affairs was changing under the
weight of its own contradiction.

> This change may be regarded as the necessary, though very late
> consequence of the extraordinary encouragement given to the in-
> dustry of the towns. The stock accumulated in them comes in time to
> be so great, that . . . by increasing the competition, necessarily
> reduces the profit. The lowering of profit in the town forces out
> stock to the country, where, by creating a new demand for country
> labor, it necessarily raises its wages. It then spreads itself . . . over the
> face of the land, and by being employed in agriculture is in part
> restored to the country, at the expence of which, in a great measure, it
> had originally been accumulated in the towns.[46]

Smith's advice to the legislator is to facilitate this spontaneous
convergence of the "unnatural" towards the "natural" path. In
summing up the reasons for this advice, he states that "the great
object of the political œconomy of every country, is to increase the
riches and power of that country." And yet, the capital "acquired to
any country by commerce and manufactures, is all a very precarious
and uncertain possession," unless at least in part "has been secured
and realized in the cultivation and improvement of its lands."

---

45 Ibid., pp. 141–2, 410–19.
46 Ibid., pp. 142–3. On the greater rewards of agricultural relative to industrial
labor in China than in Europe, see also vol. II, p. 201.

A merchant, it has been said very properly, is not necessarily the citizen of any particular country. It is in a great measure indifferent to him from what place he carries on his trade; and a very trifling disgust will make him remove his capital, and together with it all the industry which it supports, from one country to another. No part of it can be said to belong to any particular country, till it has been spread as it were over the face of that country, either in buildings, or in the lasting improvements of lands. . . . The ordinary revolutions of war and government easily dry up the sources of that wealth which arises from commerce only. That which arises from the more solid improvements of agriculture, is much more durable, and cannot be destroyed but by those more violent convulsions occasioned by the depredations of hostile and barbarous nations for a century or two together.[47]

Wealth and Power

The connection between "riches" and "power" that Smith establishes in summing up the reasons for advocating a greater convergence of the European "unnatural" developmental path towards a more "natural" one, brings us back to his conception of political economy "as a branch of the science of a statesman or legislator." "Wealth, as Mr. Hobbes says, is power." Immediately after quoting Hobbes, Smith qualifies his agreement by adding that "the person who either acquires, or succeeds to a great fortune, does not necessarily acquire or succeed to any political power, either civil or military." Wealth may provide its possessor with "the means of acquiring both," but "does not necessarily convey to him either." The power that it does convey "immediately and directly" is "the power of purchasing; a certain command over all the labor, or all the produce of labor which is then in the market."[48]

As Albert Hirschman has underscored, the displacement of the power conveyed by control over means of violence by the power conveyed by possession of wealth was for Smith the most positive effect of the development of commerce and industry.[49] Prior to this

---

47 Ibid., vol. I, pp. 394, 444–5.
48 Ibid., p. 35.
49 Albert O. Hirschman, *The Passions and the Interests: Political Arguments for Capitalism before its Triumph* (Princeton, NJ, Princeton University Press, 1977), pp. 100–2.

development, the great proprietors of land had no better use for their surplus produce than to support large numbers of retainers, who were entirely dependent on the great landlords and constituted their private armies. Under these circumstances it was very difficult for the central government to restrain the violence of the great lords "who [made] war according to their own discretion, almost continually upon one another, and very frequently upon the king," turning the open country into "a scene of violence, rapine, and disorder." But what the political and military power of the central government could not achieve, "the silent and insensible operation of foreign commerce and manufactures gradually brought about."

> These gradually furnished the great proprietors with something for which they could exchange the whole surplus of produce of their lands, and which they could consume themselves without sharing it with either their tenants or retainers. . . . For a pair of diamond buckles perhaps, or for something as frivolous and useless, they exchange the maintenance . . . of a thousand men for a year, and with it the whole weight and authority which it could give them . . . and thus, for the gratification of the most childish, the meanest and the most sordid of all vanities, they gradually bartered their whole power and authority . . . [and] became as insignificant as any substantial burgher or tradesman in a city. A regular government was established in the country as well as in the city, nobody having sufficient power to disturb its operations in the one, any more than in the other.[50]

Smith seems here to forget that, although wealth does not immediately and directly translate into political power, it provides the means of acquiring it in more roundabout ways, and that he elsewhere described urban merchants and manufacturers (whose power and authority here is said to be insignificant) as having the capacity to impose on state and society their particular interest against the national interest. As we shall see in Chapter 3, Smith's reductive conception of money as mere means of payment limits his ability to see the longer-term and larger-scale relationship between the pursuit of profit and the pursuit of power. In the present context, however, we can resolve the seeming contradiction between Smith's opposite claims concerning the operation of foreign commerce and manufactures—that it strengthened the hand of the central government and

---

50 Smith, *Wealth of Nations*, vol. I, pp. 433–9.

that it created powerful forces that interfered with the capacity of the central government to pursue the national interest—by noticing that they refer to different functions and "stages" of national development.

The first claim refers to the centralization of the legitimate use of violence over the territory of an existing or would-be national state. In this respect, Smith condemns warlordism, and welcomes the role that the operation of foreign commerce and manufactures played in overcoming its peculiar European form ("feudalism") through the spread of market exchanges from the urban to the rural areas. The second claim, in contrast, refers to a situation in which the legitimate use of violence has been successfully centralized and a national market economy has been fully established. Under these circumstances, the "unnatural" overdevelopment of foreign commerce and manufactures becomes the major obstacle to the central government's capacity to pursue the national interest. Hence Smith's advice to the legislator to countervail the power of merchants and manufacturers by making them compete with one another in driving down prices and profits. In one situation the main limit on the power of the central government comes from the landlords' control over means of violence; in the other situation, it comes from the merchants' and manufacturers' control over wealth. But in both situations, Smith's overwhelming preoccupation is with the establishment and preservation of the central government's capacity to pursue the national interest.

The pursuit of the national interest against domestic threats and resistance is, of course, closely related to its pursuit in the international arena, and Smith never leaves any doubt that "protecting the society from the violence and invasion of other independent societies" is "the first duty of the sovereign" and "is of much more importance than opulence." In the interest of national defense, he is therefore willing to support policies that in his view have negative effects on the wealth of the nation.

> If any particular manufacture was necessary . . . for the defence of the society, it might not always be prudent to depend upon our neighbors for the supply; and if such manufacture could not otherwise be supported at home, it might not be unreasonable that all the other branches of industry should be taxed in order to support it.

Similarly, Smith characterizes the Navigation Act of 1651, which gave British ships a monopoly of British trade, "perhaps the wisest of all the commercial regulations of England," even if it "proceeded from national animosity" rather than economic considerations. "National animosity at that particular time aimed at the very same object which the most deliberate wisdom would have recommended, the diminution of the naval power of Holland, the only naval power which could endanger the security of England."[51]

Smith saw a major contradiction between the needs of national defense and national economic development. Increasing national wealth makes the country a more attractive target to poorer neighbors. But the division of labor on which increasing national wealth depends undermines the martial virtues of the great body of the population. Among nations of shepherds and nations of husbandmen with little foreign commerce and only household manufactures, "every man . . . either is a warrior, or easily becomes such." Not so among nations of specialized industrial, commercial, and agricultural workers, who are neither prepared for war by their employments nor have the time to engage in martial exercises. With the progress of national wealth and of the division of labor, "the great body of the people [thus] becomes altogether unwarlike . . . and unless the state takes some new measures for the public defence, the natural habits of the people render them altogether incapable of defending themselves."[52]

In advising the legislator on the measures of public defense to take in order to solve the contradiction between the tendencies of economic development to make the nation both more likely to be attacked and more incapable of defending itself, Smith relies primarily on an extension to the "art of war" of his theory of the advantages of the social division of labor.

> The state of the mechanical, as well as of some other arts, with which it is necessarily connected, determines the degree of perfection to which [the art of war] is capable of being carried at any particular time. But in order to carry it to this degree of perfection, it is necessary that it should become the sole or principal occupation of a particular class of citizens, and the division of labor is as necessary for the improvement of this, as of every other art.[53]

---

51 Ibid., vol. I, pp. 486–7; vol. II, pp. 28, 213. For a detailed discussion, see Haakonssen, *Science of a Legislator*, pp. 93–5, 180ff.
52 Smith, *Wealth of Nations*, vol. II, pp. 216–20.
53 Ibid., p. 219.

The extension of the division of labor to the art of war, however, cannot rely on private initiative. In the other arts "the division of labor is naturally introduced by the prudence of individuals," but only the state can induce the private citizen "to give up the greater part of his time to this peculiar occupation." From this standpoint, the creation of a modern standing army has several advantages over reliance on militias. It affords greater specialization in military activities; it inculcates the qualities of regularity, order, and prompt obedience to command that "in modern armies, are of more importance . . . than the dexterity and skill of the soldiers in the use of arms"; and it "establishes, with an irresistible force, the law of the sovereign through the remotest provinces of the empire, and maintains some degree of regular government in countries which could not otherwise admit of any."[54]

Even in discussing national defense, Smith thus returns to his overwhelming concern with the centralization of power in the hands of national governments. But, in concluding that discussion with the "great change introduced into the art of war by the invention of fire-arms," he raises questions for which *The Wealth of Nations* provides no coherent answer. The main effect of that great change, we are told, was to enhance "still further both the expence of exercising and disciplining any particular number of soldiers in time of peace, and of employing them in time of war." Their arms and ammunition had become much more expensive, and so had the fortifications that towns needed "to resist even for a few weeks the attack of [modern] artillery." The unavoidable result was a true revolution in international relations.

> In modern war the great expence of fire-arms gives an evident advantage to the nation which can best afford that expence; and consequently, to an opulent and civilized, over a poor and barbarous nation. In ancient times the opulent and civilized found it difficult to defend themselves against the poor and barbarous nations. In modern times the poor and barbarous find it difficult to defend themselves against the opulent and civilized. The invention of fire-arms . . . is certainly favorable both to the permanency and to the extension of civilization.[55]

Two sets of questions immediately arise. First, is it possible that the advantages conferred to wealthy nations by modern warfare, other

---

54 Ibid., pp. 219–22, 228–9.
55 Ibid., pp. 230–1.

things being equal, are greater for the "unnatural" than for the "natural" path of economic development, given the greater role that manufacturing, foreign trade, and navigation play in the former? And, if this is the case, how can Smith's preference for the "natural" path of development be reconciled with the priority he assigns to defense over opulence? Or, to rephrase, would not "opulent and civilized" nations developing along the "natural" path expose themselves to the aggression of less "opulent and civilized" nations developing along the "unnatural" path, as was already happening to India in Smith's own times and would soon happen to China as well? Second, and closely related to the above, if wealth procured along the "unnatural" path is a source of superior military force, and if superior military force was the reason why Europeans could appropriate the benefits of the greater integration of the global economy at the expense of non-European "barbarous" and "civilized" nations alike, as Smith maintains in the passage quoted in the Introduction of this book, how could "commerce from all countries to all countries" bring about the "equality of force" among the world's nations as Smith claimed? What forces, if any, would prevent this commerce from generating a virtuous circle of enrichment and empowerment for the peoples of European descent and a vicious circle of impoverishment and disempowerment for most other peoples?

These questions fall beyond the horizon of Smith's historical sociology. They are, nonetheless, central to our concerns. In order to answer them, we must now take a step backward to re-examine the different conceptions of economic development discussed in Chapter 1, and a step forward to see what light Marx's and Schumpeter's theories of capitalist development can throw on the eclipse and resurgence of East Asia as a leading region of world development.

3

MARX, SCHUMPETER, AND THE "ENDLESS" ACCUMULATION OF CAPITAL AND POWER

The foregoing reconstruction of the historical sociology of Adam Smith confirms that the "discovery" of Smith in Beijing discussed in Chapter 1 is no mirage. Not only did Smith himself see late imperial China as an exemplar of market-based development; he also saw it as having gone *almost* as far as that development could go. I say "almost" because Smith thought that greater involvement in foreign trade, especially if carried out on Chinese ships, could have further increased China's national wealth. Despite this shortcoming, Smith upheld China rather than Europe as a model of the kind of market-based economic development that was most advisable for governments to pursue.

In this respect, Frank's contention that, according to Smith, "Europe was a Johnny-come-lately in the development of the wealth of nations" is only partially true. Smith did see economic development in Europe as taking place both within smaller national economies than in China and along an "unnatural" path, which he considered less favorable to the national interest than China's "natural" path. However, in his view, Holland had attained a condition of opulence similar to China's, albeit on an incomparably smaller geographical scale.

More generally, the problem with the notion of Smithian growth used by Wong, Frank, and Pomeranz, as well as by their critics (see Chapter 1), is that Smith theorized economic development as occurring, not along a single path, but along two distinct paths: the "unnatural" or foreign-trade-based path typical of Europe, and the "natural" or home-trade-based path typical of China. Like de Vries, Huang, and Brenner, Smith thus saw China and Europe developing along distinct paths; unlike them, however, he did not see the European path as having a greater growth potential than the Chinese. On the contrary, he saw both paths leading to a stationary state or

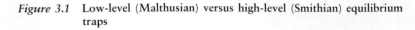

Figure 3.1   Low-level (Malthusian) versus high-level (Smithian) equilibrium traps

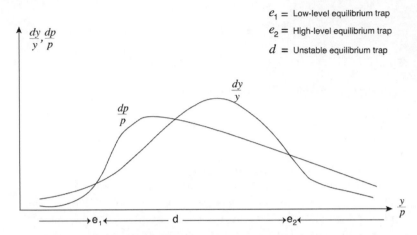

Note: y/p = per capita income, dy/y = rate of income growth, dp/p = rate of population growth. Adapted from Richard Nelson, "A Theory of the Low-Level Equilibrium Trap in Underdeveloped Economies," *The American Economic Review*, 46, 4 (1956).

high-level equilibrium. China and Holland had already reached that state; but economic growth in all countries, including the still "under-stocked" and "under-populated" Northern American colonies, would eventually taper off into a similar state.

Smith's notion of a stationary state (and the notion of a high-level equilibrium trap derived from it) should not be confused, as they often are, with the Malthusian notion of population checks on economic growth. The difference between the two can be clarified by means of Figure 3.1, in which e_1 represents a low-level equilibrium similar to that theorized by Malthus, while e_2 represents a high-level equilibrium similar to the stationary state theorized by Smith.[1] The horizontal x axis shows levels of per capita income (y/p), y being income and p population. The vertical y axis shows both the rate of income growth (dy/y) and the rate of population growth (dp/p). The curve dy/y thus describes the relationship between the rate of income

---

   1 Figure 3.1 is derived from a similar one originally conceived by Richard Nelson to illustrate his theory of the low-level equilibrium trap. See Nelson, "A Theory of the Low-Level Equilibrium Trap in Underdeveloped Economies," *The American Economic Review*, 46, 4 (1956), and for more elaborate representations of the same idea, Harvey Leibenstein, *Economic Backwardness and Economic Growth* (New York, Wiley, 1963).

growth (dy/y) and the level of per capita income (y/p). It posits that increasing levels of per capita income are associated up to a point with rising, and after that point with declining rates of income growth. The curve dp/p describes instead the relationship between the rate of population growth (dp/p) and the level of per capita income (y/p). It posits that increasing levels of per capita income are associated, up to a point with rising, and after that point with declining rates of population growth. Although the two curves have a similar shape, as the figure shows, rates of population growth are assumed to rise more steeply than rates of income growth at low levels of per capita income, and to decrease less steeply at high levels. When the curve dy/y is higher than the curve dp/p, the rate of income growth exceeds the rate of population growth, and therefore per capita income (y/p on the horizontal axis) increases; and when the curve dy/y is lower than the curve dp/p, the rate of population growth exceeds the rate of income growth, and therefore per capita income (y/p on the horizontal axis) decreases.

These assumptions generate three points of equilibrium (e_1, d, and e_2)—points, that is, at which the rates of income and population growth are equal and, therefore, per capita income does not change. Point d, however, represents an unstable equilibrium, in the sense that even a small increase (decrease) in per capita income results in a higher (lower) rate of income than population growth and, therefore, in a rise (decline) of per capita income until it reaches e_2 (e_1). Points e_1 and e_2, in contrast, represent stable equilibria, because any departure from them, to the left or to the right, will result in differentials in rates of income and population growth that bring per capita income back to them. Although they are both stable equilibria, e_1 represents a low-level and e_2 a high-level equilibrium. The low-level equilibrium best represents the Malthusian notion of population checks on economic growth, because what prevents per capita income from rising above e_1 is a steep rise in the rate of population growth; the Smithian notion of stationary state is instead best represented by the high-level equilibrium, because what prevents per capita income from rising above e_2 is a steep decline in the rate of income growth.

Figure 3.1 can also clarify Schumpeter's notion of an economic development that has no inherent tendency to transform the social framework within which it takes place. Once an economy has somehow managed to get unstuck from the low-level equilibrium e_1 by attaining a per capita income higher that d, economic growth proceeds until decreasing returns bring down the rate of increase of per capita income to the same level as the rate of population growth.

When that happens, the economy settles in the high-level equilibrium e_2 (Smith's stationary state), and further growth is possible only if the visible hand of the state (or some other exogenous process or action) brings into existence a social framework with a greater growth potential—a change that would be represented in Figure 3.1 by an upward shift to the right of the curve dy/y. The change, however, only enables the economy to move to a higher equilibrium; it does not generate a process of boundless growth. A representation like that of Figure 3.1, therefore, cannot portray what Schumpeter considers the most important characteristic of *capitalist* development: its tendency to destroy the social frameworks within which it occurs and to create the conditions for the emergence of new frameworks with greater growth potential.

In claiming that, prior to the Great Divergence, England was already developing along a path of unbound growth, Huang and Brenner have in mind a development characterized by a tendency of this kind. For Brenner, the key ingredient of such development was the separation of direct producers from the means of production, which was necessary to force workers to sell their labor-power in competition with one another to large production units. The absence of this condition, he claims, is the reason why market-based development in China did not assume the boundless character it did in England. Huang acknowledges that large, wage-labor-based farms existed also in China up to the seventeenth century. But he similarly views their subsequent displacement by small-scale household production as the main reason why China's market-based development did not acquire the more dynamic characteristics of the European path.

The positions of Huang and Brenner—being derived from Marx's critique of political economy, to which we shall presently turn—are in sharp contrast with those expressed in *The Wealth of Nations*. By elevating large-scale production and the technical division of labor to conditions of boundless economic development, they turn Smith's negative view of both phenomena on its head. Sugihara's thesis of the lasting significance of the East Asian Industrious Revolution does not question the competitive advantages of the wage-labor-based, large-scale production typical of the European path. It nonetheless maintains, first, that development along this path has its own limits, and, second, that when these limits are reached the East Asian Industrious Revolution path holds the greatest promise for further economic development. Although Sugihara does not cite Smith in this context, his positive assessment of the advantages of small-scale household production typical of the East Asian path—most notably, the preservation of a labor force capable of performing multiple tasks well; of responding flexibly to variations in the natural and social environment of production; and of anticipating, preventing, and solving problems relating to the management of production—is eminently Smithian. As we shall see in Chapter 6, it is also typical of recent theories of so-called flexible production. Is it possible that the East Asian resurgence is vindicating at least some aspects of the Smithian view of market-based development?

In order to answer this question, we must preliminarily clarify the concept of market-based *capitalist* development and its relevance to an understanding of the Great Divergence and the present East Asian economic resurgence. My argument in this chapter is that Marx's and Schumpeter's theories of capitalist development do indeed provide crucial insights into the specificity of the European developmental path. But they are even less useful than Smith's historical sociology in resolving the issue of the relationship between Europe's foreign-trade-based development and the superiority of military force that, for at least three centuries, enabled Europeans to appropriate most of the benefits of the increasing integration of the global economy. I shall therefore recast Marx's and Schumpeter's theories in an analytical framework that will enable us to deal with this issue in the rest of the book.

The "Endless" Accumulation of Capital

In his critique of political economy—the subtitle of *Capital*—Marx does not just express different views than Smith on specific issues, such as the accumulation of capital and the falling rate of profit, or the social and technical division of labor. He pursues an altogether different research program: he changes, so to say, the nature and topic of the conversation. His interlocutors are not governments—Smith's legislators—but social classes. His subject matter is not the enrichment and empowerment of nations, but the enrichment and empowerment of the possessors of capital vis-à-vis the possessors of labor-power. His research strategy does not privilege competition in the marketplace but class conflict and technical change in the workplace.

This shift in the nature and topic of the conversation has been the source of great confusion concerning Marx's *implicit* theory of national development. I say implicit because, explicitly, Marx has no such theory. What he has is a theory of the development of capitalism on a world scale which, as noted in Chapter 1, insightfully anticipated today's understanding of "globalization" but mistakenly predicted that generalized capitalist development would "flatten" the world, in Thomas Friedman's sense of the expression. Indeed, so confident was Marx in an imminent flattening of the world, that he based his entire theory of capitalist production on the premise of a borderless world, in which the labor force is fully dispossessed of the means of production and all commodities, including labor-power, exchanged freely at prices more or less equal to their production costs.[2]

Although Marx has no explicit theory of national development, the theory implicit in his analysis of capitalist development differs from Smith's in several respects. A first difference, which conditions all others, is that for Marx capitalist agencies participate in market exchanges for a purpose other than transforming commodities into commodities of greater utility. Smith rules out this possibility on the ground that, while commodities are in themselves useful, "money serves no other purpose besides purchasing goods."

> The man who buys, does not always mean to sell again, but frequently to use or consume; whereas he who sells, always means to buy again. The one may frequently have done the whole, but the other can never have done more than the one-half of his business. It is not for its own sake that men desire money, but for the sake of what they can purchase with it.[3]

Marx symbolizes Smith's logic with the formula of commodity exchange C–M–C', in which money (M) is mere means in the

---

2 However unrealistic, this premise was justified by Marx's theoretical purpose of demonstrating that, *even in an ideal world of perfect competition*, the increasing subordination of labor to capital in the workplace, along with an ever decreasing cost of the commodities needed to reproduce the labor force, could be expected to result in a relative enrichment and empowerment of the possessors of capital vis-à-vis the possessors of labor-power. The premise, however, made (and still makes) no sense at all as a description of the actual conditions of capitalist development at different times and in different places. Indeed, in some of his historical analyses—most notably, of the class struggle in France—Marx himself retreats from his critique of political economy, defines class interests with reference to a national political-economic space (as Smith does), and never mentions the hidden abodes of production. See Giovanni Arrighi, Terence K. Hopkins, and Immanuel Wallerstein, *Antisystemic Movements* (London, Verso, 1989), ch. 1.

3 Adam Smith, *An Inquiry into the Nature and Causes of the Wealth of Nations*, 2 vols (London, Methuen, 1961), vol. I, p. 460.

transformation of a set of commodities (C) into another set (C') of greater utility. He then contrasts this logic with that of the capitalist, whose business is completed (that is, has attained its purpose) when the money (M) invested in the purchase of a particular combination of commodities (C) yields, through sales in the market, a greater amount of money (M'). Hence, Marx's general formula of capital M–C–M', which simply means that for capitalist investors the purchase of commodities is strictly instrumental to an increase in the monetary value of their assets from M to M'. Indeed, if and when circumstances create more profitable opportunities in the credit system than in the trade and production of commodities, the transformation of money into commodities may be skipped altogether (as in Marx's abridged formula of capital, M–M').[4]

Marx never clearly explains why capitalist agencies pursue the seemingly irrational objective of accumulating money for its own sake. Indeed, his *dictum* "Accumulate, accumulate! That is Moses and the prophets," appears to be an admission that he has no rational explanation for the accumulation of money as an end in itself. Nevertheless, shortly before uttering the *dictum* he states that "the love of power is an element in the desire to get rich."[5] We are thus back to Hobbes's equation of wealth and power, which Smith quoted approvingly only to reduce the power associated with money to "purchasing power." Marx explicitly rejects this reduction, and although he does not tell us exactly what kind of power money confers, and how it relates to other kinds of power, his entire work implies that the "endless" accumulation of money is the primary source of power in a capitalist society.

This is evident from a second difference between Marx's implicit and Smith's explicit theories of market-based national development. Marx agrees with Smith that the European path of economic development was based on long-distance (foreign) trade rather than short-distance (domestic) trade. Both in the *Manifesto* and in *Capital*, he states categorically that the "modern history of capital"—that is, the rise to dominance of the bourgeoisie and modern industry in Europe—"dates from the creation in the sixteenth century of a world-embracing commerce and world-embracing market."[6]

---

4 Karl Marx, *Capital*, vol. I (Moscow, Foreign Languages Publishing House, 1959), pp. 146–55; *Capital*, vol. III (Moscow, Foreign Languages Publishing House, 1962), pp. 343–4.

5 Marx, *Capital*, vol. I, pp. 592–5.

6 Ibid., p. 146.

The East-Indian and Chinese markets, the colonization of America, trade with the colonies, the increase in the means of exchange
and in commodities generally, gave to commerce, to navigation, to
industry, an impulse never before known. . . . The guild-masters
were pushed on one side by the manufacturing middle class; [the
social] division of labor between different guilds vanished in the
face of [the technical] division of labor in each single workshop.[7]

However, what for Smith is an "unnatural" path of economic
development, for Marx is the capitalist path. More important,
Smith's preoccupation with the need to countervail capitalist power
through government action, as well as his preference for a development based on agriculture and home trade, are completely alien to
Marx. In his view, with the establishment of modern industry and the
world market, governments lost all capacity to countervail the power
of the bourgeoisie, who "conquered for itself, in the modern representative State, exclusive political sway," virtually reducing governments to the role of committees for managing its affairs. As for the
Asian nations and civilizations, which Smith took as the exemplars of
his "natural" developmental path, and which, in Marx's own account, had provided the markets that made possible the emergence of
the European capitalist path, they had no chance of surviving the
onslaught of the European bourgeoisie. "Just as [the bourgeoisie]
made the country dependent on the towns, so it has made barbarian
and semi-barbarian countries dependent on civilized ones, nations of
peasants on nations of bourgeois, the East on the West."[8]
    Being entirely focused on class power, Marx forgets to tell us how
the wealth of the bourgeoisie could so easily translate into political
power both nationally and internationally. Nationally, he probably
agreed with Smith that wealth and geographical concentration gave
the bourgeoisie the power to impose on the state its particular class
interest at the expense of the general national interest. Evidently,
however, he thought that this power had grown so massively since the
publication of *The Wealth of Nations* that all attempts to countervail
it in the short to medium run had been vanquished. It is also possible,
however, that Marx disagreed with Smith, and thought that, at least
in some European countries, the bourgeois interest had come to
coincide with the national interest, in the sense that the capitalist

---

7 Karl Marx and Frederick Engels, *The Communist Manifesto* (Harmondsworth, Penguin, 1967), p. 80.
    8 Ibid., pp. 82, 84.

path, of which the bourgeoisie was the bearer, had come to be "conceived of, and presented, as being the motor force of a . . . development of all the 'national' energies" (to paraphrase Antonio Gramsci).[9]

Marx is more explicit, but not particularly consistent, on the mechanisms through which the economic power of the bourgeoisie translates into the power of some nations vis-à-vis other nations. The mechanism mentioned in the *Manifesto*, and on several occasions in *Capital*, is the competitive superiority of capitalist production. "The cheap prices of its commodities are the heavy artillery with which [the bourgeoisie] batters down all Chinese walls." However, in one of the concluding chapters of the first volume of *Capital*, Marx explicitly mentions the opium wars against China as an example of the continuing significance of military force as the "midwife" of the capitalist transformation of world society.[10]

As we shall see in Chapter 11, even after British gunboats had battered down the wall of governmental regulations that enclosed China's market economy, British merchants and manufacturers had a hard time in out-competing their Chinese counterparts in most activities. Insofar as China is concerned, actual military force, rather than the metaphorical artillery of cheap commodities, was the key to the subjugation of East to West. If so, however, we need to know what made "nations of bourgeois" militarily superior to "nations of peasants"—or, to put it more precisely, whether and how economic development along the capitalist path was associated with a greater increase in military power than development along a market-based, non-capitalist path. On this issue, Marx has even less to say than Smith. By focusing exclusively on the connection between capitalism and industrialism, Marx ends up by paying no attention to the close connection between both phenomena and militarism. But even what he says about the economic superiority of capitalist development is less straightforward than Huang and Brenner imply in the passages quoted in Chapter 1.

This brings us to a third major difference between Marx and Smith. As noted in Chapter 2, while Smith's research program takes him out of the pin factory to investigate the market and the social division of labor, Marx's research program takes him into the hidden abodes of production to investigate the relationship between labor and capital

---

9 Antonio Gramsci, *Selections from the Prison Notebooks* (New York, International Publishers, 1971), pp. 181–2.

10 Marx and Engels, *Communist Manifesto*, p. 84; Marx, *Capital*, vol. I, p. 751.

and the technical division of labor. In these abodes, Marx discovers that technical and organizational change originate, not just in the competition among capitalists and in the emergence of new specialized branches of trade and production, as Smith had already theorized, but also in the incessant conflict between capital and labor over wages and working conditions. In this respect, the concentration of production in units of increasing size and the greater technical division of labor that goes with it—which Smith considers inimical to economic efficiency and to the intellectual quality of the labor force—appear to Marx as essential conditions of the innovations that enable capitalists to shift competitive pressures onto workers, by making them vulnerable to replacement by other workers, by machines, and by knowledge embodied in the organization controlled by capital.

> If, at first, the workman sells his labor-power to capital, because the material means of producing a commodity fail him, now his very labor-power refuses its services unless it has been sold to capital. Its functions can be exercised only in an environment that exists in the workshop of the capitalist after the sale.[11]

This is the central statement of Marx's critique of Smith's political economy. Whatever their effect on economic efficiency and on the intellectual quality of the labor force, the increasing size of production units and the greater technical division of labor are, for Marx, essential conditions of the empowerment and enrichment of the possessors of capital vis-à-vis the possessors of labor-power. Technical and organizational change are not class-neutral: they are the instrument of an ever more substantive subordination of labor to capital. Although this process of class subordination involves a constant increase in the productivity of the labor force *actually employed by the capitalist enterprise*, it is less clear what Marx thought of the efficacy of the process in promoting economic development at the national, regional, and global levels.

For one thing, he explicitly agrees with Smith that the technical division of labor has deleterious effects upon the moral and intellectual qualities of the labor force. The technical division of labor, he tells us, "converts the laborer into a crippled monstrosity, by forcing his detail dexterity at the expense of a world of productive capabilities and instincts." This tendency, in turn, may become an obstacle to

---

11 Marx, *Capital*, vol. I, p. 360.

further economic development, because the ever expanding and changing division of labor in society "incessantly launches masses of capital and of workpeople from one branch of production to another," and "therefore necessitates variation of labor, fluency of function, universal mobility of the laborer," rather than the "crippled monstrosities" created by the capitalistic form of modern industry.[12]

Thus, implicitly, Marx seems here to agree with Smith that the technical division of labor is ultimately less beneficial than the social division of labor for economic development. Moreover, even in describing the unfolding of the Industrial Revolution across industries in the nineteenth century, his emphasis is almost entirely on the social rather than the technical division of labor. In this description, technological change spreads across spheres of industry "connected together by being separate phases of a process, and yet . . . isolated by the social division of labor."

> Thus spinning by machinery made weaving by machinery a necessity, and both together made the mechanical and chemical revolution that took place in bleaching, printing and dyeing, imperative. So too . . . the revolution in cotton-spinning called forth the invention of the gin, for separating the seeds from the cotton fibre; it was only by means of this invention, that the production of cotton became possible on the enormous scale at present required. But more especially, the revolution in the modes of production of industry and agriculture made necessary a revolution in the general conditions of the social process of production, i.e., in the means of communication and transport. . . . [T]he means of communication and transport handed down from the manufacturing period soon became unbearable trammels on Modern Industry, with its feverish haste of production, its enormous extent, its constant flinging of capital and labor from one sphere of production to another, and its newly created connexions with the markets of the whole world. Hence . . . the means of communication and transport became gradually adapted to the modes of production of mechanical industry, by the creation of a system of river steamers, railways, ocean steamers, and telegraphs. But the huge masses of iron that had now to be forged, to be welded, to be cut, to be bored, and to be shaped, demanded, on their part, cyclopean machines, [which could only be constructed by means of other machines].[13]

---

12 Ibid., pp. 360–3, 486–9.
13 Ibid., pp. 383–4.

Except for its global scope, there is nothing in this particular description that would not fit into Smith's account of economic development as a process driven by an increasing social division of labor, including the emergence of sectors specializing in the production of capital goods and of individuals and organizations specializing in the production of scientific knowledge. If there is anything specifically capitalistic about this process of diffusion of the Industrial Revolution, it is not the employment of wage labor in units of ever increasing scale. Rather, it is the self-expansion of capital that underlies the process and continually upsets whatever equilibrium exists among branches of production at any particular time: "The different spheres of production, it is true, constantly tend to equilibrium . . . But this constant tendency to equilibrium . . . is exercised only in the shape of a reaction against the constant upsetting of this equilibrium."[14] This continual upsetting of equilibria is what Schumpeter later called capitalism's "creative destruction."

Capitalist Crises and Creative Destruction

As anticipated in Chapter 2, the idea that the accumulation of capital over time tends to drive down the rate of profit, eventually bringing economic expansion to an end, is not Marx's but Smith's idea. For Marx, this tendency is real but by no means the insurmountable obstacle to further expansion that it is for Smith. On the contrary, "as representative of the general form of wealth—[that is,] money—capital is the endless and limitless drive to go beyond its limiting barrier. . . . Every limit appears as a barrier to be overcome."

> In accord with this tendency, capital drives beyond national barriers and prejudices . . . as well as all traditional, confined, complacent, encrusted satisfactions of present needs, and reproductions of old ways of life. It is destructive towards all of this, and constantly revolutionizes it, tearing down all the barriers which hem in the development of the forces of production, the expansion of needs . . . and the exploitation and exchange of natural and mental forces.[15]

14 Ibid., pp. 355–6.

15 Karl Marx, *Grundrisse: Foundations of the Critique of Political Economy* (New York, Vintage, 1973), pp. 334, 408, 410.

This endless and limitless drive is inseparable from the crisis-prone tendencies of capitalist development. Smith does not speak of crisis to characterize the situation of over-accumulation, intensifying competition among capitals, and declining profitability that eventually brings expansion to an end. For him, such a situation is the natural outcome of a process of economic development embedded in, and limited by, a particular geographical and institutional environment. For Marx, in contrast, a general and persistent fall of the rate of profit in an economy in which trade, production, and accumulation are all undertaken in view of a profit, is bound to be experienced as a crisis— that is, a time of instability and disordered function. More important, having ruled out the possibility that capitalist agencies accumulate money as an end in itself—or, more correctly, because of the social and political power it conveys—and having disregarded the ever more substantive subordination of labor to capital in the production process, Smith rules out also the possibility of so-called over-production crises. Marx, in contrast, attributes at least as much importance to this kind of crisis, as he did to crises associated with the over-accumulation of capital and the falling tendency of the rate of profit.

> *Over-production* is specifically conditioned by the general law of production of capital: to produce to the limit set by the productive forces, that is to say, to exploit the maximum amount of labor with the given amount of capital, without any consideration for the actual limits of the market or the needs backed by the ability to pay; and this is carried out through . . . constant reconversion of revenue into capital, while on the other hand, the mass of the producers remain tied to the average level of needs, and must remain tied to it according to the nature of capitalist production.[16]

The notion of over-production crises is based on opposite assumptions concerning the capacity of real wages to keep up with increases in labor productivity than the notion of over-accumulation crises. Over-accumulation crises occur because there is such an overabundance of capital seeking investment in established channels of trade and production that competition among its possessors enables real wages to rise in step with, or even faster than, increases in labor productivity. Over-production crises, in contrast, occur because the possessors of capital are so successful in shifting competitive pres-

---

16 Karl Marx, "Crisis Theory (from *Theories of Surplus Value*)," in R.C. Tucker, ed., *The Marx–Engels Reader* (New York, Norton, 1978), p. 465.

sures onto labor that real wages fail to keep up with increases in labor productivity, thereby preventing effective aggregate demand from expanding in step with aggregate supply.

As Paul Sweezy has underscored, the assumption that real wages fail to keep up with increases in labor productivity is more consistent with Marx's theory of an ever more substantive subordination of labor to capital than the opposite assumption.[17] Marx's theoretical consistency, however, does not concern us here.[18] In any event, for our present purposes what is most interesting in Marx's account of capitalist crises is not their origin, but their consequences—the fact, that is, that Marx conceives of them as moments of fundamental capitalist reorganization.

Like Smith, Marx emphasizes how a persistent and generalized fall in the rate of profit transforms inter-capitalist competition from a positive-sum game—in which capitals benefit from one another's expansion—into a zero-sum (or even a negative-sum) game—that is, into "cutthroat competition," the primary objective of which is to drive other capitals out of business, even if it means sacrificing one's own profits for as long as it takes to attain the objective. Underlying the transformation is the existence of an excess or surplus of capital seeking investment in the purchase and sale of commodities above the level that would prevent the rate of profit from falling below what has come to be regarded as a "reasonable" or "tolerable" level. To prevent or counter such a fall, surplus capital must be crowded out.

> So long as things go well, competition affects an operating fraternity of the capitalist class . . . so that each [capitalist] shares in the common loot in proportion to the size of his respective investment. But as soon as it no longer is a question of sharing profits, but of sharing losses, everyone tries to reduce his own share to a minimum and to shove it off upon another. The class as such must inevitably lose. How much the individual capitalist . . . must share in [the loss] at all, is decided by strength and cunning, and competition then becomes a fight among hostile brothers. The antagonism between each individual capitalist's interest and those

---

17 Paul Sweezy, *The Theory of Capitalist Development* (London, Dobson, 1946), pp. 100–8, 133–86.

18 As Sweezy himself points out, whether the introduction of machinery and other labor-saving devices does or does not succeed in preventing real wages from increasing as fast as labor productivity is an issue that cannot be settled on general theoretical grounds: ibid., pp. 105–6. As we shall see in Chapters 5 and 6, the issue can be settled on empirical grounds.

of the capitalist class as a whole, then comes to the surface, just as previously the identity of those interests operated in practice through competition.[19]

The fall in the rate of profit and the intensification of the competitive struggle, however, do not end in a stationary state. On the contrary, they lead to the destruction of the social framework in which accumulation is embedded and to the creation of a new one. In Marx's account, this creative destruction takes three main forms: an increase in the size of capitals and the reorganization of business enterprise; the formation of surplus population and a new international division of labor; and the emergence of new and larger centers of capital accumulation. Let us briefly examine each in turn.

Marx draws a distinction between *concentration* of capital—the increase in size of individual capitals arising from accumulation—and *centralization* of capital, which transforms "many small into few large capitals." When competition intensifies and the rate of profit falls, small capitals "partly pass into the hands of their conquerors, [and] partly vanish."

> The so-called plethora of capital always applies essentially to a plethora of the capital for which the fall in the rate of profit is not compensated through the mass of profit . . . or to a plethora which places capitals incapable of action on their own at the disposal of the managers of large enterprises in the form of credit.[20]

Crucial in this respect is the role of the credit system, which "becomes a new and terrible weapon in the battle of competition and is . . . transformed into an enormous social mechanism for the centralization of capitals." The centralization, in turn, extends and speeds up technological and organizational change:

> Accumulation . . . is clearly a very slow procedure compared with centralization. . . . The world would still be without railways if it had to wait until accumulation had got a few individual capitals far enough to be adequate for the construction of a railway. Centralization, [in contrast,] accomplished this in the twinkling of an eye, by means of joint-stock companies.[21]

---

19 Marx, *Capital*, vol. III, p. 248.
20 Marx, *Capital*, vol. I, pp. 625–6; vol. III, p. 246.
21 Marx, *Capital*, vol. I, pp. 626–8.

The centralization and reorganization of capital go hand in hand with the formation of a reserve army of labor and a reorganization of the international division of labor. The extension and speed-up of technological and organizational change strengthens the capital-intensive and labor-saving bias of capitalist development, generating a "relatively redundant population of laborers"—relatively, that is, to the normal needs of capital accumulation. This surplus population is then available for new rounds of capitalist development on an ever increasing scale.

> The mass of social wealth, overflowing with the advance of accumulation, and transformable into additional capital, thrusts itself frantically into old branches of production, whose market suddenly expands, or into newly formed branches, such as railways . . . the need for which grows out of the development of the old ones. In all such cases, there must be the possibility of throwing great masses of men suddenly on the decisive points without injury to the scale of production in other spheres. Overpopulation supplies these masses.[22]

By creating an "unlimited" supply of labor endogenously—that is, as a result of the process of capitalist development itself—"the modern industrial system . . . acquires an elasticity, a capacity for sudden expansion by leaps and bounds that finds no hindrance except in the supply of raw material and the disposal of the produce." And yet, also this impediment is nothing but a barrier to be overcome. Not only does machinery "increase the supply of raw material in the same way, for example, as the cotton gin augmented the production of cotton," more fundamentally,

> the cheapness of the articles produced by machinery, and the improved means of transport and communication furnish the weapons for conquering foreign markets. By ruining handicraft production in other countries, machinery forcibly converts them into fields for the supply of its raw material. In this way . . . India was compelled to produce cotton, wool, hemp, jute, and indigo for Great Britain. By constantly making a part of the hands "supernumerary," modern industry, in all countries where it has taken root, gives a spur to emigration and to the colonization of foreign lands, which are thereby converted into settlements for growing

---

22 Ibid., pp. 628–32.

the raw material of the mother country; just as Australia, for example, was converted into a colony for growing wool. A new and international division of labor, a division suited to the requirements of the chief centers of modern industry springs up, and converts one part of the globe into a chiefly agricultural field of production, for supplying the other part which remains a chiefly industrial field.[23]

Marx repeats here the *Manifesto*'s contention that the cheap prices of modern industry were the main weapon through which the European bourgeoisie conquered and restructured the global market. In this context, however, the destruction of the non-capitalist economies of other countries and the colonization of foreign lands through the resettlement of surplus population, create, not a world after the image of bourgeois Europe, as in the *Manifesto*, but a world of suppliers of raw material for the benefit of European industry. We shall return in future chapters to this discrepancy, which reflects the very different outcome of the European remaking of the world in market economies newly created through European settlement, such as the Americas, and in market economies long caught in a Smithian high-level equilibrium trap, such as India or China. For now, let us note that Marx's observation that the credit system is "an enormous social mechanism for the centralization of capitals" does not refer only to capitalists operating within a given political jurisdiction but also to capitalists operating across jurisdictions.

This brings us to the third main outcome of Marx's process of creative destruction. Since the research program pursued in *Capital* abstracts from the role of states in the economic process, Marx discusses national debts and the credit system under the rubric of "primitive accumulation"—that is, "an accumulation not the result of the capitalist mode of production, but its starting point." He nonetheless acknowledges the continuing significance of national debts as means of transferring surplus capital from declining to rising centers of capitalist accumulation.

> With the national debt arose an international credit system, which often conceals one of the sources of primitive accumulation in this or that people. Thus the villainies of the Venetian thieving system formed one of the secret bases of the capital-wealth of Holland to whom Venice in her decadence lent large sums of money. So was it

---

23 Ibid., pp. 450–1.

with Holland and England. By the beginning of the 18th century
. . . Holland had ceased to be the nation preponderant in commerce and industry. One of its main lines of business, therefore,
[became] the lending out of enormous amounts of capital, especially to its great rival England. [And the] same thing is going on
to-day between England and the United States.[24]

Marx never developed the theoretical implications of this historical
observation. Despite the considerable space dedicated to "money-
dealing capital" in the third volume of *Capital*, he never rescued
national debts from their confinement to the mechanisms of an
accumulation that is "not the result of the capitalist mode of
production but its starting point." And yet, in the above passage,
what appears as a "starting point" in emerging centers (Holland,
England, the United States) is also the "result" of long periods of
capital accumulation in incumbent centers (Venice, Holland, England). In one important respect, the conception of national development implicit in this historical observation converges with that of
Smith, because it acknowledges that the size of the jurisdictional
"containers" within which capital accumulates matters. Although all
four containers in the sequence (Venice, Holland, England, and the
United States) have to different degrees developed along the foreign-
trade-based, extroverted path—which Smith calls "unnatural" and
Marx calls capitalist—over time they became too small to accommodate the "endless" accumulation of capital without provoking a
persistent decline in profitability. Marx only lived long enough to see
the beginning of the decline in England. As we shall see in Part II of
the book, however, a persistent decline occurred, not just in Britain,
but one century later in the United States as well.

Despite his optimistic expectations concerning capitalism's endless
drive to go beyond all limiting barriers, Marx had to admit that,
historically, this drive has been subject to the kind of physical and
institutional constraints that Smith emphasized. This is true, however, only if we read Marx's sequence of leading capitalist states as a
series of discrete, spatially and temporally bounded, national episodes
of capitalist development. But, if we read the sequence as a series of
connected stages of capitalist development on a world scale, we get a
different picture—a picture which reiterates the idea of capitalism's
drive to go beyond all limiting barriers. Marx, that is to say, implicitly
agrees with Smith that all the jurisdictional containers that have

---

24 Ibid., pp. 713, 755–6.

housed the leading capitalist organizations of any given epoch eventually have become "over-stocked" with capital, and thus experienced a decline of profitability and a tendency towards stagnation. He nonetheless sees the international credit system as providing capital with an escape from stagnation through migration to a larger container—as the United States was in relation to England, England in relation to Holland, and Holland in relation to Venice—where its self-expansion could resume on a larger scale. Even for Marx, therefore, the tendency towards endless expansion refers only to the development of capitalism on a world scale, not within any particular state.

Schumpeter's analysis of capitalism's creative destruction, as he readily conceded, covers only a small part of Marx's ground but has the advantage of highlighting key insights that Marx's research agenda did not foreground or tended to obscure. One such insight is the conception of prosperity and depression as obverse sides of the process of creative destruction. For Schumpeter, the incessant destruction of old economic structures and creation of new ones through innovation is "not only the most important immediate source of gain, but also indirectly produces, through the process it sets going, most of those situations from which windfall gains and losses arise and in which speculative operations acquire significant scope."[25] In this process, excess profits—"spectacular prizes" far beyond those necessary to call forth the effort of the small minority who receive them—play a double role. They provide constant incentive to innovation but they also propel

> much more efficaciously than a more equal and more "just" distribution would, the activity of that large majority of businessmen who receive in return very modest compensation or nothing or less than nothing, and yet do their utmost because they have the big prizes before their eyes and overrate their chances of doing equally well.[26]

Instead of reaping spectacular prizes, however, the "large majority" propelled into the field activate the competition, which does not just eliminate excess profits, but inflicts widespread losses by destroying

---

25 Joseph Schumpeter, *Capitalism, Socialism, and Democracy* (London, George Allen & Unwin, 1954), p. 83; *Business Cycles: A Theoretical, Historical, and Statistical Analysis of the Capitalist Process* (New York, McGraw Hill, 1964), p. 80.
26 Schumpeter, *Capitalism, Socialism, and Democracy*, pp. 73–4.

pre-existing productive combinations. Schumpeter accordingly divides the incessant working of the process of creative destruction
into two phases: the phase of revolution proper and the phase of
absorption of the results of the revolution.

> While these things are being initiated we have brisk expenditure
> and predominating "prosperity" . . . and while [they] are being
> completed and their results pour forth we have the elimination of
> antiquated elements of the industrial structure and predominating
> "depression."[27]

In Schumpeter's representation, profit-oriented innovations (and
their impact on competitive pressures) cluster *in time*, generating
swings in the economy as a whole from long phases of predominating
"prosperity" to long phases of predominating "depression." As
argued elsewhere, however, it is just as plausible to hypothesize that
they also cluster *in space*. We can then substitute "where" for
"while" in the above quotation and read it as a description of a
spatial polarization of zones of predominating "prosperity" and
zones of predominating "depression."[28]

Despite his frequent references to industrial structures, Schumpeter's conception of creative destruction has the further advantage of
defining the innovations that underlie the process very broadly, as
"the carrying out of new combinations." These include, not just
technological and organizational innovations in industry, but all
commercial innovations—such as the opening up of a new market,
a new trading route, a new source of supply, the marketing of a new
product, or the introduction of a new organization in the procurement and disposal of merchandise—which succeed in "leading" the
economy into new channels. Schumpeter calls the agents of this
leadership "entrepreneurs"—individuals who may or may not be
"capitalists," in the sense of having substantial command over means
of production and payment, but who have the capacity to detect and
seize the opportunities for excess profits that can be reaped through a
rerouting of the established flow of economic life. As an illustration
of what he has in mind, Schumpeter points to "the modern type of
'captain of industry' . . . especially if one recognizes his identity on

---

27 Ibid., p. 68.

28 Giovanni Arrighi, Beverly J. Silver, and Benjamin D. Brewer, "Industrial
Convergence and the Persistence of the North-South Divide," *Studies in Comparative
International Development*, 38, 1 (2003), pp. 17–18. See also Chapter 8 below.

the one hand with, say, the commercial entrepreneur of twelfth-century Venice . . . and on the other hand with the village potentate who combines with his agriculture and his cattle trade, say, a rural brewery, an hotel and a store."

> But whatever the type, everyone is an entrepreneur only when he actually "carries out new combinations," and loses that character as soon as he has built up his business, when he settles down to running it as other people run their businesses.[29]

Capitalists are owners of money, claims to money, or material goods, who may themselves perform entrepreneurial functions, but are not defined by it. Their specific function is to provide entrepreneurs with the means of payments necessary to force the economic system into new channels. Typically, this is done through the provision of credit; and since all reserve funds and savings usually flow to credit institutions, and the total demand for purchasing power, whether existing or to be created, concentrates on these institutions, the "banker" is "the capitalist par excellence. He stands between those who wish to form new combinations and the possessors of productive means."

> Granting credit in this sense operates as an order on the economic system to accommodate itself to the purposes of the entrepreneur, as an order on the goods which he needs: it means entrusting him with productive forces.[30]

Producers of, and dealers in, purchasing power meet entrepreneurs in the money or capital market, where they exchange present against future purchasing power. "In the daily price struggle between the two parties the fate of new combinations is decided."

> All plans and outlooks for the future in the economic system affect [the money market], all conditions of the national life, all political, economic, and natural events. . . . *The money market is always*, as

---

29 Joseph Schumpeter, *The Theory of Economic Development* (New York, Oxford University Press, 1961), pp. 66, 78, 131–6. Schumpeter underscores that entrepreneurs "do not form a social class," in the way landowners or capitalists or workers do. They may come from any social class and, if successful, move into a more privileged class position. But "the class position which may be attained is not as such an entrepreneurial position, but is characterized as landowning or capitalist, according to how the proceeds of the enterprise are used" (ibid., pp. 78–9).

30 Ibid., pp. 69, 74, 107.

it were, *the headquarters of the capitalist system* from which orders go out to its individual divisions, and that which is debated and decided there is always in essence the settlement of plans for future development.[31]

Different as they might seem, Marx's and Schumpeter's conceptions of capitalist development complement rather than contradict each other. Schumpeter himself confessed that what he had to say about the performance of capitalism merely developed the "nothing short of glowing [account] of the achievements of capitalism" that Marx offered in the *Manifesto*.[32] And, indeed, I cannot see anything in Schumpeter's account of creative destruction reported above with which Marx might have disagreed. Differences between Schumpeter and Marx concerned primarily the contradictions and the agencies that would eventually lead to the supersession of capitalism as a social system. But insofar as the capitalist dynamic is concerned, they simply observed it from different angles of vision and thus saw different but compatible facets of the phenomenon.[33]

Reprise and Preview

Our reconceptualization of Smith's "unnatural" developmental path as the capitalist path suggests that the European escape from entrapment in a high-level equilibrium was no novelty of the nineteenth-century. Rather, the nineteenth-century escape of the Industrial Revolution was preceded and prepared by earlier escapes brought about through major reorganizations of the centers and networks of European capitalism. This tendency is inseparable from what both Smith and Marx singled out as the key specificity of the European path: its extroversion, its embedding in the global market, and the "retrograde" direction of its progression from foreign trade, to industry, to agriculture. From this perspective, the widespread practice of seeking the origins of the capitalist dynamic, or lack thereof, in agriculture is misleading. To use a metaphor dear to Frank, it brings to mind the proverbial search for the lost watch under the wrong lamppost: the wealth and power of the European

---

31 Ibid., pp. 125–6, emphasis added.

32 Schumpeter, *Capitalism, Socialism, and Democracy*, p. 7.

33 See John E. Elliott, "Marx and Schumpeter on Capitalism's Creative Destruction: A Comparative Restatement," *The Quarterly Journal of Economics*, XCV, 1 (1980).

bourgeoisie did not originate in agriculture but in foreign, long-distance trade; and even industry became their main foundation only after several centuries.[34]

Equally widespread and misleading is the practice of attributing to capitalist development at the national level features that, historically, belong to capitalist development at the global level, and vice versa. Marx's theory of the centralization of capital and increasing technical division of labor in ever larger production units, for example, is valid only at the global level. Although railways were invented and first introduced in Britain, it was only when they were introduced on an incomparably larger geographical scale in the United States—with the decisive contribution of British surplus capital—that they led to the reorganization of capital into vertically integrated corporations. Had the center of capitalist development not shifted from Britain to the United States, the great leap forward in the technical division of labor prompted by that reorganization might have never occurred. Indeed, despite or, perhaps, because of the Industrial Revolution, throughout the nineteenth century Britain experienced a consolidation of family capitalism and a decrease, rather than an increase, in the vertical integration of production processes.[35]

Conversely, the contention that capitalist development presupposes the separation of agricultural producers from the means of producing their subsistence—which Brenner derives from Marx—has some validity as a description of the conditions that facilitated the development of capitalism in Britain. At the global level, however, such separation appears to be more a *consequence* of capitalism's creative destruction—that is, the production of a relative surplus population—than one of its preconditions. In any event, it was definitely not a precondition of capitalist development in other European countries—such as France and Switzerland—or in the United States, where the agricultural foundations of the greatest technical and organizational advances in capitalist history were laid by the destruction of the

---

34 See Giovanni Arrighi, *The Long Twentieth Century: Money, Power and the Origins of our Times* (London, Verso, 1994), chs 2–3, and Chapter 8 below. On the "lost watch" metaphor, see Andre Gunder Frank, *ReOrient: Global Economy in the Asian Age* (Berkeley, CA, University of California Press, 1998), pp. 338–9.

35 On the role of railways in promoting the vertical integration and bureaucratic management of capitalist enterprise, see Alfred Chandler, *The Visible Hand: The Managerial Revolution in American Business* (Cambridge, MA, The Belknap Press, 1977), chs 3–5. For evidence on the persistence of family business and the decrease in vertical integration in nineteenth-century Britain, see Giovanni Arrighi and Beverly J. Silver, *Chaos and Governance in the Modern World System* (Minneapolis, MN, University of Minnesota Press, 1999), ch. 2.

native population, the forcible transplant of enslaved African peoples, and the resettlement of European surplus population.

The difficulties involved in pinning down the capitalist nature of the European developmental path have led Frank to see its quest as "not much better than the alchemist's search for the philosopher's stone that transforms base metal into gold."[36] Frank's frustration is understandable, and he is on firm empirical grounds in rejecting attempts to trace differences between the European and the East Asian developmental paths to the presence of "capitalists" in one region and their absence in the other. As William Rowe has noted, and our analysis in Chapter 11 will confirm, "Whatever the reason, the divergences between Chinese and Western social histories since 1500 are not due to the fact that the progressive West discovered capitalism and the modern state and China did not."[37]

As will be argued in greater detail in Chapter 11, the feature that enables us to distinguish between the European and East Asian market-based developmental paths is not the presence of particular business and governmental institutions as such, but their combination in different power structures. Thus, Smith's "unnatural" path differs from the "natural," not because it has a larger number of capitalists, but because capitalists have greater power to impose their class interest at the expense of the national interest. In Marx's reconceptualization of Smith's "unnatural" path as the capitalist path, this greater power has turned governments into committees for managing the affairs of the bourgeoisie. Although this is at best an exaggeration and at worst a false characterization of most European states, it is probably as accurate a description as any other of the states that have been the leaders of the European developmental path. As Fernand Braudel put it,

> Capitalism only triumphs when it becomes identified with the state, when it is the state. In its first great phase, that of the Italian city-states of Venice, Genoa, and Florence, power lay in the hands of the moneyed elite. In seventeenth-century Holland the aristocracy of the Regents governed for the benefit and even according to

36 Frank, *ReOrient*, p. 332, quoting K.N. Chaudhuri, *Asia before Europe: Economy and Civilization of the Indian Ocean from the Rise of Islam to 1750* (Cambridge, Cambridge University Press, 1990), p. 84, on the analogy with the alchemist's search for the philosopher's stone.

37 William Rowe, "Modern Chinese Social History in Comparative Perspective," in P.S. Ropp, ed., *Heritage of China: Contemporary Perspectives on Chinese Civilization* (Berkeley, CA, University of California Press, 1990), p. 262.

the directives of the businessmen, merchants, and money-lenders. Likewise, in England the Glorious Revolution of 1688 marked the accession of business similar to that in Holland.[38]

Except for the addition of Genoa and Florence to Venice, and the omission of the latest leader of capitalist development (the United States), this is the same sequence of declining and emerging capitalist centers that, according to Marx, were linked to one another by a recycling of surplus capital through the international credit system. In both sequences, the states that became identified with capitalism—the Italian city-states, the Dutch proto-nation-state, and eventually a state, the English, that was in the process of becoming, not just a national state, but the center of a world-encircling maritime and territorial empire—were larger and more powerful than their predecessor. Our contention will be that it is this *sequence* of endless accumulation of capital and power, more than anything else, that defines the European developmental path as "capitalist"; and conversely, the absence of anything comparable to such a sequence in East Asia can be taken as the clearest sign that, prior to the Great Divergence, the East Asian developmental path was as market-based as the European but was not the bearer of a capitalist dynamic.

We shall further maintain that this specificity of the European developmental path can only be understood in conjunction with two other tendencies. One is the tendency of over-accumulation crises to bring about long periods of financial expansions which, to paraphrase Schumpeter, provide the means of payments necessary to force the economic system into new channels. As Braudel underscores, this tendency is no novelty of the nineteenth century. In sixteenth-century Genoa and eighteenth-century Amsterdam, no less than in late nineteenth-century Britain and the late twentieth-century United States, "following a wave of growth . . . and the accumulation of capital on a scale beyond the normal channels for investment, finance capitalism was already in a position to take over and dominate, for a while at least, all the activities of the business world."[39] While, initially, this domination tends to revive the fortunes of incumbent capitalist centers, over time it is a source of political, economic, and social turbulence, in the course of which the existing social frameworks of accumulation are

---

38 Fernand Braudel, *Afterthoughts on Material Civilization and Capitalism* (Baltimore, MD, Johns Hopkins University Press, 1977), pp. 64–5.

39 Fernand Braudel. *Civilization and Capitalism, 15th–18th Century, Volume III: The Perspective of the World* (New York, Harper & Row, 1984), p. 604.

destroyed; the "headquarters of the capitalist system," in Schumpeter's sense of the expression, are relocated to new centers; and more encompassing social frameworks of accumulation are created under the leadership of ever more powerful states.[40] Whether and to what extent the US-led financial expansion of the 1980s and 1990s fits this pattern is the subject matter of Part II of this book.

Neither the recurrent financial expansions of historical capitalism, nor the sequence of ever more powerful states with which capitalism has become identified, can nonetheless be understood except in relation to another tendency: the intense interstate competition for mobile capital, which Max Weber has called "the world-historical distinctiveness of [the modern] era."[41] This tendency is the key to solving the issue of the relationship between capitalism, industrialism, and militarism, which was implicitly raised but not resolved by Smith and on which neither Marx nor Schumpeter have anything interesting to say. As noted in Chapter 2, Smith's observation that the great expense of modern warfare gives a military advantage to wealthy over poor nations raises two closely related questions. First, given the greater role that manufacturing, foreign trade, and navigation played in his "unnatural" developmental path—which, following Marx, we have renamed the capitalist path—would not countries developing along that path acquire a military advantage, not just towards poor nations, but also towards wealthy market economies developing along Smith's "natural" path? And, second, if wealth procured along the capitalist path is a source of superior military force, and if superior military force is the reason why Europeans could appropriate the benefits of the greater integration of the global economy at the expense of non-European nations, as Smith maintains, what forces can prevent this integration from reproducing the joint operation of a virtuous circle of enrichment and empowerment for the peoples of European descent and a vicious circle of impoverishment and disempowerment for most other peoples?

---

40 For different aspects of this pattern, see Arrighi, *The Long Twentieth Century*, and Arrighi and Silver, *Chaos and Governance*.

41 Max Weber, *Economy and Society* (Berkeley, CA, University of California Press, 1978), p. 354. According to Weber, whereas in pre-modern times the formation of world empires swept away freedoms and powers of the cities that constituted the main loci of capitalist expansion, in the modern era these loci came under the sway of "competing national states in a condition of perpetual struggle for power in peace or war. . . . The separate states had to compete for mobile capital, which dictated to them the conditions under which it would assist them to power." It is this competitive struggle that has created the largest opportunities for modern capitalism. Max Weber, *General Economic History* (New York, Collier, 1961), p. 249.

These questions will be answered in Parts III and IV of the book. Part III will focus specifically on the seemingly "endless" accumulation of capital and power along the capitalist path, which has culminated in the US attempt to create, for the first time in world history, a truly global state. It will show that the synergy between capitalism, industrialism, and militarism, driven by interstate competition, did indeed engender a virtuous circle of enrichment and empowerment for the peoples of European descent and a corresponding vicious circle of impoverishment and disempowerment for most other peoples. Integral to this tendency was the spatial polarization of the process of creative destruction into a zone of predominating prosperity, which eventually became the global North, and a zone of predominating depression, which eventually became the global South. But it will also show, first, that this polarization posed increasingly insurmountable problems of social and political legitimacy for the reproduction of Northern domination, and second, that the attempt by the United States to overcome these problems through coercive means has backfired and created unprecedented opportunities for the social and economic empowerment of the peoples of the global South.

Part IV, the concluding chapters of the book, will focus on the world-historical conditions that have enabled China to pioneer this empowerment. Sugihara's contention that the intense competition between the United States and the Soviet Union during the Cold War and the surge of nationalism in the former colonial world jointly created in East Asia a favorable geopolitical environment for the hybridization of the Industrious and Industrial Revolution paths, will be reformulated in my own terms and developed in two new directions. I shall argue, first, that the Industrious and Industrial Revolution paths themselves originated in the contrasting geopolitical environments that emerged in East Asia and Europe in the course of what Braudel calls the "extended" sixteenth century with reference to European history (1350–1650),[42] and which corresponds almost exactly to the Ming era in East Asian history (1368–1643). I shall show that this difference in geopolitical environments provides a simple but compelling explanation of the emergence of two distinct developmental paths in Europe and East Asia, which in due course led to the Great Divergence. But I shall also argue that the superiority of the European vis-à-vis the East Asian path depended critically on a synergy between financial and military capabilities that was hard to sustain in an increasingly integrated and competitive global economy.

---

42 Braudel, *Capitalism and Civilization, 15th–18th Century, Volume 3*, p. 79.

Once the synergy ceased to function, as it did in the closing decades of the twentieth century, Japan became the harbinger and China the bearer of the hybrid, market-based, developmental path which, to paraphrase Fairbank, continues to confuse people both inside and outside China.

Part II

TRACKING GLOBAL TURBULENCE

4

THE ECONOMICS OF
GLOBAL TURBULENCE

"Depression," wrote Thorstein Veblen shortly after the end of the Great Depression of 1873–96, "is primarily a malady of the affections of the businessmen. That is the seat of the difficulty. The stagnation of industry and the hardship suffered by the workmen and other classes are of the nature of symptoms and secondary effects." To be efficacious remedies must, therefore, be such "as to reach this emotional seat of the trouble and . . . restore profits to a 'reasonable' rate."[1] Between 1873 and 1896, prices had fallen unevenly but inexorably, in what David Landes has called "the most drastic deflation in the memory of man." Along with prices, the rate of interest fell "to the point where economic theorists began to conjure with the possibility of capital so abundant as to be a free good. And profits shrank, while what was now recognized as periodic depressions seemed to drag on interminably. The economic system appeared to be running down."[2]

In reality, the economic system was not "running down." Production and investment continued to grow not just in the newly-industrializing countries of the time (most notably, in Germany and the US) but in Britain as well—so much so that, writing at the same time as Landes, another historian could declare that the Great Depression of 1873–1896 was nothing but a "myth."[3] Nevertheless, as Veblen suggests, there is no contradiction in saying that there was a "great depression" at a time of continuing expansion in production and investment. On the contrary, the Great Depression was not a myth

---

1 Thorstein Veblen, *The Theory of Business Enterprise* (New Brunswick, NJ, Transaction Books, 1978), p. 241.

2 David S. Landes, *The Unbound Prometheus: Technological Change and Industrial Development in Western Europe from 1756 to the Present* (Cambridge, Cambridge University Press, 1969), p. 231.

3 S.B. Saul, *The Myth of the Great Depression, 1873–1896* (London, Macmillan, 1969).

precisely *because* production and trade in Britain and in the world economy at large had expanded and were still expanding too rapidly for profits to be maintained at what was considered a "reasonable" rate.

More specifically, the great expansion of world trade of the middle of the nineteenth century had led to a system-wide intensification of competitive pressures on the agencies of capital accumulation. An increasing number of business enterprises from an increasing number of locations across the UK-centered world economy were getting into one another's way in the procurement of inputs and in the disposal of outputs, thereby destroying one another's previous "monopolies"— that is, their more or less exclusive control over particular market niches.

> This shift from monopoly to competition was probably the most important single factor in setting the mood for European industrial and commercial enterprise. Economic growth was now also economic struggle—struggle that served to separate the strong from the weak, to discourage some and toughen others, to favour the new . . . nations at the expense of the old. Optimism about the future of indefinite progress gave way to uncertainty and a sense of agony.[4]

But then, all of a sudden, as if by magic,

> the wheel turned. In the last years of the century, prices began to rise and profits with them. As business improved, confidence returned—not the spotty, evanescent confidence of the brief booms that had punctuated the gloom of the preceding decades, but a general euphoria such as had not prevailed since . . . the early 1870s. Everything seemed right again—in spite of rattlings of arms and monitory Marxist references to the "last stage" of capitalism. In all of western Europe, these years live on in memory as the good old days—the Edwardian era, *la belle époque*.[5]

As we shall see, there was nothing magic in the sudden restoration of profits to a more "reasonable" level, and the consequent recovery of the British and Western bourgeoisies from the malady provoked by "excessive" competition. For now, let us simply note that not all

---

4 Landes, *Unbound Prometheus*, p. 240.
5 Ibid., p. 231.

benefited from the "beautiful times" of 1896–1914. Internationally, the main beneficiary of the recovery was Britain. As its industrial supremacy waned, its finance triumphed and its services as shipper, trader, insurer broker, and intermediary in the world's system of payments became more indispensable than ever before.[6] But, even within Britain, not everybody benefited. Particularly noteworthy was the overall decline of British real wages after the mid 1890s, which reversed the rapidly rising trend of the previous half century.[7] For the working class of the then hegemonic power, the *belle époque* was thus a time of containment of the preceding half century of improvement in its economic condition. This, no doubt, gave an additional boost to the renewed euphoria of the British bourgeoisie. Soon, however, the "rattling of arms" got out of hand precipitating a crisis from which the British-centered world capitalist system would never recover.

Robert Brenner's analysis of what he calls the "persistent stagnation" of 1973–93 and the subsequent "revival" of the US and world economies does not refer to this earlier experience of world capitalism with depression, revival, and crisis, but his central argument continually invites a comparison between the two.[8] I shall, therefore, take it as the starting point of a comparative analysis of two long periods of global turbulence, one century apart from each other, aimed at determining what is truly novel and anomalous in the global turbulence of our days. In this chapter, I reconstruct Brenner's argument focusing on its most interesting and essential aspects. In Chapter 5, I re-examine the argument critically focusing on its weaknesses and limits, and in Chapter 6, I incorporate these critiques into my own interpretation of the global turbulence that has set the stage for both the terminal crisis of US hegemony and the economic resurgence of East Asia. I shall conclude Part II by making explicit the connections of my argument concerning global turbulence with the theoretical framework developed in the first part of the book.

---

6 Eric J. Hobsbawm, *Industry and Empire: An Economic History of Britain since 1750* (London, Weidenfeld & Nicolson, 1968), p. 125.

7 Saul, *Myth of the Great Depression*, pp. 28–38; Michael Barrat Brown, *The Economics of Imperialism* (Harmondsworth, Penguin, 1974), table 14.

8 Robert Brenner, "The Economics of Global Turbulence: A Special Report on the World Economy, 1950–1998," *New Left Review*, I, 229 (1998); *The Boom and the Bubble: The U.S. in the World Economy* (London, Verso, 2002); *The Economics of Global Turbulence: The Advanced Capitalist Economies from Long Boom to Long Downturn* (London, Verso, 2006). The 2006 book consists of the 1998 book-length manuscript published as a special issue of *New Left Review*, a new preface and a new afterword. Except when referring to the preface and the afterword, I have retained the references to the 1998 publication.

Uneven Development: From Boom to Crisis

Brenner conceives of the long boom of the 1950s and 1960s and the crisis of profitability that brought the boom to an end between 1965 and 1973 as both being rooted in what he calls "uneven development." In his definition, uneven development is the process whereby laggards in capitalist development seek to catch up, and eventually succeed in catching up, with the leaders of that development.[9] Focusing on Germany and Japan as the most successful among the laggards that after the Second World War attempted to catch up with prior developmental achievements of the United States, Brenner argues that it was the capacity of these two countries to combine the high-productivity technologies, pioneered by the United States, with the large, low-wage and elastic labor supplies crowding their rural and small business sectors, that pushed up their rate of profit and investment. Through the early 1960s, this tendency did not affect negatively US production and profit, because "goods produced abroad remained for the most part unable to compete in the US market and because US producers depended to only a small extent on overseas sales."[10]

Indeed, although "uneven economic development did entail the *relative* decline of the US domestic economy . . . it was also a precondition for the continued vitality of the dominant forces within the US political economy."

> US multinational corporations and international banks, aimed at expanding overseas, needed profitable outlets for their foreign direct investment. Domestically based manufacturers, needing to increase exports, required fast-growing overseas demand for their goods. An imperial US state, bent on "containing communism" and keeping the world safe for free enterprise, sought economic success for its allies and competitors as the foundation for the

---

9 Brenner, "Economics of Global Turbulence," pp. 39–137; *The Boom and the Bubble*, pp. 9–24. Brenner's use of the expression "uneven development" echoes Trotsky's and Lenin's but differs radically from the more common contemporary use to designate the tendency of capitalist development to polarize and diversify geographical space. See especially Samir Amin, *Unequal Development* (New York, Monthly Review Press, 1976) and Neil Smith, *Uneven Development: Nature, Capital and the Production of Space* (Oxford, Basil Blackwell, 1984). Unless otherwise specified, I shall use this expression in the same sense as Brenner.

10 Brenner, "Economics of Global Turbulence," pp. 91–2.

political consolidation of the postwar capitalist order. . . . All these forces thus depended upon the economic dynamism of Europe and Japan for the realization of their own goals.[11]

In short, up to the early 1960s, uneven development was a positive-sum game that buttressed "a symbiosis, if a highly conflictual and unstable one, of leader and followers, of early and later developers, and of hegemon and hegemonized."[12] To paraphrase Landes's account of the Great Depression of 1873–96, it had not yet become "economic struggle"—a zero- or even negative-sum game that would benefit some at the expense of others. In Brenner's own account of the onset of the long downturn of 1973–93, this is precisely what uneven development became between 1965 and 1973. By then, Germany and Japan had not just caught up but had "forge[d] ahead of the US leader . . . in one key industry after another—textiles, steel, automobiles, machine tools, consumer electronics." More important, the newer, lower-cost producers based in these and other follower countries began "invading markets hitherto dominated by producers of the leader regions, especially the US and also the UK."[13]

This irruption of lower-priced goods into the US and world markets undermined the ability of US manufacturers "to secure the established rate of return on their placements of capital and labor," provoking, between 1965 and 1973, a decline in the rate of return on their capital stock of over 40 percent. US manufacturers responded to this intensification of competition at home and abroad in various ways. They priced products below full cost—that is, they sought the established rate of profit only on their circulating capital; they repressed the growth of wage costs; and they updated their plant and equipment. Ultimately, however, the most decisive US weapon in the incipient competitive struggle was a drastic devaluation of the dollar relative to the Japanese yen and the German mark.[14]

To some extent, the devaluation was itself the result of the deterioration in the US balance of trade that ensued from the loss of competitiveness of American vis-à-vis German and Japanese manufacturers. Nevertheless, the effects of this trade balance on the values of the three currencies were considerably amplified by government policies that destabilized (and eventually disrupted) the

---

11 Brenner, *The Boom and the Bubble*, pp. 14–15.
12 Ibid., p. 15.
13 Brenner, "Economics of Global Turbulence," pp. 41, 105–8.
14 Ibid., pp. 93–4; *The Boom and the Bubble*, pp. 17–18.

international gold–dollar-standard regime, established at the end of the Second World War. For the German and the Japanese governments responded to the inflationary pressures engendered in their domestic economies by the export-led production boom with a repression of domestic demand, which further increased their trade surpluses and speculative demand for their currencies.[15] At the end of Johnson's administration and at the beginning of Nixon's, the US government did attempt to turn the tide of growing international monetary instability through fiscal austerity and tight monetary policies. Soon, however,

> the political costs of sustaining a serious anti-inflationary policy— not to mention the alarming fall in the stock market . . . proved unacceptable to the Nixon Administration. Well before the defeat of the Republicans in the congressional elections of November 1970, and as high interest rates threatened to choke off the recovery, the government turned once again to fiscal stimulus and the Fed accommodated with a policy of easy credit. As Nixon was to put it several months later, "We are all Keynesians now."[16]

The US turn to macroeconomic expansionary policies in mid 1970 sounded the death knell for the gold–dollar standard. As interest rates fell in the United States while remaining high or increasing in Europe and Japan, short-term speculative money fled the dollar sending the US balance-of-payments deficit (short and long term) through the roof. The half-hearted attempt of the Smithsonian Agreement of December 1971 to preserve fixed exchange rates through a 7.9 percent devaluation of the dollar against gold, and a revaluation of the mark by 13.5 percent and of the yen by 16.9 percent against the dollar, failed to contain the renewed downward pressure that the Nixon administration put on the US currency through another round of economic stimulus. By 1973, the pressure became unbearable, resulting in a further major devaluation of the dollar and the formal abandonment of the fixed-rate system of exchange in favor of the float.[17]

The massive devaluation of the dollar against the mark (by a total of 50 percent between 1969 and 1973) and the yen (by a total of 28.2 percent between 1971 and 1973)—Brenner claims—secured "the kind of turnaround in relative costs that [the US manufacturing sector] had

---

15 Brenner, "Economics of Global Turbulence," pp. 94, 116, 119, 126–30.
16 Ibid., pp. 120–1.
17 Ibid., pp. 121–3.

been unable to achieve by way of productivity growth and wage restraint." The turnaround had a galvanizing effect on the US economy. Profitability, investment growth, and labor productivity in manufacturing staged a comeback, and the US trade balance was restored to a surplus. The impact on the German and Japanese economies was just the opposite. The competitiveness of their manufacturers was sharply curtailed, making it their turn "to forgo their high rates of return if they wished to maintain their sales." The global crisis of profitability had not been overcome. But its burden was now more evenly shared among the chief capitalist countries.[18]

In sum, uneven economic development—understood as a process of successful catching up of laggard with leading economic powers—produced both the long postwar boom and the crisis of profitability of the late 1960s and early 1970s. As long as the catching-up was going on, it sustained a worldwide virtuous circle of high profits, high investments, and increasing productivity. But, once the laggards—or at least two of the most sizeable ones—had actually caught up with the former leader, the result was a worldwide glut of productive capacity and a consequent downward pressure on rates of profit. Initially, US manufacturers bore the brunt of the pressure. Soon, however, a US enormous, government-supported devaluation of the dollar against the mark and the yen distributed the fall in profitability more evenly among the three main capitalist powers.

Over-Capacity and Persistent Stagnation

Uneven development generated the excess capacity that provoked the general fall in the rate of profit between 1965 and 1973. But it was the failure of capitalist enterprises and governments to restore profitability to its previous level through the elimination of excess capacity that was primarily responsible for the persistence of comparative stagnation from 1973 to 1993. In Brenner's conceptualization, there is "over-capacity and over-production" (two terms he always uses together) when "there is insufficient demand to allow higher-cost firms to maintain their former rates of profit." These firms are thus "obliged to cease using some of their means of production and can make use of the rest only by lowering their prices and thus their profitability. There is over-capacity and over-production, *with re-*

---

18 Ibid., pp. 123–4, 137.

spect to the hitherto-existing profit rate."[19] Either the over-supply of productive capacity is eliminated, or the rate of profit must fall, with all the dire consequences that such a fall entails in a capitalist economy, from drops in the rates of investment and productivity growth to the decline of real wages and levels of employment. Brenner's contention is that, at least up to 1993, the over-supply of productive capacity that underlay the crisis of profitability of 1965–73, far from being eliminated, if anything increased further, continually depressing profitability.

The contention is based on two lines of argument, one concerning capitalist enterprises and one concerning governments. In Brenner's conceptualization of world capitalism, there is no spontaneous market mechanism that will prevent over-capacity from developing in a large number of industries, or from becoming a chronic feature of the world economy once it has developed. Higher-cost incumbent firms have both the means and the incentive to resist exit from overcrowded industries, while over-capacity and falling profits do not necessarily discourage new entry. Higher-cost incumbents resist exit because many of their tangible and intangible assets "can be realized only in their established lines of production and would be lost were [the incumbents] to switch lines." Moreover, "the slowed growth of demand that is the unavoidable expression of the reduced growth of investment and wages that inevitably result from falling profit rates makes it increasingly difficult to reallocate to new lines." These firms, therefore, "have every reason to defend their markets [by seeking the average rate of return on their circulating costs only] and counterattack by speeding up the process of innovation and investment in additional fixed capital." The adoption of such a strategy, in turn, "will tend to provoke the original cost-reducing innovators to accelerate technical change themselves, further worsening the already existing over-capacity and over-production."[20]

---

19 Ibid., pp. 25–6, emphasis in the original. As noted, Brenner invariably uses the terms "over-capacity" and "over-production" together, occasionally replacing them with the term "over-accumulation" (e.g. *The Boom and the Bubble*, pp. 32, 159). As we shall see in Chapters 5 and 6, what he is describing is a crisis of over-accumulation, of which over-capacity and over-production are distinct manifestations. However, by not clarifying conceptually the difference between over-capacity and over-production, Brenner creates considerable difficulties in assessing empirically their actual importance, both in absolute terms and relative to other manifestations of the underlying crisis of over-accumulation.

20 Brenner, "Economics of Global Turbulence," pp. 32–3.

At the same time, the aggravation of over-capacity does not deter new entry and a consequent further downward pressure on the rate of profit. "On the contrary, the initial fall in profitability . . . can be expected to intensify the worldwide drive for even lower production costs through the combination of even cheaper labor with even higher levels of techniques in still later-developing regions." The most conspicuous instance of such new entry during the long downturn were producers based in a limited number of so-called Less Developed Countries—especially in East Asia, but also in such places as Mexico and Brazil—who managed to make significant inroads in world markets of manufactured goods, further intensifying the downward pressure on prices and profitability. "There was, in short, not only too little exit, but too much entry."[21]

This first line of argument is, for the most part, developed deductively on the basis of circumstantial empirical evidence. The bulk of the empirical evidence and historical narrative concerns the second line of argument, according to which the governments of the main capitalist powers, especially the United States, share responsibility for aggravating rather than alleviating the market tendency towards too little exit and too much entry. In this respect, Brenner's main contribution to our understanding of the long downturn is to have shown that the governments in question acted not so much as regulators—though they did that too—as active participants, even protagonists, of the system-wide competitive struggle that has set capitalists against one another since the late 1960s.

As previously noted, in his account of the crisis of profitability, Brenner already saw the US government's active pursuit of a major devaluation of the US dollar against the mark and yen as contributing decisively to a shift of the burden of the crisis from US to German and Japanese manufacturers. Similarly, in his account of the long downturn, Brenner shows how the ebb and flow of currency devaluations and revaluations have been key instruments of governmental action in the inter-capitalist competitive struggle. Three major political-economic turning points mark this ebb and flow of currency devaluation and revaluation: the Reagan–Thatcher monetarist "revolution" of 1979–80, which reversed the devaluation of the US dollar of the 1970s; the Plaza Accord of 1985, which resumed the dollar devaluation; and the so-called "reverse Plaza Accord" of 1995, which again reversed the devaluation. Let us briefly examine Brenner's account of the relationship between these turning points and the persistence of over-

---

21 Ibid., p. 34; *The Boom and the Bubble*, pp. 26, 31, 37.

production and over-capacity in manufacturing, which underlies his long downturn.

By the late 1970s, the US macro-policy of federal deficits, extreme monetary ease, and "benign neglect" with respect to the dollar's exchange rate reached the limit of its ability to sustain economic expansion and restore US manufacturing competitiveness and profitability. The policy had "enabled the advanced capitalist economies to transcend the oil crisis recession of 1974–5 and to continue to expand during the remainder of the decade." Nevertheless, in their effects, "Keynesian stimuli proved to be profoundly ambivalent." While sustaining the growth of demand domestically and internationally, "Keynesian remedies helped to perpetuate over-capacity and over-production, preventing the harsh medicine of shakeout, indeed depression, that historically had cleared the way for new upturns [in profitability.]" Reduced profitability, in turn, made firms "unable and unwilling . . . to bring about as great an increase in supply as in the past when profit rates were higher . . . with the result that the ever-increasing public deficits of the 1970s brought about not so much increases in *output* as rises in *prices*." The escalation in inflationary pressures was accompanied by record-breaking deficits in the US balance-of-payments. By 1977–78 these deficits "precipitated a devastating run on the US currency that threatened the dollar's position as an international reserve currency, [clearing the path] for a major change in perspective." This major change came with the Reagan–Thatcher monetarist revolution of 1979–80.[22]

----

22 Brenner, *The Boom and the Bubble*, pp. 33–4, emphasis in the original. Brenner's account of the sequence of events that led to the monetarist revolution (or counterrevolution, as I prefer to characterize it) is the weakest link in his story of the long downturn. For one thing, he leaves us wondering why under conditions of over-capacity and over-production Keynesian stimuli brought about increases in prices rather than output, and having done so, why price increases did not result in higher rates of profit. More important, he does not tell us how and why US policies "designed to restore US manufacturing competitiveness" resulted instead in record-breaking US trade deficits, despite a simultaneous escalation in protectionist measures (the Multi-Fiber Arrangement of 1973, the Trade Act of 1974 against "unfair trade," and the tightening of so-called "voluntary export restraints" imposed on East Asian countries). In his earlier text, he does suggest three reasons for this perverse outcome: a US macroeconomic policy "more stimulative than that of its rivals," a slower growth of US labor productivity, and an apparently greater "tolerance of rival capitalists abroad for reduced profitability." See Brenner, "Economics of Global Turbulence," pp. 179–80. Nevertheless, these are *ad hoc* explanations that do not clearly fit his "too-little-exit, too-much-entry" thesis and, as we shall see in Chapters 5 and 6, they miss the most fundamental causes of the devastating run on the dollar of 1979–80.

According to Brenner, the main objective of the change was to revive profitability, not just or even primarily in manufacturing, but in the low-productivity service sector and, especially, in the domestic and international financial sectors, through reduced corporate taxation, increased unemployment, and the elimination of controls on capital. Unlike earlier, Keynesian solutions, however, monetarist remedies sought to restore profitability by administering the harsh medicine of shakeout. Unprecedented tight credit provoked "a purge of that great ledge of high-cost, low-profit manufacturing firms that had been sustained by the Keynesian expansion of credit." Although inflationary pressures were rapidly brought under control, record-high US real interest rates and the rising dollar associated with them "threatened to precipitate a worldwide crash, starting in the US."[23]

The crash was avoided by the "fortuitous" return of Keynesianism—with a vengeance. Reagan's "monumental programme of military spending and tax reduction for the rich . . . partly offset the ravages of monetarist tight credit and kept the economy ticking over." Reaganite policies did, of course, bring back trade and current-account deficits, also with a vengeance, especially "since, from this point onward, most of the rest of the world increasingly eschewed Keynesian public deficits." As in the 1970s, unprecedented deficits provided "the injections of demand that were needed . . . to pull the world economy out of the recession of 1979–82." In contrast to the 1970s, however, even larger US deficits did not now provoke a run on the dollar. On the contrary, the pull of extremely high real interest rates and a push from the Japanese Ministry of Finance resulted in a huge inflow of capital into the United States from all over the world, leading to a sharp appreciation of the US currency.[24]

The synergy of reduced inflationary pressures, high real interest rates, massive inflows of capital, and a rising dollar was in keeping with the Reagan administration's objective of strengthening US finance capital. It nonetheless "proved catastrophic for large sections of US manufacturing." Under strong pressure from Congress and many of the country's leading corporate executives, the Reagan administration "had little choice but to undertake an epoch-making reversal of direction." The centerpiece of this epoch-making reversal was the Plaza Accord of September 22, 1985, whereby the G5 powers, under US pressure, agreed to take joint action to bring relief to US manufacturers by reducing the exchange rate of the dollar. The very

---

23 Brenner, *The Boom and the Bubble*, pp. 35–6.
24 Ibid., pp. 36, 54–5.

next day, the Accord was complemented by stepped-up US denunciations of the "unfair" trading practices of other countries. The
denunciations soon materialized in an escalation of threats, supported
by new legislation (most notably, the Omnibus Trade and Competition Act of 1988 and the Structural Impediments Act of 1989), to close
off the US market to leading (mostly East Asian) foreign competitors,
"as a bludgeon both to limit their imports [through 'voluntary
exports restraints'] and to force the opening of their markets to
US exports and foreign direct investment."[25]

In seeking a radical devaluation of the dollar while stepping up
protectionist and "market opening" measures, the Reagan administration was following in the footsteps of the Nixon, Ford, and
Carter administrations. The outcome of these initiatives in the
1980s and early 1990s was nonetheless quite different than in the
1970s.

> The Plaza Accord and its sequels, proved to be the turning point in
> the US manufacturing turnaround, and a major watershed for the
> world economy as a whole. It set off ten years of more or less
> continuous, and major, devaluation of the dollar with respect to
> the yen and the mark, which was accompanied by a decade-long
> freeze on real wage growth. It thereby opened the way simulta-
> neously for the recovery of competitiveness, along with the speed-
> up of export growth, of US manufacturing, a secular crisis of
> German and Japanese industry, and an unprecedented explosion of
> export-based manufacturing expansion throughout East Asia,
> where economies for the most part tied their currencies to the
> dollar and thereby secured for the manufacturing exporters a
> major competitive advantage vis-à-vis their Japanese rivals when
> the dollar fell between 1985 and 1995.[26]

By 1993, the tendencies set off by the Plaza Accord, along with the
prior shakeout of the US industrial structure provoked by the unprecedented tight credit of the early 1980s, resulted in a revival of US
profitability, investment, and production. To paraphrase Veblen, the
remedies concocted by the government to cure the malady of the
affections of US business seemed to have at long last reached the
emotional seat of the trouble and restored profits to a "reasonable"
rate. The cure, however, had some serious side effects.

---

25 Ibid., pp. 54, 59–60.
26 Ibid., pp. 60–1.

In Brenner's view, the main problem was that the US revival had occurred primarily at the expense of its Japanese and Western European rivals and had done little to overcome the underlying over-capacity and over-production in manufacturing that haunted the global economy. This zero-sum nature of the US revival was problematic for the United States itself. For one thing, "the ever slower growth of world demand, and in particular the related intensification of international competition in manufacturing" limited the revival there, too. More compellingly, the United States could hardly afford "a truly serious crisis of its leading partners and rivals," especially Japan.

This contradiction surfaced starkly in the wake of the Mexican peso crisis of 1994–95. The crisis, and the US rescue of the Mexican economy, led to a new run on the dollar, sharply accentuating its downward trend of the preceding decade. With the yen reaching an all-time high of 79 to the dollar in April 1995, "Japanese producers could not even cover their variable costs, and . . . the Japanese growth machine appeared to be grinding to a halt." Still under the shock of the Mexican collapse and its disastrous impact on international financial stability (and with the upcoming 1996 presidential election looming in the background) the Clinton administration simply could not risk a Japanese version of the Mexican debacle.

> Even if a Japanese crisis could be contained, it would probably entail the large-scale liquidation of Japan's enormous holdings of US assets, especially Treasury Bonds. Such a development would chase up interest rates, frighten the money markets, and possibly endanger a recession at the very moment that the US economy appeared finally ready to right itself.[27]

Led by Treasury Secretary Robert Rubin, the United States entered into an arrangement with Germany and Japan to take joint action aimed at reversing the upward trend of the yen and the downward trend of the dollar. This double reversal was to be achieved by lowering further interests rates in Japan relative to those in the United States, and by substantially enlarging Japanese purchases of dollar-denominated instruments such as Treasury bonds, as well as German and US purchases of dollars in currency markets. Later called the "reverse Plaza Accord," the agreement represented "a stunning—and entirely unexpected—about-face in the policy stance of both the US

---

27 Ibid., pp. 130–1.

and its main allies and rivals, in much the same way as had the
original Plaza Accord of 1985."[28]

Through this volte-face, the governments of the world's largest
economies switched roles in their minuet of mutual help. "Just as
Japan and Germany had had to accede to the Plaza Accord . . . to
rescue US manufacturing from its crisis of the first half of the 1980s,
at great cost to themselves, so the US [was now] obliged to accept a
quite similar bailout of Japan's crisis-bound manufacturing sector—
again with epoch-making results."[29] These epoch-making results
transformed the ongoing US economic revival into the boom and
bubble of the second half of the 1990s.

Unsustainable Revival

Even before 1995, the recovery of profitability in US manufacturing
had translated into an increase in stock prices. The "reverse Plaza
Accord" amplified this increase for foreign investors by pushing up
the value of the dollar. More important, the Accord "unleashed a
torrent of cash from Japan, East Asia, and overseas more generally
into US financial markets, which sharply eased interest rates and
opened the way for a mighty increase in corporate borrowing to
finance the purchase of shares on the stock market." Crucial in this
respect were Japanese policies. Not only did Japanese authorities
directly pump money into US government securities and the dollar,
and encourage Japanese insurance companies to follow suit by
loosening regulations on overseas investment. In addition, by slashing
the official discount rate to 0.5 percent, they enabled investors—
including, above all, US investors, to borrow yen in Japan almost for
free, convert them into dollars, and invest them elsewhere, especially
in the US stock market.[30]

This flood of US-bound foreign capital and the associated appreciation of the dollar were essential ingredients in the transformation
of the pre-1995 boom in equity prices into the subsequent bubble. In
Brenner's account, however, the transformation would have probably
not occurred without the encouragement of the US Federal Reserve.
Despite his famous December 1996 warning about the stock market's
"irrational exuberance," Greenspan "did nothing to indicate by his

---

28 Ibid.
29 Ibid., p. 127.
30 Ibid., pp. 139–41.

actions any serious worry about orbiting equity prices." On the contrary, while steadily expanding the domestic money supply, he did not raise interest rates significantly or impose greater reserve requirements on banks; nor did he raise margin requirements on equity purchases. Worse still, as the bubble gained momentum, Greenspan went much further.

> By spring 1998, he would be explicitly rationalizing tearaway equity prices in terms of "New Economy" productivity gains that he saw as at once keeping down inflation and giving credence to investors' expectations of the "extraordinary growth of profits into the distant future." He would also be expressing his warm appreciation of the stepped-up corporate investment and household consumption that flowed from the wealth effect of exploding asset values, and which strengthened the boom. . . . Equity speculators could hardly be faulted if they drew the conclusion that the Fed Chairman, despite his professed caution, found their exuberance not just not irrational, but also sensible and beneficial.[31]

The inrush of capital unleashed by the "reverse Plaza Accord" and the Fed's easy credit regime were necessary conditions of the equity market bubble. But "the main active force" in the dilation of the bubble were US non-financial corporations, which exploited those conditions "to vastly ratchet up their borrowing for the purpose of buying shares in colossal quantities—either to accomplish mergers and acquisitions or to simply re-purchase (retire) their own outstanding equities." Entering upon "the greatest wave of accumulation of debt in their history," US corporations pushed up equity prices at unprecedented rates. "Since rising equity prices, by providing growing paper assets and thereby increased collateral, facilitated still further borrowing, the bubble was enabled to sustain itself, as well as to fuel the strong cyclical upturn already in progress."[32]

Spectacular as it was, the revival did not signal the overcoming of the secular problem of manufacturing over-capacity and over-production. On the contrary, the inflation of the paper value of their assets, and the bubble-induced "wealth effect" on consumer demand, led corporations to invest well above what was warranted by their actually realized profits. As a result, as soon as the wealth effect ceased to subsidize productivity growth, investment and consumer

31 Ibid., pp. 143–6.
32 Ibid., pp. 146–7, 151–2.

demand, "firms . . . were bound to suffer truly excruciating down-ward pressure on their rates of return." Indeed, writing in mid 2001, Brenner already observed the initial impact on the US and world economies of the bursting of the bubble and of "the huge glut of productive capacity left in its wake"—most notably, a disastrous decline in the non-financial corporate profit rate that wiped out "virtually all of the gains in profitability achieved in the expansion of the 1990s"; and a sharp contraction in capital accumulation.[33]

In speculating on how serious the ensuing downturn would be, Brenner pointed out that the "underlying question" is "whether the big recessions and crises . . . that had punctuated the 1990s, as well as the rise of new industries all across the advanced capitalist world, had finally rid international manufacturing of its tendency to redundant production and made for the . . . increase in complementarity" that was required "to finally support a dynamic international expansion." On balance, he found that no such shakeout had actually occurred. On the contrary, in his judgment, the bursting of the bubble left the US economy "weighed down by many of the same stagnationist forces that held back the Japanese economy at the end of its bubble"—that is, "*both* the downward spiral set off by the bubble-in-reverse *and* an international manufacturing sector still constrained by over-capacity and over-production." The US economy might have been in a position to avoid the banking crisis that had crippled Japan, but it lacked "the enormous savings and current-account surpluses that have enabled Japan—so far—to muddle through." It was therefore vulnerable, not just to the "destructive reductions in demand" that would ensue from attempts to reduce the huge indebtedness of US corporations and households, but also to the possibility of violent withdrawals of investment by foreigners and consequent runs on the dollar.[34]

Under these circumstances, Brenner thought that the United States was more likely to lead the world economy into a self-reinforcing recession than a recovery. In a sense, such a self-reinforcing recession would constitute a "continuation of the international crisis of 1997–98, which was temporarily postponed by the last phase of the US stock market run-up but never fully resolved." As in that earlier crisis, "East Asia will once again prove the world's powder keg," with vast over-capacity in Japan and elsewhere in the region exercising a strong downward pressure on profitability locally and globally.[35] Prudently,

---

33 Ibid., pp. 209–17, 248–53, 261–4.
34 Ibid., pp. 269, 276–8, emphasis in the original.
35 Ibid., pp. 278–82.

Brenner did not commit himself to any particular scenario. But the central thesis that underlies all his contentions leaves us with the overwhelming impression that the long downturn is far from over, and indeed, that the worst has yet to come.[36]

This central thesis is that the persistence of relative stagnation in the world economy at large over the last thirty years has been due to "too little exit" and "too much entry"—too little and too much, that is, relative to what would be required in order to restore profitability in manufacturing to the level it had attained during the long boom of the 1950s and 1960s. As we have seen, Brenner traces this tendency to the mutually reinforcing action of the behavior of higher-cost incumbent firms and to the policies of the governments of the world's three largest economies. As a result of this combination, each of these three, and the world economy at large, were prevented "from purging superfluous, high-cost means of production by the *standard capitalist methods* of bankruptcy, downsizing, and layoffs."

> Higher cost/lower profit firms were thus able to long occupy economic positions that could, in the abstract, have eventually been assumed by more productive, higher profit, and more dynamic enterprises. But allowing the less productive, less profitable firms to go out of business by *letting the business cycle take its natural course* would very likely have turned the long downturn, with its relatively serious but nonetheless limited recessions, into *outright depression*. Simply put, the precondition for restoring the system to health was a debt-deflation, leading to what Marx called "a slaughtering of capital values." But since the only systematic way to achieve this was through depression, the only real alternative was continuing debt expansion, which contributed both to stagnation and financial instability.[37]

In his account of the long downturn, Brenner mentions two moments when the "standard" capitalist method of structural shakeout was

---

36 This view has been reiterated in the 2006 version of the 1998 essay. "The truth is that even today, nearly five years into the new, post-New Economy business cycle that began in February 2001, the standard macroeconomic indicators provide no clear sign that the long downturn has been overcome. . . . Meanwhile, financial imbalances and asset price bubbles exceeded even their record-breaking predecessors of the later 1990s and loomed like dark clouds over the global economy" (Brenner, *The Economics of Global Turbulence*, pp. xxviii–xxix).

37 Brenner, *The Boom and the Bubble*, p. 113; "Economics of Global Turbulence," p. 152, emphases added.

briefly at work: the early 1980s under Reagan and the mid 1990s under Clinton. But, as soon as the shakeout threatened to trigger a system-wide depression, the concerted action of the main capitalist states cut short the "slaughter of capital values" through an expansion of public and private debt. "But while the growth of debt . . . was helping to stave off depression, it was also slowing down that recovery of profitability which was the fundamental condition for economic revitalization."[38]

Brenner never tells us what a "depression"—as opposed to the "comparative stagnation" of the long downturn—would look like. In the passages just quoted, the context makes clear that it would be a far more destructive occurrence. But the difference is never made explicit, leaving us wondering, first, whether world capitalism actually ever experienced this allegedly "classical," "natural," "standard" shakeout and outright depression; second, if it did, what alteration in historical conditions has enabled contemporary capitalism to avoid the same experience; and finally, what are the implications of this change for the future of world capitalism and world society?

Two Long Downturns Compared

In seeking answers to such questions, it is helpful to compare the sketch of the Great Depression of 1873–96, set out at the beginning of this chapter, with Brenner's account of the long downturn or persistent stagnation of 1973–93. Notwithstanding the widespread designation of the earlier period as a *depression*,[39] such a comparison immediately reveals striking similarities. Both were lengthy periods of reduced profitability; both were characterized by a system-wide intensification of competitive pressures on capitalist enterprise; and both were preceded by an exceptionally sustained and profitable expansion of world trade and production. Moreover, in both periods, the crisis of profitability and the intensification of competition sprang from the same sources as the preceding expansion: the successful

---

38 Brenner, "Economics of Global Turbulence," pp. 151–2.

39 As noted earlier, the Great Depression of 1873–96 has been called a "myth" precisely because it was characterized by a slowdown in the rate of growth rather than a collapse of production, trade, and investment, as in the truly "great depression" of the 1930s. But, in the 1870s and 1880s, profitability did collapse and remained depressed through the early 1890s. Brenner does not deal with this semantic ambiguity of "depression" but it is clearly an issue that must be confronted to make sense of his frequent use of the term.

"catching-up" of laggard countries with developmental achievements previously "monopolized" by a leading country. Once we substitute the United Kingdom for the United States as the leading country, and the United States and Germany for Germany and Japan as the laggards, Brenner's interpretation of the late twentieth-century long downturn can equally well be applied to that of the late nineteenth. Interestingly, the notion of "excessive competition," which surfaced in Japan during the crisis of profitability of the late 1960s and early 1970s and which Brenner occasionally uses to characterize the underlying condition of the long downturn of 1973–93, first gained currency in business circles in the late nineteenth-century downturn, especially in the United States.[40]

Differences between the two long downturns are, in key respects, even more important than similarities, as we shall see. Yet, faced with a situation of intensifying competition comparable to that of the late twentieth century, world capitalism in the late nineteenth century experienced relative stagnation for more than twenty years—with plenty of local or short-lived crises and recessions, but without the kind of system-wide shakeout that according to Brenner is the standard capitalist method of restoring profitability. In manufacturing, in particular, there continued to be "too much entry" and "too little exit," as well as major technological and organizational innovations which intensified rather than alleviated competitive pressures system-wide. Not only did the long downturn of the late nineteenth century witness the beginning of the so-called Second Industrial Revolution. More important, it saw the emergence in the United States of the modern, multi-unit, vertically integrated enterprises that became dominant over the next century. "Almost non-existent at the end of the 1870s, these integrated enterprises came to dominate many of the [US's] most vital industries within less than three decades."[41]

In spite of the absence of a system-wide shakeout, in the closing years of the century profitability was restored, generating the upturn of the Edwardian *belle époque*. As noted in Chapter 3, and further specified in future chapters, this upturn can be traced to a response to

---

40 See Terutomo Ozawa, *Multinationalism, Japanese Style: The Political Economy of Outward Dependency* (Princeton, NJ, Princeton University Press, 1979), pp. 66–7; Veblen, *Theory of Business Enterprise*, p. 216; Martin J. Sklar, *The Corporate Reconstruction of American Capitalism, 1890–1916: The Market, the Law, and Politics* (Cambridge, Cambridge University Press, 1988), pp. 53–6.

41 Alfred Chandler, *The Visible Hand: The Managerial Revolution in American Business* (Cambridge, MA, The Belknap Press, 1977), p. 285.

system-wide intensifications of competition that has characterized world capitalism from its earliest, pre-industrial beginnings right up to the present. This response consists of a system-wide tendency, centered on the leading capitalist economy of the epoch, towards the "financialization" of processes of capital accumulation. Integral to the transformation of inter-capitalist competition from a positive- into a negative-sum game, this tendency has also acted as a key mechanism of the restoration of profitability, at least temporarily, in the declining but still hegemonic centers of world capitalism. From this standpoint, we can detect resemblances, not just between the Great Depression of 1873–96 and the long downturn of 1973–93, but also between the Edwardian *belle époque* and the US economic revival and great euphoria of the 1990s.[42]

While a verdict on the eventual outcome of the US economic revival of the 1990s might be premature, we know that the Edwardian *belle époque* ended in the catastrophes of two world wars and the inter-vening global economic collapse of the 1930s. This collapse is, in fact, the only occurrence of the last century and a half that corresponds to Brenner's image of a system-wide shakeout or "outright depression." If this is indeed what is signified by Brenner's image, we must conclude that such a process appears to have been an exceptional occurrence rather than the "standard" or "natural" capitalist method of restoring profitability. What has recurred thus far is the tendency for uneven development in Brenner's sense to generate a long boom, followed by a long period of intensifying competition, reduced profitability, and comparative stagnation; itself followed by an upturn of profitability, based on a financial expansion centered on the epoch's leading economy. The one and only systemic breakdown of the last 150 years has occurred in the transition from the first to the second round of uneven development.

The question then arises of whether a comparable breakdown is now in the making, and whether such an occurrence is as "funda-mental" a condition for the revitalization of the global economy as Brenner seems to think. In order to answer this question, we must highlight not just similarities but also differences between the two long downturns—which are, indeed, equally striking. Although both downturns were characterized by an escalation of competitive strug-

42 Giovanni Arrighi, *The Long Twentieth Century: Money, Power and the Origins of our Times* (London, Verso, 1994); Giovanni Arrighi and Beverly J. Silver, *Chaos and Governance in the Modern World System* (Minneapolis, MN, University of Minnesota Press, 1999) and "Capitalism and World (Dis)Order," *Review of International Studies*, 27 (2001).

gles, these unfolded along radically different paths. As previously noted, in 1873–96 the main form of inter-enterprise competition was a "price war," resulting in "the most drastic deflation in the memory of man." Closely related to this tendency, the governments of the main capitalist countries subjected their currencies to the self-regulating mechanisms of a metallic standard, thereby surrendering devaluations and revaluations as a means of competitive struggle.

Increasingly, however, governments became active supporters of their domestic industries through protectionist and mercantilist practices, including the construction of overseas colonial empires—thereby undermining the unity of the world market. Although Britain continued to practice free trade unilaterally, it also remained in the vanguard of territorial expansion and empire-building overseas. From the 1880s, this trajectory of intensifying interstate competition in overseas empire-building translated into the escalation of the armament race among rising and declining capitalist powers, which eventually came to a head in the First World War. Although Britain was an active participant in this scramble, it continued to provide the world economy with capital through two major waves of overseas investment—in the 1880s and in the 1900s—which included pouring significant funds in the United States.

In all these respects, the competitive struggle during the late twentieth century's long downturn unfolded along a radically different path. During the 1970s, in particular, commodity prices generally rose rather than fell, in what was probably one of the greatest system-wide inflations in a time of peace. Although inflationary pressures were contained in the 1980s and 1990s, prices continued to rise throughout the long downturn. At its outset, the last tenuous link between monetary circulation and a metallic standard—the gold–dollar exchange standard established at Bretton Woods—was severed and never again restored. As Brenner underscores, the governments of the main capitalist countries were thus in a position to use the devaluation and revaluation of currencies as means of the competitive struggle. And while they did so systematically, they nonetheless continued to promote the integration of the world market through a series of negotiations that further liberalized global trade and investment, eventually resulting in the formation of the World Trade Organization.

Far from being undermined, the unity of the world market was thus further consolidated during this period. Nor was there any sign of an armament race among rising and declining capitalist powers. On the contrary, during and especially after the final escalation of the Cold

War arms build-up in the 1980s, global military capabilities became even more centralized in the hands of the United States than they had been previously. At the same time, instead of providing capital to the rest of the world economy, as Britain had throughout the previous long downturn and financial expansion, since the 1980s the United States has been absorbing capital at historically unprecedented rates, as Brenner himself notes. In all these respects, the trajectory of the competitive struggle in the latest long downturn differs radically from the previous one. Our next task is to account for this combination of similarities and differences between the two periods and to find out what new light this kind of comparison throws on Brenner's account of global turbulence over the last thirty years.

SOCIAL DYNAMICS OF GLOBAL TURBULENCE

Brenner presents his account of the long downturn as a critique of what he calls "supply side" theories of capitalist crises. Advanced in various forms by left and right alike, these theories contended that, by the 1960s, labor had acquired a leverage in the wealthier capitalist countries sufficient to squeeze profits and thereby undermine the mechanisms of capitalist accumulation. While acknowledging that labor may indeed be in such a position locally and temporarily, Brenner finds it inconceivable that labor can wield the power necessary to provoke a long-term, system-wide downturn.

> Labor cannot, as a rule, bring about a temporally extended, systemic downturn because, as a rule, what might be called the potential sphere of investment for capital in any line of production generally extends beyond the labor market that is affected by unions and/or political parties or is regulated by norms, values, and institutions supported by the state. So firms can generally circumvent and thereby undermine the institutionalized strength of workers at any given point by investing where workers lack the capacity to resist. Indeed, they must do so, or they will find themselves outflanked and competitively defeated by other capitalists who will.[1]

It follows that, as Brenner puts it, "vertical" pressure on capital from below—that is, from labor—could not and did not bring about the spatially generalized and temporally extended squeeze on profits that

---

1 Although Brenner mentions immigration—"unless . . . restrained by political means"—as another mechanism through which workers' power can be undermined, his overwhelming emphasis is on the mobility of capital. Robert Brenner, "The Economics of Global Turbulence: A Special Report on the World Economy, 1950–1998," *New Left Review*, I/229 (1998), pp. 18–20.

underlie the long downturn. Only "horizontal" pressure from inter-capitalist competition could do so.[2]

This hypothesis is based on the assumption that there is in fact "cheaper labor that can be combined with means of production embodying something like the current level of technology without loss of efficiency (that is, at lower unit costs)." According to Brenner, this assumption is justified for two reasons. First, "labor forces in regions with long histories of economic development tend to receive wages that are substantially higher than can be explained simply by reference to their level of productiveness"; and second, "over similarly extended time periods, technical change tends to reduce the skill required to produce any given array of products, with the result that the labor force that can make those products without loss of efficiency is continually enlarged, and the wage required to pay it correspondingly reduced."[3]

In short, for historical reasons that Brenner does not explore, labor forces in "advanced" capitalist countries have secured rewards for effort far higher than warranted by their productivity. This in itself makes them vulnerable to the competition of labor forces that—for equally unexplored historical reasons—work for wages lower than their actual or potential productivity might warrant. At the same time, technical change continually enlarges this global pool of underpaid workers, or would-be workers, who can be mobilized to outflank the pressure on profitability coming from overpaid workers. The only pressure on profitability that capitalists cannot outflank is the pressure coming from the competition of other capitalists.

There are two main problems with this argument. Firstly, it appears to be logically inconsistent because it claims that, in the past, workers in the "advanced" capitalist countries were able to gain greater rewards than warranted by their productivity, in contradiction to the theoretical claim that any attempt to do so would price workers out of the world market. In addition, the argument overestimates the ease with which, in the present no less than in the past, cheaper labor supplies can be mobilized to outflank more expensive ones. Let us clarify these problems by looking once again at the historical record.

---

2 Ibid., p. 23.
3 Ibid., p. 18.

Class Conflict and Inter-Capitalist Competition

An analysis of the long downturn of 1873–96 provides strong evidence both in favor and against Brenner's thesis of the predominance of horizontal (inter-capitalist) relations over vertical (labor–capital) relations in bringing about a long-term and generalized squeeze on profits. In support of Brenner's argument, it could be pointed out that intense labor–capital conflicts—either in the form of sustained strike activity, as in Britain and the United States, or in the form of working-class party formation, as in Germany and elsewhere—*followed* rather than preceded the onset of the long downturn in profitability. There can be little doubt that intense inter-capitalist competition, in the form of a relentless price war, was the main, and prior, driving force for the substantial increase in real wages that occurred during the depression, especially in Britain. It is also plausible to assume that rising real wages at home were at least in part responsible for the explosive growth of British overseas investment in the 1880s. Brenner's argument for the late twentieth century thus fits key features of the late nineteenth-century experience. The fit, however, is far from perfect.

Although inter-capitalist competition was undoubtedly the primary force squeezing profitability and pushing up real wages through drastic price deflation, did not workers' resistance in the form of increasing strike activity and class-based organization contribute in a major way to that outcome by preventing nominal wages from decreasing as rapidly as prices? And did not this resistance itself affect the trajectory of inter-capitalist competition by strengthening the tendency, not just towards the export of capital from Britain and the import of labor to the United States, but also towards the "politicization" of that competition through a revival of neo-mercantilist practices and overseas empire-building on an unprecedented scale? Whatever the exact answer to these questions, Brenner's hard and fast distinction between horizontal and vertical conflicts, and his *a priori* exclusion of the latter as a possible contributing factor of general and persistent downturns in profitability, are ill-suited to unravel the complex historical interaction between the two kinds of conflicts.[4]

Similarly, Brenner's contention concerning the inevitable outflanking of workers' leverage in core capitalist countries through interna-

---

4 See Beverly J. Silver, *Forces of Labor: Workers' Movements and Globalization since 1870* (Cambridge, Cambridge University Press, 2003), pp. 131–8, for one set of answers to these questions.

tional factor mobility ignores key aspects of how that mobility actually functioned during the earlier long downturn. Most of the capital exported from Britain and lesser core countries in this period did not involve a relocation of industrial production but the building of infrastructures in overseas territories, expanding demand for the output of British and other metropolitan industries while increasing the supply of cheap raw materials and wage goods. Far from undermining the leverage of labor in the main capitalist centers, this pattern of overseas investment consolidated it. At the same time, while constant immigration may have helped contain the growing leverage of US labor, massive emigration—especially from Britain—surely helped the empowerment of European labor. As Göran Therborn notes, in the nineteenth century Europe in general and Britain in particular enjoyed practically unlimited migration outlets for its labor. "Even the English center of global industry was an out-migration area. . . . A conservative estimate is that about 50 million Europeans emigrated out of the continent in the period 1850–1930, which corresponds to about 12 percent of the continent's population in 1900."[5]

All things considered, the persistence and generality of the late nineteenth-century profit squeeze appear to have been due, not just to the intensification of inter-capitalist competition, but also to the effective resistance of workers against attempts to make them bear the costs of that competition and to the difficulties which capitalists encountered in outflanking that resistance. Partly related to these difficulties, in the half century following the end of the long downturn of 1873–96, inter-capitalist competition became increasingly politicized: literal wars among rising and declining capitalist powers, rather than price wars among capitalist enterprises, came to dominate the dynamics of horizontal and vertical conflicts alike. From the late 1890s until the First World War, this transformation was instrumental in reviving profitability. Eventually, however, it resulted in the breakdown of the UK-centered world market and a new and more vicious round of inter-imperialist conflicts. For all practical purposes, in the 1930s and 1940s there was no world market to speak of. In Eric Hobsbawm's words, world capitalism had retreated "into the igloos of its nation-state economies and their associated empires."[6]

Under these circumstances, labor–capital conflicts developed along two distinct and increasingly divergent paths. One was the predo-

---

5 Göran Therborn, *European Modernity and Beyond: The Trajectory of European Societies, 1945–2000* (London, Sage, 1995), p. 40.

6 Eric J. Hobsbawm, *Nations and Nationalism since 1780: Programme, Myth, Reality* (Cambridge, Cambridge University Press, 1991), p. 132.

minantly "social" path of movements nesting at the point of production, whose main weapon of struggle was the disruptive power that mass production puts in the hands of strategically placed workers. This originated in late nineteenth-century Britain but assumed almost idea-typical form in the United States. The other was the predominantly "political" path of movements nesting in the bureaucratic structures of political parties, whose main weapon was the seizure of state power and the rapid modernization of the states that fell under their control. It originated in continental Europe, most notably in Germany, but assumed its idea-typical form in the USSR.[7]

The course of struggle along both paths was thoroughly shaped by the two world wars. Each of these was characterized by a similar pattern: overt labor militancy rose on the eve of both wars, declined temporarily during the conflicts themselves, and then exploded in their aftermath. The Russian Revolution took place during the First World War's wave of labor militancy, while that of the Second World War saw the spread of Communist regimes to Eastern Europe, China, North Korea, and Vietnam. It was in this context of escalating labor militancy in the core, and advancing communist revolution in peripheral and semi-peripheral regions, that the social parameters of the US postwar world order were established.[8] The form and intensity of inter-capitalist competition—that is, inter-imperialist rivalries and world wars—shaped the form and intensity of workers' struggles during this period. But the "feedback" of workers' struggles on the trajectory of inter-capitalist conflicts was even more powerful in the first half of the twentieth century than it had been during the long downturn of 1873–96. Indeed, in the absence of this powerful feedback, the establishment at the end of the Second World War of what Aristide Zolberg has called a "labor friendly" international regime would be hard to explain.[9]

---

7 Giovanni Arrighi and Beverly J. Silver, "Labor Movements and Capital Migration: The US and Western Europe in World-Historical Perspective," in Charles Bergquist, ed., *Labor in the Capitalist World-Economy* (Beverly Hills, CA, Sage, 1984).

8 Silver, *Forces of Labor*, pp. 125–31, 138–61.

9 Aristide R. Zolberg, "Response: Working-Class Dissolution," *International Labor and Working-Class History*, 47 (1995). To be sure, the "labor friendly" reforms instituted with the establishment of US hegemony—e.g., macroeconomic policies favoring full employment—went hand in hand with fierce repression of any sectors of the labor movement that sought a deeper social transformation than the postwar social contract offered. Nevertheless, the reforms instituted under the pressure of escalating labor unrest and advancing communist revolution marked a significant transformation in comparison with the laissez-faire regime characteristic of the period of British world hegemony. See Giovanni Arrighi and Beverly J. Silver, *Chaos and Governance in the Modern World System* (Minneapolis, MN, 1999) pp. 202–7; Silver, *Forces of Labor*, pp. 157–8.

Along with the US-sponsored reconstitution of the world market on new and more solid foundations, this regime created the institutional conditions for the system-wide revival of profitability that underlay the long boom of the 1950s and 1960s. I have no particular disagreement with Brenner's contention that "uneven development," in his sense of the term, was a key determinant of the long boom and of the long downturn that followed. But his insistence that labor–capital conflicts played no significant role in determining the extent, length, and shape of the downturn seems even less warranted than for earlier comparable periods.

Let us begin by noting that, in the late twentieth century, workers' struggles played a far more proactive role vis-à-vis inter-capitalist competition than they did in the late nineteenth century. Whereas in the earlier period, the intensification of labor–capital conflicts, and the most significant increases in real wages, *followed* the onset of the downturn, in the second half of the twentieth century they *preceded* it. In arguing his case against the role of workers' leverage in bringing about a system-wide and persistent squeeze on profits, Brenner focuses almost exclusively on the containment of workers' power in the United States in the late 1950s and early 1960s: since the containment occurred before the crisis of profitability, he argues, the crisis could not be due to workers' pressures.[10] Unfortunately, this narrow focus on the single "tree" of a short-term and local episode of class conflict, prevents Brenner from seeing the "forest" of the *multinational* rising tide of conflicts over wages and working conditions that in 1968–73 culminated in what E.H. Phelps Brown aptly called the "pay explosion."[11] Coming in the wake of twenty years of rising real wages in the core regions of the world economy, and at a time of intensifying inter-capitalist competition worldwide, this pay explosion did not merely exercise a system-wide downward pressure on profitability, as many have emphasized.[12] More important, it had a major and lasting impact on the subsequent trajectory of inter-capitalist competition.

---

10 Brenner, "Economics of Global Turbulence," pp. 52–4, 58–63.

11 E.H. Phelps Brown, "A Non-Monetarist View of the Pay Explosion," *Three Banks Review*, 105 (1975).

12 See, among others, Makoto Itoh, *The World Economic Crisis and Japanese Capitalism* (New York, St Martin's Press, 1990), pp. 50–3; Philip Armstrong, Andrew Glyn, and John Harrison, *Capitalism since World War II: The Making and Breakup of the Great Boom* (London, Fontana, 1984), pp. 269–76; Philip Armstrong and Andrew Glyn, *Accumulation, Profits, State Spending: Data for Advanced Capitalist Countries 1952–83* (Oxford, Oxford Institute of Economics and Statistics, 1986).

This brings us to a second observation concerning differences between the two end-of-century long downturns. Although he occasionally mentions price inflation, Brenner is generally oblivious to the peculiarly inflationary character of the downturn he describes—all the more remarkable when contrasted with the strong deflationary character of the late nineteenth-century downturn. Brenner never questions this peculiarity; nor does he raise the closely related question of why the 1965–73 crisis of profitability witnessed the severance of the last tenuous link between monetary circulation and a metallic standard, in sharp contrast with the tendency of the 1870s and 1880s towards the diffusion of the gold and other metallic-based regimes.

To be sure, Brenner does implicitly acknowledge that Washington's final abandonment, in 1970, of half-hearted attempts to stem the tide of speculation against the gold–dollar system was not just a ploy to shift the downward pressure on profits from US to Japanese and German manufacturers through a radical realignment of exchange rates. As he mentions in passing, "the political costs of sustaining a serious anti-inflationary policy . . . quickly proved unacceptable to the Nixon administration."[13] What these "political costs" were, and whether they had anything to do with labor–capital relations, we are not told. As we shall see in the next section of this chapter, in the case of the United States such costs were world-systemic as well as domestic. Nevertheless, even in the United States—torn as it was by intense social conflicts over war in Vietnam and civil rights at home—the political price of subjecting monetary circulation to the discipline of a metallic standard clearly had a social component, including the costs and risks of alienating labor from the ideologies and practices of the dominant social bloc.[14]

In fact, the most compelling evidence for the role played by labor leverage in the final demise of the gold standard comes, not from the United States, but from the country that had been the staunchest advocate of a return to a pure gold-based regime in the 1960s: de Gaulle's France. French advocacy of the gold standard ended abruptly, never to be revived again, in May 1968, when de Gaulle had to grant a huge wage hike to prevent labor from siding with the rebellious students. Had monetary circulation been subject to the automatic mechanism of a metallic standard, such a wage hike would have been impossible. Being perfectly aware of this, de Gaulle did

---

13 Brenner, "Economics of Global Turbulence," pp. 120–1.
14 Silver, *Forces of Labor*, pp. 161–3.

what was necessary to restore social peace and stopped daydreaming about a return to gold.[15]

As the US and French experiences suggest, the leverage of labor during the transition from boom to relative stagnation in the late 1960s and early 1970s was not a mere reflection of inter-capitalist competition, as it largely had been at the onset of the late nineteenth-century downturn.[16] On the contrary, it was significant enough to make its own independent contribution, not just to the squeeze of profitability that underlay the transition, but also towards launching the downturn along an inflationary rather than deflationary path. This does not mean that inter-capitalist competition was not also at work in squeezing profits, nor that workers and their social power benefited from the inflationary nature of the downturn—they clearly did not. All it means is that Brenner's model—near-absolute pre-dominance of inter-capitalist competition over labor–capital conflict—fits the latest long downturn even less than it did the previous one.

A closer examination of the effects of capital mobility on labor leverage provides further evidence for such an assessment. In the 1970s, in particular, there was indeed a strong tendency for capital, including industrial capital, to "migrate" to lower-income, lower-wage countries. Nevertheless, as Beverly Silver has documented in great detail, the relocation of industrial activities from richer to poorer countries has more often than not led to the emergence of strong, new labor movements in the lower-wage sites of investment, rather than an unambiguous "race to the bottom." Although corporations were initially attracted to particular Third World sites—Brazil, South Africa, South Korea—because they appeared to offer a cheap and docile labor force, the subsequent expansion of capital-intensive, mass-production industries created new and militant working classes with significant disruptive power. This tendency was already in evidence in the late nineteenth and early twentieth centuries in textiles, the chief industry of British capitalism. But it has been far

---

15 Completely forgotten today, the connection between the May events and the abrupt end of French advocacy of the gold standard was also little noticed at the time. I nonetheless remember quite vividly from newspaper accounts how May 1968 brought about a sudden reversal in French support of the gold standard as a means of challenging US dollar supremacy.

16 As noted in Chapter 4, real wages rose throughout the Great Depression of 1873–96. Although in the 1880s and 1890s, the increase could be attributed to workers' resistance against cuts in nominal wages, initially it was entirely due to inter-capitalist competition driving prices down more quickly than wages.

stronger in the leading industries of US capitalism, such as the automobile industry.[17]

Thus capitalist attempts to outflank labor pressures on profitability through industrial relocation tended to deprive capital of the considerable benefits associated with producing close to the wealthier markets and in safer political environments, without actually providing many of the expected benefits of abundant, low-waged, and easy-to-discipline labor supplies. Acting in conjunction with other tendencies to be discussed later, this tendency made its own contribution to the massive redirection of transnational capital flows in the 1980s from low- and middle-income destinations to the United States. Again, I am not denying that industrial relocation helped in undermining workers' leverage in the countries that experienced the greatest net outflow of capital. I am simply saying that, generally speaking, it tended to backfire on profitability; and, insofar as the United States was concerned, the net outflow soon turned into a huge net inflow. If labor's leverage declined in the course of the long downturn, as it certainly did, capital mobility is not a very convincing explanation.

Labor migration does not provide a very plausible explanation either. It is true that labor migration over the last thirty-five years has come predominantly from poor countries, to a far greater extent than in the late nineteenth century—thereby constituting a greater competitive threat for workers in the wealthier industrial centers. Nevertheless, in the late twentieth century the capacity of workers in the richer countries to forestall competition from immigrant labor forces (often through adherence to racist ideologies and practices) has been far greater.[18]

---

17 Silver, *Forces of Labor*, esp. chs 2 and 3. Brenner and Silver both make use of Raymond Vernon's product cycle model (see "International Investment and International Trade in the Product Cycle," *Quarterly Journal of Economics*, 80, 2 [1966]). Brenner ("Economics of Global Turbulence," p. 18) uses it to buttress on *a priori* grounds the assumptions of his own model, whereas Silver (*Forces of Labor*, pp. 77–97) uses it to show empirically the limits of industrial relocation in outflanking labor resistance.

18 This greater capacity is reflected in the fact that, proportionately speaking, migratory flows in the late nineteenth century were larger than today's, despite the technological advances in transportation since then. See David Held et al., *Global Transformations* (Stanford, CA, Stanford University Press, 1999), ch. 6. Moreover, immigrant workers have been the protagonists in some of the most militant and successful labor struggles in the US in the 1990s, for example, the Justice for Janitors campaigns. See Roger Waldinger et al., "Helots No More: A Case Study of the Justice for Janitors Campaign in Los Angeles," in K. Bronfenbrenner et al., eds, *Organizing to Win* (Ithaca, NY, Cornell University Press, 1998), ch. 6.

In sum, Brenner's argument for the absolute predominance of inter-capitalist competition over labor–capital struggles in determining system-wide and persistent contractions in profitability misses the complex historical interaction between horizontal and vertical conflicts. Although, world-historically, inter-capitalist competition has indeed been the predominant influence—provided that we include inter-capitalist wars among the most important forms of that competition—labor–capital conflicts never were a mere "dependent variable," above all on the eve and early stages of the latest long downturn.[19] Not only did conflicts over wages and working conditions in core regions contribute to the initial squeeze on profitability in the crucial 1968–73 period; more importantly, they forced the ruling groups of core capitalist countries to choose an inflationary rather than a deflationary strategy of crisis management.

To put it bluntly, at the end of the long postwar boom, the leverage of labor in core regions was sufficient to make any attempt to roll it back through a serious deflation far too risky in social and political terms. An inflationary strategy, in contrast, promised to outflank workers' power far more effectively than international factor mobility could. It was, indeed, the great stagnation-cum-inflation of the 1970s—"stagflation," as it was called at the time—and its effects on inter-capitalist competition and labor–capital relations, that effectively wore down workers' power in the core, opening the way for its collapse under the impact of the Reagan–Thatcher counterrevolution. In order to capture the full significance of this development and its impact on the subsequent trajectory of the long downturn, however, it is not enough to focus on labor–capital relations. Even more important were North–South relations, to which we now turn.

Southern Exposure

In his critique of supply-side theorists, Brenner contrasts their disposition to view the world economy as the mere sum of its national components with his own attempt to see systemic processes as having a logic of their own.

> [T]he emphasis of the supply-side theorists on institutions, policy and power has led them to frame their analyses too heavily on a country-by-country basis, in terms of national states and national

---

19 See Arrighi and Silver, *Chaos and Governance*, ch. 3.

economies—to view the international economy as a sort of spill-over of national ones and to see systemic economic problems as stemming from an agglomeration of local ones. In contrast, I shall take the international economy—*the capital accumulation and profitability of the system as a whole*—as a theoretical vantage point from which to analyze its crises and those of its national components.[20]

Laudable as this intent is, Brenner's analysis falls short of its promises, being focused almost exclusively on three national states/economies (the United States, Japan, and Germany) and their mutual relations, with occasional references to other Western European countries and the "miracle economies" of East Asia. China appears only fleetingly towards the end of "Global Turbulence" and in a little more detail in the closing pages of *The Boom and the Bubble*. In the 2006 Afterword to *Global Turbulence*, Brenner cannot avoid referring to the spectacular economic performance of China since the publication of the earlier texts. China's ascent, however, is said to make no difference, indeed, to strengthen the conclusions reached on the basis of the earlier analysis focused on the United States, Germany, and Japan.[21]

The vast majority of the world's states and the bulk of its population have, apparently, no bearing on the functioning of Brenner's world economy. Brenner admits that concentrating on three countries "does introduce distortions." But, without specifying what these distortions are, he goes on to justify his narrow focus on three grounds. First, in 1950, the US, German, and Japanese economies taken together "accounted for 60 per cent of the output (in terms of purchasing power parities) of the seventeen leading capitalist economies and by 1994 that figure had risen to 66 per cent." Second, each of the three economies "stood . . . at the hub of great regional blocs, which they effectively dynamized and dominated." And finally, "the interaction among these three economies was . . . one of the keys to the evolution of the advanced capitalist world throughout the post-war period."[22]

These premises are questionable on two grounds. The combined weight of the three economies in question is indeed considerable,

---

20 Brenner, "Economics of Global Turbulence," p. 23, emphasis in the original.

21 Robert Brenner, *The Economics of Global Turbulence: The Advanced Capitalist Economies from Long Boom to Long Downturn, 1945–2005* (London, Verso, 2006), pp. 323–9, 340–3.

22 Brenner, "Economics of Global Turbulence," p. 9.

though somewhat less than Brenner's sources suggest.[23] Nevertheless, as Figure 5.1 shows, their share of total world exports has been less than 30 percent for most years, and while through the 1980s the growing German and Japanese shares compensated or more than compensated the falling US share, since the mid 1990s the shares of all three countries have been declining in sharp contrast with the rapid rise of the Chinese share. Moreover, the combined share of value added in manufacturing of the three countries—the branch of activities on which Brenner concentrates—has declined significantly in the course of the long downturn. The fall has been largely due to the rapid industrialization of many countries of the world's South—what Alice Amsden has called "The Rise of the 'Rest.'" Even excluding China, the global South's share of world manufacturing value added rose from 10.7 percent in 1975 to 17.0 percent in 1998, and its share of world manufactured exports grew even faster, rising from 7.5 percent in 1975 to 23.3 percent in 1998.[24] By dealing with the world's South in a cursory way, Brenner thus tends to miss one of the most dynamic elements of the intensification of competition to which he attributes so much importance.

The second problem with Brenner's focus on three countries is more serious: the virtual eviction of world politics from the analysis of capitalist dynamics. There is no question that the interaction of the

---

23 Using the more inclusive data sets of the World Bank, their combined share of "world" GNP appears to have remained virtually constant, rising insignificantly from 53.1 per cent in 1960 to 53.6 per cent in 1999 (calculated from World Bank, *World Tables*, vols 1 and 2 [Washington DC, World Bank, 1984] and *World Development Indicators*, CD ROM [Washington DC, World Bank, 2001]). "World" GNP excludes the former Communist countries of the USSR and Eastern Europe and other countries for which there are no comparable data for both 1960 and 1999. However, all the available evidence suggests that the exclusion has the effect of raising the above figures by one or two percentage points at most.

24 Alice Amsden, *The Rise of "The Rest"* (New York, Oxford University Press, 2001), and "Good-bye Dependency Theory, Hello Dependency Theory," *Studies in Comparative International Development*, 38, 1 (2003), tables 1 and 2. By recalculating Amsden's percentages to include China, I obtain an increase in the Southern share of world manufacturing value added from 11.9 per cent in 1975 to 21.8 per cent in 1998. As shown elsewhere, this increase in the Southern share of manufacturing value added reflects a strong North–South convergence in degree of industrialization—accompanied, however, by a complete *lack* of income convergence. See Giovanni Arrighi, Beverly J. Silver, and Benjamin D. Brewer, "Industrial Convergence and the Persistence of the North–South Divide," *Studies in Comparative International Development*, 38, 1 (2003); "A Reply to Alice Amsden," *Studies in Comparative International Development*, 38, 1 (2003); and "Industrial Convergence and the Persistence of the North–South Divide: A Rejoinder to Firebaugh," *Studies in Comparative International Development*, 40, 1 (2005).

Figure 5.1   National exports as a percentage of total world exports

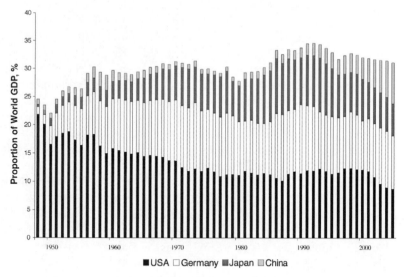

■USA □Germany ■Japan ▨China

Note: Percentages of world exports in current US dollars.
Source: WTO International Trade Statistics.

United States, Japan, and Germany has been "one of the keys" to the
evolution of world capitalism since the Second World War; but it has
certainly not been the only one, or even the most important. As Brenner
implicitly recognizes in one of the passages quoted in Chapter 4,
throughout the long boom US interaction with Germany and Japan
was thoroughly embedded in, and dominated by, the Cold War
relations between the United States, the USSR, and China. The crisis
of profitability that marked the transition from the long boom to the
long downturn, as well as the great stagflation of the 1970s, were
themselves deeply affected by the parallel crisis of American hegemony
which ensued from the escalation of the Vietnam War and eventual US
defeat. As for the Reagan–Thatcher neo-liberal counterrevolution, it
was not just, or even primarily, a response to the unsolved crisis of
profitability but also—and especially—a response to the deepening
crisis of hegemony. All along, the trajectories of inter-capitalist competition and of the interaction among the world's three largest economies were shaped by the broader political context. The almost complete
absence of this context in Brenner's story is indeed the source not just of
distortions but of indeterminateness as well.

Consider the connection between the crisis of profitability of the late
1960s and early 1970s and the contemporaneous breakdown of the

gold–dollar exchange standard. As we have seen, Brenner implicitly acknowledges that "political costs" played a role in the abandonment of gold, but nonetheless upholds the thesis that its primary determinant was the competitive struggle between US manufacturers and their German and Japanese rivals. We have already criticized this argument for ignoring the relatively autonomous role that workers' leverage played in the crisis. Nevertheless, the most important determinant was neither inter-capitalist competition nor labor–capital relations but the direct and, especially, the indirect effects of the escalation of the Vietnam War on the US balance-of-payments. Although Vietnam is conspicuous for its absence in Brenner's story, these effects do creep in on a few occasions. Thus, "stepped-up Vietnam War spending" is said to be the reason for the sudden acceleration of price inflation in the United States which, between 1965 and 1973, slowed down but did not stop the growth of real wages. This acceleration of inflation, in turn, is held responsible for the weakening of the competitive position of American manufacturers, both at home and abroad, vis-à-vis their German and Japanese rivals in the same period.[25]

These casual observations show that even Brenner is forced to acknowledge that behind the intensification of competition between US and foreign manufacturers, and the vagaries of labor–capital conflicts in the United States and elsewhere, there lurks an eminently systemic but political variable, which his research design has ruled out of consideration. This lurking variable is the power struggle in which the US government sought to contain, through the use of force, the joint challenge of nationalism and communism in the Third World. As the escalation of the war in Vietnam failed to break the back of Vietnamese resistance, and provoked instead widespread opposition to the war in the United States itself, this struggle reached its climax in the same years as the crisis of profitability. As I have argued else-where, the costs of the war—including the costs of programs aimed at stemming the tide of domestic opposition—not only contributed to the profit squeeze, but were the most fundamental cause of the collapse of the Bretton Woods regime of fixed exchange rates and the precipitous devaluation of the US dollar that ensued.[26]

As Brenner maintains, the dollar devaluation of 1969–73 did help the United States to foist the burden of the profitability crisis onto Germany

25 Brenner, "Economics of Global Turbulence," p. 97; *The Economics of Global Turbulence*, pp. 102, 119.

26 Giovanni Arrighi, *The Long Twentieth Century: Money, Power and the Origins of our Times* (London, Verso, 1994), pp. 300–8, 320–1.

and Japan and check the pressure of rising money wages on profits at home. But I would argue that this redistribution of the burden was largely a byproduct of policies aimed primarily at freeing the US government's struggle for dominance in the Third World from monetary constraints. At least initially, the liquidation of the gold–dollar exchange standard did seem to endow the US government with an unprecedented freedom of action in tapping the resources of the world simply by issuing its own currency.[27] However, this free hand could not prevent the defeat of the United States in Vietnam nor stop the steep decline of US prestige and power in its wake. Indeed, if anything, it worsened that decline by provoking a worldwide inflationary spiral which threatened to destroy the entire US credit structure and the worldwide networks of capital accumulation on which American wealth and power had become more dependent than ever before.[28]

The decline of US power and prestige reached its nadir in the late 1970s with the Iranian Revolution, a new hike in oil prices, the Soviet invasion of Afghanistan, and another serious crisis of confidence in the US dollar. Brenner hardly mentions this deepening crisis of US hegemony as the context in which, between 1979 and 1982, the monetary policies of the US government changed from ultra laxity to extreme tightness. He does trace the change to "a devastating run on the US currency that threatened the dollar's position as an international reserve currency." But he has no satisfactory explanation of the flight and pays no attention to the Arab fears over Afghanistan and Iran that, according to *Business Week*, were behind the surge in the price of gold to an all-time high of $875 in January 1980.[29] As in the case of the liquidation of the gold–dollar exchange standard ten years earlier, war and revolution in the South, rather than inter-capitalist competition among the world's three largest economies, were the primary driving force of the monetarist counter-revolution of 1979–82. Fundamental change in the monetary sphere once again had major implications both for the inter-capitalist and class struggles in core regions. But the strongest stimulus for the

---

27 Riccardo Parboni, *The Dollar and its Rivals* (London, Verso, 1981), pp. 47, 89–90.

28 Arrighi, *The Long Twentieth Century*, pp. 310–14, 317–20. As we shall see in Chapter 6, the so-called first "oil shock" of 1973–74 was a crucial intervening variable in the worldwide inflationary spiral that connects the crisis of US hegemony of the late 1960s and early 1970s to the devastating run on the US dollar of the late 1970s.

29 Cited in Michael Moffitt, *The World's Money: International Banking from Bretton Woods to the Brink of Insolvency* (New York, Simon & Schuster, 1983), p. 178.

change came from the unsolved crisis of US hegemony in the Third World rather than the crisis of profitability as such.

Here too, the peculiarities of the late twentieth-century long downturn may be usefully highlighted through a comparison with that of 1873–96. Though seldom remarked upon, differences in North–South relations between the two long downturns are even more significant than those of labor and capital. The most important and all-encompassing difference is that the earlier long downturn occurred in the midst of the latest and greatest wave of Northern territorial conquest and colonization of the South, whereas the later long downturn occurred at the tail-end of the greatest wave of decolonization in world history.[30] In between there stood the great "revolt against the West" of the first half of the twentieth century which, according to Barraclough's view quoted in the Introduction, marked the beginning of an entirely new era in world history. Although, in the 1990s, the seemingly unlimited power of the West made the earlier Southern revolt look insignificant, if not futile, neither the origins, nor the trajectory, nor the consequences of the latest long downturn can be accurately deciphered except in the light of the fundamental change in North–South relations that occurred in the preceding half century. To illustrate the point, I shall focus once again on the monetary aspects of the two long downturns.

In the preceding section we traced the inflationary character of the latest long downturn to the social and political impossibility of subjecting labor–capital relations in core regions to the discipline of a metallic standard, as they had been during the late nineteenth century. The nature and strength of this social constraint within core regions, however, themselves depend critically on the particular political arrangements that link the core to the peripheries. Nothing illustrates this better than the close connection between Britain's adherence to the gold standard and its extraction of tribute from the Indian subcontinent. Britain's Indian empire was critical in two main respects.

First, militarily: in Lord Salisbury's words, "India was an English barrack in the Oriental Seas from which we may draw any number of troops without paying for them."[31] Funded entirely by the Indian taxpayer, these forces were organized in a European-style colonial

---

30 On waves of colonization and decolonization, see Albert Bergesen and Ronald Schoenberg, "Long Waves of Colonial Expansion and Contraction, 1415–1969," in A. Bergesen, ed., *Studies in the Modern World-System* (New York, Academic Press, 1980).

31 Quoted in B.R. Tomlinson, "India and the British Empire, 1880–1935," *The Indian Economic and Social History Review*, 12, 4 (1975).

army and used regularly in the endless series of wars through which Britain opened up Asia and Africa to Western trade, investment, and influence.[32] They were "the iron fist in the velvet glove of Victorian expansionism . . . the major coercive force behind the internationalization of industrial capitalism."[33] As late as 1920, soldiers from India accounted for more than 87 percent of the troops Britain deployed in Iraq to quell a full-scale insurgency against British military occupation. "Perhaps, then, the greatest problem faced by the Anglophone empire of our time is very simple: the United Kingdom had the Indian Army; the United States does not."[34]

Second, and equally important, the infamous Home Charges and the Bank of England's control over India's foreign-exchange reserves, jointly turned India into the "pivot" of Britain's global financial and commercial supremacy. India's balance-of-payments deficit with Britain, and surplus with all other countries, enabled Britain to settle its deficit on current-account with the rest of the world. Without India's forcible contribution to the balance-of-payments of imperial Britain, it would have been impossible for the latter "to use the income from her overseas investment for further investment abroad, and to give back to the international monetary system the liquidity she absorbed as investment income." Moreover, Indian monetary reserves "provided a large *masse de manœuvre* which British monetary authorities could use to supplement their own reserves and to keep London the center of the international monetary system."[35]

---

32 If we take Asia and Africa together, there were as many as seventy-two separate British military campaigns between 1837 and 1900. Brian Bond, ed., *Victorian Military Campaigns* (London, Hutchiuson, 1967), pp. 309–11. By a different count, between 1803 and 1901 Britain fought fifty major colonial wars (Anthony Giddens, *The Nation-State and Violence* (Berkeley, CA, University of California Press, 1987), p. 223.

33 David Washbrook, "South Asia, the World System, and World Capitalism," *The Journal of Asian Studies*, 49, 3 (1990), p. 481.

34 N. Ferguson, "Cowboys and Indians," *New York Times*, May 24, 2005. In 2003, the United States exerted heavy pressure on the Indian government to commit a full division of 17,000 troops. Even if the Indian government had been willing to do so, the domestic political environment simply did not allow it. "In retrospect, this was one of the key events of the first thirty months of the Iraq war. No Indian commitment meant that no other major troop offerings [ironically, with the exception of the British army] were forthcoming" (P. Rogers, "Fragments of the 'War on Terror'," *openDemocracy*, August 25, 2005).

35 Marcello de Cecco, *The International Gold Standard: Money and Empire*, 2nd edn (New York, St Martin's Press, 1984), pp. 62–3. For a full account of the tribute that Britain extracted from India in the late nineteenth and early twentieth centuries, see Amiya K. Bagchi, *Perilous Passage: Mankind and the Global Ascendancy of Capital* (Lantham, MD, Rowman & Littlefield, 2005), pp. 239–43.

In enforcing monetary discipline at home on workers and capitalists alike, Britain's ruling groups thus faced an altogether different
situation to that of US leaders a century later. For one thing, the
exercise of world-hegemonic functions—including the endless series
of wars fought in the world's South—did not involve the kind of
inflationary pressures that the Vietnam War engendered in the United
States. Not only were the wars financed by Indian money but, fought
by Indian and other colonial troops, they did not require the kind of
social expenditure the US government had to incur in order to contain
domestic opposition to escalating casualties.

Costs of war aside, unlike the United States in the late twentieth
century, Britain could internalize the benefits (for its metropolitan
subjects) and externalize the costs (on its colonial subjects) of the ceaseless
"structural adjustments" involved in the subjection of its currency to a
metallic standard. Coercive control over the surplus of India's balance-
of-payments enabled Britain to shift the burdens of its own persistent
trade deficits onto Indian taxpayers, workers, and capitalists.[36] In a post-
colonial world, in contrast, no such blatant coercion was available. The
United States faced the stark choice of either balancing its trade and
current-accounts deficits through a drastic downsizing of its national
economy and expenditures abroad, or alienating a growing share of its
future incomes to foreign lenders. The inflationary strategy of crisis
management was not dictated solely by the social and political impossibility of subjecting the American national economy to a drastic downsizing, or by the relief from foreign competitive pressures that the strategy
could bring to US manufacturers. It was also a more or less conscious
attempt *not* to choose between the two equally unpalatable alternatives
of downsizing or debt. The deepening crisis of US hegemony of the late
1970s and the devastating run on the dollar it provoked were a shocking
reminder that the choice could no longer be postponed.

The monetary counterrevolution initiated in the closing year of the
Carter administration, and pursued with greater force under Reagan,
was a pragmatic response to this situation. As Brenner notes, the
turnaround deepened rather than alleviated the crisis of profitability.
But, as he does not note, it did reverse—beyond the rosiest expectations of its perpetrators—the precipitous decline of US world power
of the preceding fifteen years.[37] In order to understand this unex-

36 On Britain's persistent trade deficits, see, among others, Andre Gunder
Frank, "Multilateral Merchandise Trade Imbalances and Uneven Economic Development," *Journal of Economic History*, 5, 2 (1978) and de Cecco, *The International
Gold Standard*.
37 Arrighi, *The Long Twentieth Century*, pp. 323–4.

pected reversal, we must once again shift focus and re-examine critically the processes of inter-capitalist competition that are at the center of Brenner's analysis.

The Financial Underpinnings of US Revival

Brenner, as we have seen, attributes the persistence of "over-production and over-capacity" after 1973 partly to the behavior of higher-cost incumbent firms—which had "every reason to defend their markets and counterattack by speeding up the process of innovation and investment in additional fixed capital"—and partly to actions of the US, Japanese, and German governments that aggravated rather than alleviated the underlying tendency towards too little exit and too much entry. We also noted that, while governmental action occupies center-stage in Brenner's historical narrative, the theoretically more crucial argument about firms is for the most part developed deductively, on the basis of circumstantial evidence.

The main problem with this crucial argument is that it is almost exclusively focused on manufacturing. Brenner does not give an explicit justification for this, as he does for his focus on the US, Japanese, and German economies. The theoretical and historical identification of capitalism with *industrial* capitalism appears to be for him—as for most social scientists, Marxist and non-Marxist alike—an article of faith which requires no justification. Yet, the share of value added generated in manufacturing worldwide has been comparatively small, shrinking steadily from 28 percent in 1960, to 24.5 percent in 1980, to 20.5 percent in 1998. Moreover, the contraction has been greater than average in Brenner's "advanced" capitalist countries, the share for North America, Western Europe, Australasia, and Japan combined having declined from 28.9 percent in 1960, to 24.5 percent in 1980, to 19.7 percent in 1998.[38]

Brenner does seem to be aware of this problem but he sees it as a symptom of economic crisis rather than a reason for questioning the relevance and validity of his focus on manufacturing. Thus, in commenting on the "huge expansion" experienced by the US non-manufacturing sector in the 1980s, he interprets it as "a symptom of the broad economic decline that accompanied the crisis of manu-

---

38 The percentages have been calculated from World Bank 1984 and 2001. The figures for the world include all the countries for which data are available for 1960, 1980, and 1998. Value added is GDP.

facturing in the US economy, which can usefully be called 'deindus-trialization,' with all its negative connotations."[39] At one point, however, he does feel it necessary to provide some justification for his narrow focus on manufacturing.

> It has become standard to downplay the importance of the manufacturing sector, by pointing to its shrinking share of total employment and GDP. But, during the 1990s, the US corporate manufacturing sector still accounted for 46.8 percent of total profits accruing to the non-financial corporate sector (the corporate economy minus the corporate financial sector), and in 1999 it took 46.2 percent of that total. The climb of pre-tax manufacturing profitability was in fact *the* source of the parallel recovery of pre-tax profitability in the private economy as a whole.[40]

Leaving aside the fact that it is not clear why profits in the corporate financial sector are not included in the comparison, this justification does not stand up to a close empirical scrutiny. As Greta Krippner has shown on the basis of a thorough analysis of the available evidence, not only had the share of total US corporate profits accounted for by finance, insurance, and real estate (FIRE) in the 1980s nearly caught up with and, in the 1990s, surpassed the share accounted for by manufacturing; more important, in the 1970s and 1980s, *non-financial firms themselves* sharply increased their investment in financial assets relative to that in plant and equipment, and became increasingly dependent on financial sources of revenue and profit relative to that earned from productive activities. Particularly significant is Krippner's finding that manufacturing not only dominates but *leads* this trend towards the "financialization" of the non-financial economy.[41]

Brenner does not provide any indicator of his "over-capacity and over-production" concept comparable to Krippner's multiple indicators for the financialization of the non-financial economy. Nevertheless, Anwar Shaikh does provide two indicators of "capacity utilization" in US manufacturing—one based on his own measure,

---

39 Robert Brenner, *The Boom and the Bubble: The U.S. in the World Economy* (London, Verso, 2002), p. 79.

40 Ibid., pp. 68–70, emphasis in the original.

41 Greta R. Krippner, "The Financialization of the American Economy," *Socio-Economic Review*, 3 (2005). Krippner's analysis is based on data provided by the Federal Reserve Flow of Funds Accounts; the Bureau of Economic Analysis National Income and Product Accounts; the IRS Corporation Income Tax Returns; Balance-of-Payments data; and the IRS Corporate Foreign Tax Credit data.

and one on that of the Federal Reserve Board—which we may take as imperfect *inverse* indicators of over-capacity.[42] Across the entire period 1947–95, both indicators show a great deal of fluctuation but no clear long-term trend. More specifically, in line with Brenner's argument, both indicators—especially Shaikh's—suggest that over-capacity in US manufacturing decreased sharply during the closing years of the long boom and increased even more sharply during the crisis of profitability that marked the transition from the long boom to the long downturn. After 1973, in contrast, both indicators continue to show considerable fluctuations but provide no evidence in support of Brenner's contention that the long downturn was characterized by above-normal over-capacity. The Federal Reserve Board figures show capacity utilization settling back to where it was in the 1950s with no trend either way, while Shaikh's show capacity utilization in the 1970s at higher levels than in the 1950s and rising further in the 1980s and 1990s—suggesting a comparatively low and declining over-capacity.

Supplemented with what can be gauged from these imperfect indicators, Krippner's unambiguous findings throw serious doubts on Brenner's *a priori* assumptions concerning the behavior of incumbent, higher-cost manufacturers. The predominant response of these firms to the irruption in their markets of lower-cost competitors does not appear to have been a strenuous defense of their sunk capital, and a counterattack through additional investment in fixed capital that further increased over-capacity. Although this kind of response was certainly present, the predominant response was, in capitalist terms, far more rational. Confronted with heightened international competition (especially in trade-intensive sectors like manufacturing) higher-cost incumbent firms responded to falling returns by diverting a growing proportion of their incoming cash flows from investment in fixed capital and commodities to liquidity and accumulation through financial channels.

This is what Krippner observes empirically. But this is also what

---

42 Anwar Shaikh, "Explaining the Global Economic Crisis," *Historical Materialism*, 5 (1999), pp. 140–1. A major problem in using these two indicators, or indeed any other indicator, to gauge Brenner's "over-capacity" is that, as previously noted, he always uses this term together with the term "over-production," and never tells us how to disentangle the concepts denoted by the two terms. This conflation makes it impossible to know what would be a valid indicator of either over-capacity or over-production. But, unless the use of the term over-capacity is completely redundant and has no meaning of its own, it is reasonable to suppose that *increases* in Brenner's over-capacity are reflected in *decreases* in capacity utilization and vice versa.

we should expect theoretically, whenever returns to capital invested in trade and production fall below a certain threshold and inter-capitalist competition becomes a zero- or negative-sum game. Under these conditions—precisely those which, according to Brenner, have characterized the long downturn—the risks and uncertainties involved in reinvesting incoming cash flows into trade and production are high, and it makes good business sense to use them to increase the liquidity of assets as a defensive or offensive weapon in the escalating competitive struggle, both within the particular industry or sphere of economic activity in which the firm had previously specialized and outside it. For liquidity enables enterprises not just to escape the "slaughtering of capital values" which, sooner or later, ensues from the over-accumulation of capital and the intensification of competition in old and new lines of business, but also to take over at bargain prices the assets, customers, and suppliers of the less prudent and "irrationally exuberant" enterprises that continued to sink their incoming cash flows into fixed capital and commodities.

In a sense, this competitive strategy is nothing but the continuation by other means of the logic of the product cycle that Brenner himself invokes in another context. The logic of the product cycle for the leading capitalist organizations of a given epoch is to shift resources ceaselessly through one kind or another of "innovation" from market niches that have become overcrowded (and therefore less profitable) to those that are less crowded (and therefore more profitable). When escalating competition reduces the availability of relatively empty, profitable niches in the commodity markets, the leading capitalist organizations have one last refuge, to which they can retreat and shift competitive pressures onto others. This final refuge is Schumpeter's "headquarters of the capitalist system"—the money market.[43]

In this respect, US capital in the late twentieth century was following a trajectory analogous to that of British capital a century before, which had also responded to the intensification of competition in manufacturing through financialization. As Halford Mackinder pointed out in a speech delivered to a group of London bankers at the turn of the century, when the financialization of British capital was already at an advanced stage: the industrialization of other

---

43 As already suggested in Chapter 3, and elaborated further in Chapter 8, this tendency of intense, system-wide inter-capitalist competition to result in a persistent financialization of capital has been the clearest sign of continuity among the various organizational forms that historical capitalism has assumed before and after the Industrial Revolution. For a detailed discussion of the tendency, see Arrighi, *The Long Twentieth Century*, pp. 220–38.

countries enhanced the importance of a single clearinghouse, which "will always be where there is the greatest ownership of capital. . . . [W]e are essentially the people who have capital, and those who have capital always share in the activity of brains and muscles of other countries."[44] This was certainly the case during the Edwardian *belle époque*, when nearly one-half of Britain's assets were overseas and about 10 percent of its national income consisted of interest on foreign investment.[45]

In spite of the far greater economic, military, and political power of the United States in comparison to the British empire, sharing in the "activity of brains and muscles" in other countries through financialization has been more arduous for US capital. To be sure, American primacy in the formation of vertically integrated, multinational corporations has been a highly effective means of putting such sharing into operation throughout the twentieth century; and immigration, of course, has "drained" brains and muscles from all over the world, throughout US history.[46] Unlike Britain in the nineteenth century, however, the United States was not structurally oriented to playing the role of global clearinghouse; its relationship to the global economy was rather that of a self-centered and largely self-sufficient continental economy.

This difference was underscored by a Study Group established in

---

44 Quoted in Peter J. Hugill, *World Trade since 1431: Geography, Technology, and Capitalism* (Baltimore, MD, Johns Hopkins University Press, 1993), p. 305.

45 A.K. Cairncross, *Home and Foreign Investment, 1870–1913* (Cambridge, Cambridge University Press, 1953), pp. 3, 23. As Peter Mathias noted, British foreign investment "was not just 'blind capital' but the 'blind capital' of *rentiers* organized by financiers and businessmen very much with a view to the trade that would be flowing when the enterprise was under way." British railway building in the United States, and *a fortiori* in countries like Australia, Canada, South Africa, and Argentina "was instrumental in opening up these vast land masses and developing export sectors in primary produce . . . for Britain" (Peter Mathias, *The First Industrial Nation: An Economic History of Britain, 1700–1914* [London, Methuen, 1969], p. 329); see also Stanley D. Chapman, *Merchant Enterprise in Britain: From the Industrial Revolution to World War I* (New York, Cambridge University Press, 1992), pp. 233ff.

46 US corporations became multinational almost as soon as they had completed their continental integration. See Stephen Hymer, "The Multinational Corporation and the Law of Uneven Development," in J.N. Bhagwati, ed., *Economics and the World Order* (New York, Macmillan, 1972), p. 121. By 1902 Europeans were already speaking of an "American invasion"; and by 1914 US direct investment abroad amounted to 7 per cent of US GNP—the same percentage as in 1966, when Europeans once again felt threatened by an "American challenge." See Mira Wilkins, *The Emergence of Multinational Enterprise* (Cambridge, Cambridge University Press, 1970), pp. 71, 201.

the early 1950s under the sponsorship of the Woodrow Wilson Foundation and of the National Planning Association. In challenging the assumption "that a sufficiently integrated world economic system could be again achieved by means essentially similar to those employed in the 19th century," it pointed out that the United States—although a "mature creditor" like nineteenth-century Britain—had an altogether different relationship to the world than Britain. The latter was "fully integrated into the world economic system and in large measure making possible its successful functioning owing to [its] dependence on foreign trade, the pervasive influence of its commercial and financial institutions, and the basic consistency between its national economic policies and those required for world economic integration." The United States, in contrast, is "only partially integrated into the world economic system, with which it is also partly competitive, and whose accustomed mode and pace of functioning it tends periodically to disturb. No network of American commercial and financial institutions exists to bind together and to manage the day-to-day operations of the world trading system."[47]

Under the conditions of the increasing fragmentation and eventual breakdown of the world market that characterized inter-capitalist struggles in the first half of the twentieth century, the scale, self-centeredness, and relative self-sufficiency of the US economy provided American capital with decisive competitive advantages. US primacy in the formation of vertically integrated, multinational corporations enabled it to outflank, through direct investment, the rampant protectionism of the period. Nevertheless, the very success of the United States in promoting the reunification and expansion of the global market after the end of the Second World War diminished those advantages; and the intensification of international competition that ensued turned them, in some respects, into handicaps.

An expanded and unified world market enabled enterprises based in smaller, less self-centered and self-sufficient countries to enjoy economies of scale and scope comparable to those of US firms. The advantages of vertically integrated, bureaucratically managed, multinational corporations—which were overwhelming when there were

---

47 William Y. Elliott, ed., *The Political Economy of American Foreign Policy: Its Concepts, Strategy, and Limits* (New York, Henry Holt, 1955), p. 43. This difference is important in explaining why, even at the height of its liberal crusade of the 1980s and 1990s, the United States did not adhere unilaterally to the precepts of the liberal creed, as Britain did in the late nineteenth and early twentieth centuries. See Beverly J. Silver and Giovanni Arrighi, "Polanyi's 'Double Movement': The Belle Époques of British and U.S. Hegemony Compared," *Politics and Society*, 31, 2 (2003).

hundreds of them, and mostly American—quickly vanished when their number and variety (including their national origin) experienced an explosive growth. By 1980, it was estimated that there were over 10,000 of them, and by the early 1990s three times as many.[48] As their mutual competition intensified, they were forced to subcontract to small businesses activities previously carried out within their own organizations. The tendency towards the vertical integration and bureaucratization of business, which had made the fortunes of US capital since the 1870s, thus began to be superseded by a tendency towards informal networking and the subordinate revitalization of small business.[49]

As we shall see in future chapters, this reversal of tendencies in business organization has been crucial in bolstering the competitiveness of East Asian economies vis-à-vis the United States. For now, however, let us note that the lack of organic integration of the United States in the global economy—which had been a major advantage for US capital in the first half of the twentieth century—turned into a constraint on the capacity of American capital to take full advantage of the tendency towards financialization that gained momentum, at home and abroad, in the 1970s. Also in this respect the inflationary crisis-management strategy that the United States adopted under Nixon was counterproductive. Whatever its success in redistributing the burden of the profitability crisis from US capital to US labor and foreign competitors, the strategy backfired because it repelled from the US economy and its currency the growing mass of liquidity released by the financialization of capital. And conversely, the main reason why the monetarist counterrevolution was so stunningly successful in reversing the decline in US power is that it brought about a massive rerouting of global capital flows towards the United States and the dollar.

---

48 John M. Stopford and John H. Dunning, *Multinationals: Company Performance and Global Trends* (London, Macmillan, 1983), p. 3; Satoshi Ikeda, "World Production," in T.K. Hopkins, I. Wallerstein et al., *The Age of Transition: Trajectory of the World-System 1945–2025* (London, Zed Books, 1996).

49 Arrighi and Silver, *Chaos and Governance*, ch. 2; cf. Manuel Castells and Alejandro Portes, "World Underneath: The Origins, Dynamics, and Effects of the Informal Economy," in A. Portes, M. Castells, and L.A. Benton, eds, *The Informal Economy: Studies in Advanced and Less Developed Countries* (Baltimore, MD, Johns Hopkins University Press, 1989), pp. 27–9; Michael J. Piore and Charles F. Sable, *The Second Industrial Divide: Possibilities for Prosperity* (New York, Basic Books, 1984), pp. 4–5, 15, 19–20; Bennett Harrison, *Lean and Mean: The Changing Landscape of Corporate Power in the Age of Flexibility* (New York, Basic Books, 1994), pp. 244–5.

Figure 5.2   Current-account balance, 1980–2005

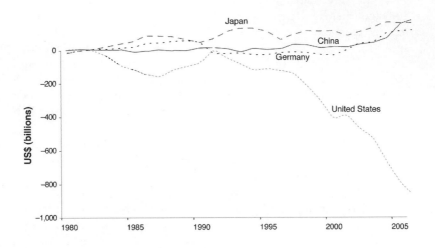

Note: Figures in billions of current US dollars.
Source: International Monetary Fund, World Economic Outlook Database, September 2006.

This rerouting transformed the United States from being the main source of world liquidity and foreign direct investment, as it had been in the 1950s and 1960s, into the world's main debtor nation and absorber of liquidity, from the 1980s through the present. The extent of the rerouting can be gauged from the change in the current-account of the US balance-of-payments shown in Figure 5.2. Brenner is probably right in doubting that levels of indebtedness of this order are sustainable in the long run. Nevertheless, for about twenty years, an escalating foreign debt enabled the United States to turn the deteriorating crisis of the 1970s into a *belle époque* wholly comparable to, and in some respects far more spectacular, than Britain's Edwardian era.

It has, first of all, enabled the United States to achieve through financial means what it could not achieve by force of arms—to defeat the USSR in the Cold War and tame the rebellious South. Massive borrowing from abroad, mostly Japan, was essential to the escalation under Reagan of the armament race (primarily, though not exclusively, through the Strategic Defense Initiative) well beyond what the USSR could afford. Combined with generous support to Afghan resistance against Soviet occupation, the escalation forced the Soviet

Union into a double confrontation, neither side of which it could win: in Afghanistan, where its high-tech military apparatus found itself in the same difficulties that had led to the defeat of the United States in Vietnam; and in the arms race, where the United States could mobilize financial resources wholly beyond the Soviet reach.

At the same time, the enormous redirection of capital flows to the United States turned the flood of capital that Southern countries had experienced in the 1970s into the sudden "drought" of the 1980s. First signaled by the Mexican default of 1982, this drought was probably the single most important factor in shifting competitive pressures from North to South and in provoking a major bifurcation in the fortunes of Southern regions in the 1980s and 1990s. Regions that, for historical reasons, had a strong advantage in competing for a share of the expanding US demand for cheap industrial products—most notably East Asia—tended to benefit from the redirection of capital flows, because the improvement in their balance-of-payments lessened their need to compete with the United States in world financial markets, and indeed turned some of them into major lenders to the United States. Other regions—most notably Sub-Saharan Africa and Latin America—were, for historical reasons, particularly disadvantaged in competing for a share of the North American demand. These tended to run into balance-of-payments difficulties that put them into the hopeless position of having to compete directly with the United States in world financial markets.[50] Either way, the United States benefited both economically and politically as American business and governmental agencies were best positioned to mobilize in the global competitive and power struggles for the cheap commodities and credit that Southern "winners" eagerly supplied, as well as the assets that Southern "losers" had to alienate at bargain prices.

Finally, massive inflows of foreign capital were essential to the "Keynesianism with a vengeance" that rescued the US and world economies from the deep recession provoked by the switch from extremely lax to extremely tight monetary policies. This deep recession, and the ideological and practical liquidation of the welfare state that accompanied it, was the true turning point in the collapse of workers' leverage in the US and other core regions. To be sure, the stagflation of the 1970s had already worn down workers' resistance

---

50 For a preliminary analysis of the comparative advantages of East Asia and disadvantages of Sub-Saharan Africa in the new global environment of the 1980s and 1990s, see Giovanni Arrighi, "The African Crisis: World Systemic and Regional Aspects," *New Left Review*, II/15 (2002), pp. 24–31.

against attempts to shift the burden of intensifying competition onto their shoulders. But it was only in the 1980s that, in core countries in general and in the United States in particular, pressure from below on money wages subsided, and workers came to rely on governmental control of price inflation as their best chance of protecting their standards of living. As Margaret Thatcher's advisor Alan Budd publicly admitted in retrospect, "What was engineered in Marxist terms was a crisis of capitalism which re-created a reserve army of labor, and has allowed the capitalists to make high profits ever since."[51]

As Brenner maintains, the weakening of labor's leverage was greater in the United States than in other core regions and thereby contributed to the revival of US profitability in the 1990s. In a similar vein, Alan Greenspan later attributed the greater success of US in comparison with Japanese and European companies in increasing productivity and profits to Japan's and Europe's "relatively inflexible and, hence, more costly labor markets." "Because our costs of dismissing workers are lower"—he went on to explain—"the potential costs of hiring and the risks associated with expanding employment are less."[52] Yet, although this was undoubtedly a factor in the revival of US profitability in the 1990s, Brenner's (and Greenspan's) narrow focus on manufacturing is again misleading, because the turnaround was primarily due, not to the comparatively slower growth of US real wages, but to the overall reorientation of the US economy to take full advantage of financialization, both at home and in the world at large. From this point of view, the "deindustrialization" of the United States and other core regions certainly had negative connotations for the workers most directly affected by it; but it had no such dire meaning for the US economy as a whole, and especially its wealthier strata. Rather, it was a necessary condition of the great revival of US wealth and power of the 1990s, when—to paraphrase Landes's characterization of the Edwardian era—in spite of rattlings of arms in the South and former East or monitory references to a coming clash of civilizations, everything seemed right again.

---

51 Quoted in David Harvey, *Spaces of Hope* (Berkeley, CA, University of California Press, 2000), p. 7.

52 "For Greenspan, Flexibility Key to U.S. Gains," *International Herald Tribune*, July 12, 2000.

6

A CRISIS OF HEGEMONY

In underscoring the difficulties involved in attributing causal priority to any of the interacting elements that have propelled the economic expansion of East Asia in the 1970s and 1980s, Robert Wade has invited us to think "more in terms of opening a combination lock than a padlock."[1] What is true of the East Asian expansion is *a fortiori* true of the global turbulence that set the stage for its unfolding. Brenner's uneven development is undoubtedly an element of the combination; but it is by no means the key that unlocks the mechanisms of capital accumulation on a world scale over the second half of the twentieth century—from boom through crisis to relative stagnation and *belle époque*.

The combination that does unlock those mechanisms is the establishment and crisis of US world hegemony, within which uneven development, inter-capitalist competition, and state action were all embedded. In recasting Brenner's account of global turbulence in the broader social and political perspective advocated in Chapter 5, I shall use Gramsci's definition of hegemony as something different than sheer domination. According to this definition, hegemony is the *additional* power that accrues to a dominant group by virtue of its capacity to *lead* society in a direction that not only serves the dominant group's interests but is also perceived by subordinate groups as serving a more general interest. It is the inverse of the notion of "power deflation" used by Talcott Parsons to designate situations in which a society cannot be governed except through the widespread use or threat of use of force. If subordinate groups have confidence in their rulers, systems of domination can be governed without resorting to force. But if that confidence wanes, they no longer can. By the same token, Gramsci's notion of hegemony may be said to consist of the "power inflation" that ensues from the capacity

---

1 Robert Wade, "East Asian Economic Success: Conflicting Perspectives, Partial Insights, Shaky Evidence," *World Politics*, 44 (1992), p. 312.

of dominant groups to present their rule as credibly serving not just their interests but those of subordinate groups as well. When such credibility is lacking or wanes, hegemony deflates into sheer domination, that is, into what Ranajit Guha has called "dominance without hegemony."[2]

As long as we speak of leadership in a national context, as Gramsci does, an increase in the power of a state vis-à-vis other states is an important component—and in itself a measure—of the successful pursuit of a general (that is, "national") interest. But, when we use the term leadership in an international context to designate the fact that a dominant state leads the *system* of states in a desired direction, the general interest cannot be defined in terms of an increase in the power of an individual state over others, because by definition this power cannot increase for the system as a whole. A general interest for the system as a whole can, nonetheless, be identified by focusing on "collective" rather than "distributive" aspects of power. Distributive aspects of power refer to a zero-sum-game relationship whereby an agency can gain power only if others lose some. Collective aspects of power, in contrast, refer to a positive-sum-game relationship, whereby cooperation among distinct agencies increases their power over third parties or over nature. Thus, while the general interest of a system of states cannot be defined in terms of changes in the distribution of power among the states, it can be defined in terms of an increase in the collective power of the entire system's dominant groups over third parties or nature.[3]

We shall speak of crisis of hegemony to designate a situation in which the incumbent hegemonic state lacks the means or the will to continue leading the system of states in a direction that is widely perceived as expanding, not just its power, but the collective power of the system's dominant groups. Crises do not necessarily result in the end of hegemonies. Especially germane to our concerns is the distinction between crises of hegemony that signal problems that are

---

2 Giovanni Arrighi and Beverly J. Silver, *Chaos and Governance in the Modern World System* (Minneapolis, MN, University of Minnesota Press, 1999), pp. 26–7; Talcott Parsons, "Some Reflections on the Place of Force in Social Process," in H. Eckstein, ed., *Internal War* (Glencoe, IL, Free Press, 1964); Ranajit Guha, "Dominance without Hegemony and its Historiography," in R. Gupta, ed., *Subaltern Studies*, IV (New York, Oxford University Press, 1992), pp. 231–2.

3 Arrighi and Silver, *Chaos and Governnance*, pp. 27–8. On the distinction between distributive and collective aspects of power, see Talcott Parsons, "The Distribution of Power in American Society," in *Structure and Process in Modern Societies* (New York, Free Press, 1960), pp. 199–225.

nonetheless resolved for fairly long periods of time—which we shall call "signal crises"—and crises that are not resolved and thus mark the end of hegemonies—which we shall call "terminal crises." As our definition of hegemony implies, a state may remain dominant even after the terminal crisis of its hegemony—a situation which, following Guha, we shall characterize as one of domination without hegemony.

In this chapter we retell the story of Brenner's boom, relative stagnation, and bubble as the story of the establishment, signal crisis, and temporary revival (*belle époque*) of US hegemony. In Part III of the book I shall turn to the forces that, in the wake of September 11, have precipitated the terminal crisis of US hegemony and consolidated China's leadership of the East Asian economic renaissance.

US Hegemony and its Signal Crisis

The particular form that uneven development assumed after the Second World War—as opposed to the forms that it took, let us say, in the nineteenth century, or in the first half of the twentieth century—was thoroughly embedded in, and shaped by, the formation and evolution of US world hegemony in the Cold War era. This hegemony, in turn, had a peculiar social character, reflected in system-wide institutional arrangements quite different from those that underlay the nineteenth-century UK-centered global economy. These arrangements were eminently political in origin and social in orientation. They were based on the widespread belief among US government officials that "a new world order was the only guarantee against chaos followed by revolution" and that "security for the world had to be based on American power exercised through international systems."[4] Equally widespread was the belief that the lessons of the New Deal were relevant to the international sphere.

> Just as the New Deal government increasingly took active responsibility for the welfare of the nation, US foreign policy planners took increasing responsibility for the welfare of the world. . . . It

---

4 Franz Schurmann, *The Logic of World Power: An Inquiry into the Origins, Currents, and Contradictions of World Politics* (New York, Pantheon, 1974), pp. 44, 68.

could not insulate itself from the world's problems. As at home, moreover, it could not neatly pick and choose among those problems, distinguishing politics from economics, security from prosperity, defense from welfare. In the lexicon of the New Deal, taking responsibility meant government intervention on a grand scale.[5]

In Franklin Roosevelt's original vision, the New Deal would be "globalized" through the United Nations, and the USSR would be included among the poor nations of the world to be incorporated into the evolving Pax Americana, for the benefit and security of all. In the shoddier but more realistic political project that materialized under Truman, in contrast, the containment of Soviet power became the main organizing principle of US hegemony, and US control over world money and military power became the primary means of that containment.[6] This more realistic model was not so much a negation of the original notion of creating a global welfare state, as its transformation into a project of creating a "warfare–welfare state" on a world scale, in competition with and in opposition to the Soviet system of communist states.[7]

The speed and extent of the process of uneven development, to which Brenner traces both the postwar boom and the subsequent downturn, cannot be understood without reference to the successes and failures of this project. The model was highly successful in launching one of the greatest system-wide expansions in capitalist history. In its absence, world capitalism might well have gone through a long period of stagnation, if not outright depression. Such a contraction was avoided through the joint operation of both military and social Keynesianism on a world scale. Military Keynesianism—that is, massive expenditures on the rearmament of the United States and its allies and the deployment of a far-flung network of quasi-permanent military bases—was undoubtedly the most dynamic and conspicuous element of the combination. But the US-sponsored spread of social Keynesianism—that is, the governmental pursuit of full employment and high mass consumption in the West/North

---

5 Ann-Marie Burley, "Regulating The World: Multilateralism, International Law, and the Projection of the New Deal Regulatory State," in J.G. Ruggie, ed., *Multilateralism Matters: The Theory and Praxis of an Institutional Form* (New York, Columbia University Press, 1993), pp. 125–6, 129–32.

6 Schurmann, *Logic of World Power*, pp. 5, 67, 77.

7 To borrow James O'Connor's expression. See James O'Connor, *The Fiscal Crisis of the State* (New York, St Martin's Press, 1973).

and of "development" in the global South—was also an essential factor.[8]

The reconstruction and upgrading of the German and Japanese industrial apparatuses—the centerpiece of Brenner's uneven development—were integral aspects of the internationalization of the US warfare–welfare state. As Cumings notes, commenting specifically on the American approach to Japanese reindustrialization, "George Kennan's policy of containment was always limited and parsimonious, based on the idea that four or five industrial structures existed in the world: the Soviet had one and the United States had four, and things should be kept this way." Kennan's "idea" was translated into US government sponsorship of Japanese reindustrialization. The Korean War became " 'Japan's Marshall Plan' . . . War procurement propelled Japan along its war beating industrial path."[9] US promotion of the reconstruction and upgrading of the German industrial apparatus occurred through different but equally effective channels. Germany was, of course, among the main beneficiaries of the Marshall Plan and US military expenditure abroad. But the most important contribution was US sponsorship of Western European economic union. As John Foster Dulles declared in 1948, "a healthy Europe" could not be "divided into small compartments." It had to be organized into a market "big enough to justify modern methods of

---

8 On the critical role of military Keynesianism in launching the expansion see, among others, Fred Block, *The Origins of International Economic Disorder: A Study of the United States International Monetary Policy from World War II to the Present* (Berkeley, CA, University of California Press, 1977), pp. 103–4; Thomas J. McCormick, *America's Half Century: United States Foreign Policy in the Cold War* (Baltimore, MD, Johns Hopkins University Press, 1989), pp. 77–8, 98; Giovanni Arrighi, *The Long Twentieth Century: Money, Power and the Origins of our Times* (London, Verso, 1994), pp. 295–8. On the Northern and Southern variants of social Keynesianism, see Arrighi and Silver, *Chaos and Governance*, pp. 202–11; Beverly J. Silver, *Forces of Labor: Workers' Movements and Globalization since 1870* (Cambridge, Cambridge University Press, 2003), pp. 149–61.

9 Bruce Cumings, "The Origins and Development of the Northeast Asian Political Economy: Industrial Sectors, Product Cycles, and Political Consequences," in F.C. Deyo, ed., *The Political Economy of the New Asian Industrialism* (Ithaca, NY, Cornell University Press, 1987), p. 60, and "The Political Economy of the Pacific Rim," in R.A. Palat, ed., *Pacific-Asia and the Future of the World-System* (Westport, CT, Greenwood Press, 1993), p. 31. See also Jerome B. Cohen, *Japan's Postwar Economy* (Bloomington, IN, Indiana University Press, 1958), pp. 85–91; Takafusa Nakamura, *The Postwar Japanese Economy* (Tokyo, Tokyo University Press, 1981), p. 42; Makoto Itoh, *The World Economic Crisis and Japanese Capitalism* (New York, St Martin's Press, 1990), p. 142.

cheap production for mass consumption." A reindustrialized Germany was an essential component of this new Europe.[10]

Far from being a spontaneous process originating from the actions of capitalist accumulators "from below"—as it had been in the nineteenth century under British hegemony—uneven development under US hegemony was a process consciously and actively encouraged "from above" by a globalizing US warfare–welfare state. This difference accounts not just for the speed and extent of the long post-Second World War boom but also for the particular combination of limits and contradictions that transformed it into the relative stagnation of the 1970s and 1980s. Brenner's account of the onset of the long downturn points to one such limit and contradiction: successful catching-up creates new competitors, and intensifying competition exercises a downward pressure on the profits of incumbent firms. To the extent that this was an unanticipated outcome of the Cold War project, it was not just a limitation but also a contradiction of American policies. It is nonetheless more plausible to suppose that the outcome was an anticipated but unavoidable economic cost of policies whose primary objectives were not economic but social and political—that is, the containment of communism, the taming of nationalism and the consolidation of US hegemony.

The most serious contradiction of US policies lay elsewhere: that is, precisely in the difficulties involved in attaining these social and political objectives. To be sure, in the rising centers of capital accumulation, rapid economic growth, low levels of unemployment and the actual spread of high mass consumption consolidated the hegemony of one variant or another of liberal capitalism. As previously noted, however, even in these centers the political triumph of liberal capitalism did not lessen and, on the whole, actually strengthened the disposition of workers to seek a greater share of the social product through direct struggle or electoral mobilization. Washington's Cold War policies thus put a double squeeze on profits—a first squeeze from the intensification of inter-capitalist competition, which they promoted by creating conditions favorable to the upgrading and expansion of the Japanese and Western European productive apparatuses; and a second squeeze deriving from the social empowerment of labor, which they promoted through the pursuit of near full employment and high mass consumption throughout the Western world.

This double squeeze was bound to produce a system-wide crisis of

---

10 Quoted in McCormick, *America's Half Century*, pp. 79–80.

profitability but there is no reason why, in itself, it should have produced the crisis of US hegemony which became the dominant event of the 1970s. If the problems of profitability came to be subsumed within this broader hegemonic crisis, the reason is that in the global South the US warfare–welfare state attained neither its social nor its political objectives. Socially, the "Fair Deal" that Truman promised to the poor countries of the world in his 1949 inaugural address never materialized in an actual narrowing of the income gap that separated North and South. As Third World countries stepped up their industrialization efforts—the widely pre-scribed means to "development"—there was indeed industrial con-vergence between North and South; but, as previously noted, there was no income convergence at all. Third World countries were thus bearing the costs without reaping the expected benefits of industria-lization. Worse still, in 1970, Robert McNamara, then president of the World Bank, acknowledged that even high rates of growth of GNP did not result in the expected improvements in welfare in Third World nations.[11]

Partly related to this social failure, the political failure of the US welfare–warfare state was far more conspicuous. The epicenter of this was, of course, the war in Vietnam, where the United States was unable to prevail, despite escalating US casualties and the deployment of military hardware and firepower without historical precedent for a conflict of this kind. The upshot was that the United States lost much of its political credibility as global policeman, thereby emboldening the nationalist and social revolutionary forces that Cold War policies were meant to contain. Along with much of the political credibility of its military apparatus, the United States also lost control of the world monetary system. As contended in Chapter 5, the escalation of public expenditures to sustain the military effort in Vietnam and to over-come opposition to the war at home—through the Great Society program—strengthened inflationary pressure in the United States and the world economy at large, deepened the fiscal crisis of the US state, and eventually led to the collapse of the US-centered system of fixed exchange rates.

It is, of course, impossible to know whether the Bretton Woods regime would have survived without the effects of the Vietnam War. Nor is it possible to know what would have happened to world capitalism had uneven development been driven "from below," as in

---

11 Robert McNamara, "The True Dimension of the Task," *International Development Review*, 1 (1970), pp. 5–6.

the nineteenth century, rather than "from above" as under the US
Cold War regime. All I am saying in contrast to Brenner is that,
historically, uneven development after the Second World War was
embedded from beginning to end in Cold War rivalries, and was
therefore thoroughly shaped by the successes and failures of the
strategies and structures deployed by the hegemonic US warfare–
welfare state. The intensification of inter-capitalist competition and
the associated crisis of profitability were important as a sign that the
long postwar boom had reached its limits. But they were only an
element of the broader signal crisis of hegemony that contempor-
aneously revealed the limits and contradictions of US Cold War
policies.[12]

Financialization and the Monetarist Counterrevolution

As suggested in Chapter 5, the monetarist counterrevolution of 1979–
82 was a far more decisive turning point in the evolution of US and
world capitalism than either the Plaza Accord of 1985 or the reverse
Plaza Accord of 1995, to which Brenner seems to attribute equal or
even greater importance. Important as they were in other respects, the
Accords of 1985 and 1995 were moments of adjustment within a
process of revival of US hegemony that had already begun with the
switch from ultra lax to extremely tight monetary policies. Before the
switch, US monetary and fiscal policies tended to repel rather than
attract the growing mass of capital that sought accumulation through
financial channels. Worse still, in spite of the positive effects on the
competitiveness of US manufacturers that Brenner emphasizes, they
created conditions of accumulation on a world scale that benefited
neither the US state nor US capital.

Crucial in this respect was the explosive growth of the Eurodollar
and other extraterritorial financial markets. Curiously, Brenner
hardly mentions this development, even though it originated in the
same years as his transition from boom to downturn and left an
indelible mark on the 1970s. Established in the 1950s to hold dollar
balances of Communist countries unwilling to risk depositing them in
the United States, the Eurodollar market grew primarily through the
deposits of US multinationals and the offshore activities of New York
banks. Having grown steadily through the 1950s and early 1960s, it

---

12 On the Vietnam War as the central event of the signal crisis of US hegemony, see
Chapter 5 above and Arrighi, *The Long Twentieth Century*, pp. 215–17, 300, 320–2.

started growing exponentially in the mid and late 1960s, with euro-currency assets more than quadrupling between 1967 and 1970.[13]

Hard as it is to know exactly what lay behind this explosion, it is plausible to suppose that it was triggered by the joint crisis of profitability and US hegemony of those years. Although Brenner focuses on US manufacturers producing at home, we know that US corporations operating abroad had also begun to face tougher competition from their European rivals.[14] Moreover, Europe was the epicenter of the pay explosion of 1968–73. Horizontal pressure from intensifying competition and vertical pressure from labor demands must have given a major boost to the liquidity preference of US multinational corporations operating abroad. Since conditions for the profitable reinvestment of cash flows in production were even less favorable in the United States than in Europe, it made good business sense for US multinationals to "park" their growing liquid assets in euro-currency and other offshore money markets rather than repatriate them.

Be that as it may, the explosive growth of euro-currency markets provided currency speculators—including US banks and corporations—with a huge *masse de manoeuvre* with which to bet against, and thereby undermine, the stability of the US-controlled system of fixed exchange rates. And once that system actually collapsed, the gates were open for an ever growing mass of privately controlled liquidity to compete with the US and other state actors in the production of world money and credit. Three mutually reinforcing tendencies were at work in this particular competitive struggle.

First, the breakdown of the regime of fixed exchange rates added a new momentum to the financialization of capital, by increasing the risks and uncertainties of commercial-industrial activities. Fluctuations in exchange rates became a major determinant of variations in corporate cash-flow positions, sales, profits, and assets in different countries and currencies. In hedging against these variations, or in trying to profit from them, multinationals tended to increase the mass of liquidity deployed in financial speculation in extraterritorial money

13 Engène L. Versluysen, *The Political Economy of International Finance* (New York, St Martin's Press, 1981), pp. 16–22; Marcello de Cecco, "Inflation and Structural Change in the Euro–Dollar Market," *EUI Working Papers*, 23 (Florence, European University Institute, 1982), p. 11; Andrew Walter, *World Power and World Money* (New York, St Martin's Press, 1991), p. 182.

14 Alfred Chandler, *Scale and Scope: The Dynamics of Industrial Capitalism* (Cambridge, MA, The Belknap Press, 1990), pp. 615–16.

markets where freedom of action was greatest and specialized services most readily available.[15]

Second, combined with the loss of credibility of the United States as global policeman, the massive devaluation of the US currency in the early 1970s prompted Third World governments to adopt a more aggressive stance in negotiating the prices of their exports of industrial raw materials—oil in particular. Intensifying inter-capitalist competition and the stepping-up of low- and middle-income countries' industrialization efforts had already led to significant increases in raw material prices before 1973. In 1973, however, the virtual acknowledgment of defeat by the US government in Vietnam, followed immediately by the shattering of the myth of Israeli invincibility during the Yom Kippur War, energized OPEC into protecting its members more effectively from the depreciation of the dollar through a fourfold increase in the price of crude oil in a few months. Coming as it did at the tail end of the pay explosion, this so-called first "oil shock" deepened the crisis of profitability and strengthened inflationary tendencies in core capitalist countries. More important, it generated a $80 billion surplus of "petrodollars," a good part of which was parked or invested in the euro-currency and other offshore money markets. The mass of privately controlled liquidity that could be mobilized for financial speculation and new credit creation outside publicly controlled channels thereby received an additional powerful stimulus.[16]

Finally, the tremendous expansion in the supply of world money and credit, due to the combination of extremely lax US monetary policies and the explosive growth of privately controlled liquidity in offshore money markets, was not matched by demand conditions capable of preventing the devaluation of money capital. To be sure, there was plenty of demand for liquidity, not only on the part of multinational corporations—to hedge against or speculate on exchange rate fluctuations—but also on the part of low- and middle-income countries, to sustain their developmental efforts in an increasingly competitive and volatile environment. For the most part, however, this demand added more to inflationary pressures than it did to the expansion of solvent indebtedness.

---

15 See, among others, Susan Strange, *Casino Capitalism* (Oxford, Basil Blackwell, 1986), pp. 11–13.

16 Itoh, *World Economic Crisis*, pp. 53–4, 60–8, 116; de Cecco, "Inflation and Structural Change," p. 12; Strange, *Casino Capitalism*, p. 18.

Formerly, countries other than the United States had to keep their balance-of-payments in some sort of equilibrium. They had to "earn" the money they wished to spend abroad. Now they could borrow it. With liquidity apparently capable of infinite expansion, countries deemed credit-worthy no longer had any external check on foreign spending. . . . Under such circumstances, a balance-of-payments deficit no longer provided, in itself, an automatic check to domestic inflation. Countries in deficit could borrow indefinitely from the magic liquidity machine. . . . Not surprisingly, world inflation continued accelerating throughout the decade, and fears of collapse in the private banking system grew increasingly vivid. More and more debts were "rescheduled," and a number of poor countries grew flagrantly insolvent.[17]

In short, the interaction between the crisis of profitability and the crisis of hegemony, in combination with the US inflationary strategy of crisis management, resulted in a ten-year-long increase in world monetary disorder, escalating inflation and steady deterioration in the capacity of the US dollar to function as the world's means of payment, reserve currency, and unit of account. Brenner's narrow focus on profitability in manufacturing misses this broader context of collapsing monetary foundations of the world capitalist order. What was the point of taking some of the pressure off profits in US manufacturing through lax monetary policies if, in the process, money capital—the beginning and end of capitalist accumulation—was made so abundant as to be a free good? Was not the abuse of US seigniorage privileges in fact chasing capital into alternative monetary means, thereby depriving the US state of one of its main levers of world power?

The root of the problem of US and world capitalism in the 1970s was not low rates of profit as such. After all, the driving down of profit *rates* in the pursuit of a larger *mass* of profits has been a long established tradition of historical capitalism.[18] The real problem throughout the 1970s was that US monetary policies were trying to entice capital to keep world trade and production expanding, even though such an expansion had become the primary cause of rising costs, risks, and uncertainty for corporate capital in general, and US corporate capital in particular. Not surprisingly, only a fraction of the

---

17 David Calleo, *The Imperious Economy* (Cambridge, MA, Harvard University Press, 1982), pp. 137–8.

18 On this, Marx and Smith were in full agreement. See Karl Marx, *Capital*, vol. III (Moscow, Foreign Languages Publishing House, 1962), pp. 245–6.

liquidity created by the US monetary authorities found its way into new trade and production facilities. Most of it turned into an extraterritorial money supply, which reproduced itself many times over through the mechanisms of private inter-bank money creation, and promptly re-emerged in world markets to compete with the dollars issued by the Federal Reserve.

In the last resort, this growing competition between private and public money did not benefit the US government, because the expansion of the private supply of dollars set an increasingly large group of countries free from balance-of-payments constraints, and thereby undermined Washington's seigniorage privileges. Nor did it benefit US capital, since the expansion of the public supply of dollars fed offshore money markets with more liquidity than could possibly be recycled safely and profitably. It therefore forced the US banks and other financial intermediaries that controlled these markets to compete fiercely with one another in pushing money on countries deemed credit-worthy, and indeed in lowering the standards by which this credit-worthiness was assessed.

Unfolding as it did in the context of a deepening crisis of US hegemony, this mutually destructive competition culminated in the devastating run on the dollar of 1979–80. Whatever the actual motivations and ostensible rationale of the sudden reversal in US monetary policies that followed the run, its true long-term significance—and the main reason why it eventually revived US fortunes beyond anyone's expectations—is that it brought this mutually destructive competition to an abrupt end. Not only did the US government stop feeding the system with liquidity; more important, it started competing aggressively for capital worldwide—through record-high interest rates, tax breaks, increasing freedom of action for capitalist producers and speculators and, as the benefits of the new policies materialized, an appreciating dollar—provoking the massive rerouting of capital flows towards the United States discussed in Chapter 5. To put it crudely, the essence of the monetarist counter-revolution was a shift of US state action from the supply side to the demand side of the ongoing financial expansion. Through this shift, the US government stopped competing with the growing private supply of liquidity and instead created brisk demand conditions for the latter's accumulation through financial channels.

The monetarist counterrevolution was not an isolated event but an ongoing process which had to be managed. Brenner's account of interstate cooperation and competition among the leading capitalist countries in the 1980s and 1990s is particularly useful in highlighting the swings that have characterized this management. Whenever the process threatened to get out of hand and provoke a systemic breakdown, the leading capitalist states cooperated to avert the danger by bringing relief from competitive pressures to the producers most immediately threatened with collapse—US manufacturers on the eve of the Plaza Accord of 1985; Japanese and, to a lesser extent, Western European manufacturers on the eve of the reverse Plaza Accord of 1995. But once the danger was averted, interstate competition resumed until the threat of a new breakdown loomed on the horizon. Illuminating as it is, this account does not tell us whether this process has any limits—and if it does, what these limits might be.

Belle Époque as Prelude to Terminal Crisis

Writing in the early 1990s—before the take-off of the revival analyzed by Brenner, but after the monetarist counterrevolution had already succeeded in transforming the crisis of the 1970s into a new *belle époque* of US and world capitalism—I contended that "the most striking similarity [between this new *belle époque* and the Edwardian one] has been the almost complete lack of realization on the part of their beneficiaries that the sudden and unprecedented prosperity that they had come to enjoy did not rest on a resolution of the crisis of accumulation that had preceded the beautiful times." Rather, "the newly found prosperity rested on a shift of the crisis from one set of relations to another set of relations. It was only a question of time before the crisis would reemerge in more troublesome forms."[19]

This diagnosis resembles Brenner's assessment that the US economic revival of the second half of the 1990s did not constitute "a definitive transcendence of the long downturn;" and that, indeed, the worst had yet to come. There are nonetheless two main differences between Brenner's diagnosis of the crisis of profitability underlying the global turbulence of the last thirty years, and my own. One is that I interpret the crisis of profitability as an aspect of a broader crisis of hegemony. And the other is that I see the financialization of capital, rather than persistent "over-capacity and over-production" in manufacturing, as the predominant capitalist response to the joint crisis of profitability and hegemony.

As we shall see in the third part of the book, the response of the Bush administration to the events of September 11 has already

---

19 Arrighi, *The Long Twentieth Century*, p. 324.

precipitated the terminal crisis of US hegemony, thereby bringing the US *belle époque* to an end sooner rather than later. Nevertheless, the main reason why the US *belle époque* was bound to be a temporary phenomenon, regardless of what Bush or any other US president might have done, is that financial expansions have a fundamentally contradictory impact on systemic stability. In the short run—with the understanding that, in this context, a short run encompasses decades rather than years—financial expansions tend to stabilize the existing order, by enabling incumbent hegemonic groups to shift onto sub-ordinate groups, nationally and internationally, the burdens of the intensifying competition that challenges their hegemony. I have sketched above the process through which the US government suc-ceeded in turning the financialization of capital from a factor of crisis of US hegemony—as it was through the 1970s—into a factor of reflation for US wealth and power. Through different mechanisms, analogous—if less spectacular—reversals can be detected not just in the course of the UK-centered financial expansion of the late nine-teenth and early twentieth centuries, but even in the course of the Dutch-centered financial expansion of the mid eighteenth century.[20]

Over time, however, financial expansions tend to destabilize the existing order through processes that are as much social and political as they are economic. Economically, they systematically divert pur-chasing power from demand-creating investment in commodities (including labor-power) to hoarding and speculation, thereby exacer-bating realization problems. Politically, they tend to be associated with the emergence of new configurations of power, which under-mine the capacity of the incumbent hegemonic state to turn to its advantage the system-wide intensification of competition. And so-cially, they entail the massive redistribution of rewards and social dislocations, which tend to provoke movements of resistance and rebellion among subordinate groups and strata, whose established ways of life are coming under attack.

The form that these tendencies take, and the way in which they relate to one another in space and time, have varied from financial expansion to financial expansion. But some combination of the three tendencies can be detected in each of the two so far completed hegemonic transitions of historical capitalism—from Dutch to British and from British to US hegemony. In the past transitions, they eventually resulted in a complete and seemingly irremediable break-down in the system's organization, which was not overcome until the

---

20 Arrighi and Silver, *Chaos and Governance*, ch. 1 and conclusion.

system was reconstituted under a new hegemony.[21] The Crash and Great Depression of the 1930s—the only occurrence in the last 150 years that corresponds to Brenner's image of a system-wide shakeout or "outright depression"—was an integral element of the latest breakdown. The success of the monetarist counterrevolution in transforming the financial expansion of the 1970s into the driving force of the reflation of US wealth and power of the 1980s and 1990s was not in itself a guarantee that an analogous systemic breakdown would not occur again. On the contrary, the very scale and scope of the transformation might have exacerbated realization problems worldwide to such an extent as to make an "outright depression" more rather than less likely.[22]

Once again, however, the economics of the situation evolved in combination with the political and social dimensions of the ongoing transition. And while the economics of the present transition is in key respects similar to that of past transitions—as witnessed by the intensification of inter-capitalist competition and associated financialization of capital—its politics and sociology are quite different. As previously noted, in the course of the latest long downturn and *belle époque* there has been no tendency—as there was in the course of the long downturn and *belle époque* of the late nineteenth and early twentieth centuries—towards the transformation of inter-enterprise competition into a world-scale interstate struggle over territory, with its associated escalation of the armaments race among rising and declining capitalist powers. On the contrary, global military capabilities have become even more centralized in the hands of the United States than they already were, while rising and declining capitalist powers have continued to work towards the consolidation of the unity of the world market. It is of course impossible to tell how this might change, were increasing realization problems to precipitate a major system-wide depression. For the time being, however, the increasing segmentation of the world market that contributed decisively to the economic breakdown of the 1930s does not appear to be a factor in the present transition.

Closely related to the above, the social forces that have shaped and constrained inter-capitalist competition in the late twentieth century

---

21 Ibid., chs 1, 3, and conclusion.

22 In response to a critique by James Crotty, Brenner acknowledges that tight monetary policies exacerbated realization problems in 1969–70. See James Crotty, "Review of *Turbulence in the World Economy* by Robert Brenner," *Challenge*, 42, 3 (1999) and Robert Brenner's reply, pp. 119–30. Curiously, however, he hardly mentions the much more serious realization problems that have been created by the far more persistent, widespread, and tight monetary policies of the 1980s and 1990s.

are significantly different from those at work in the previous transition. Although the monetarist counterrevolution was quite successful
in undermining the capacity of labor in core regions, and of most
Southern nations in the world at large, to obtain a larger share of the
national and global pies, respectively, this success has its own limits
and contradictions. Chief among these, as Brenner himself emphasizes, is the fact that the US economic revival of the 1990s, and the
continuing dependence of the world economy on a growing US
economy, have been based on an increase in US foreign indebtedness
that has no precedent in world history. A situation of this kind can
hardly be reproduced for any length of time without transforming
into an outright tribute, or "protection payment," the more than $2
billion (and counting) that the United States needs *daily* to balance its
current accounts with the rest of the world. And yet, as we shall see in
Part III of the book, US attempts to make the extraction of such a
tribute the foundation of a new, and for the first time in history, truly
universal empire, have failed miserably, creating a situation of global
political instability with no precedent since the 1920s and 1930s.

Towards the end of the *belle époque* of Dutch capitalism in 1778,
the periodical *De Borger* wrote: "Each one says 'it will last my time
and after me the deluge!' as our [French] neighbors' proverb has it,
which we have taken over in deeds if not in words."[23] This pretty
much sums up the philosophy that underlies all financial expansions
and *belles époques* of historical capitalism, including the latest. The
main difference between then and now is the incomparably greater
power wielded by the declining hegemonic state.

As David Calleo has argued, international systems break down, not
only because unbalanced and aggressive new powers challenge the
existing order, but also because declining powers, rather than adjusting
and accommodating, try to cement their slipping hegemony into an
exploitative domination.[24] In 1999, Beverly Silver and I concluded a
comparison of current and past hegemonic transitions in the Western
world by underscoring a historical reversal in the role played by Calleo's
two causes of systemic breakdowns. At the time of the *belle époque* of
Dutch capitalism, Dutch world power was already so diminished that

---

23 Quoted in Charles R. Boxer, *The Dutch Seaborne Empire 1600–1800* (New
York, Knopf, 1965), p. 291.

24 David P. Calleo, *Beyond American Hegemony: The Future of the Western
Alliance* (New York, Basic Books, 1987), p. 142. I have changed Calleo's expressions
"slipping preeminence" and "exploitative hegemony" into "slipping hegemony" and
"exploitative domination," respectively, to match the Gramscian distinction between
hegemony and domination adopted in this chapter and throughout the book.

Dutch resistance to adjustment and accommodation played virtually no role in the subsequent systemic breakdown, in comparison with the role played by the emerging, aggressive, empire-building national states, first and foremost Britain and France. Today, in contrast, we have reached the other end of the spectrum.

> There are no credible aggressive new [military] powers that can provoke the breakdown of the US-centered world system but the United States has even greater capabilities than Britain did a century ago to convert its declining hegemony into an exploitative domination. If the system eventually breaks down, it will be primarily because of US resistance to adjustment and accommodation. And conversely, US adjustment and accommodation to the rising economic power of the East Asian region is an essential condition for a non-catastrophic transition to a new world order. An equally essential condition is the emergence of a new global leadership from the main centers of the East Asian economic expansion . . . willing and able to rise up to the task of providing system-level solutions to the system-level problems left behind by US hegemony.[25]

Since this was written, US resistance to adjustment and accommodation has materialized in a more extreme form than anyone expected in the Project for a New American Century, whose disastrous first trial in Iraq has already precipitated the terminal crisis of US hegemony and consolidated further the shift of global economic power to East Asia. But whether the catastrophic outcome of the Iraqi adventure is a prelude to even greater catastrophes, or has taught the American people and government to adjust to the new realities of world power, remains an open question. And so does the question of whether a new global leadership is emerging in East Asia with the capacity to provide system-level solutions to the problems left behind by US hegemony. These issues are addressed in Parts III and IV of the book. But, before we proceed, I shall further clarify my argument concerning global turbulence by making explicit its connections with the theoretical framework developed in Part I.

Reprise and Preview

Despite Brenner's characterization of the late twentieth-century long downturn as a situation of over-production, what he actually de-

---

25 Arrighi and Silver, *Chaos and Governance*, pp. 288–9.

scribes is a variant of the kind of over-accumulation of capital that, in Smith's theory of economic development, drives down the rate of profit and brings economic expansions to an end. As argued in Chapter 3, Marx's notion of over-production should be reserved for situations in which the labor-saving dispositions of capitalist accumulators prevent aggregate demand from expanding in step with aggregate supply. A situation of this kind may have been the *result* of the monetarist counterrevolution, but was definitely not the *cause* of the joint crisis of profitability and hegemony that prompted the counterrevolution itself.

The match between the decline of profitability of the late twentieth century and Smith's theory of economic development is far from perfect, because Smith's theory presupposes the existence of a sovereign who activates and regulates inter-capitalist competition in the general interest, whereas the decline of profitability of the late twentieth century occurred in a global context characterized by multiple sovereignties. In our conceptualization, however, hegemonic states play governmental functions at the global level, and in so doing pursue policies that may or may not heed Smith's advice to governments. Thus early US Cold War policies followed the spirit, if not the letter, of Smith's advice, both because they created the conditions of the subsequent intensification of inter-capitalist competition—by upgrading and expanding the Japanese and Western European productive apparatuses—and because they constrained the capacity of capitalists to shift onto labor the burden of intensifying competition—by promoting near full employment in the North and development in the South. The US-sponsored monetarist counterrevolution of the 1980s, in contrast, did exactly the opposite of what Smith advised governments to do because, under the infamous slogan "There Is No Alternative" (TINA), it promoted the re-establishment of profitability through policies that empowered capitalists to shift the burden of competitive pressures onto labor and subordinate groups worldwide.

As noted in Chapter 5, both Brenner and Greenspan point out that the greater weakening of labor's leverage in the United States than in Europe and Japan contributed to the revival of US profitability in the 1990s and beyond. Smith's theory of the falling rate of profit nonetheless invites us to address the more important issue of whether this revival may, in turn, have contributed to a deterioration of the competitiveness of US business at home and abroad. The balance of the current account of a country's payments is as good a measure as any other of this overall competitiveness. As Figure 5.2 shows, after the revival of US profitability of the mid 1990s the US deficit experienced a veritable explosion, while Germany and Japan continued to generate a surplus. Does not this divergence suggest that Smith might have been right in claiming that high profits have more "pernicious effects" on the competitiveness of business than the high wages capitalists always complain about, especially in view of the huge increase in the ratio of the average income of American CEOs to that of the average manufacturing employee that has accompanied the deterioration of the global competitiveness of US business? In 1980, this ratio was 40:1; twenty years later, it was 475:1, that is, twenty to thirty times greater than in European countries and Japan, despite the fact that these countries had either almost caught up with or surpassed the United States in productivity per hour worked. The extravagant rewards thrown at US CEOs, far from being part of the solution, may well have been part of the problem of the declining competitiveness of US corporations.[26]

Be that as it may, the most fundamental probable cause of the decline in US competitiveness has been the reversal of the tendency towards the vertical integration and bureaucratization of business mentioned in Chapter 5. The intensification of competitive pressures of the late nineteenth century—as Smith had theorized a century earlier—drove profits down to a barely "tolerable" level, provoking widespread reactions among capitalists against "excessive competition." US manufacturers in particular—wrote Edward S. Meade in 1900—were "tired of working for the public"; they wanted "a larger profit without such a desperate struggle to get it," and sought ways "to stop this worrisome struggle, whose benefits [were] nearly all of them gained by the consumer in low prices."[27]

One obvious way of restraining competition was horizontal combination—the fusion through association, merger, or takeover of enterprises using much the same inputs to make much the same outputs for much the same markets. Through combinations of this kind, competing enterprises could set their combined production, purchases, and sales at levels that would guarantee larger profits and pool resources to break into unregulated markets, to develop new technologies, and to organize more effectively their operations. Horizontal combinations, however, were hard to enforce in over-

---

26 Cf. Robin Blackburn, *Banking on Death; Or Investing in Life: The History and Future of Pensions* (London, Verso, 2002), p. 201; Tony Judt, "Europe vs. America," *New York Review*, February 10, 2005; M. Reutter, "Workplace Tremors," *Washington Post*, October 23, 2005.

27 Quoted in Martin J. Sklar, *The Corporate Reconstruction of American Capitalism, 1890–1916: The Market, the Law, and Politics* (Cambridge, Cambridge University Press, 1988), p. 56.

crowded markets—that is, precisely where they were most needed—
especially in the absence of support by governments.

Where feasible, a more effective way of restraining competition was
vertical integration—the fusion, that is, of an enterprise's operations
with those of its suppliers and customers, so as to ensure supplies
"upstream" from primary production, and outlets "downstream"
towards final consumption. The multi-unit enterprises that resulted
from this fusion could reduce the transaction costs, risks, and uncertainties involved in moving inputs and outputs through the sequen-
tial subprocesses of production and exchange that linked the
procurement of primary inputs to the disposal of final outputs. While
a more effective scheduling of flows enabled them to use facilities and
personnel in production and distribution more intensively, administrative coordination provided them with a more certain cash flow and
a more rapid repayment for services rendered. As the large and steady
cash flows ensured by this kind of centralization were plowed back in
the creation of managerial hierarchies to monitor and regulate markets
and labor processes, the vertically integrated enterprises gained decisive competitive advantages vis-à-vis single-unit enterprises or less
specialized multi-unit enterprises. Once established, these hierarchies
constituted imposing barriers to entry in the industries that had been
successfully reorganized through vertical integration.[28]

The tendencies towards horizontal combination and vertical integration set off by the cut-throat competition of the late nineteenth
century developed unevenly in the three main industrial countries of
the time—Britain, the United States, and Germany. German business,
with crucial government support, moved most successfully in both
directions, giving rise to the highly centralized and cohesive system of
business enterprise that became the model of Marxist theories of state
monopoly capitalism. British business, in contrast, was driven to
specialize further in global commercial and financial intermediation,
and was least successful in moving towards horizontal combination
and, especially, vertical integration. US business fell somewhere in
between, being less successful than German business in creating
horizontal combinations but eventually emerging as the most successful in practicing vertical integration.[29]

Thus, while the intensification of competitive pressures and declin-

28 Alfred Chandler, *The Visible Hand: The Managerial Revolution in American
Business* (Cambridge, MA, The Belknap Press, 1977), pp. 7, 299.

29 Chandler, *Scale and Scope*; Arrighi and Silver, *Chaos and Governance*, pp.
121–30.

ing profitability of the late nineteenth century vindicated Smith's contention that economic expansions are limited by the particular institutional setting in which they are embedded, the outcome of the competitive struggle in Germany and in the United States vindicated Marx's contention that the concentration and centralization of capital would destroy the old institutional setting and create a new one of greater growth potential. Although Marxists remained long fixated on the German model of state monopoly capitalism, it was in the United States that vertical integration had created the kind of business organization and technical division of labor that Marx theorized in *Capital*—as Tronti's "discovery" of Marx in Detroit discussed in Chapter 1 eventually suggested.

The late twentieth-century long downturn, in contrast, appears to be vindicating Smith's predictions, not just from the standpoint of its causes (over-accumulation within a particular institutional setting), but also of its outcome: a revival of more decentralized forms of business, which rely far more on the social division of labor among production units than on the technical division of labor within units. Already in the late 1960s, Peter Drucker foresaw that the dominance of big US corporations like General Motors and US Steel was about to end in an era of "turbulence" comparable to that of the half century before the First World War. As Krugman notes, Drucker's forecast proved prophetic.[30]

By the 1980s, the crisis of vertically integrated, bureaucratically managed corporations had become a reality. "The large corporation, with its national vertical structure and the separation of its functions between staff and line," wrote Manuel Castells and Alejandro Portes, "does not appear any more as the last stage of a necessary evolution toward rationalized industrial management. Networks of economic activities, networks of firms, and coordinated clusters of workers appear to comprise an emergent model of successful production and distribution." In a similar vein, Michael Piore and Charles Sable argued that the triumph of mass production, undertaken in bureau-cratically managed, giant corporations, over the "flexible specializa-tion" of small-batch craft production, carried out in small and medium-sized business units coordinated by market relationships, was neither complete nor irreversible.[31]

---

30 Peter Drucker, *The Age of Discontinuity* (New York, Harper & Row, 1969); P. Krugman, "Age of Anxiety," *New York Times*, November 28, 2005.

31 Manuel Castells and Alejandro Portes, "World Underneath: The Origins, Dynamics, and Effects of the Informal Economy," in A. Portes, M. Castells, and L.A. Benton, eds, *The Informal Economy: Studies in Advanced and Less Developed Countries* (Baltimore, MD, Johns Hopkins University Press, 1989), pp. 29–30; *cont'd over*/

As Bennett Harrison has underscored, the portrait of the large corporation as "something of a dinosaur, increasingly unable to compete in a 'post-industrial' world characterized by continually fluctuating consumer demands, heightened international competition, and the need for more 'flexible' forms of work and interfirm interaction," has been greatly exaggerated. Rather than dwindling away, "concentrated economic power is changing its shape, as the big firms create all manner of alliances, short- and long-term financial and technology deals—with one another, with governments at all levels, and with legions of generally (although not invariably) smaller firms who act as their suppliers and subcontractors." In the process, they cut to the bone permanent ("core") jobs and relocate as much as possible contingent ("peripheral") ones to the outer reaches of their networks, often in different geographical locations. The large corporations themselves thus resorted to networking to decentralize production outside their organizational domains, retaining as much as possible control over markets and technological and financial resources.[32]

Granted all this, the world-historical significance of the change should not be underestimated for at least two reasons. First, the change shows how dependent the competitive advantages of vertically integrated and bureaucratically managed corporations were on two peculiar historical conditions: the segmentation of the world market in the first half of the twentieth century on the one side, and the spatial and natural resource endowment of the continent-sized US national economy on the other. Those advantages were considerable as long as the

---

31 cont'd   Michael J. Piore and Charles F. Sable, *The Second Industrial Divide: Possibilities for Prosperity* (New York, Basic Books, 1984), pp. 4–5, 15, 19–20. Claims of this kind revived interest in Alfred Marshall's notion of "industrial districts" as the locus of "external economies" (external, that is, to individual business units), which enabled small business to survive and prosper without exploiting the "internal economies" of scale and scope available to big business. See Alfred Marshall, *Industry and Trade* (London, Macmillan, 1919); Giacomo Becattini, "The Marshallian Industrial District as a Socio-Economic Notion," in F. Pyke, G. Becattini, and W. Sengenberger, eds, *Industrial Districts and Inter-Firm Cooperation in Italy* (Geneva, International Institute for Labor Studies, 1990); Sebastiano Brusco, "Small Firms and Industrial Districts: The Experience of Italy," in D. Keeble and F. Weaver, eds, *New Firms and Regional Development* (London, Croom Helm, 1986). As should be evident from Chapter 2, however, behind Marshall's notion stood, largely unnoticed, Smith's skepticism concerning the competitive advantages of corporate business, because of the inevitable "negligence and profusion" of managers, their lack of flexibility in adapting to local conditions, and the deleterious effects of the technical division of labor on the quality of the labor force.

32 Bennett Harrison, *Lean and Mean: The Changing Landscape of Corporate Power in the Age of Flexibility* (New York, Basic Books, 1994), pp. 8–12.

number and variety of such corporations were small, and trade was a poor substitute for direct investment as a means of penetrating the world's relatively protected national and colonial markets. But, as soon as US hegemony promoted the reunification of the world market, and the number and variety of corporate structures proliferated worldwide, the advantages of vertical integration and bureaucratic management began to wane, while the advantages of informally coordinated social divisions of labor emphasized by Smith and Marshall increased correspondingly. The result is not a return to the family capitalism of the nineteenth century, but a great variety of hybrid forms of corporate and non-corporate business, all of which differ radically from the dominant business organization of the twentieth century.

Second, the strategy of big business to turn the advantages of small business into an instrument of the consolidation and expansion of its own power has been in evidence everywhere. But nowhere has this strategy resulted in rapid and widespread economic growth as it has in East Asia. As we shall see in Part III of the book, this outcome lies at the roots of the shift of economic power to East Asia and can be traced to the hybridization of the region's tradition of market-based, non-capitalist development with the Western tradition of capitalist development. In the United States, however, the outcome of the strategy in question has been quite different, deepening rather than solving the crisis of the previously dominant industrial corporation.

The most dramatic manifestation of this deepening crisis has been the displacement of General Motors by Wal-Mart as the nation's "business template." In the 1950s, G.M. was the largest US corporation, its revenues making up 3 percent of US GDP. Today, Wal-Mart has taken its place with a workforce of 1.5 million and revenues equal to 2.3 percent of US GDP. But the two templates differ in fundamental ways. G.M. was a vertically integrated industrial corporation, which established production facilities throughout the world, but remained deeply rooted in the US economy, where the bulk of its products were manufactured and sold. Wal-Mart, in contrast, is primarily a commercial intermediary between foreign (mostly Asian) subcontractors, who manufacture most of its products, and US consumers, who buy most of them. The change of guard between the two corporations as the template of US business can thus be taken as a symbol and a measure of the transformation of the United States from a nation of producers to a nation whose role as global financial entrepôt enables it, to paraphrase Mackinder, to "share in the activity of brain and muscles of other countries."

As apologists for the new template of US business insist, Wal-Mart has been a highly innovative exploiter of the cheapest sources of

supply and of the most efficient techniques of procurement and
distribution, which have enabled it to provide its 20 million or so
daily customers with a wide variety of products at low prices and to
make a significant contribution to the boom in US productivity since
the 1990s. But as the detractors of the new template have argued, Wal-
Mart has been a leader, not just of lower prices and higher productivity, but also and especially of the redistribution of income from
labor to capital and of the transformation of workers, to paraphrase
Marx, into "crippled monstrosities" and disposable commodities.
Taking advantage of its position as the biggest retailer in world
history, writes Barry Lynn, Wal-Mart has driven down wages and
benefits not just in retailing but in manufacturing and shipping as
well. "Wal-Mart and a growing number of today's dominant firms
. . . are programmed . . . to dictate downward the wages and profits
of the millions of people and smaller firms who make and grow what
they sell, to break down entire lines of production in the name of
efficiency." "Once upon a time," comments Krugman in reporting
Wal-Mart's brutal treatment of its own employees, "a company that
treated its workers this badly would have made itself a prime target
for union organizers." These days, however, employers like Wal-
Mart "don't worry that angry workers will respond to their war on
wages by forming unions, because they know that government
officials, who are supposed to protect workers' rights, will do
everything they can to come down on the side of wage-cutters."[33]

In short, the rise of Wal-Mart and its anti-labor strategies are
manifestations of the crisis of the previously dominant industrial
corporations on the one side, and of the monetarist counterrevolution
that has facilitated the financialization of US capital on the other.
Wal-Mart did not create these circumstances; but, in exploiting them,
it did become an active agent of their consolidation. By contributing
to the revival of profitability at the expense of labor, in other words, it
has strengthened the position of the United States as the world's
financial clearinghouse, thereby enabling a growing and influential
minority of the US population to share in the activity of brain and
muscles of other countries without having to use their own brain and
muscles.

33 J. Madrick, "Wal-Mart and Productivity," *New York Times*, September 2,
2004; Barry Lynn, "The Case for Breaking Up Wal-Mart," *Harper's Magazine*, July 24,
2006; P. Krugman, "The War Against Wages," *New York Times*, October 6, 2006.

Part III

HEGEMONY UNRAVELING

7

DOMINATION WITHOUT HEGEMONY

At the turn of the twenty-first century, the "E" and "I" words, empire and imperialism, came back in fashion. Their return was not due, *pace* John Ikenberry, to the advent of the "American unipolar age" in which, "[f]or the first time in the modern era, the world's most powerful state can operate on the global stage without the constraints of other great powers."[1] That age had begun with the collapse of the Soviet bloc in 1989, yet throughout the 1990s the buzzword was "globalization," not empire or imperialism; and, as Ikenberry himself notes, the unparalleled global power of the United States was generally discussed under the rubric of "hegemony." Even critical thinkers—including many Marxists—found the concepts of empire and imperialism of little analytical use.[2] In the aftermath of the 1991 Gulf War, Cumings claimed that it would have taken an electron microscope to detect the use of the word "imperialism" to describe the United States's role in the world.[3] Hyperbole, of course; but the exaggeration contained an important element of truth.

Nor did the publication of *Empire* in 2000 significantly alter the situation, for Hardt's and Negri's work simply repackaged and gave a radical twist to the central tenets of globalization-speak, including the proposition that, under the present conditions of global economic and informational integration, no national state, not even the US, can form the center of an imperialist project. Indeed, Hardt and Negri presented Empire as a logic and structure of world rule that was in key respects

---

1 G.J. Ikenberry, "Illusions of Empire: Defining the New American Order," *New York Times*, March 16, 2004.

2 Leo Panich and Sam Gindin, "Global Capitalism and American Empire," in L. Panich and C. Leys, eds, *The New Imperial Challenge* (London, Merlin Press, 2003), pp. 2–3.

3 Bruce Cumings, "Global Realm with No Limit, Global Realm with No Name," *Radical History Review*, 57 (1993), pp. 47–8.

antithetical to the imperialism that Marxists had theorized in the twentieth century.[4]

A real break with the 1990s occurred only in 2001, when the Bush administration responded to the events of September 11 by embracing a new imperial program—that of the Project for a New American Century. There is a curious resemblance between this reflex and the actions that, sixty years earlier, had ushered in the first American century. The Great Depression of the 1930s and the rise of fascism in Europe and Japan had convinced Roosevelt that a Pax Americana was necessary to ensure domestic security and prosperity. But non-interventionist currents in foreign policy were hard to challenge, as long as the American people believed that continental isolation ensured their safety. Between the outbreak of the European war and Pearl Harbor, Schurmann has argued, "Roosevelt undoubtedly prayed for some dramatic demonstration that this was not so." When his prayers were answered, "Roosevelt made astute use of the ideological sentiments of nationalism aroused by Pearl Harbor to elaborate an ideology of imperialism through which he promised Americans order, security, and justice."[5]

Once the Second World War was over, however, isolationist dispositions reasserted themselves. Truman and Secretary of State Acheson knew very well that appeals to *raison d'état* and US economic interests would not be enough to overcome them. In drafting the text that became the Truman doctrine, they accordingly followed Arthur Vandenberg's notorious advice to "scare hell out of the American people" by inflating the notion of global communist menace.[6] The trick worked in winning Congress support for the Marshall Plan. But something more was needed to secure funding for the large-scale US and European rearmament envisaged in National Security Council document 68, which Truman approved in principle in April 1950. The NSC document gave no precise figure, but estimates suggested annual expenditures 300 percent above that originally requested by the Pentagon for 1950.

How to get that kind of money from a fiscally conservative Congress, even in the name of anticommunism, presented no small

---

4 Michael Hardt and Antonio Negri, *Empire* (Cambridge, MA, Harvard University Press, 2000), pp. xiv, 327–32. For a variety of critical assessments of the book, see Gopal Balakrishnan, ed., *Debating Empire* (London, Verso, 2003).

5 Franz Schurmann, *The Logic of World Power: An Inquiry into the Origins, Currents, and Contradictions of World Politics* (New York, Pantheon, 1974), pp. 40–1.

6 Thomas J. McCormick, *America's Half Century: United States Foreign Policy in the Cold War* (Baltimore, MD, Johns Hopkins University Press, 1989), pp. 77–8.

task for the administration. What was required was an international emergency, and since November 1949, Secretary Acheson had been predicting that one would occur sometime in 1950 in the Asian rimlands—in Korea, Vietnam, Taiwan, or all three. Two months after the President examined NSC-68, that crisis happened. Acheson was to say later, "Korea came along and saved us."[7]

It is hard to tell what President Bush may have been praying for in the eight months between his inauguration and September 11, but we know that the promoters of the Project for a New American Century within his administration were waiting for a chance to implement the new imperial strategy they had long been working on.[8] Their first months in office were not propitious, but Osama bin Laden, to paraphrase Acheson, saved them. As Michael Mann has observed, he provided both "the popular mobilizing power and the targets."[9] The menace of Muslim "fundamentalists" and "rogue states" became the new fear factor, scaring hell out of the American people and winning almost unanimous Congress support for the invasion of Iraq that Cheney, Rumsfeld, and Wolfowitz had been unsuccessfully advocating for the best part of a decade.[10]

It is this development that revived the fortunes of the "E" and "I" words to describe the emergent imperial project of the United States. The project has failed in its objectives more rapidly and abysmally than even its critics expected, so that the "E" and "I" words may lose currency as quickly as they gained it. Nevertheless, even if they do, the social, political, and economic circumstances that led to the emergence of the Project for a New American Century and its adoption by the Bush administration can be expected to persist in one form or another. Of particular interest is whether and how these circumstances relate to the turbulence of the global political economy

---

7 Ibid., p. 98.

8 For details on the Project for a New American Century see the website http://www.newamericancentury.org. On the rise of its promoters to power, see Arthur Schlesinger Jr, "The Making of a Mess," *New York Review*, September 22, 2004.

9 Michael Mann, *Incoherent Empire* (London, Verso, 2003), p. 9.

10 On the determination of the neo-conservatives to wage war on Iraq long before September 11, see Ron Suskind, *The Price of Loyalty: George W. Bush, the White House, and the Education of Paul O'Neill* (New York, Simon & Schuster, 2004) and Richard Clarke, *Against All Enemies: Inside America's War on Terror* (New York, Free Press, 2004). Clarke reports on the now (in)famous cabinet-level meeting in which, less than a day after the attacks, Rumsfeld pointed out that there were "no decent targets for bombing in Afghanistan" and therefore "we should consider bombing Iraq instead" because it had "better targets."

discussed in Part II of the book and how they have changed under the impact of the War on Terrorism.

In this chapter, I shall analyze the unraveling of the neo-conservative imperial project and the transformation of US hegemony into what, following Guha, we earlier called domination without hegemony. I focus first on the double failure of the war on Iraq to end the so-called Vietnam syndrome and to lay the foundations of a new American century. I then turn to the failure of the neo-conservative imperial project to counter the economic decline of the United States and conclude by suggesting that the most important unintended consequence of the Iraqi adventure has been the consolidation of the tendency towards the recentering of the global economy on East Asia and, within East Asia, on China.

The Persistence of the Vietnam Syndrome

Within six months of the official declaration of the end of hostilities, many commentators were observing that, although Iraq is not Vietnam, the ever more frequent use of images like "quagmire," "attrition," "credibility gap," "Iraqification" made the current debate seem to be "almost as much about Vietnam as about Iraq."[11] In Iraq, as in Vietnam, increasing US difficulties in overcoming the resistance of a comparatively insignificant military adversary were jeopardizing the credibility of US military might in the world at large. But precisely because Iraq is not Vietnam, I shall contend, failure in Iraq poses a far more serious challenge to US power than did failure in Vietnam.

As previously noted, the Vietnam War was the central event of the "signal crisis" of US hegemony; but, in the 1980s and especially in the 1990s, the signal crisis of 1968–73 gave way to a remarkable resurgence of US wealth and power—a *belle époque* wholly comparable to that enjoyed by Britain a century before. The resurgence reached its apogee after the collapse of the USSR, when the US began to present itself—and to be widely perceived—as the greatest military power the world had ever seen. Behind this façade, however, there lurked the problem that the verdict of Vietnam had never really been reversed, nor the actual credibility of US military might fully restored.

The long series of military confrontations the United States engaged in after its defeat in Vietnam were remarkable for their careful

---

11 C.R. Whitney,"Watching Iraq, and Seeing Vietnam," *New York Times*, November 9, 2003.

avoidance of the conditions that had led to that debacle. Exemplary in this respect was the US flight from Lebanon after the 1983 bombing of the Marine compound in Beirut killed 241 Americans. From then on, until the collapse of the USSR, the United States either fought wars by proxy (as in Nicaragua, Cambodia, Angola, Afghanistan, and in supporting Iraq in the war against Iran),[12] or against insignificant enemies (Grenada, Panama), or from the air, where the US high-tech apparatus had an absolute advantage (Libya).[13]

At the same time, the US escalated the armament race with the USSR—primarily, though not exclusively, through the Strategic Defense Initiative—well beyond what Moscow could afford economically. The escalation trapped the USSR into a double confrontation: in Afghanistan, where its high-tech military apparatus encountered the same difficulties that had led to the defeat of the US in Vietnam, and in the armament race, where the United States could mobilize financial resources that were wholly beyond the Soviet reach. The Soviet Union's eventual defeat, however, did nothing to dispose of the Vietnam syndrome. To the extent that it was caused by US power, it was due not to US military might but to superior financial capabilities. And to the extent that it had military origins, it confirmed rather than reversed the Vietnam verdict. It showed that, in Afghanistan no less than in Vietnam, the high-tech military apparatuses controlled by the Cold War superpowers were ineffectual in policing the Third World on the ground, however well they had succeeded in reproducing the "balance of terror."

---

12 In March 1984, undeterred by Saddam Hussein's atrocities, Rumsfeld flew to Baghdad as Reagan's envoy to offer him US support, on the very day that Iraq launched a chemical weapons attack on Iran. Four years later, while Hussein was razing hundreds of villages in northern Iraq and killing thousands of Kurds, Washington offered him $500 million in subsidies to buy US farm products. The following year, the US government doubled the subsidy to $1 billion and provided him with high-quality germ seed for anthrax and dual-use material that could be used to manufacture chemical and biological weapons. See S. Milne, "We Are Sleepwalking into a Reckless War of Aggression," *Guardian*, September 27, 2002; and A. Roy, "Not Again," *Guardian*, September 27, 2002.

13 The fact that "Third World Rollback," as the Reagan doctrine that inspired these confrontations was sometimes called, eventually backfired does not mean that it did not inflict unspeakable damage and suffering on the countries singled out. To give just one example, 300,000 children died directly or indirectly as a result of the prolongation of the Angolan civil war by the murderous Unita organization with US support. D. Aaronovitch, "The Terrible Legacy of the Reagan Years," *Guardian*, June 8, 2004. On the longer-term effects of the Reagan doctrine in breeding future terrorists, see Mahmood Mamdani, *Good Muslim, Bad Muslim: America, the Cold War, and the Roots of Terror* (New York, Pantheon, 2004).

The collapse of the USSR nonetheless created the opportunity to test the widely held assumption that, without Soviet assistance, the Vietnamese could not have defeated the United States, just as the Afghani warlords and the Mujahideen could not have defeated the USSR without US aid. Moreover, the subjugation of Moscow cleared the ground for the mobilization of the UN Security Council to legitimate US police actions to an extent that had not been possible since the Korean War. Saddam Hussein's 1990 invasion of Kuwait immediately created an ideal opportunity for such a mobilization, which the United States promptly seized, putting on a televised show of its high-tech firepower.[14] Nevertheless, as John McCain has pointed out, victory in the first Gulf War "did not end the hold of the Vietnam syndrome over [the American] national consciousness"—in his view, because Saddam Hussein was not removed from power.[15] The first Gulf War, other commentators noted, "was intended to be everything that Vietnam was not. Instead of a long, gradual use of force the goal was to overpower the enemy and quickly withdraw."[16] Known as the Powell doctrine, this strategy was the culmination of US endeavors not to reverse but more to avoid another Vietnam verdict.

An attempt to test the US military's ability to police the Third World on the ground came soon after the first Gulf War, under the cover of a "humanitarian" mission in Somalia. It failed abysmally: televised footage of a dead American being pulled through the streets of Mogadishu revived the Vietnam syndrome at home and led to the immediate withdrawal of US troops. But, under Clinton, the Powell doctrine became an increasing embarrassment, leading Secretary of State Madeleine Albright to ask her famous question: "What's the point of having this great army you're always talking about if we can't use it?"

---

14 According to General Anthony Zinni, Desert Storm in 1991 "left the impression that the terrible mess that awaits us abroad can somehow be overcome by good, clean soldiering, just like in World War Two. In reality, the only reason Desert Storm worked was because we managed to go up against the only jerk on the planet who was stupid enough to challenge us to refight World War Two" (Tom Clancy with Anthony Zinni and Tony Koltz, *Battle Ready* [New York, Putnam, 2004]).

15 Quoted in C.R. Whitney, "Watching Iraq, and Seeing Vietnam," *New York Times*, November 9, 2003. A similar view undoubtedly loomed large in the fixation of the promoters of the New American Century with the removal of Hussein. Wolfowitz, for example, had criticized the first Bush administration, in which he served as undersecretary of defense for policy, for failing to "deal with Saddam" after the 1991 Gulf War: "Democrats Target Wolfowitz on Iraq Crisis," *New York Times*, May 18, 2004.

16 M.R. Gordon, "A Sequel, Not a Re-run," *New York Times*, March 18, 2003.

The overriding objective of the "humanitarian" missions in Bosnia and against what remained of Yugoslavia was precisely to show that there was a point in "having this great army." The Kosovo War was also meant to demonstrate that prior UN endorsement of the police actions the US chose to undertake was welcome but dispensable. The more reliable NATO endorsement was enough. Militarily, however, all the Kosovo War could prove was what everybody already knew: that Washington has the technological capabilities to bomb out of existence any country it chooses. It nonetheless failed to demonstrate that the US government was willing to risk the lives of American citizens in overseas police actions that made little sense to the US public.

On the eve of 9/11, the unwillingness to take such risks still constituted the clay feet of the US military colossus. The shock of attacks on the World Trade Center and the Pentagon changed the situation, providing a *casus belli* that made sense to the American public. But, even in the Afghanistan War, which enjoyed widespread domestic and international support, the Bush administration showed little inclination to risk American casualties, even if this reluctance meant compromising the avowed US war aim of getting bin Laden "dead or alive." Instead, Afghans did most of the fighting on the ground, leaving a *Washington Post* commentator to jeer that:

> America has fought this war on the cheap. The response to the worst attack on American soil amounted to the hiring of Hessians. The United States would not even commit troops to sealing the border with Pakistan. Who knows how many of bin Laden's fighters got through? Who knows if bin Laden himself was among them?[17]

Incompetence and ideology-driven irrationality are common and sometimes plausible explanations of the many instances of puzzling behavior on the part of the Bush administration. Fighting the war in Afghanistan "on the cheap" and risking no casualties in the hunt for bin Laden was nonetheless a perfectly rational choice, if the objective of the War on Terror was not merely capturing terrorists but remaking the political geography of West Asia in the pursuit of a new American century. From the standpoint of this broader objective, Afghanistan was a most unpropitious place to test the greater

---

17 R. Cohen, "Even a Low-Risk War Brings its Own Cost," *International Herald Tribune*, January 9, 2002.

disposition of Americans to suffer casualties in foreign wars, after 9/11. It was quite reasonable to suppose that "finishing the job" in Afghanistan would cost more US lives, and would bring much lower political and economic returns per casualty, than moving on and conquering Iraq.

The successful blitzkrieg on Baghdad seemed to bear out these expectations, with Iraqi armed forces offering virtually no resistance. By June 2003, however, US casualties started to add up relentlessly. Worse still, political and economic returns per casualty declined precipitously, as US plans to remake Iraq, let alone the West Asian region, to suit American interests clashed with realities on the ground and had to be revised, downsized, or altogether abandoned. Yet, on this occasion Washington seemed determined to "finish the job," even though it kept redefining the nature of the "job." A year after the invasion, in the midst of growing difficulties, Bush launched the slogan "We must stay the course in Iraq," despite the open criticism of his generals. "The course," retorted former CENTCOM commander General Zinni, "is headed over the Niagara Falls."[18] By 2005, not only did the US army appear to be wholly incapable of finishing the job, whatever that was; it began facing a collapse in quality and morale similar to that experienced in Vietnam, and without a draft. The alternative no longer seemed to be between winning and losing; as a Marine officer put it: "We can lose in Iraq and destroy our Army, or we can just lose." By December 2006, former Secretary of State Colin Powell said on CBS News that "the active Army is about broken," while Bush for the first time admitted that the US was not winning the war in Iraq and ordered his new Defense Secretary Robert Gates to develop a plan to increase the troop strength of the Army and Marine Corps—a plan that he had dismissed only a few months before.[19] By then, however, crisis management had supplanted principled policy.

The world's only superpower no longer acts; instead, it reacts, usually to whatever happens to be the latest bad news out of Baghdad. As events in Iraq slip out of his control, President George W. Bush's strategy for waging his "global war on terror" lies in

---

18 Chalmers Johnson, "Why I Intend to Vote for John Kerry," *The History News Network*, June 14, 2004, p. 1.

19 P. Krugman, "Time to Leave," *New York Times*, November 21, 2005; Editorial, "Army Stretched to Breaking," *Minneapolis-St. Paul Star Tribune*, February 20, 2006; P. Rogers, "A Tale of Two Insurgencies," *openDemocracy*, June 1, 2006; P. Baker, "U.S. Not Winning War in Iraq, Bush Says for First Time," *Washington Post*, December 20, 2006.

ruins. He is navigating without a compass . . . Iraq constituted step one. Success there would pave the way for the Bush administration to proceed along similar lines to steps two, three and four. The disappointments and frustrations resulting from that first step now leaves the entire project in a shambles.[20]

Already in 2004, a defense expert at the conservative Lexington Institution saw how serious the problem was for the United States "because the whole world can see the pattern of Vietnam and Somalia in Iraq now." By October 2006, even Bush had to concede that the ongoing surge of violence in Iraq "could be" comparable to the Tet Offensive, which had turned the American public against the Vietnam War.[21] In reality, the problem the US has been facing in Iraq is far more serious than the one it faced in Vietnam. The situation of political blockage is similar. Then, Washington had felt unable to bring the war to an end long after its futility had become evident because withdrawal, in Nixon's words, would show the United States to be "a pitiful helpless giant," and would inspire "totalitarianism and anarchy throughout the world."[22] Similarly, despite today's "grave and deteriorating" situation in Iraq, even war critic Brent Snowcroft has claimed that withdrawal without somehow finishing the job would show that "the American colossus has stumbled, was losing its resolve," thereby emboldening terrorists and extremists everywhere.[23] But the loss of power that the United States faces from its inability to carry out its will against Iraqi resistance is far greater

---

20 A. Bacevich, "Bush's Illusions," *International Herald Tribune*, December 22, 2006.

21 B. Bender, "Study Ties Hussein, Guerrilla Strategy," *Boston Globe*, October 11, 2004; M. Fletcher and P. Baker, "Iraq Violence, 'No Child' Occupy Bush," *Washington Post*, October 19, 2006.

22 W. Pfaff, "Reclaiming the U.S. Army," *International Herald Tribune*, July 24–25, 2004.

23 B. Snowcroft, "Why America Can't Just Walk Away," *International Herald Tribune*, January 4, 2007. In reality, US actions evoked the image of "a pitiful helpless giant" well before its withdrawal was even considered. Thus, in a more colorful formulation, Saudi Arabia's *Arab News* described US military power in the wake of the Abu Ghraib disclosures as "a behemoth with the response speed of a muscle-bound ox and the limited understanding of a mouse," quoted in P. Kennicott, "A Wretched New Picture of America," *Washington Post*, May 5, 2004. This image is reminiscent of the "ghastly metaphor" with which Mann illustrated his prescient assessment that the "American Empire will turn out to be a military giant, a back-seat economic driver, a political schizophrenic and an ideological phantom. The result is a disturbed, misshapen monster stumbling clumsily across the world" (Mann, *Incoherent Empire*, p. 13).

and less remediable than that which it experienced from defeat in Vietnam.

The main reason is not US dependence on West Asian oil, as many commentators maintain, including early critics of the war like George Soros.[24] Rather, as previously noted, it is that despite the similarities Iraq is not Vietnam. In purely military terms, the Iraqi insurgents, unlike the Vietnamese, do not field heavily armored vehicles, nor do they have a long experience with guerrilla warfare in a favorable natural environment, or enjoy the support of a superpower like the USSR. In these and other respects, they are a far less formidable adversary than the Vietnamese. Furthermore, during the three decades that separate the US withdrawal from Vietnam and the invasion of Iraq, the US military underwent a fundamental restructuring aimed specifically at reversing the Vietnam verdict. This "professionalization" of the armed forces was intended both to improve their combat-readiness and simultaneously to free them from the constraints that a constant turnover of civilian soldiers and temporary officers imposed on military action and discipline. Combined with the extraordinary technological improvements in US weaponry that occurred in that same thirty-year period, the restructuring turned the US military apparatus into a far more lethal force than it had been at the time of the Vietnam War.

In short, the disparity of forces between the US invaders and the local resistance in Iraq has been incomparably greater than in Vietnam. This is why the Bush administration hoped the invasion of Iraq would reverse the Vietnam verdict; but it is also the reason why the failure to do so constitutes a far greater blow to the credibility of US military might than defeat in Indochina. If the Powell doctrine had raised the issue of what the point was of having a great army if it could not be used, the Iraqi quagmire, as Andrew Bacevich has noted, raised a far more troubling question: "What's the point of using this great army if the result is Fallujah, Najaf, and Karbala?"[25]

To be sure, the United States will remain the world's dominant military power for some time to come, regardless of the outcome of

---

24 "Having invaded Iraq, we cannot extricate ourselves. Domestic pressure to withdraw is likely to build, as in the Vietnam war, but withdrawing would inflict irreparable damage on our standing in the world. In this respect, Iraq is worse than Vietnam because of our dependence on Middle Eastern oil" (G. Soros, "The US Is Now in the Hands of a Group of Extremists," *Guardian*, January 26, 2004).

25 Andrew Bacevich, "A Modern Major General," *New Left Review*, II/29 (2004), p. 132.

the Iraqi War. But, just as US difficulties in Vietnam precipitated the signal crisis of US hegemony, in all likelihood US difficulties in Iraq will, in retrospect, be seen as having precipitated its terminal crisis.[26] This crisis has long been in the making, and was bound to come, sooner or later, in one form or another, regardless of the actions of the Bush or any other administration. But the particular form in which it is now occurring has been determined by the decision to invade Iraq in the hope that an easy victory would reverse the Vietnam verdict and lay the foundations of a new American century.

As previously noted, Clinton's Kosovo War was meant to demonstrate, among other things, that UN support for US police actions backed by NATO was dispensable. Bush's Iraq War was now meant to demonstrate that even NATO was dispensable. The assumption, in the words of one neo-conservative foreign policy expert, was that

in the past 500 years or more, no greater gap had ever existed between the No. 1 and the No. 2 power in the world. Given this American domination, [the Bush administration] believed that it was enough to express the American national interest firmly and everyone would accommodate themselves.[27]

As it turned out, almost no one that mattered did. Except for Britain, increasingly behaving like the fifty-first state of the Union, and a pitiful "coalition of the willing,"[28] the rest of the world rejected American leadership to an extent that had no precedent in the annals

---

26 From a different perspective Fred Halliday made a similar point in claiming that "in the spring of 2004 we are in the midst of one of the greatest, most intractable and *global* crises of modern times. It is not a world war, a strategic military conflict between major states—the form of conflict that, with two world wars and the cold war, dominated the 20th century; nor is it a major international economic crisis, as was 1929 and (less seriously) 1973. But at every level of social and political life, we confront a situation that is likely to affect everyone on earth and have serious global consequences." See his "America and Arabia after Saddam," *openDemocracy*, May 13, 2004.

27 Norman Ornstein, American Enterprise Institute, quoted in R. Cohen, D.E. Sanger and S.R. Weisman, "Challenging the Rest of the World with a New Order," *New York Times*, October 12, 2004.

28 Already at the end of 2004, the coalition was reported to be a "joke." Of the 28 allied countries that still had troops in Iraq, "only eight have more than 500. Most are there as window dressing. And because of language and equipment difficulties, some contingents—like Macedonia's 28 or Kazakhstan's 29—may be more trouble than they are worth" (N. Kristof, "Brother, Can You Spare a Brigade?" *New York Times*, December 11, 2004). Since then, all contingents of any significance, except Britain's and Australia's, have withdrawn or announced their withdrawal.

of US hegemony. To be sure, many foreign critics of the invasion of Iraq found little to rejoice over in the US predicament. A senior advisor at the French Institute for International Relations explained:

> When the US finds itself bogged down abroad, it poses a big challenge to the rest of the world. If America simply pulled out now, other countries would find themselves in the strange position of having to put pressure on the Americans to stay, having previously begged them not to risk invasion without a United Nations resolution. In the aftermath of a rapid withdrawal, the focus of international concern would quickly switch from the perils of US global domination, to the dangers of a world deprived of US international engagement. The problem is that if the present strategy in Iraq does not really work, there is no convincing alternative. It is unlikely that sending more US troops or handing over power to the Iraqis would make a serious difference. America is in a mess, but so are we.[29]

Reasoning along these lines probably motivated the unanimous UN Security Council resolution of October 16, 2003 that provided the US-led occupation with some juridical legitimacy and called on the world's governments to lend it their support. Juridical legitimacy as such, however, mattered to the US primarily, if not exclusively, as a means of extracting resources from other states to cover the escalating human and financial costs of the Iraqi occupation. Indeed, the main purpose of rushing the resolution through the UN Security Council was to ensure the success of the "donors conference" that the United States had convened in Madrid for the following week—the poor results of which, as we shall see in Chapter 9, provide a good measure of the deflation that US power had experienced as a result of its transformation from hegemony into sheer domination.

An even better measure was the decline of US influence in the West Asian region, whose political geography the invasion of Iraq was supposed to remake to suit US interests and values. By the spring of 2004, the problems in Iraq had deprived of all practical significance the issue of how the United Sates would use the occupation, leaving Thomas Friedman to lament that:

> We are in danger of losing something much more important than just the war in Iraq. We are in danger of losing America as an

---

29 Dominique Moisi, "The World Is Trapped in the Iraqi Quagmire," *Financial Times*, November 14, 2003.

instrument of moral authority and inspiration in the world. I have never known a time in my life when America and its president were more hated around the world than today. . . . [T]he war on terrorism is a war of ideas, and to have any chance of winning we must maintain the credibility of our ideas. . . . We cannot win a war of ideas against [the people who hit us on 9/11] by ourselves. Only Arab and Muslims can. . . . But it is hard to partner someone when you become so radioactive no one wants to stand next to you.[30]

Indeed, the US had become so "radioactive" that plans to promote a raft of cosmetic political reforms in the so-called Greater Middle East had to be scrapped. When, in February 2004, an Arabic newspaper published a draft of the Bush administration's call for the world's wealthiest nations to press for political change in West Asia, several Arab leaders erupted in anger, with even Mubarak calling the plan "delusional"; the administration quickly withdrew it. A few months later, Washington tried to use the tools of "soft power" by sponsoring a multilateral agenda based on a UN report on human development in the Arab world at the G8 summit meeting on Sea Island, Georgia. The drafters of the report, however, were harshly critical of the initiative, pointing out that the US had little credibility in the Arab world and that, the more it associated itself with the UN development report, the more it undermined the authority of their work. By December 2004, when Secretary of State Colin Powell arrived at a summit meeting in Morocco intended to promote democracy across the Arab world, the US had given up trying to take the lead. Arab leaders, noted an American official, are "willing to take the aid, but they are not willing to carry out the reforms."[31]

The problem for the US was not just the widespread perception among Arabs and Muslims that the invasion of Iraq was aimed at strengthening Israel's hand vis-à-vis Palestinian resistance and the Arab world in general, nor their resentment at the larger-scale reproduction in Iraq of the kind of coercive domination that Israel had pioneered in the Palestinian territories: the "striking symmetry in military tactics"; the "similar inattention to the plight of the victims";

---

30 "Restoring our Honor," *New York Times*, May 6, 2004.
31 J. Brinkley, "U.S. Slows Bid to Advance Democracy in Arab World," *New York Times*, December 5, 2004; F. Heisbourg, "Mideast Democracy Is a Long-Term, Global Project," *International Herald Tribune*, March 23, 2004.

and the "excessive solicitude towards the misfortunes of the aggressors."[32] The problem was also, and especially, the perception among the ruling groups of the Arab and Muslim world that subservience to the US had higher costs and risks than defiance. While difficulties in Iraq made US threats to use military force against other Muslim states mostly empty, the state that was most empowered by the war in Iraq was Iran, itself next on the list of US targets for regime change in the West Asian region.

> The United States has destroyed Iran's arch enemy, while itself doing great damage to its own credibility in the region; Iran's own political allies in Iraq, among Kurds and Shi'a, are integrated into the new government structure and have never been stronger; and the country is now poised to play a major, if not decisive, role in the formation of any new Iraqi political and social system. Iran . . . is not unhappy to see the Americans bogged down [in Iraq] for a lengthy period, at considerable cost. It is delighted that, for the first time in the politics of any Arab country, the Shi'a community . . . has now acquired public, legitimate, internationally recognized status.[33]

Shiite dominance in Iraq, coupled with Shiite rule in Iran, is particularly threatening to Sunni-ruled states that border Iraq and down the Persian Gulf, carrying as it does the threat of increasing unrest among long suppressed Shiite populations. "If Iraq goes Islamic Republic," warned King Abdullah of Jordan, "we've opened ourselves to a whole set of new problems that will not be limited to the borders of Iraq." These fears have created an opening for the United States to mobilize Sunni rulers in the region against Iran, but the opening is strictly limited by a growing perception that it is dangerous for all Arab leaders to ally themselves too closely with the US.[34]

---

32 In the months before the war, US and Israeli officials expressed quite openly the hope that a swift US victory over Iraq would bolster the safety and security of Israel by demonstrating to Arab leaders that defiance did not pay. For a good selection of statements to this effect, see Sukumar Muralidharan, "Israel: An Equal Partner in Occupation of Iraq," *Economic and Political Weekly*, October 9, 2004.

33 F. Halliday, "America and Arabia after Saddam," *openDemocracy*, May 13, 2004.

34 R. Khalaf, "Iranian Nuclear Ambitions Worry Gulf Arab States," *Financial Times*, December 18/19, 2004; J.F. Burns and R.F. Worth, "Iraqi Campaign Raises Questions of Iran's Sway," *New York Times*, December 15, 2004; B. Daragahi, "Jordan's King Risks Shah's Fate, Critics Warn," *Los Angeles Times*, October 1, 2006; B. Snowcroft, "Why America Can't Just Walk Away," *International Herald Tribune*, January 4, 2007.

It is hard to tell what the eventual outcome of the US invasion of Iraq will be in the wider West Asian region. Even the Iranian "victory" may prove temporary, given the growing atrophy and unpopularity of the Ayatollah regime and the possibility of yet another ill-considered action on the part of the United States. Indeed, according to Seymour Hersh and reports in the *New York Times*, it appears that the Bush White House was closely involved in the planning of Israel's 2006 bombardment and invasion of Lebanon and backed the offensive against Hezbollah. This move, however, also backfired. Instead of creating a credible *casus belli* with Iran, it demonstrated Israel's own vulnerability to the chaos generated in the region by the invasion of Iraq. Although this new failure—along with US dependence on Shiite goodwill in Iraq—makes a military attack on Iran implausible, the dispatch in January 2007 of two aircraft carriers and their accompanying battle groups into the Persian Gulf was meant, in the words of a senior US military official, "to remind the Iranians that we can focus on them, too."[35] Under these circumstances, the only safe bet is that, whatever the eventual outcome of the Iraqi adventure, it will bear no resemblance to its blueprint. Far from being the opening act of a new American century, in all likelihood it will be the closing act of the first and only American century, the "long" twentieth century.

The Strange Death of the Globalization Project

The idea that we are witnessing the terminal crisis of US hegemony becomes more compelling when we turn to the impact of the Iraqi War on the US centrality in the global political economy. As Harvey has underscored, the objectives of the neo-conservative imperial project, both at home and on the world stage, were only in part consistent with neo-liberal proclamations of belief in allegedly self-regulating markets. Should the operation of free markets threaten to undermine US centrality, neo-conservatives were prepared to transform the low-intensity warfare waged around the globe under neo-

---

35 Z. Mian, "Choosing War, Confronting Defeat," *Economic and Political Weekly*, October 7, 2006; D.E. Sanger, "On Iran, Bush Confronts Haunting Echoes of Iraq," *New York Times*, January 28, 2007; M. Slackman, "Iraqi Ties to Iran Create New Risks for Washington," *New York Times*, June 8, 2006; F. Halliday, "Lebanon, Israel, and the 'Greater West Asian Crisis'," *openDemocracy*, August 18, 2006; W. Pfaff, "Can Bush Forestall Defeat?" *International Herald Tribune*, January 13–14, 2007; G. Kolko, "The Great Equalizer. Lessons from Iraq and Lebanon," *Japan Focus*, August 25, 2006.

liberalism into a dramatic confrontation capable of eliminating the threat once and for all. The invasion of Iraq was meant to be such a confrontation: a first tactical move in a longer-term strategy aimed at using military might to establish US control over the global oil spigot, and thus over the global economy, for another fifty years or more.[36]

The unexpectedly disastrous results of the Iraqi invasion raise the question of what was so threatening to US power in the outcome of the "globalization project" of the 1980s and 1990s as to drive neo-conservatives into the risky Iraqi adventure. Had not the US-sponsored liberalization of world trade and capital movements resulted in a major reflation of American power after the multiple crises of the 1970s? Was not reliance on the verdict of a US-centered and US-regulated global market, supplemented by a prudent use of low-intensity warfare, the best guarantee of the reproduction of US centrality in the global political economy?

For all its free-market rhetoric, the Bush administration was never as enthusiastic as the Clinton administration about the process of multilateral liberalization of trade and capital movements that constituted the central institutional aspect of so-called globalization. Indeed, the word "globalization" has rarely, if ever, cropped up in President Bush's speeches. According to a senior presidential aide, the word "makes him uncomfortable." Speaking, in December 2003, as the Bush administration was being fined by the WTO for its 2002 tariffs on imported steel, under threat of $2.3 billion in retaliatory sanctions, the aid explained that the White House "thinks what went wrong in the 90's is that we forgot to put American interests first. So globalization sounds like the creation of a lot of rules that may restrict the president's choices, that dilute American influence."[37]

---

36 David Harvey, *The New Imperialism* (New York, Oxford University Press, 2003), pp. 24–5, 75–8, 84–5, 190–2; 201–2.

37 Quoted in D. Sanger, "While America Sells Security, China Is Buying Its Dollars," *New York Times*, December 7, 2003. See also Chalmers Johnson, *The Sorrows of Empire: Militarism, Secrecy, and the End of the Republic* (New York, Metropolitan Books, 2004), p. 272. "September 11 was the ultimate blow to globalization's promise. . . . Threafter . . . the United States retreated into full national-interest-first mode. . . . Now, to the extent that President Bush talks with any conviction about cross-border cooperation or integration, it's always in the context of the war on terrorism, and in the narrowest of terms" (A. Martinez, "The Borders Are Closing," *Los Angeles Times*, June 1, 2005). The Bush administration accordingly switched from multilateral to bilateral free-trade agreements. The only multilateral negotiation it supported—the new global trade round initiated at Doha, Qatar, shortly after the attacks of 9/11—broke up spectacularly two years later at Cancun, in large part over US and European farm subsidies.

The Bush administration's attempt to set itself free from the constraints that globalization imposed on US power has been most evident in the financial sphere. Niall Ferguson, contrasting the financial position of the United States and that of Britain a century earlier, has pointed out that, in Britain's case, hegemony "also meant hege*money*." As the world's banker, Britain in its imperial heyday "never had to worry about a run on the pound," whereas the US, as it "overthrows 'rogue regimes,' first in Afghanistan and now in Iraq, is the world's biggest debtor." This condition was the result of the escalating deficits in the current-account of the US balance-of-payments discussed in Chapters 5 and 6.

> Thus President Bush's vision of a world recast by military force to suit American tastes has a piquant corollary: the military effort involved will be (unwillingly) financed by the Europeans—including the much reviled French—and the Japanese. Does that not give them just a little leverage over American policy, on the principle that he who pays the piper calls the tune? Balzac once said that if a debtor was big enough then he had power over his creditors; the fatal thing was to be a small debtor. It seems that Mr. Bush and his men have taken this lesson to heart.[38]

In fact, it was not Europeans who were the main financiers of the huge US current-account deficit. As Figure 7.1 shows, since the Asian crisis of 1997–98 the current-accounts of the countries of the global North *taken together* (i.e., the former First World, including Japan) have experienced an escalating deficit—for the most part due to the US deficit—to which corresponds an escalating surplus in the current-account of the rest of the world (i.e., of the former Third and Second Worlds). As we shall see in the Epilogue, this striking bifurcation involves a growing dependence of Northern and especially US global financial domination on a flow of money and credit from the very countries that are most likely to become the victims of that domination. Unsurprisingly, the director of research at a US think tank has warned against the dangers of the emerging situation: "We are increasingly counting on a group of creditors who are not our closest friends but have a bigger and bigger stake in America."[39]

---

38 Niall Ferguson, "The True Cost of Hegemony," *New York Times*, April 20, 2003. The argument is developed further in Niall Ferguson, *Colossus: The Price of America's Empire* (New York, Penguin, 2004), pp. 261–95.

39 Quoted in F. Kempe, "Why Economists Worry about Who Holds Foreign Currency Reserves," *Wall Street Journal*, May 9, 2006.

won militarily but lost financially, for Britain to lose its prior position as the world's leading creditor nation.[41]

The US, in contrast, has become a debtor nation much earlier and more substantially than the UK, not just because of its consumerist orientation, but also because it had no India from which to draw, gratis, all the troops it needed to wage as endless a series of wars in the global South as Britain did during its own hegemony. Not only did Washington have to pay for those troops and their highly capital-intensive weaponry; in addition, instead of extracting tribute from an overseas empire, it had to compete aggressively in world financial markets for the capital needed to balance the explosive growth of its current-account deficit. Although the United States was highly successful in this during the 1980s and 1990s, the capital it attracted—unlike Indian contributions to the British balance-of-payments—did not come for free. On the contrary, it generated a self-expanding flow of incomes to foreign residents that has made the US current-account deficit increasingly hard to balance.[42]

It follows that the US *belle époque* of the 1990s was based on a virtuous circle that could, at any time, turn vicious. This virtuous-but-potentially-vicious circle rested on the synergy of two conditions: the US capacity to present itself as performing the global functions of market of last resort and indispensable political-military power; and the capacity and willingness of the rest of the world to provide the US with the capital it needed to continue to perform those two functions on an ever-expanding scale. The collapse of the Soviet bloc, the spectacular "victories" in the first Gulf and Yugoslav wars, and the emergence of the new-economy bubble all gave a tremendous impulse to the synergy between US wealth and power on the one side, and the influx of foreign capital on the other. But if any of those conditions

---

41 Giovanni Arrighi and Beverly J. Silver, *Chaos and Governance in the Modern World System* (Minneapolis, MN, University of Minnesota Press, 1999), pp. 72–87.

42 Thus, in late September 2006, the *Wall Street Journal* reported that, for the first time in at least ninety years, the United States was paying noticeably more to foreign creditors than it received from its investments abroad, thereby reverting to its nineteenth-century condition when it was borrowing vast sums from Europe. Besides the fact that the vast sums are now borrowed from Asia instead of Europe, there is a fundamental difference between the debtor-nation condition of the United States in the nineteenth century and today: in the nineteenth century, borrowing financed the building of railroads and other infrastructure, which strengthened the productiveness of the US economy, whereas today they finance private and public consumption that the United States can no longer produce competitively. M. Whitehouse, "US Foreign Debt Shows its Teeth as Rates Climb," *Wall Street Journal*, September 7, 2005; P. Krugman, "Debt and Denial," *New York Times*, February 8, 2006.

changed, the synergy might go into reverse and turn the virtuous circle into a vicious one.

Coming to power just after the bursting of the new-economy bubble, Bush had plenty of reasons to be "uncomfortable" about the policies of the Clinton era.[43] During the bubble's expansion, most of the foreign capital that flowed into the United States had been private capital in search of profits, and the private investors themselves consisted of an amorphous mass that gained little or no leverage over US policies. As noted, however, after the bubble burst, the inflow of capital into the United States became more political, and the governments that financed the escalating US current-account deficit necessarily gained more than a little leverage over US policies. This greater leverage posed no immediate problem for Washington, because most of the East Asian creditor states, first and foremost Japan, felt deeply dependent on the US for their security and prosperity. As we shall see, this situation changed radically with the emergence of China as an alternative destination for East Asian exports and investment, and as a significant creditor of the United States. But even abstracting from the China factor, growing financial dependence on foreign governments necessarily constrained US ability to pursue its national interest in the multilateral and bilateral negotiations that promoted and regulated global economic integration. In June 1997, for example, on his way back from a G8 meeting in Denver that featured considerable chest-thumping by the Clinton administration about the booming US economy, the Japanese prime minister told a New York audience that Japan had been tempted to sell large lots of US treasuries during Japan's negotiations with the US over auto sales, and again when exchange rates were fluctuating wildly while the United States appeared preoccupied only with domestic issues. As one commentator noted, Hashimoto "was simply reminding Washington that while it had created a robust . . . economy, Asian central banks held the deed."[44]

---

43 Prior to the invasion of Iraq, foreboding comparisons between post-bubble United States and Japan gained currency. The fact that in 2002 US stocks declined for the third consecutive year, the longest losing streak since 1939–41, did not help. D. Leonhardt, "Japan and the U.S.: Bubble, Bubble, Toil and Trouble," *New York Times*, October 2, 2002; S. Roach, "The Next Japan?" http://www.morganstanley. com (accessed October 21, 2002). The unprecedented combination of fiscal and financial stimuli that was put in place by the Bush administration (see below) allayed but never completely disposed of fears that the United States in the 2000s might repeat the Japanese experience of the 1990s.

44 W. Pesek, "Commentary: Across Asia, the Sounds of Sharpening Knives," *International Herald Tribune*, December 7, 2004.

The Bush administration's decision to respond to 9/11 with a protracted war on multiple fronts added a new urgency to the need to switch from the policies of the 1990s, for how could such a war be financed from a starting point of heavy indebtedness to other countries? There were four possible answers to this question: raise taxes; borrow more heavily from foreigners; make war pay for itself; or exploit the seigniorage privileges that the United States enjoyed by virtue of the general acceptance of the US dollar as international currency.

Raising taxes was out of the question. Having won the elections on a platform of extensive tax reductions, the Bush administration could not raise them without alienating its core electoral base, thus committing political suicide. Moreover, the popularity of the war effort rested in good part on the belief, fostered by the administration, that the US did not have to choose between guns and butter but could have more of both. Indeed, the 9/11 crisis was used to launch two wars while taking advantage of the surpluses built by the previous administration to spend while cutting taxes. In retrospect, laments Friedman, the United States "followed the dot-com bubble with the 9/11 bubble. . . . The first was financed by reckless investors, and the second by a reckless administration and Congress."[45]

Borrowing more heavily from abroad was possible but within economic and political limits. Economically, the limits were set by the need to keep interest rates low in order to revive the domestic economy after the 2000–01 crash on Wall Street, which 9/11 had further aggravated. Politically, the limits were set by the Bush administration's reluctance to give foreign governments more leverage over US policies. Borrowing from foreign (especially East Asian) governments did however increase after 9/11–as did their leverage. The funding of the deficit was thus left increasingly at the mercy of East Asian central banks. But this situation was not so much the result of a conscious US policy to increase borrowing, as of foreign governments' decisions, for reasons of their own, to keep financing current-account deficits spiraling out of US control.[46]

Making the war pay for itself was more easily said than done. The previously noted switch from the unfinished war in Afghanistan to Iraq was due not just to the expectation that Iraq provided a more favorable terrain for an easy US victory, as famously epitomized in

---

45 T. Friedman, "The 9/11 Bubble," *New York Times*, December 2, 2004.

46 F. Norris, "Is It Time for the Dollar to Fall in Asia?" *International Herald Tribune*, October 22, 2004; E. Porter, "Private Investors Abroad Cut their Investments in the U.S," *New York Times*, October 19, 2004.

Rumsfeld's remark that Iraq had "better targets" than Afghanistan. It was due also to the expectation that Iraqi oil would provide the wherewithal for the consolidation of US power in Iraq and the West Asian region at large. As we now know, both expectations have gone unfulfilled. Once the "better Iraqi targets" had been taken out, Iraqi oil could not even begin to cover the rapidly escalating costs of a war that dragged on without end in sight.

Before the war, officials refused to discuss costs, except to insist that

> they would be minimal. It was only after shooting started, and Congress was in no position to balk, that the administration demanded $75 billion for the Iraq Freedom Fund. Then, after declaring "mission accomplished" and pushing through a big tax cut . . . Mr. Bush told Congress that he needed an additional $87 billion. . . . and warned that American soldiers would suffer if the money wasn't forthcoming.

A year later he came back with the same warning, asking Congress for another $25 billion.[47] By the end of 2006, Congress had approved more than $500 billion for the wars in Iraq and Afganistan, as well as for terrorism-related operations elsewhere, and the War on Terror was projected to surpass in 2007 the cost (adjusted for inflation) of all US wars except for the Second World War.[48]

Since taxes could not be raised, further borrowing from abroad had limits, and the war was not paying for itself, the exploitation of US seigniorage privileges became the main source of finance for Bush's wars. As one commentator wrote, shortly after the invasion of Iraq, a cynic might view the way foreign countries were providing the US with goods, services, and assets in return for overpriced pieces of paper, "as a brilliant US conspiracy."

> In the 1980s and 1990s, [US] policymakers persuaded a host of economies to liberalize their financial markets. Such liberalizations generally ended with financial crises, currency crises, or a combination of the two. These disasters lowered domestic investment in the afflicted countries, instilled deep fear of current-account deficits and engendered a strong desire to accumulate foreign-exchange reserves.

---

47 P. Krugman, "The Wastrel Son," *New York Times*, May 18, 2004.

48 P. Baker, "U.S. Not Winning War in Iraq, Bush Says for the First Time," *Washington Post*, December 20, 2006; "Costs of Major U.S. Wars," *CounterPunch*, May 5, 2006.

The safest way was to invest surplus funds in the country with the world's biggest economy and most liquid capital markets. When gullible foreigners can no longer be persuaded to finance the US, the dollar will decline. Since US liabilities are dollar-denominated, the bigger the decline, the smaller net US liabilities to the rest of the world will then turn out to be. In this way, the last stage of the "conspiracy" will be partial default through dollar depreciation.[49]

At the end of 2004 *The Economist* put the decline of the dollar over the previous three years at 35 percent against the euro and 24 percent against the yen, and estimated the stock of dollar assets held by foreigners at nearly $11 trillion. "If the dollar falls by another 30 percent, as some predict, it would amount to the biggest default in history: not a conventional default on debt service, but default by stealth, wiping trillions off the value of foreigners' dollar assets."[50] As it turns out, this "biggest default in history" has yet to occur. But whether it will or not, US exploitation of seigniorage privileges in order to consume both guns and butter far beyond its means, can postpone but not avoid indefinitely a fundamental structural adjustment of the United States needed to reflect its substantially diminished competitiveness in the global economy.

The longer-term causes of this diminished competitiveness before the invasion of Iraq have already been discussed in Chapter 6. Since the invasion, an increasing number of US observers have lamented this loss of competitiveness, not just in low-technology, labor-intensive activities, but also in the high-technology, knowledge-intensive activities that constitute the backbone of US comparative advantage.[51] US multi-

---

49 M. Wolf, "A Very Dangerous Game," *Financial Times*, September 30, 2003. For more complex accounts of the US "conspiracy," see R.H. Wade, "The Invisible Hand of the American Empire," *openDemocracy*, March 13, 2003, and Andre Gunder Frank, "Meet Uncle Sam—Without Clothes—Parading around China and the World," available at http://www.rrojasdatabank.info/agFrank/noclothes.htm.

50 "The Disappearing Dollar," *The Economist*, December 2, 2004.

51 See, among others, Adam Segal, "Is America Losing its Edge?" *Foreign Affairs* (November–December 2004); J. Kumagi and W. Sweet, "East Asia Rising," *IEEE Spectrum Online*, October 19, 2004; W.J. Broad, "U.S. Is Losing Its Dominance in the Sciences," *New York Times*, May 3, 2004; E. Porter, "Innovation and Disruption Still Going Hand in Hand," *New York Times*, December 6, 2004; D. Baltimore, "When Science Flees the U.S," *Los Angeles Times*, November 29, 2004; T. Friedman, "Fly Me to the Moon," *New York Times*, December 5, 2004; K. Bradsher, "Made in U.S., Shunned in China," *New York Times*, November 18, 2005; P.C. Roberts, "Another Grim Jobs Report. How Safe Is Your Job?" *CounterPunch*, April 18, 2006; J. Perry and M. Walker, "Europeans' Appetite for Imports Benefits China at the Expense of the U.S," *Wall Street Journal*, September 11, 2006.

nationals did see their revenues and profits grow; but the growth occurred primarily abroad, and these firms could only hold on to their global market shares by reinvesting profits abroad.[52] The revaluation of the currencies of other countries (most notably China)—widely held as the remedy for the loss of competitiveness—might help, but past experience is not encouraging.

> There is an abundance of evidence that the US obsession with currencies is misplaced. Since 1976 the yen has roughly trebled in value against the dollar. But there has been no significant improvement in the US bilateral position against Japan—the long standing *bête noire* of US manufacturers.[53]

US adjustment to the new realities of the global economy will involve some combination of further depreciation of the US dollar, appreciation of the currencies of the countries with the largest current-account surpluses, and a rerouting of these surpluses from the financing of US deficits to the creation of demand elsewhere, especially in East Asia. This eventual adjustment may be "brutal," through a dollar rout, or "smooth."[54] Either way, the adjustment will inevitably result in a further decrease of US command over world-economic resources, a reduction of the weight and centrality of the US market in the global economy, and a diminished role for the dollar as international means of payment and reserve currency.

The Bush administration has shown some awareness of the risks involved in relying too heavily on a depreciating dollar and default on US liabilities to foreigners to buttress US competitiveness. Thus, at the Doha meeting in June 2003, Treasury Secretary John Snow persuaded the finance ministers of the other G7 countries to sign a joint statement arguing that the market should determine exchange rates. The statement was taken as a signal that Washington was

---

52 L. Uchitelle, "Increasingly, American-Made Doesn't Mean in the U.S.A.," *New York Times*, March 19, 2004.

53 J. Kynge and C. Swann, "US Risks Paying High Price for Calls over Currency Flexibility," *Financial Times*, September 26, 2003. Similarly, between July 2001 and March 2006, the euro rose 44 percent against the dollar but the US bilateral deficit with the euro zone grew by 75 percent: C. Swann, "Revaluation of the Renminbi 'Will Do Little to Reduce US Deficit,' " *Financial Times*, March 28, 2006. More generally, the massive dollar depreciation of 2001–04, far from narrowing the US trade deficit, sent it to a new record of $617.7 billion. As Figure 5.2 shows, the US current-account deficit since the mid 1990s has been escalating regardless of whether the dollar was appreciating (as in 1995–2000) or depreciating (as in 2001–04).

54 M. Wolf, "A Very Dangerous Game," *Financial Times*, September 30, 2003.

officially abandoning the strong dollar policy of the Clinton era, and the dollar promptly dived against all major currencies. But whenever the dive has threatened to become a rout, US officials have repeated the mantra about the importance of a strong currency: "Nobody in the markets quite knows what [that] means anymore, but just in case it could signal a burst of intervention, they take cover and stop selling greenbacks."[55]

Confusion in the markets has been fully justified in light of the contradiction between rhetorical adherence to the importance of a strong currency and the extreme monetary and fiscal laxity through which the Bush administration sustained the recovery of the US economy after the crash of 2001 and financed the escalating costs of the War on Terror. This extreme laxity is reminiscent of US policies in the closing years of the Vietnam War, when Nixon's Treasury Secretary, John B. Connally, famously told a worried world: "The dollar is our currency, but your problem."[56] Eventually, however, the sinking dollar did become a US problem. For a brief moment in January 1980, the rise of the price of gold to an all-time high of $875 an ounce seemed to signal an imminent end of the *de facto* dollar standard inaugurated in 1971—the year in which the US finally abandoned its commitment to buy gold at the fixed price of $35 an ounce. As it turned out, the dollar quickly recovered from the rout and the *de facto* dollar standard has remained in place ever since. In light of this experience, the Bush administration's willingness to push to its limits the abuse of seigniorage privileges may reflect the belief that, if the worse comes to the worst, Washington can pull back from the brink and enjoy another twenty years of uncontested seigniorage.[57]

In the event of a new dollar rout comparable to that of the late 1970s, however, it would be far more difficult, if at all possible, for the United States to regain the upper hand in the world monetary system. In the 1980s, the US dollar recouped its position as the world's money by virtue of a sudden and radical reversal of US monetary policies, from extreme laxity to extreme tightness, accompanied by a stepping-up of US competition for capital worldwide—through re-

---

55 C. Denny, "Trap a Dragon, Mr. Bush, and Lose an Election," *Guardian*, November 3, 2003.

56 M. Landler, "Sidelined by U.S. and Asia, Singing the Euro Blues," *New York Times*, December 12, 2004.

57 This belief seems to be implicit in Cheney's contention, as reported by Paul O'Neill, that "Reagan proved that deficits don't matter" (quoted in J. Cassidy, "Taxing," *The New Yorker*, January 26, 2004).

cord-high interest rates, tax breaks, and increasing freedom of action for capitalist producers and speculators.[58] But the very success of this policy reversal in attracting gargantuan amounts of capital has turned the US from a creditor nation into the world's leading debtor. US creditors may pause—as they certainly do—at the idea of pulling the rug from under the feet of such a big debtor. *Pace* Balzac, it would nonetheless make no sense at all for them to redouble their lending to a country that has partially defaulted on its debt through massive currency depreciation.[59] Moreover, having already granted extraordinary incentives to capital, the United States has little left to offer in the situation of a new dollar rout. Under these circumstances— unprecedented indebtedness and exhaustion of incentives—a hike in interest rates like the one engineered under Reagan would provoke a far more severe domestic contraction, without any guarantee that it would be followed by a robust recovery. A major increase in interest rates would thereby aggravate, rather than alleviate, the relative downsizing of the US economy that would ensue from the dollar rout.

To this we should add that in the late 1970s there were few, if any, viable alternatives to the US dollar as international currency. The euro was still a project rather than a reality. The rapidly appreciating German mark and Japanese yen had neither the global economic weight nor the national institutional support needed to become significant means of international payment and reserve currencies. Having nowhere else to go, capital taking flight from the dollar thus went primarily into gold. But no capitalist power had any interest in a remonetization of gold at a time of world economic stagnation, especially in view of the leverage that such a remonetization would have put in the hands of the USSR. Under these circumstances, US attempts to preserve the dollar standard could count on the active cooperation of all the governments that mattered in world monetary regulation.

Also in this respect the situation today is quite different. The governments that matter may still be willing, to a large extent, to cooperate with the US government in preserving the dollar standard. But this willingness rests on foundations that are different—and less favorable to the US— than they were in the 1980s. As former Treasury Secretary Lawrence Summers has recently put it, US dependence on foreign cash is "even more distressing" than US dependence on foreign energy.

---

58 As we have seen in Chapters 5 and 6, the policy reversal began under Carter but materialized fully only under Reagan.

59 M. Wolf, "The World Has a Dangerous Hunger for American Assets," *Financial Times*, December 8, 2004.

In a real sense, the countries that hold U.S. currency and securities in their banks also hold U.S. prosperity in their hands. That prospect should make Americans uncomfortable. There is something odd about the world's greatest power being the world's greatest debtor. It is true, of course, that the foreign governments and investors financing the superpower spending spree have no incentive to bankrupt the U.S. economy by suddenly dumping their dollar reserves. The ensuing financial crisis would seriously damage their own economies as well. But having finally emerged from the Cold War's military balance of terror, the United States should not lightly accept a new version of mutually assured destruction if it can be avoided.[60]

Indeed, it is far more difficult for the United States to resolve the new "balance of terror" in its favor than was the case with the USSR. As previously noted, the decisive advantage of the US during the Cold War was financial. But, in the new confrontation, financial power is stacked not in favor but against the United States. Should US abuses of seigniorage privileges once again result in a dollar rout, European and East Asian governments are in a far better position than they were twenty-five years ago to create viable alternatives to the dollar standard. We should nonetheless bear in mind that, in these matters, inertia is the rule and the dethroning of the dollar does not require that any other single currency take its place.

Dislodging an incumbent currency can take years. Sterling maintained a central international role for at least half a century after America's GDP overtook Britain's at the end of the nineteenth century. But it did eventually lose that status. If America continues on its current profligate path, the dollar is likely to suffer a similar fate. But in future no one currency, such as the euro, is likely to take over. Instead the world might drift towards a multiple reserve-currency system shared among the dollar, the euro and the yen (or indeed the yuan at some time in the future). . . . A slow, steady shift out of dollars could perhaps be handled. But if America continues to show such neglect of its own currency, then a fast-falling dollar and rising American interest rates would result.[61]

In sum, like many of its critics, the Bush administration may well think that a sinking US dollar is not a US problem but rather a very effective

---

60 Lawrence H. Summers, "America Overdrawn," *Foreign Policy*, 143 (2004).
61 "The Passing of the Buck?" *The Economist*, December 2, 2004.

means of forcing friends and foes to finance the US war effort and economic growth. In reality, the sinking dollar of the 2000s is the expression of a far more serious crisis of US hegemony than the sinking dollar of the 1970s. Whether gradual or brutal, it is the expression (and a factor) of a relative and absolute loss of the nation's capacity to retain its centrality within the global political economy. In order to fully appreciate the extent and nature of this loss, we must switch our focus to what, in retrospect, may well appear to have been the greatest failure of the neo-conservative imperial project: the failure to prevent China from becoming a potential new center of the global political economy.

The China Syndrome

On the eve of 9/11, John Mearsheimer concluded *The Tragedy of Great Power Politics*—the most ambitious product of recent US international relations theorizing—with a prognosis and a prescription concerning the implications for US power of the Chinese economic ascent.

China is still far away from the point where it has enough [economic] power to make a run at regional hegemony. So it is not too late for the United States to . . . do what it can to slow the rise of China. In fact, the structural imperatives of the international system, which are powerful, will probably force the United States to abandon its policy of constructive engagement in the near future. Indeed, there are signs that the new Bush administration has taken the first steps in this direction.[62]

---

62 John J. Mearsheimer, *The Tragedy of Great Power Politics* (New York, W.W. Norton, 2001), p. 402. Mearsheimer's argument echoed Wolfowitz's 1992 contention that the objective of foreign policy should be "to prevent any hostile power from dominating a region whose resources would, under consolidated control, be sufficient to generate global power" (quoted in Chalmers Johnson, *The Sorrows of Empire: Militarism, Secrecy, and the End of the Republic* [New York, Metropolitan Books, 2004], pp. 85–6). Mearsheimer reiterated his position in an interview given eight months after 9/11. "The United States will go to great lengths . . . to contain China and to cut China off at the knees, the way it cut Imperial Germany off at the knees in World War I, the way it cut Imperial Japan off at the knees in World War II, and the way it cut the Soviet Union off at the knees during the Cold War." At the same time, he acknowledged that "it would be almost impossible to slow down Chinese economic growth." A more effective strategy, he claimed, would be for the United States to put in place a political and military "balancing coalition" that included Japan, Vietnam, Korea, India, and Russia. The United States could then back Russia in a border dispute with China; it could back Japan in a dispute with China over sea lines of communication; or it could "go to war on behalf of Taiwan" (Harry Kreisler, "Through the Realist Lens," *Conversations with History, Conversation with John Mearsheimer* [Institute of International Studies, UC Berkeley, April 8, 2002]).

As it turns out, by getting bogged down in the Iraqi quagmire, the Bush administration has been forced to deepen, rather than abandon, the constructive engagement with China. On his way to and from the 2003 Asia-Pacific Economic Cooperation (APEC) meeting in Bangkok, Bush skirted—geographically and rhetorically—the country that once was at the center of his administration's national security policy.[63] As the *Financial Times* noted, this is "a significant shift for a president who came into office touting his break from Clintonian policies of engagement with China, insisting in the first weeks of his presidency that China was a 'strategic competitor' to the United States." As security issues in West Asia weighed more heavily on the US government, so warnings of the Chinese threat gave way to an even greater engagement with Beijing than under Clinton. The reversal was so complete that the White House began boasting that it had better relations with China than any administration since Richard Nixon resumed relations with the PRC.[64]

As we shall see in Chapter 10, Washington has by no means given up on the idea of containing China through a variety of strategies, including the kind of political and military "balancing coalition" favored by Mearsheimer. Nevertheless, the more the US became entangled in the War on Terror and dependent on cheap foreign credit and commodities, the more successful was China in bringing to bear a different kind of "structural imperative" to those envisaged by Mearsheimer. As Krugman has pointed out, when the US Treasury Secretary went to Beijing to request a revaluation of the yuan and got no satisfaction, one reason was that China's trade surplus with the United States was largely offset by trade deficits with other countries. But another reason was that:

> the U.S. currently has very little leverage over China. Mr. Bush needs China's help to deal with North Korea. . . . Furthermore, purchases of Treasury bills by China's central bank are one of the

---

63 "In the first draft of the 1992 *Defense Policy Guidance* drafted by Paul Wolfowitz and Lewis Libby, it was unclear where the new rival to U.S. supremacy would most likely emerge. Europe and Japan as well as China were among the candidates. By the time the Bush administration came into office, however, the proponents of this doctrine of supremacy saw only one possible peer competitor emerging in the foreseeable future: China" (John Gershman, "Remaking Policy in Asia?" *Foreign Policy in Focus* [November 2002], available at http://www.fpif.org).

64 J. Harding and P. Spiegel, "Beijing Looms Large in the White House's Defence Strategy," *Financial Times*, October 17, 2003. See also R. Cohen, "The Iraqi Silver Lining: Closer U.S.–China Ties," *International Herald Tribune*, December 13, 2006.

main ways the U.S. finances its trade deficit. . . . Just four months
after Operation Flight Suit, the superpower has become a suppli-
cant to nations it used to insult. Mission accomplished![65]

Moreover, the Bush administration has been quite aware of the
danger that imposing tariffs on Chinese imports, as a way to press
revaluation, is a move that could backfire. As Bush's economic
advisor Greg Mankiw repeatedly stated, most US jobs have been
lost in industries—machinery, transport equipment, and semicon-
ductors—where Chinese competition is slight. More important, a
revaluation of the yuan would merely replace Chinese imports with
those of other, more expensive foreign suppliers. The result for the US
would be rising inflation, a further loss of competitiveness, and a
reduction rather than an increase in jobs.[66]

The combined effects of China's strong economic hand and
Washington's troubles in West Asia were soon reflected not just in
the two countries' mutual relations but also in their respective
standing with third parties. On the eve of the 2003 APEC meeting
in Bangkok, the New York Times reported that political and business
leaders in Asia saw US hegemony "subtly but unmistakably eroding
as Asian countries [looked] toward China as the increasingly vital
regional power." Although the US was still the region's biggest
trading partner, China was rapidly catching up, and soon became
a bigger trading partner of America's two most important strategic
allies, Japan and South Korea. More important, local perceptions of
the politics of the situation experienced a radical turnabout. A
prominent Singaporean businessman who, a year earlier, had accused
China of being a juggernaut poised to smother the weaker economies
of Southeast Asia, in the fall of 2003 drew an altogether different
picture. "The perception is that China is trying its best to please,
assist, accommodate its neighbors while the United States is perceived
as a country involved more and more in its own foreign policy, and
strong-arming everyone onto that agenda."[67] By 2006, the turnabout
in perceptions had resulted in an equally radical change in the
geopolitics of the situation.

---

65 P. Krugman, "The China Syndrome," New York Times, September 5, 2003.
66 "Mr. Wen's Red Carpet," The Economist, December 11, 2003.
67 J. Perlez, "Asian Leaders Find China a More Cordial Neighbor," New York
Times, October 18, 2003; "With U.S. Busy, China Is Romping with Neighbors," New
York Times, December 3, 2003; P. Pan, "China's Improving Image Challenges U.S. in
Asia," Washington Post, November 15, 2003; G. Kessler, "U.S., China Agree to
Regular Talks," Washington Post, April 8, 2005.

Many of the arrangements that have inspired security measures in Southeast Asian security over the past 50 years were designed as bulwarks against Chinese Communist expansion. Now Southeast Asia, whose leaders have traditionally looked to the United States as the anchor of regional security, are speaking out about the need to strengthen their relationships with Beijing.[68]

There were signs of waning US influence even in the cultural sphere where—from Hollywood movies to MTV—the American appeal remained strongest. Deterred from visiting the US by the difficulties of getting visas after 9/11, an increasing number of Asians began traveling to China, as students and tourists. Cultural exchanges flowed both ways: the Chinese became the dominant tourist group in the region; Asian students took advantage of proliferating opportunities for higher education in China, while middle-class Chinese students who could not afford the steep American fees went to campuses in Southeast Asia.[69]

But it is in the economic sphere that the ascent of Chinese influence was most remarkable. In 2001–04, China accounted for one-third of the total increase in world-import volume, thereby becoming "a locomotive for the rest of East Asia" and playing a big part in Japan's economic recovery.[70] This leading economic role of China was taken as "one more piece of evidence pointing to the shift of geopolitical power underway in Asia."

> In the space of a few years, China has become an economic power and increasingly potent political force in a region where the United States once stood unchallenged. . . . Much of China's new status stems from its emergence as one of the world's major trading nations and, in the process, an important market for export-oriented neighbors. But there is a strong political dimension to this power as Beijing's new leaders show themselves prepared to set aside old disputes and engage, rather than bully, other nations.[71]

---

68 D. Greenlees, "Asean Hails the Benefits of Friendship with China," *International Herald Tribune*, November 1, 2006.

69 J. Perlez, "Chinese Move to Eclipse U.S. Appeal in South Asia," *New York Times*, November 18, 2004.

70 "The Passing of the Buck?" *The Economist*, December 2, 2004. In 2004, China surpassed the United States to become Japan's biggest trading partner since records began.

71 T. Marshall, "China's Stature Growing in Asia," *Los Angeles Times*, December 8, 2003.

Integral to this shift was China's growing importance relative to the US even outside the East Asian region. In South Asia, trade with India has grown from $300 million in 1994 to more than $20 billion in 2005, leading to a "complete U-turn" in the relationship between the two countries and to an unprecedented mutual engagement at the governmental and business level alike.[72] Washington's failure to tighten its control over the "global oil spigot" in West Asia was signaled most spectacularly by the signing of a major oil agreement between Beijing and Tehran in October 2004.[73] Further south, oil fuels China's push into Africa. In 2000 Beijing voluntarily waived $1.2 billion in sovereign African debt, and, over the next five years, trade between Africa and China increased from just under $10 billion to over $40 billion. Each year, more Chinese entrepreneurs—in 2006 ten times as many as in 2003–arrive in Africa to invest where Western companies are uninterested to do business, while the Chinese government (except for requesting that Taiwan not be recognized) provides development assistance with none of the strings that are attached to Western aid. Increasingly, African leaders looked East for trade, aid, and political alliances, shaking up the continent's historical links with Europe and the United States.[74] Equally significant were Chinese inroads in South America. While Bush paid only a fleeting visit to the 2004 APEC meeting in Chile, Hu Jintao spent two weeks visiting Argentina, Brazil, Chile, and Cuba, announced more than $30 billion in new investments, and signed long-term contracts that will guarantee China supplies of vital raw materials. Political spin-offs seemed to be advancing most rapidly with Brazil, where Lula repeatedly floated the idea of a "strategic alliance" with Beijing, and with Venezuela, where Chavez celebrated increasing oil sales to China as a way for Venezuela to break free of dependence on the American market.[75]

---

72 A. Greenspan, "When Giants Stop Scuffling and Start Trading," *International Herald Tribune*, September 14, 2004; N. Vidyasagar, "Meet India's Future No 1 Bilateral Trade Partner," *The Times of India*, February 9, 2005; S. Sengupta and H. French, "India and China Poised to Share Defining Moment," *New York Times*, April 10, 2005; W.N. Dawar, "Prepare Now for a Sino-Indian Trade Boom," *Financial Times*, October 31, 2005.

73 K. Afrasiabi, "China Rocks the Geopolitical Boat," *Asia Times Online*, November 6, 2004.

74 J. Murphy, "Africa, China Forging Link," *Baltimore Sun*, November 23, 2004; K. Leggett, "Staking a Claim," *Wall Street Journal*, March, 29, 2005; E. Economy and K. Monaghan, "The Perils of Beijing's Africa Strategy," *International Herald Tribune*, November 1, 2006; "Africa and China," *The Economist*, November 3, 2006.

75 L. Rohter, "China Widens Economic Role in Latin America," *New York Times*, November 20, 2004; J. Forero, "China's Oil Diplomacy in Latin America," *New York Times*, March 1, 2005. See also R. Lapper, "Latin America Quick to Dance to China's Tune," *Financial Times*, November 10, 2004.

By 2004, the European Union and China were on their way to becoming each other's leading trading partner. Combined with their mutual designation as "strategic partners" and frequent joint meetings and state visits, these increasingly closer economic ties prompted talks of an emerging "China–Europe" axis in world affairs. "Axis" may be too strong a word; but if such an alliance actually emerges, it will be largely because of a common perception that US financial and military policies constitute a serious threat to world security and prosperity. As one European Commission official described: "The US is the silent party at the table in all EU–China meetings, not in terms of pressure but in terms of our mutual interest in developing multilateralism and constraining American . . . behavior."[76]

China also began to overshadow the United States in the promotion of multilateral trade liberalization. Regionally, it successfully sought integration with ASEAN countries, while simultaneously seeking economic ties with Japan, South Korea, and India. Globally, it joined Brazil, South Africa, and India in leading the G20 offensive at the 2003 WTO meeting in Cancun against Northern double standards—imposing market-opening on the South while remaining fiercely protectionist itself, especially in activities where the South has the greatest comparative advantage. In this respect, too, China's stance contrasted sharply with the US abandonment of multilateral trade negotiations in favor of bilateral agreements aimed at breaking up the Southern alliance that emerged at Cancun, or at gaining support for the War on Terror.[77]

As we shall see in Chapter 9, only in 2006 did the abysmal failure of the neo-conservative imperial project become a generally accepted fact. But already on July 4, 2004, US Independence Day, the *New York Times* magazine, already countered the neo-conservatives' New American Century by announcing the probable coming of a "Chinese Century" as its cover story:

> The U.S. economy is about eight times the size of China's. . . . Americans, per capita, earn 36 times what the Chinese do. And there is no shortage of potential roadblocks in China's path, either.

---

76 David Shambaugh, "China and Europe: The Emerging Axis," *Current History* (September 2004), pp. 243–8.

77 R.L. Smith, and C.G. Cooper, "The US and Economic Stability in Asia," *Asia Times Online*, December 6, 2003; A. Kwa, "The Post-Cancun Backlash and Seven Strategies to Keep the WTO off the Tracks," *Focus on Trade*, 95, November 2003; M. Vatikiotis and D. Murphy, "Birth of a Trading Empire," *Far Eastern Economic Review*, March 20, 2003.

Its banks may collapse. Its poor and its minorities may rebel. Uppity Taiwan and lunatic North Korea may push China to war. The U.S. could slap taxes on everything China ships to us. Still, barring . . . nuclear cataclysm, nothing is likely to keep China down for long. Since 1978 . . . [it] has gone from being virtually absent in international trade to the world's third-most-active trading nation, behind the U.S. and Germany and ahead of Japan. . . . 21 recessions, a depression, two stock-market crashes and two world wars were not able to stop the U.S. economy's growth, over the last century. . . . China is poised for similar growth in this century. Even if China's people do not, on average, have the wealth Americans do, and even if the United States continues to play a strong economic game and to lead in technology, China will still be an ever more formidable competitor. If any country is going to supplant the U.S. in the world marketplace, China is it.[78]

In sum: far from laying the foundations of a second American century, the occupation of Iraq has jeopardized the credibility of US military might, further undermined the centrality of the US and its currency in the global political economy, and strengthened the tendency towards the emergence of China as an alternative to US leadership in East Asia and beyond. It would have been hard to imagine a more rapid and complete failure of the neo-conservative imperial project. But if the Bush administration's bid for global supremacy is most likely to go down in history as one of the several "bubbles" to have punctuated the terminal crisis of US hegemony, the bursting of this bubble transformed but did not erase the world-historical circumstances that generated the Project for a New American Century.[79] Although no longer hegemonic in the sense in which we have used the term, the US remains the world's preeminent military power and retains considerable leverage in the new "balance

---

78 T.C. Fishman, "The Chinese Century," *New York Times Magazine*, July 4, 2004.

79 "Iraq was supposed to signal the US's new global might: in fact it may well prove to be the harbinger of its decline. . . . Once the bubble of US power has been pricked in a global context already tilting in other directions, it could deflate rather more quickly than has been imagined" (M. Jacques, "The Disastrous Foreign Policies of the US Have Left it More Isolated than Ever, and China Is Standing by to Take Over," *Guardian*, March 28, 2006). George Soros, *The Bubble of American Supremacy: Correcting the Misuse of American Power* (New York, Public Affairs, 2004), characterized the neo-conservative bid for global supremacy as a "bubble" well before its unraveling became evident.

of terror" that links its economic policies to those of its foreign competitors and financiers. In order to identify the possible future uses of this residual power, we must now turn to the historical processes that underlie the relationship between capitalism and imperialism.

8

THE TERRITORIAL LOGIC OF
HISTORICAL CAPITALISM

"Imperialism is a word that trips easily off the tongue." Like John A. Hobson one century earlier, Harvey notes that the term has assumed so many different meanings that its analytic, as opposed to polemical, use requires some clarification.[1] Its most general meaning is an extension or imposition of the power, authority or influence of a state over other states, or stateless communities. Thus understood, imperialism has been around for a very long time under a great variety of forms. But the special brand of imperialism that Harvey calls "capitalist imperialism" or "imperialism of the capitalist sort" is what we need to investigate in order to understand why the greatest capitalist power in world history, the United States, has developed a military apparatus of unparalleled and unprecedented destructiveness and has shown a strong disposition to deploy that apparatus in the pursuit of the most ambitious project of world rule ever conceived.

Harvey defines imperialism of the capitalist sort as a "contradictory fusion" of two components: "the politics of state and empire" and "the molecular processes of capital accumulation in space and time." The first component refers to "the political, diplomatic and military strategies invoked and used by a state (or some collection of states operating as a political power bloc) as it struggles to assert its interests and achieve its goals in the world at large." This struggle is driven by a "territorial logic of power"—a logic, that is, in which command over a territory and its human and natural resources constitutes the basis of the pursuit of power. The second component, in contrast, refers to the flow of economic power "across and through continuous space, towards and away from territorial entities . . .

---

1 David Harvey, *The New Imperialism* (New York, Oxford University Press, 2003), p. 26. On Hobson's classic definition of imperialism and its usefulness in mapping analytically the different (often opposite) meanings that the term has assumed historically, see Giovanni Arrighi, *The Geometry of Imperialism* (London, Verso, 1983).

through the daily practices of production, trade, commerce, capital flows, money transfers, labor migration, technology transfer, currency speculation, flows of information, cultural impulses, and the like." The driving force of these processes is a "capitalist logic of power"—a logic, that is, in which command over economic capital constitutes the basis of the pursuit of power.[2]

The fusion of these components is always problematic and often contradictory (that is, dialectical). Neither logic can be reduced to the other. Thus, "it would be hard to make sense of the Vietnam War or the invasion of Iraq . . . solely in terms of the immediate requirements of capital accumulation," because it can be plausibly argued that "such ventures inhibit rather than enhance the fortunes of capital." By the same token, however, "it is hard to make sense of the general territorial strategy of containment of Soviet power by the United States after the Second World War—the strategy that set the stage for US intervention in Vietnam—without recognizing the compelling need felt on the part of business interests in the United States to keep as much of the world open to capital accumulation through the expansion of trade . . . and opportunities for foreign investment."[3]

While the territorial and the capitalist logics of power are not reducible to each other, and at times the territorial logic comes to the fore, "what sets imperialism of the capitalist sort apart from other conceptions of empire is that it is the capitalistic logic that dominates." But, if this is the case, Harvey asks, "how can the territorial logics of power, which tend to be awkwardly fixed in space, respond to the open dynamics of endless capital accumulation?" And if hegemony within the global system is a property of a state or collection of states, "how can the capitalist logic be so managed as to sustain the hegemon?" Does not the attempt of hegemonic states to maintain their position in relation to endless capital accumulation

---

2 Harvey, *New Imperialism*, pp. 26–7. Harvey refers to my own distinction between a capitalist and a territorialist logic of power. See Giovanni Arrighi, *The Long Twentieth Century: Money, Power and the Origins of our Times* (London, Verso, 1994). His use of the distinction, however, differs from mine in two important ways. In his, the territorialist logic refers to state policies, while the capitalist logic refers to the politics of production, exchange, and accumulation. In mine, in contrast, both logics refer primarily to state policies. Moreover, Harvey seems to assume that all market processes (including trade, commerce, labor migration, technology transfer, information flows, and the like) are driven by a capitalist logic. I make no such assumption. As we shall see, these differences result in a historical account of the relationship between capitalism and imperialistic practices that departs in key respects from Harvey's account.

3 Harvey, *New Imperialism*, pp. 29–30.

inevitably induce them to extend, expand, and intensify their powers militarily and politically to a point where they endanger the very position they are trying to maintain? Was not the United States under George W. Bush falling in this trap, despite Paul Kennedy's 1987 warning that overextension and overreach have again and again proven the Achilles heel of hegemonic states and empires? And finally, "if the US is no longer in itself sufficiently large and resourceful to manage the considerably expanded world economy of the twenty-first century, then what kind of accumulation of political power under what kind of political arrangement will be capable of taking its place, given that the world is heavily committed still to capital accumulation without limit?"[4]

In seeking answers to these questions, Harvey interprets the Bush administration's adoption of the Project for a New American Century as a high-risk approach to sustaining US hegemony under the conditions of unprecedented global economic integration created by endless capital accumulation at the end of the twentieth century. If the United States could install a friendly regime in Iraq; move on to do the same in Iran; consolidate its strategic presence in Central Asia and so dominate Caspian Basin oil reserves—"then it might, through control of the global oil spigot, hope to keep effective control over the global economy for the next fifty years." Since all the economic competitors of the United States, both in Europe and in East Asia, are heavily dependent on West Asian oil,

> What better way for the United States to ward off that competition and secure its own hegemonic position than to control the price, conditions, and distribution of the key economic resource upon which those competitors rely? And what better way to do that than to use the one line of force where the US still remains all-powerful—military might?[5]

Nevertheless, even if such a strategy could have succeeded militarily, it would have not been sufficient to maintain the *hegemonic* position of the United States. Thus, on the eve of the US invasion of Iraq, Thomas Friedman had contended that there was "nothing illegitimate or immoral about the US being concerned that an evil, megalomaniac

---

4 Ibid., pp. 33–5; Paul Kennedy, *The Rise and Fall of the Great Powers: Economic Change and Military Conflict from 1500 to 2000* (New York, Random House, 1987).

5 Harvey, *New Imperialism*, pp. 24–5, 75–8.

dictator might acquire excessive influence over the natural resource that powers the world's industrial base." But the US had to be careful to convey to the public and reassure the world that the intention was "to protect the world's right to economic survival" rather than our own right to indulge ourselves, that the United States was "acting for the benefit of the planet, not simply to fuel American excesses. . . . If we occupy Iraq and simply install a more pro-US autocrat to run the Iraqi gas station (as we have in other Arab oil states), then this war would be immoral."[6]

Harvey uses Friedman's argument to illustrate the difference—which we have already discussed in Chapter 6—between hegemony in a Gramscian sense and sheer domination. He then goes on to note that over the last half century the United States relied frequently on coercive means to subjugate or liquidate antagonistic groups at home and—especially—abroad. Coercion was nonetheless, "only a partial, and sometimes counterproductive, basis for US power." An equally indispensable foundation was the US capacity to mobilize consent and cooperation internationally, by acting in such a way as to make plausible to others the claim that it was acting in the general interest, even when it was really putting narrow American interests first.[7] Also in justifying the invasion of Iraq, the Bush administration did all it could to persuade the world that the US was "acting for the benefit of the planet, not simply to fuel American excesses," as Friedman had suggested. Outside the US, however, few took the claim seriously. From the start, the main problem was not that the "weapons of mass destruction" and the "Iraq–al Qaeda connection" rationalizations lacked credibility, but rather that the invasion was inscribed in a broader political project of US global domination that explicitly emphasized the preservation of US power for another century regardless of the interests of other power-holders. The attempted implementation of the plan through the unilateral decision to invade Iraq "created a bond of resistance . . . between France, Germany and Russia, even backed by China." This sudden geopolitical realignment made it "possible to discern the faint outlines of a Eurasian power bloc that Halford Mackinder long ago predicted could easily dominate the world geopolitically."[8]

In light of Washington's longstanding fears that such a bloc might

---

6 As quoted in ibid., p. 24.

7 Ibid., pp. 39–40.

8 Ibid., pp. 84–5. On the current significance of Mackinder for geostrategic thought, see also Paul Kennedy, "Mission Impossible?" *New York Review*, June 10, 2004.

actually materialize, the occupation of Iraq took on an even broader meaning.

> Not only does it constitute an attempt to control the global oil spigot and hence the global economy through domination over the Middle East. It also constitutes a powerful US military bridgehead on the Eurasian land mass which, when taken together with its gathering alliances from Poland down through the Balkans, yields it a powerful geostrategic position in Eurasia with at least the potentiality to disrupt any consolidation of a Eurasian power that could indeed be the next step in that endless accumulation of political power that must always accompany the equally endless accumulation of capital.[9]

It was these far-reaching plans that led observers to speak of a "new" imperialism. Yet, as Harvey notes, "the balance of forces at work within the capitalistic logic point in rather different directions."[10] The interaction of these forces with the logic of territorial expansionism constitutes the subject matter of this chapter. I begin by introducing Harvey's concepts of "spatial fix" and "accumulation by dispossession," and then use them to tell my own story of the long historical process of capitalist development and territorial expansion that has culminated—and reached its limits—in the failed project of a truly universal US empire.

Over-Accumulation and the Production of Space

One of the most essential (and theoretically neglected) features of historical capitalism is the "production of space." This process has not only been essential to the survival of capitalism at especially critical conjunctures, as Henri Lefebvre contended.[11] It has also been the most fundamental condition for the formation and increasing global reach of capitalism as a historical social system. Harvey's theory of a "spatial-temporal fix" or, for brevity, of a "spatial fix" applied to the crisis-prone tendencies of the endless accumulation of capital provides a compelling explanation of why the production of

---

9 Harvey, *New Imperialism*, p. 85.
10 Ibid., p. 86.
11 Henri Lefebvre, *The Survival of Capitalism: Reproduction of the Relations of Production* (New York, St Martin's Press, 1976).

space has been such an essential ingredient of the enlarged reproduction of capitalism.[12] In *The New Imperialism*, this theory is deployed
to highlight the connection between the emergence of the Project for
the New American Century and the over-accumulation crisis of the
1970s and 1980s, as well as the contradictions between the territorial
logic that underlies this project and the capitalist logic. The term
"fix" has a double meaning:

> A certain portion of the total capital is literally fixed in and on the
> land in some physical form for a relatively long period of time
> (depending on its economic and physical lifetime). Some social
> expenditures (such as public education or a health-care system)
> also become territorialized and rendered geographically immobile
> through state commitments. The spatio-temporal "fix", on the
> other hand, is a metaphor for a particular kind of solution to
> capitalist crises through temporal deferral and geographical ex-
> pansion.[13]

The literal meaning of the term "fix" draws attention to the reliance
of capital accumulation on the existence of a particular built environment of facilities (such as ports, railways, roads, airports, cable
networks, optic-fiber systems, pipelines, electricity grids, water and
sewage systems, as well as factories, offices, housing, hospitals, and
schools) that constitute fixed capital *embedded* in the land, as
opposed to forms of fixed capital (such as ships, trucks, aircraft,
and machinery) that can be moved around. It is only by fixing certain
physical infrastructures *in* space that capital, in all its physically
mobile forms, can actually move *over* space in search of maximum
profit.[14]

The metaphorical meaning of the term "fix," in contrast, underscores the tendency of successful capital accumulation to drive
incessantly towards the reduction if not the elimination of spatial
barriers—what Marx called "the annihilation of space through
time"; thus unwittingly undermining the monopolistic privileges
attached to specific locations through the intensification of competition across geographical space. As a result of this tendency, capital
recurrently accumulates over and above what can be profitably

---

12 David Harvey, *Limits to Capital* (Oxford, Basil Blackwell, 1982) and the
essays collected in *Spaces of Capital: Towards a Critical Geography* (New York,
Routledge, 2001).
13 Harvey, *New Imperialism*, p. 115.
14 Ibid., pp. 99–100.

reinvested in the production and exchange of commodities within existing territorial systems. This surplus of capital materializes in inventories of unsold commodities that can only be disposed of at a loss, in idle productive capacity and in liquidity that lacks outlets for profitable investment. The incorporation of new space into the system of accumulation "fixes" (i.e., provides a solution for) the ensuing crisis of over-accumulation by absorbing these surpluses, first through "temporal deferral" and then through a spatial enlargement of the accumulation system. Absorption through temporal deferral refers specifically to the production of space, that is, to the utilization of surplus capital in opening up and endowing the new space with the necessary infrastructure, both physical and social. Absorption through spatial enlargement, for its part, refers to the utilization of surplus capital in the new productive combinations that are made profitable by the geographical expansion of the system of accumulation after the new space has been adequately produced.[15]

The combined effect of the tendencies to which the two meanings of spatial fix draw our attention is a geographical variant of Schumpeter's process of "creative destruction," which we discussed in Chapter 3. As Harvey puts it,

> The aggregate effect is . . . that capitalism perpetually seeks to create a geographical landscape to facilitate its activities at one point of time only to have to destroy it and build a wholly different landscape at a later point in time to accommodate its perpetual thirst for endless capital accumulation. Thus is the history of creative destruction written into the landscape of the actual historical geography of capital accumulation.[16]

Schumpeter's own list of the kind of innovations that drive the process of creative destruction did include changes in the spatial configuration of trade and production. But Schumpeter never spelled out the relationship between innovations that altered the spatial configuration of trade and production and other kinds of innovations. This is what Harvey does by underscoring the interrelated roles that technological and locational advantages play in generating the excess profits that drive the Schumpeterian dynamic. In this dynamic, as noted in Chapter 3, excess profits (Schumpeter's "spectacular prizes") play a double role. On the one side, they provide a constant incentive

---

15 Ibid., pp. 98–9, 109–12.
16 Ibid., p. 101.

to innovation and, on the other, they propel the activity of that vast majority of businessmen who enter the field that yields excess profits and in the process set off the competition that not only eliminates excess profits, but also inflicts widespread losses by destroying pre-existing productive combinations. Harvey theorizes a similar process but focuses on the fact that individual capitalists can acquire excess profits not just by adopting superior technologies, but also by seeking out superior locations.

> A direct trade-off exists, therefore, between changing technology or location in the competitive search for excess profits. . . . [In] both cases the excess profit that accrues to individual capitalists . . . disappears as soon as other capitalists adopt the same technology or shift to equally advantageous locations. . . . To the degree that opportunities for excess profits from location are eliminated . . . the greater the competitive incentive for individual capitalists to disrupt the basis of [the resulting] equilibrium through technological change. . . . Competition [thus] simultaneously promotes shifts in spatial configurations of production, changes in technological mixes, the re-structuring of value relations and temporal shifts in the overall dynamic of accumulation. The spatial aspect to competition is a volatile ingredient in this volatile mix of forces.[17]

The spatial-temporal shifts in the overall dynamic of accumulation that absorb surplus capital generally "threaten . . . the values already fixed in place (embedded in the land) but not yet realized." Hence,

> The vast quantities of capital fixed in place act as a drag upon the capacity to realize a spatial fix elsewhere. . . . If capital does move out, then it leaves behind a trail of devastation and devaluation; the deindustrializations experienced in the heartlands of capitalism . . . in the 1970s and 1980s are cases in point. If capital does not or cannot move . . . then overaccumulated capital stands to be devalued directly through the onset of a deflationary recession or depression.[18]

---

17 Harvey, *Limits to Capital*, pp. 390–3; also *New Imperialism*, pp. 96–8. *Mutatis mutandis*, Harvey's considerations concerning the relationship between technological innovations and the struggle for locational advantage apply also to product innovations.

18 Harvey, *New Imperialism*, p. 116.

Either way, spatial fixes involve interregional volatility and the redirection of capital flows from one space to another. The redirection may occur smoothly, or it may involve what Harvey calls "switching crises."[19] Harvey does not spell out what, exactly, these crises are. The drift of his argument nonetheless seems to be that switching crises are moments of impasse that stem from resistance to the relocations involved in the spatial-temporal fixes that recurrently revolutionize the historical geography of capitalism. In part, resistance originates from the contradictory logic of capital accumulation itself. Indeed, "the more capitalism develops," argues Harvey, "the more it tends to succumb to the forces making for geographical inertia."

> The circulation of capital is increasingly imprisoned within immobile physical and social infrastructures which are crafted to support certain kinds of production . . . labor processes, distributional arrangements, consumption patterns, and so on. Increasing quantities of fixed capital . . . check uninhibited mobility. . . . Territorial alliances, which often become increasingly powerful and more deeply entrenched, arise . . . to conserve privileges already won, to sustain investments already made, to keep a local compromise intact, and to protect itself from the chill winds of spatial competition. . . . New spatial configurations cannot be achieved because regional devaluations are not allowed to run their course.[20]

In part, however, the forces of geographical inertia may originate in resistance, not to economic change as such, but to the real or imagined political and social consequences of spatial fixes. Discussing resistance to political consequences, Harvey focuses on China as the most promising site for an effective spatial fix to the ongoing overaccumulation crisis. Not only has China become the most rapidly growing attractor of foreign direct investment, but its internal market has been growing faster than any other. Even more dramatic, in Harvey's view, are the prospects for long-term infrastructural investment. The effort involved in building new subway systems, highways, railroads and the upgrading of urban infrastructures "is far larger *in toto* than that which the United States undertook during the 1950s and 1960s, and has the potential to absorb surpluses of capital for several years to come."[21]

---

19 Ibid., pp. 121–3; *Limits to Capital*, pp. 428–9.
20 Harvey, *Limits to Capital*, pp. 428–9.
21 Harvey, *New Imperialism*, p. 123.

Being largely deficit-financed, this enormous production of new space entails the risk of a major fiscal crisis of the Chinese state. Nevertheless, assuming that such a crisis can be avoided or successfully weathered, this spatial-temporal fix "has global implications not only for absorbing overaccumulated capital, but also for shifting the balance of economic and political power to China . . . and perhaps placing the Asian region, under Chinese leadership, in a much more competitive position vis-à-vis the United States." It is this possibility that makes US resistance to a smooth spatial fix all the more likely, despite the fact that this process holds out the best prospect for a solution of the underlying over-accumulation crisis.[22] The association between spatial fixes and hegemonic shifts thus strengthens the catch-22 that always confronts incumbent centers of capitalist development. The unconstrained development of new regions brings devaluation to these centers through intensified international competition. Constrained development abroad limits international competition, but blocks off opportunities for the profitable investment of surplus capital and so sparks internally generated devaluations.[23]

If the competitively challenged center is also a hegemonic center, either outcome threatens to deflate not just the value of its assets but its power as well. Worse still, it may threaten the social stability of the challenged center, because spatial fixes to over-accumulation crises always have a social dimension which affects their impetus, both positively and negatively. Harvey originally derived this social dimension from Hegel's observation in *The Philosophy of Right* that bourgeois society appears to be incapable of solving through *internal* mechanisms the problem of social inequality and instability that arises from its tendency to over-accumulate wealth at one pole and deprivation at the other. A "mature" civil society is thus driven to seek *external* solutions through foreign trade and colonial or imperial practices.[24] In *The New Imperialism*, Harvey supplements this observation with Hannah Arendt's contention that "Hobbes's Commonwealth is a vacillating structure and must always provide itself with new props from outside; otherwise it would collapse overnight into the aimless, senseless chaos of the private interests from which it sprang."[25]

22 Ibid., pp. 123–4.

23 Harvey, *Limits to Capital*, p. 435.

24 G.W.F. Hegel, *The Philosophy of Right* (New York, Oxford University Press, 1967), pp. 149–52; Harvey, *Spaces of Capital*, ch. 14; *Limits to Capital*, pp. 414–15.

25 Hannah Arendt, *The Origins of Totalitarianism* (New York, Harcourt, Brace & World, 1966), p. 142.

Harvey finds Arendt's proposition especially applicable to the United States. In this "quite extraordinary multicultural immigrant society . . . a fierce competitive individualism . . . perpetually revolutionizes social, economic, and political life . . . [rendering] democracy chronically unstable." The difficulty of achieving internal cohesion in such an ethnically mixed and intensely individualistic society produced the tradition that Richard Hofstadter described in the early 1960s as "the paranoid style" of American politics—the tradition, that is, whereby fear of some "other" (such as communism, socialism, anarchism, "outside agitators" or, for the left, capitalist or state conspiracies) is essential to the creation of political solidarities on the home front.[26] At times, "the whole country appears so unruly as to be ungovernable." Despite (or because of) a booming economy and the disappearance of the communist threat with the end of the Cold War, in Harvey's assessment the 1990s were such a time, and part of George W. Bush's electoral appeal in 2000 "was his promise of providing a strong-minded and tough moral compass to a civil society spiraling out of control." Be that as it may, September 11 "provided the impetus to break with the dissolute ways of the 1990s." In this respect, the war on Iraq was no mere diversion from difficulties at home; "it was a grand opportunity to impose a new sense of social order at home and bring the commonwealth to heel." Once again, the "evil enemy without became the prime force through which to exorcize or tame the devils lurking within."[27]

These observations suggest that spatial fixes are constrained, not just by resistance to economic relocation and associated geopolitical realignments, but by resistance to social change as well. For both meanings of spatial fix have inescapable social aspects. The literal fixing of capital in the form of ports, roads, airports, electricity grids, water and sewage systems, factories, housing, hospitals, schools, etc., in and on the land creates something more than a geographical landscape that facilitates the accumulation of capital. It also brings into being a particular human habitat of social interaction and

---

26 Harvey, *New Imperialism*, pp. 15–16, 49; R. Hofstadter, *The Paranoid Style in American Politics and Other Essays* (Cambridge, MA, Harvard University Press, 1996). Hofstadter introduced the notion of a paranoid style of American politics with specific reference to the radical right-wingers who succeeded in nominating Barry Goldwater at the 1964 convention of the Republican Party. Today, notes Krugman, those radicals control both Congress and the White House so that "political paranoia . . . has gone mainstream" ("The Paranoid Style," *New York Times*, October 9, 2006).

27 Harvey, *New Imperialism*, pp. 16–17.

reproduction. And conversely, the metaphorical spatial fix to over-accumulation crises involves much more than a devaluation of the capital fixed in and on the land that is made obsolete by the creation of a new geographical landscape. It involves also a devastation of the human habitat embedded in the obsolescent landscape of capital accumulation.

As Polanyi pointed out long ago with special reference to the over-accumulation crisis of the late nineteenth and early twentieth centuries, devastations of this kind inevitably call forth the "self-protection of society" in both progressive and reactionary political forms, mobilized by forces seeking to slow down or reverse the relocation of economic activities and political power involved in the spatial fix.[28] Such mobilizations strengthen geographical inertia, making the resolution of the over-accumulation crisis more problematic. There is, nonetheless, a possible way out of this impasse, namely, the use of financial means "to rid the system of overaccumulation by the visitation of crises of devaluation upon vulnerable territories." Harvey calls the deployment of these means the "sinister and destructive side of spatial-temporal fixes to the overaccumulation problem."[29] Let us briefly examine what this involves.

Accumulation by Dispossession

In discussing the absorption of surplus capital in the production of new space, Harvey points out that the conversion of unsold inventories and idle productive capacity into infrastructural investment depends crucially on the mediating role of financial and state institutions. "Surplus capital in shirts and shoes cannot be converted directly into an airport or research institute." But state and financial institutions have the capacity to generate credit commensurate to the surplus capital locked into the production of shirts and shoes, and to offer it to agencies capable and willing to invest it in airports, research institutes or whatever other forms of infrastructural investment are

---

28 Polanyi does not speak of spatial fixes or over-accumulation crises. Nevertheless, his emphasis on the opposition of "habitation versus improvement" conveys the same idea of a fundamental contradiction between the tendency of capital to relentlessly transform geographical landscapes on the one side, and the tendency of the communities embedded in those landscapes to resist such relentless transformations on the other. See Karl Polanyi, *The Great Transformation: The Political and Economic Origins of our Time* (Boston, MA, Beacon Press, 1957), ch. 3.

29 Harvey, *New Imperialism*, pp. 134–5.

involved in the production of new space. States also, of course, have
the power of converting surplus capital into the production of new
space through deficit financing, or through the allocation of tax
revenues to infrastructural investments.[30]

In the real world of capitalism, this constructive function of private
and public finance is invariably intertwined with speculative booms
and busts in both land and property markets and in government debt.
Speculative excesses divert capital from trade and production and
eventually meet their fate as devaluations. Nevertheless, the curtail-
ment of speculation would have "equally invidious results from the
standpoint of capitalism":

> The transformation of spatial configurations in the built environ-
> ment would be held in check and the physical landscape necessary for
> future accumulation could not hope to materialize. . . . Rampant
> speculation and unchecked appropriation, costly as they are for
> capital and life-sapping as they may be for labor, generate the chaotic
> ferment out of which new spatial configurations can grow.[31]

As long as speculative excesses favor—rather than hamper—the
emergence of new spatial configurations which enable trade and
production to expand further than they could have under the pre-
existing ones, they are "necessary evils" of an otherwise positive-sum
game. This is how official rhetoric justified the speculative excesses
and "irrational exuberance" of the 1990s: unfettered spatial mobility
of capital, it was claimed, was ultimately for the good of the
expanded reproduction of the global economy, including its most
vulnerable components. Underneath the official rhetoric, however,
lay the more destructive reality of a negative-sum game that hampered
rather than facilitated the emergence of new spatial configurations.

> Like war in relation to diplomacy, finance capital intervention
> backed by state power frequently amounts to accumulation by
> other means. An unholy alliance between state powers and the
> predatory aspects of finance capital forms the cutting edge of a
> "vulture capitalism" that is as much about cannibalistic practices
> and forced devaluations as it is about achieving harmonious global
> development.[32]

---

30 Ibid., p. 113; *Limits to Capital*, p. 404.
31 Ibid., p. 398; see also *New Imperialism*, pp. 131–2.
32 Harvey, *New Imperialism*, p. 136.

Harvey goes on to note that these "other means" are what Marx, following Smith, referred to as the means of "primitive" or "original" accumulation. He quotes approvingly Arendt's observation that "the emergence of 'superfluous' money . . . which could no longer find productive investment within the national borders," created a situation in the late nineteenth and early twentieth centuries whereby Marx's "original sin of simple robbery . . . had eventually to be repeated lest the motor of accumulation suddenly die down." Since a similar situation appears to have emerged again in the late twentieth and early twenty-first centuries, Harvey advocates a "general reevaluation of the continuous role and persistence of the predatory practices of 'primitive' or 'original' accumulation within the long historical geography of capital accumulation." And, since he finds it peculiar to call an ongoing process "primitive" or "original," he proposes to replace these terms with the concept of "accumulation by dispossession."[33]

Historically, accumulation by dispossession has taken many different forms, including the conversion of various forms of property rights (common, collective, state, etc.) into exclusive private-property rights; colonial, semi-colonial, neo-colonial, and imperial appropriations of assets and natural resources; and the suppression of alternatives to the capitalistic use of human and natural resources. Although much has been contingent and haphazard in the *modus operandi* of these processes, finance capital and the credit system have been major levers of dispossession, while the states, with their monopolies of violence and definitions of legality, have been crucial protagonists. But whatever its manifestations, agencies and instruments,

> What accumulation by dispossession does is to release a set of assets (including labor power) at very low (and in some instances zero) cost. Overaccumulated capital can seize hold of such assets and immediately turn them to profitable use.[34]

In Harvey's view, the rise of neo-liberal ideology and its associated politics of privatization since the late 1970s constitute the cutting edge of the present phase of accumulation by dispossession. The collapse of the Soviet Union and the savage privatization carried out under the

---

33 Ibid., pp. 142–4; Karl Marx, *Capital*, vol. I (Moscow, Foreign Languages Publishing House, 1959), p. 713; Arendt, *Origins of Totalitarianism*, p. 148.
34 Harvey, *New Imperialism*, pp. 145–9.

heading of "shock therapy," as advised by the capitalist powers and the international financial institutions, was a major episode in the release at fire-sale prices of hitherto unavailable assets. Equally important, however, has been the release of devalued assets in other lower-income countries in the wake of the financial crises that have punctuated the liberalization of capital flows in the 1980s and 1990s.[35] There is always a danger, of course, that local crises and place-based devaluations spin out of control, sparking a global collapse, or that they provoke a revolt against the system that is perceived to generate them. Even as it orchestrates the process to its own advantage, therefore, the hegemonic power must organize "bailouts" to keep global capital accumulation on track. The mixture of coercion and consent involved in such bailouts varies considerably. It nonetheless reveals, concludes Harvey,

> how hegemony gets constructed through financial mechanisms in such a way as to benefit the hegemon while leading the subaltern states on the supposedly golden path of capitalist development. The umbilical cord that ties together accumulation by dispossession and expanded reproduction is that given by finance capital and the institution of credit, backed, as ever, by state powers.[36]

As we have seen in Chapter 3, Marx also emphasized the crucial role that finance and state institutions have played in linking accumulation by dispossession (his primitive accumulation) in different locales to the expanded reproduction of historical capitalism. Unlike Harvey, however, he focused exclusively on the role of national debts and the international credit system as means of an invisible inter-capitalist cooperation, which "started" capital accumulation over and over again across the space-time of the world capitalist system, from its inception through to his own days. In Marx's sequence of cooperating capitalist states, we noted, what appears as a "starting point" in an emerging center (Holland, England, the United States) is at the same time the "result" of long periods of capital accumulation (and eventual over-accumulation) in previously established centers (Venice, Holland, England). Moreover, although Marx does not say so explicitly, each emergent leading center in his sequence consists of an agency of greater territorial scale and scope than its predecessors.

Marx's sequence—reformulated using Harvey's terminology—

---

35 Ibid., pp. 149–50, 156–61.
36 Ibid., pp. 151–2.

describes a series of spatial fixes of increasing scale and scope which provide profitable outlets for the surplus capital that over-accumulates in previously established capitalist centers and, simultaneously, *reduce* the need for accumulation by dispossession in the newly emerging centers. Were this tendency still in force today, the US and other mature centers of capital accumulation would be lending out "enormous amounts of capital" to emerging centers. Why is it then that the US, instead of lending, is borrowing enormous amounts of capital—as previously noted in Chapter 5—at the tune of more than $2 billion a day? And why is it that an increasingly large share of this capital comes from emerging centers, especially China?

This anomaly signals a blockage in the mechanisms that, in the past, facilitated the absorption of surplus capital in spatial fixes of increasing scale and scope. Harvey does not deal with this anomaly but his theory of the spatial fix suggests that the strengthening of the economic, political, and social forces of geographical inertia might be the cause of the blockage. Although this is definitely part of the explanation, another reason could be that accumulation by dispossession has reached its limits, either because the leading emerging center (China) is accumulating capital by other means—a plausible hypothesis, as we shall see in Chapter 12—or because coercive means can no longer create a spatial fix of sufficient scale and scope to absorb profitably the unprecedented mass of surplus capital that is accumulating worldwide.

Harvey does not investigate this possibility, nor does he clarify the connection between Washington's adoption of the New American Century program and accumulation by dispossession. While suggesting that "the dispossession of Iraqi oil" could mark the beginning of a continuation by military means of accumulation by dispossession, he also claims that the specific territorial logic that the neo-conservative imperial project sought to impose was deeply inconsistent with the capitalistic logic of power. Although military expenditures could boost the US economy in the short run, their more lasting effects would be greater US foreign indebtedness and therefore greater US vulnerability to capital flight. The risks for finance capital to continue to underwrite the US national debt would increase correspondingly, and if this situation did not change, sooner or later a flight of capital would force the US economy into a "structural adjustment" that would entail "an unheard of degree of austerity the likes of which have not been seen since the great depression of the 1930s."[37]

------

37 Ibid., pp. 201–2, 204–9.

Harvey speculated that under these circumstances, the United States "would be sorely tempted to use its power over oil to hold back China, sparking a geopolitical conflict at the very minimum in central Asia and perhaps spreading into a more global conflict." The only realistic alternative to such a disastrous outcome, in his view, is some sort of "new 'New Deal' " led by the United States and Europe, both domestically and internationally. "This means liberating the logic of capital . . . from its neo-liberal chains, reformulating state powers along much more interventionist and redistributive lines, curbing the speculative powers of finance capital, and decentralizing or democratically controlling the overwhelming power of oligopolies and monopolies (in particular . . . of the military-industrial complex)." This alternative project resembles the "ultra-imperialism" of cooperating capitalist powers envisaged long ago by Karl Kautsky and, as such, has its own negative connotations and consequences. It does nonetheless "seem to propose a far less violent and far more benevolent imperial trajectory than the raw militaristic imperialism currently offered up by the neo-conservative movement in the United States."[38]

In the four years since this was written, the unraveling of the neo-conservative imperial project has ruled out the possibility that the appropriation of Iraqi oil by military means could initiate a new phase of accumulation by dispossession and has further increased US foreign indebtedness and vulnerability to capital flight. Thus far, however, finance capital and foreign governments have continued to underwrite the US national debt, so that no flight of capital has forced the US economy into a structural adjustment that would entail some austerity, let alone, anything comparable to the experience of the 1930s. Although such a flight and structural adjustment remain possible, it is hard to tell how the United States would react if they actually materialize. As we shall see in the fourth part of the book, the Iraqi debacle has not discouraged the US from pursuing strategies towards China that may spark the kind of geopolitical conflicts envisaged by Harvey. But the global political economic environment has become less conducive to such an outcome, and in any event a Euro-American "ultra-imperialist" project is neither the only nor the most plausible alternative to the raw militaristic imperialism so unsuccessfully pursued by the Bush administration.

In order to identify the full range of historical possibilities opened up by the unraveling of US hegemony, the concepts of spatial fix and

---

38 Ibid., pp. 209–11.

accumulation by dispossession must be recast in a broader and longer historical perspective than Harvey does. Within this optic, the new imperialism will appear as the outcome of a protracted historical process consisting of spatial fixes of increasing scale and scope, on the one hand, and, on the other, of a US attempt to bring this process to an end through the formation of a US-centered world government. This attempt, I shall argue, was integral to US hegemony from the start. Under George W. Bush, it has simply reached its limits and in all likelihood will cease to be the primary determinant of ongoing transformations of the global political economy.

Over-Accumulation and Financialization

In *The Origins of Totalitarianism*, Arendt makes an insightful if somewhat functionalist observation concerning the relationship between the accumulation of capital and the accumulation of power.

> Hobbes's insistence on power as the motor of all things human . . . sprang from the theoretically indisputable proposition that a never-ending accumulation of property must be based on a never-ending accumulation of power. . . . The limitless process of capital accumulation *needs* the political structure of so "unlimited a Power" that it can protect growing property by constantly growing more powerful. . . . This process of never-ending accumulation of power *necessary* for the protection of a never-ending accumulation of capital determined the "progressive" ideology of the late nineteenth century and foreshadowed the rise of imperialism.[39]

After quoting this theoretical observation, Harvey writes that it corresponds "exactly" to my own empirical account of the succession of leading organizations that has promoted and sustained the formation of a world-capitalist system, from the Italian city-states through the Dutch, the British, and the US phases of hegemony.[40]

---

39 Arendt, *Origins of Totalitarianism*, p. 143. I have italicized "needs" and "necessary" to highlight for future reference the functionalist nature of Arendt's contention.

40 Harvey, *New Imperialism*, pp. 34–5. My empirical observations were made independently of Arendt's theoretical contentions. I am grateful to Harvey for pointing out their correspondence.

Just as in the late seventeenth and early eighteenth centuries the hegemonic role had become too large for a state of the size and resources of the United Provinces, so in the early twentieth century that role had become too large for a state of the size and resources of the United Kingdom. In both instances, the hegemonic role fell on a state—the United Kingdom in the eighteenth century, the United States in the twentieth century—that had come to enjoy a substantial "protection rent," that is, exclusive cost advantages associated with absolute or relative geostrategic insularity. . . . But that state in both instances was also the bearer of sufficient weight in the capitalist world-economy to be able to shift the balance of power among the competing states in whatever direction it saw fit. And since the capitalist world-economy had expanded considerably in the nineteenth century, the territory and resources required to become hegemonic in the early twentieth century were much greater than in the eighteenth century.[41]

The correspondence, though undeniable, is not as "exact" as Harvey suggests. For Arendt's observation refers to the accumulation of power and capital *within states*, whereas mine refers to the accumulation of power and capital in an evolving *system of states*. The difference is crucial in more than one respect.

Arendt draws our attention to the process whereby individual capitalist states tend to experience an accumulation of "superfluous money" (that is, of more capital than can be profitably reinvested within their national boundaries) and a need to grow more powerful in order to be able to protect growing property. From this perspective, imperialism of the capitalist sort is a policy aimed both at finding profitable external outlets for surplus capital and at strengthening the state. My observation, in contrast, draws our attention to the process whereby increasingly powerful capitalist organizations have become the agency of the expansion of a system of accumulation and rule that, from the start, encompassed a multiplicity of states. From this perspective, imperialism of the capitalist sort is an aspect of the recurrent struggles through which capitalist states have used coercive means in the attempt to turn in their favor the spatial shifts entailed in the "endless" accumulation of capital and power.[42]

---

41 Arrighi, *Long Twentieth Century*, p. 62.

42 I prefer the qualifier "endless" instead of the "never-ending" used by Arendt, because "endless" conveys the more accurate meaning of an accumulation that allegedly "never ends" and is at the same time an "end in itself," whether it actually ends or not.

As Harvey underscores, finance capital backed by state power plays a crucial mediating role both in the production of space that is involved in the enlarged reproduction of capital and in the "cannibalistic practices and forced devaluations" that constitute the essence of accumulation by dispossession. He is nonetheless vague about the world-historical coordinates of this role. Like Arendt, he seems to adhere to the view that finance capital has been an outgrowth of nineteenth-century industrial capitalism. While this may be true of capitalist development in some states, it is certainly not true of capitalist development on a world scale.

As anticipated in Chapter 3, Braudel has demonstrated that financialization (the capacity of finance capital "to take over and dominate, for a while at least, all the activities of the business world") in response to the over-accumulation of capital ("the accumulation of capital on a scale beyond the normal channels for investment") has been in evidence in the European economy long before capitalism became associated with industrialism. To this we should now add that Braudel also provides a list of dates, places, and agencies that enable us to ground in world-historical space and time Harvey's theoretical considerations concerning finance capital. Braudel suggests that the withdrawal of the Dutch from commerce around 1740 to become "the bankers of Europe" was typical of a recurrent world-systemic tendency. The same process was in evidence in Italy in the fifteenth century, and again around 1560, when the leading groups of the Genoese business diaspora gradually relinquished commerce to exercise for about seventy years a rule over European finances comparable to that exercised in the twentieth century by the Bank of International Settlement at Basle—"a rule that was so discreet and sophisticated that historians for a long time failed to notice it." After the Dutch, the British replicated the tendency during and after the Great Depression of 1873–96, when "the fantastic venture of the industrial revolution" created an overabundance of money capital. After the equally "fantastic venture" of so-called Fordism–Keynesianism, we may add, US capital since the 1970s has followed a similar trajectory. "[Every] capitalist development of this order seems, by reaching the stage of financial expansion, to have in some sense announced its maturity: it [is] *a sign of autumn*."[43]

In light of these observations, Marx's general formula of capital

---

43 Fernand Braudel, *Civilization and Capitalism, 15th–18th Century, Volume III: The Perspective of the World* (New York, Harper & Row, 1984), pp. 157, 164, 242–3, 246, emphasis added.

(MCM') may be reinterpreted as depicting, not just the logic of individual capitalist investments, but also a recurrent pattern of world capitalism. The central aspect of this pattern is the alternation of epochs of material expansion (MC phases of capital accumulation) with phases of financial expansion (CM' phases). In phases of material expansion, money capital (M) sets in motion an increasing mass of commodities (C), including labor-power and gifts of nature; and, in phases of financial expansion, an expanded mass of money capital (M') sets itself free from its commodity form, and accumulation proceeds through financial deals (as in Marx's abridged formula MM'). Taken together, the two epochs or phases constitute what I have called a *systemic cycle of accumulation* (MCM').[44]

Starting from these premises, I have identified four such cycles, each encompassing a "long" century: a Genoese–Iberian cycle, covering the period from the fifteenth through the early seventeenth centuries; a Dutch cycle, from the late sixteenth through the late eighteenth centuries; a British cycle, from the mid eighteenth through the early twentieth centuries; and a US cycle, from the late nineteenth through the latest financial expansion. Each cycle is named after (and defined by) the particular complex of governmental and business agencies that led the world capitalist system towards first the material and then the financial expansions that jointly constitute the cycle. Consecutive systemic cycles of accumulation overlap with each other at their beginnings and ends, because phases of financial expansion have not only been the "autumn" of major developments of world capitalism. They have also been periods in the course of which a new leading governmental-business complex emerged and over time reorganized the system, making its further expansion possible.[45]

Material and financial expansions are both processes of a system of accumulation and rule that has increased in scale and scope over the centuries but has encompassed from its earliest beginnings a large number and variety of governmental and business agencies. Within each cycle, material expansions occur because of the emergence of a particular bloc of governmental and business agencies capable of leading the system towards a new spatial fix that creates the conditions for the emergence of wider or deeper divisions of labor. Under

44 Arrighi, *Long Twentieth Century*, pp. 4–6.

45 On the historical and theoretical underpinning of systemic cycles of accumulation, see Arrighi, *Long Twentieth Century*. For a detailed analysis of the transitions from Dutch to British and from British to US hegemony, see Giovanni Arrighi and Beverly J. Silver, *Chaos and Governance in the Modern World System* (Minneapolis, MN, University of Minnesota Press, 1999).

these conditions, returns to capital invested in trade and production increase; profits tend to be plowed back into the further expansion of trade and production more or less routinely; and, knowingly or unknowingly, the system's main centers cooperate in sustaining one another's expansion. Over time, however, the investment of an ever-growing mass of profits in trade and production inevitably leads to the accumulation of capital over and above what can be reinvested in the purchase and sale of commodities without drastically reducing profit margins. At this point, capitalist agencies tend to invade one another's spheres of operation; the division of labor that previously defined the terms of their mutual cooperation breaks down; and competition becomes increasingly vicious. The prospects of recouping the capital invested in trade and production decrease, and capitalist agencies tend to keep in liquid form a larger proportion of their incoming cash flows. The stage is thus set for the change of phase from material to financial expansion.

In all financial expansions of systemic significance, the accumulation of surplus capital in liquid form had three main effects. First, it transformed surplus capital embodied in landscapes, infrastructures, and means of trade and production into an expanding supply of money and credit. Second, it deprived governments and populations of the revenues that they previously derived from the trade and production that were no longer undertaken because unprofitable or too risky. Finally, and largely as a corollary of the first two effects, it created highly profitable market niches for financial intermediaries capable of channeling the expanding supply of liquidity into the hands either of governments and populations in financial straits, or of public and private entrepreneurs intent on opening up new avenues of profit-making in trade and production.

As a rule, the leading agencies of the preceding material expansion were best positioned to occupy these highly profitable market niches and thus lead the system of accumulation towards the financial expansion. This capacity to switch from one kind of leadership to another has been the main reason why, after experiencing the signal crisis of their hegemonies, all incumbent centers of world capitalism enjoyed a *belle époque* of temporary but nonetheless significant reflation of their wealth and power. The reason why all these *belles époques* have been temporary phenomena is because they tended to deepen rather than solve the underlying over-accumulation crisis. They have thereby exacerbated economic competition, social conflicts, and interstate rivalries to levels that it was beyond the incumbent centers' power to control. Before we proceed to discuss the ever-changing nature of the struggles that ensued, two observations are in order.

The first is that all financial expansions entailed accumulation by dispossession. Suffice it to mention that lending surplus capital to governments and populations in financial straits was profitable only to the extent that it redistributed assets or incomes from the borrowers to the agencies that controlled surplus capital. Massive redistributions of this kind have indeed been key ingredients of all the *belles époques* of finance capitalism—from Renaissance Florence to the Reagan and Clinton eras. In and by themselves, however, they provided no solution to the underlying over-accumulation crisis. On the contrary, by transferring purchasing power from strata and communities with a lower liquidity preference (that is, with a lesser disposition to accumulate money capital) to strata and communities with a higher liquidity preference, they tended to provoke an even greater over-accumulation of capital and the recurrence of profitability crises. Moreover, by alienating the strata and communities that were being dispossessed, they tended to provoke a legitimacy crisis as well. A combination of profitability and legitimacy crises is, of course, the underlying condition to which Arendt and Harvey trace the imperialism of their respective times. Nevertheless, comparable conditions were in evidence also in earlier financial expansions, directly or indirectly exacerbating conflicts within and among states.[46]

At least initially, escalating interstate conflicts benefited incumbent centers, because it inflated states' financial needs and thereby intensified their mutual competition for mobile capital. But, once the conflicts escalated into major wars, the incumbent centers generally lost out even in the financial sphere to newly emergent centers that were better positioned to provide the endless accumulation of capital and power with a spatial fix of greater scale and scope than the previous one.

This brings us to the second observation, which concerns the transfer of surplus capital from incumbent to emerging centers of capitalist development. As previously noted, the role that Marx attributed to the credit system in promoting such a reallocation points to an invisible inter-capitalist cooperation that *reduces* the need for accumulation by dispossession in the emerging centers. We also noted that Marx's sequence of leading capitalist centers (Venice,

---

46 Arrighi, *Long Twentieth Century*; Arrighi and Silver, *Chaos and Governance*, esp. ch. 3.

Holland, England, United States) points to a series of spatial fixes of increasing scale and scope that created the conditions for the resolution of the preceding over-accumulation crisis and the take-off of a new phase of material expansion. To this we should now add that wars played a crucial role. In at least two instances (from Holland to Britain and from Britain to the United States), the reallocation of surplus capital from mature to emerging centers began long before the escalation of interstate conflicts. This early transfer, however, established claims on the assets and future incomes of the emerging centers that brought back to the mature centers flows of interest, profits, and rents that equaled or even surpassed the original investment. Instead of weakening, it therefore strengthened the position of the incumbent centers in the world of high finance. But once wars escalated, the creditor–debtor relation that linked the mature to the emerging centers was forcibly reversed and the reallocation to the emerging centers became both more substantial and permanent.

The mechanisms of the reversal varied considerably from transition to transition. In the Dutch–British reversal, the key mechanism was the plunder of India during and after the Seven Years' War, which enabled Britain to buy back its national debt from the Dutch and thus start the Napoleonic Wars nearly free from foreign debt. In the British–US reversal, the key mechanism was US wartime supply of armaments, machinery, food, and raw materials far in excess of what Britain could pay out of current incomes. But, in both cases, wars were essential ingredients in the change of guard at the commanding heights of world capitalism.[47]

Origins of the Capitalist Strategy of Power

Contrary to the reading of some critics, my concept of systemic cycles of accumulation does not portray the history of capitalism as "the

47 On Dutch–British reversal, see Ralph Davis, *The Industrial Revolution and British Overseas Trade*, (Leicester, Leicester University Press, 1979), pp. 55–6; P.J. Cain and A.G. Hopkins, "The Political Economy of British Expansion Overseas, 1750–1914," *Economic History Review*, 2nd series, 33, 4 (1980), p. 471 and Arrighi, *Long Twentieth Century*, pp. 208–12. On the British–US reversal, see Barry Eichengreen and Richard Portes, "Debt and Default in the 1930s: Causes and Consequences," *European Economic Review*, 30 (1986), pp. 601–3; Paul Kennedy, *Rise and Fall of the Great Powers*, p. 268; Arrighi and Silver, *Chaos and Governance*), pp. 73–7. The peculiarities of the ongoing US–East Asian reversal have already been hinted at in Part II and will be explored further in future chapters.

eternal return of the same."[48] It shows instead that precisely when the "same" (i.e., recurrent system-wide financial expansions) appeared to return, new rounds of inter-capitalist competition, interstate rivalries, accumulation by dispossession, and production of space on an ever-increasing scale *revolutionized* the geography and mode of operation of world capitalism, as well as its relationship to imperialistic practices. Thus, if we focus on the "containers of power"[49] that have housed the "headquarters" of the leading capitalist agencies of successive cycles of accumulation, we immediately see a progression from a city-state and a cosmopolitan business diaspora (the Genoese); to a proto-national state (the United Provinces) and its joint-stock chartered companies; to a multinational state (the United Kingdom) and its globe-encircling tributary empire; to a continent-sized national state (the United States) and its world-encompassing system of transnational corporations, military bases, and institutions of world governance.[50]

As this progression shows, none of the agencies that have promoted the formation and expansion of world capitalism correspond to the mythical national state of political and social theory: Genoa and the United Provinces were something less, the United Kingdom and the United States were something more than national states. And, from the very beginning, the networks of accumulation and power that enabled these agencies to play a leading role in the formation and expansion of world capitalism were not "contained" within the metropolitan territories that defined their proto-national, multinational, or national identities. Indeed, long-distance trade, high finance, and related imperialistic practices (that is, war-making and empire-building activities) were even more essential sources of profit for the early than for the later agencies. As Arendt maintains, imperialism must indeed be considered "the first stage in the political rule of the bourgeoisie rather than the last stage of capitalism."[51] But that first stage must be situated in early modern

48 Michael Hardt and Antonio Negri, *Empire* (Cambridge, MA, Harvard University Press, 2000), p. 239.

49 Anthony Giddens, *The Nation-State and Violence* (Berkeley, CA, University of California Press, 1987), introduced this expression to characterize states, especially national states. As the reader will notice, the expression is used here to designate a broader set of organizations.

50 For detailed accounts of this progression, see Arrighi, *Long Twentieth Century*; Arrighi and Silver, *Chaos and Governance*, ch. 1; Giovanni Arrighi and Beverly J. Silver, "Capitalism and World (Dis)Order," *Review of International Studies*, 27 (2001).

51 Arendt, *Origins of Totalitarianism*, p. 138.

city-states rather than in late nineteenth-century national states, as she suggests.

The fact that imperialistic practices were a more critical source of profit in the early than in the later stages of capitalist expansion does not mean that the policies and actions of the later agencies have been less imperialistic than those of the earlier ones. On the contrary, they have become more rather than less so, because of an increasing interpenetration of the capitalist and territorialist strategies of power. This tendency can be clearly observed by comparing the historical geography of successive systemic cycles of accumulation.

Even before the first cycle began to materialize, some Italian city-states, most notably Venice, had demonstrated the viability of a capitalist strategy of power in the early modern European context. Rulers pursuing territorialist strategies sought to accumulate power by expanding the size of their territorial domains. The bourgeoisies that controlled the Italian city-states, in contrast, sought to accumulate power by expanding their command over money capital, while abstaining from territorial acquisitions unless they were absolutely essential to the accumulation of capital. The success of this strategy rested on the interaction of two conditions. One was the balance of power among the larger territorial organizations of the European subcontinent. The other was the extroversion of the emerging European system of states—the fact, that is, that the successful pursuit of profit and power *within* Europe depended critically on privileged access to resources *outside* Europe through trade or plunder. The balance of power ensured not just the political survival of the territorially parsimonious capitalist organizations. It also ensured that the competition among the larger territorial organizations for financial resources would empower the capitalist organizations that controlled those resources. At the same time, the extroversion of the European power struggle ensured that this competition would be continually renewed by the need of the states to outdo one another in gaining privileged access to extra-European resources.[52]

Initially, the combination of these two conditions was extremely favorable to the capitalist strategy of power. Indeed, it was so favorable that its most successful agency was an almost entirely deterritorialized organization. For the Genoese–Iberian designation of the first systemic cycle of accumulation does not refer to the Republic of Genoa as such—a city-state which throughout the cycle led a politically precarious existence and "contained" very little

---

52 Arrighi, *Long Twentieth Century*, chs 1 and 2.

power. It refers instead to the transcontinental commercial and financial networks that enabled the Genoese capitalist class, organized in a cosmopolitan diaspora, to deal on a par with the most powerful rulers of Europe and to turn these rulers' mutual competition for capital into a powerful engine for the self-expansion of its own capital. From this position of strength, the Genoese capitalist diaspora entered into a highly profitable relationship of informal political exchange with the rulers of Portugal and imperial Spain. By virtue of this relationship, Iberian rulers undertook all the war- and state-making activities involved in the formation of a world-encircling market and empire, while Genoa's diaspora capitalists specialized in facilitating commercially and financially these activities. Unlike the Fuggers, who were ruined by their connection with imperial Spain, the Genoese probably gained from the relationship more than their Iberian partners did. As Richard Ehrenberg noted, "it was not the Potosí silver mines, but the Genoese fairs of exchange which made it possible for Philip II to conduct his world power policy decade after decade." But in the process, as Suarez de Figueroa lamented in 1617, Spain and Portugal were turned into "the Indies of the Genoese."[53]

In the second (Dutch) systemic cycle of accumulation, the conditions for the pursuit of a strictly capitalist strategy of power remained favorable, but not as favorable as they had been in the first cycle. To be sure, the intense conflicts that set the larger territorial states of Europe against one another were essential to the Dutch ascent, and in 1648 the Peace of Westphalia provided the European balance of power with some institutional stability. Moreover, in the seventeenth century, the Dutch could expand the spatial scale of their operations from the Baltic to the Atlantic and the Indian Ocean as easily and swiftly as they did only because the Iberians had already conquered the Americas and established a direct sea route to the East Indies. Nevertheless, the geopolitical landscape created in Europe by the Iberian world-encircling spatial fix left no room for the kind of capitalist strategy of power that had made the fortunes of the Genoese diaspora in the "long" sixteenth century. Indeed, the Dutch succeeded in carving out of the Iberian seaborne and territorial empires the Amsterdam-centered system of commercial entrepôts and joint-stock

---

53 Ehrenberg is quoted in Peter Kriedte, *Peasants, Landlords, and Merchant Capitalists: Europe and the World Economy, 1500–1800* (Cambridge, Cambridge University Press, 1983), p. 47, and de Figueroa in J. H. Elliott, *The Old World and the New 1492–1650* (Cambridge, Cambridge University Press, 1970), p. 96. For details on the Genoese–Iberian cycle, see Arrighi, *Long Twentieth Century*, pp. 109–32, 145–51.

chartered companies that became the foundation of the second systemic cycle of accumulation precisely by doing what the Genoese had not been doing, that is, by becoming self-sufficient in war- and state-making.[54]

Violet Barbour has claimed that this Amsterdam-centered system was the last instance of "a veritable empire of trade and credit . . . held by a city in her own right, unsustained by the forces of a modern state."[55] Since the United Provinces combined features of the disappearing city-states with those of the rising national states, whether it qualifies as a "modern state" is a controversial issue. But whichever features one may want to emphasize, the Dutch cycle does appear to have been the watershed between two distinct ages of historical capitalism: the age of the city on the one side, and that of the territorial state and the national economy on the other.

> At the heart of a Europe swollen with success and tending, by the end of the eighteenth century, to embrace the whole world, *the dominant central zone had to grow in size to balance the entire structure.* Cities standing alone, or almost alone, by now lacked sufficient purchase on the neighboring economies from which they drew strength; soon they would no longer measure up to the task. The territorial states would take over.[56]

We shall deal later with the issue of why the central zone had to "grow in size" so as "to balance the entire structure." For now let us note that the emergence of territorial states as the leading agencies of capitalist expansion brought about a far greater interpenetration of capitalism and imperialism than had hitherto been the case. Although the fortunes of the Genoese capitalist diaspora had been thoroughly dependent on the war-making and empire-building activities of its Iberian partners, the diaspora itself abstained completely from such activities. Genoese capitalism and Iberian imperialism sustained each other but through a relationship of political exchange that reproduced their separate organizational identities from beginning to end. While no such separation existed in the Dutch cycle, the eighty-year struggle for independence that the United Provinces waged against imperial

---

54 Arrighi, *Long Twentieth Century*, pp. 36–47, 127–51; Arrighi and Silver, *Chaos and Governance*, pp. 39–41, 99–109.

55 Violet Barbour, *Capitalism in Amsterdam in the Seventeenth Century* (Baltimore, MD, Johns Hopkins University Press, 1950), p. 13.

56 Braudel, *Civilization and Capitalism, 15th–18th Century, Volume 3*, p. 175, emphasis added.

Spain endowed Dutch capitalism with a long-lasting anti-imperialist identity. Even after that struggle had come to an end, Peter de la Court could portray Holland as a "cat" in a jungle of "wild beasts." The wild beasts were the territorial states of Europe: "Lions, Tygers, Wolves, Foxes, Bears, or any other Beast of Prey, which often perish by their own Strength, and are taken where they lie in wait for others." A cat does resemble a lion. But Holland was and would remain a cat because "we who are naturally Merchants, cannot be turned into Souldiers" and "there is more to be gotten by us in a time of Peace and good Trading, than by War, and the ruin of Trade."[57]

In reality, the Dutch system of accumulation, which would indeed have benefited more from peace than from war after Westphalia, had been previously built through war and the ruin of Iberian trade. Moreover, in the non-European world, especially in the Indonesian archipelago, the "cat of Holland" was second to none of the European "beasts of prey" in the use of violence to destroy existing landscapes of trade and production in order to create landscapes more favorable to the endless accumulation of Dutch capital. De la Court's metaphor does nonetheless draw a distinction between the imperialism of the larger territorial states of Europe and the capitalism of the territorially parsimonious Dutch Republic that remained discernible throughout the Dutch cycle. For the strategy of power of the Dutch Republic was primarily based, not on the expansion of its territorial domains, but on the expansion of its control over money capital and the international credit system. Combining the strengths of the Venetian and Genoese strategies, it relied on money and credit as the key means by which the struggles among the territorial states of Europe were turned into an engine of the self-expansion of Dutch capital. Over time, however, the escalation of these struggles undermined the success of the Dutch strategy, and simultaneously created the conditions of a complete fusion of capitalism and imperialism in the practices of the state that eventually emerged as the new leader of capitalist expansion.[58]

In order to gain some insight into the reasons for this fusion we must return to Braudel's contention that the territorial scale of the dominant center of the system of accumulation had somehow to grow in step with the increase in the spatial scale of the system. Braudel himself suggests that one of the main reasons why the small territorial

---

57 Quoted in Peter Taylor, "Ten Years that Shook the World? The United Provinces as First Hegemonic State," *Sociological Perspectives*, 37, 1 (1994), pp. 36, 38.

58 Arrighi, *Long Twentieth Century*, pp. 144–58; Arrighi and Silver, *Chaos and Governance*, pp. 48–51.

scale of Holland became a handicap in holding the center of the globalizing European system of accumulation was a structural shortage of labor. "Holland," he claims, "could only fulfil her role as freighter of the high seas if she could obtain the necessary extra labor from among the wretched of Europe." It was the poverty of the rest of Europe that "enabled the Dutch to 'set up' their Republic."[59] But once an increasing number of European states sought to internalize within their own domains the sources of Dutch wealth and power through one variant or another of mercantilism and imperialism, competition over European labor resources intensified and the size of the Dutch Republic turned into an increasingly insurmountable handicap. As Stavorinus lamented,

> ever since the year 1740, the many naval wars, the great increase of trade and navigation, particularly in many countries, where formerly these pursuits were little attended to, and the consequent great and continual demands for able seamen, both for ships of war and for merchantmen, have so considerably diminished the supply of them, that, in our own country, where there formerly used to be a great abundance of mariners, it is now, with great difficulty and expense, that any vessel can procure a proper number of able hands to navigate her.[60]

Nor could the Dutch compete with larger territorial states in settling colonies, simply because too few Dutchmen were available for the purpose. As a result, in North America most of the colonial population and nearly all of the well-to-do merchant, planter, and professional classes were of British origin, accustomed to manufactures from British sources and sales through British factors. English ports thus began to challenge and then to outdo Amsterdam's entrepôt trade. Moreover, while Dutch industries languished, English industries expanded rapidly under the joint impact of Atlantic trade and increasing governmental protection.[61] British success in out-competing the Dutch, both in over-

---

59 Braudel, *Civilization and Capitalism, 15th–18th Century, Volume 3*, pp. 192–3.

60 Quoted in Charles R. Boxer, *The Dutch Seaborne Empire 1600–1800* (New York, Knopf, 1965), p. 109.

61 Ibid., p. 109; Ralph Davis, "The Rise of Protection in England, 1689–1786," *Economic History Review*, 2nd series, 19 (1966), p. 307, and "English Foreign Trade, 1700–1774," in W.E. Minchinton, ed., *The Growth of English Overseas Trade in the Seventeenth and Eighteenth Centuries* (London, Methuen, 1969), p. 115; Minchinton, *Growth of English Overseas Trade*, p. 13.

seas commercial expansion and domestic industrial expansion, gradually reduced Amsterdam's share of entrepôt trade. But the death blow to
Dutch commercial supremacy came from the spread of mercantilism to
the Baltic region and the consequent disruption of what had all along
been the "mother trade" of Dutch capitalism.[62]

The Fusion of Capitalism and Imperialism

It was in this context that the United Kingdom emerged as the new leader
of the endless accumulation of capital and power through a complete
fusion of capitalism and imperialism. Once London had displaced
Amsterdam as the financial center of the globalizing European system
of states, as it did by the 1780s, the United Kingdom became the main
beneficiary of interstate competition for mobile capital. In this respect, it
became the heir of the capitalist tradition initiated by the Genoese in the
"long" sixteenth century and developed further by the Dutch in the
"long" seventeenth century. In other respects, however, the United
Kingdom was also the heir of the imperialist tradition initiated by the
Iberian partners of the Genoese—a tradition which the "anti-imperi-
alism" of the Dutch and the stabilization of the European balance of
power at Westphalia had reversed only temporarily and partially.[63]

This peculiar fusion of capitalism and imperialism provided the
endless accumulation of capital and power with a spatial and
organizational fix that differed from that of the Dutch cycle in
key respects. Geopolitically, the system of states established at
Westphalia under Dutch leadership was truly anarchic—characterized, that is, by the absence of central rule. The interstate system
reconstituted after the Napoleonic Wars under British leadership, in
contrast, was one in which the European balance of power was
transformed, for a while at least, into an instrument of informal

---

62 "The basic reason for the decisive decline of the Dutch world-trading system
in the 1720s and 1730s was the wave of new-style industrial mercantilism which swept
practically the entire continent from around 1720. . . . Down to 1720 countries such
as Prussia, Russia, Sweden, and Denmark–Norway had lacked the means and, with
the Great Northern War in progress, the opportunity, to emulate the aggressive
mercantilism of England and France. But in the years around 1720 a heightened sense
of competition among the northern powers, combined with the diffusion of new
technology and skills, often Dutch or Huguenot in origin, led to a dramatic change.
Within the next two decades most of northern Europe was incorporated into a
framework of systematic industrial mercantilist policy" (Jonathan Israel, *Dutch
Primacy in World Trade, 1585–1740* [Oxford, Clarendon Press, 1989], pp. 383–4).

63 See Arrighi, *Long Twentieth Century*, pp. 47–58, 159–69.

British rule. Having gained mastery over the balance of power during the wars, the British took a number of steps to ensure that it would remain in their hands. While reassuring the absolutist governments of Continental Europe organized in the Holy Alliance that changes in the balance of power would come about only through consultation in the newly established Concert of Europe, they created two counter-weights to their power. In Europe, they requested and obtained that defeated France be included among the Great Powers, albeit held in check by being ranked with second-tier powers. In the Americas, they countered the Holy Alliance's designs to restore colonial rule by asserting the principle of non-intervention in Latin America and by inviting the United States to support the principle. What later became the Monroe doctrine—the idea that Europe should not intervene in American affairs—was initially a British policy.[64]

By pursuing its national interest in the preservation and consolida-tion of a fragmented and "balanced" power structure in Continental Europe, Britain fostered the perception that its overwhelming world power was being exercised in the general interest—the interest of former enemies as well as of former allies, of the new republics of the Americas as well as of the old monarchies of Europe. This perception was consolidated by Britain's *unilateral* liberalization of its trade, which culminated in the repeal of the Corn Laws in 1848 and of the Navigation Acts in 1849. Over the following twenty years, close to one-third of the exports of the rest of the world went to Britain. The United States, with almost 25 percent of all imports and exports, was Britain's single largest trading partner, while European countries accounted for another 25 percent. Through this policy, Britain cheapened the domestic costs of vital supplies and at the same time provided the means of payment for other countries to buy its manufactures. It also drew much of the Western world into its trading orbit, fostering interstate cooperation and securing low protection costs for its overseas trade and territorial empire.[65]

---

64 See Polanyi, *Great Transformation*, pp. 5–7, 259–62; David Weigall, *Britain and the World, 1815–1986: A Dictionary of International Relations* (New York, Batsford, 1987), pp. 58, 111; Henry Kissinger, *A World Restored: Europe after Napoleon. The Politics of Conservation in a Revolutionary Age* (New York, Grosset & Dunlap, 1964), pp. 38–9; Alonso Aguilar, *Pan-Americanism from Monroe to the Present: A View from the Other Side* (New York, Monthly Review Press, 1968), pp. 23–5.

65 Michael Barrat Brown, *After Imperialism* (London, Heinemann, 1963), p. 63; Paul Kennedy, *The Rise and Fall of British Naval Mastery* (London, Scribner, 1976), pp. 156–64, 149–50; Joseph S. Nye, *Bound to Lead: The Changing Nature of American Power* (New York, Basic Books, 1990), p. 53.

Also in this respect, the UK-centered system of accumulation differed radically from its Dutch predecessor. In both systems, the metropolitan territories of the leading capitalist state played the role of central entrepôt. But soon after the Dutch system had become predominant, it began to be challenged by the aggressive mercantilism of both Britain and France. The British system, in contrast, could consolidate further through the longest peace in European history—Polanyi's Hundred Years' Peace (1815–1914). British mastery of the European balance of power and centrality in world trade were mutually reinforcing conditions of this long peace. The first reduced the chances that any state would have the capabilities to challenge British commercial supremacy in the same way the British had challenged Dutch supremacy after Westphalia. The second "caged" a growing number of territorial states in a global division of labor that strengthened each one's interest in preserving the UK-centered system. And the more general this interest became, the easier it was for Britain to manipulate the balance of power to prevent the emergence of challenges to its commercial supremacy.

This combination of circumstances depended critically on a third difference between the British and Dutch systems. Whereas the Dutch entrepôt was primarily a commercial one, the British entrepôt was also industrial, the "workshop of the world." England had long been one of the main industrial centers of Europe. But it was only in the course of the eighteenth century that the expansion of England's entrepôt trade and massive governmental expenditure during the Napoleonic Wars turned British industrial capabilities into an effective instrument of national aggrandizement.[66] The Napoleonic Wars, in particular, constituted a decisive turning point. In McNeill's words,

> government demand created a precocious iron industry, with a capacity in excess of peacetime needs, as the postwar depression 1816–20 showed. But it also created the condition for future growth by giving British ironmasters extraordinary incentives for finding new uses for the cheaper product their new, large-scale furnaces were able to turn out. Military demands on the British economy thus went far to shape the subsequent phases of the industrial revolution, allowing the improvement of steam engines and making such critical innovations as the iron railway and iron ship possible at a time and under conditions which simply

---

66 Arrighi, *Long Twentieth Century*, ch. 3.

would not have existed without the wartime impetus to iron production.[67]

In the course of the nineteenth century, railways and steamships forged the globe into a single interacting economy as never before. In 1848, there was nothing resembling a railway network outside Britain. Over the next thirty years or so, notes Eric Hobsbawm, "the most remote parts of the world [began] to be linked together by means of communication which had no precedent for regularity, for the capacity to transport vast quantities of goods and numbers of people, and above all, for speed." As this system of transport and communication took shape, world trade expanded at unprecedented rates. From the mid 1840s to the mid 1870s, the volume of seaborne merchandise between the major European states more than quadrupled, while the value of the exchanges between Britain and the Ottoman empire, Latin America, India, and Australasia increased about sixfold. Eventually, this expansion of world trade intensified interstate competition and rivalries. But in the middle decades of the century the advantages of hooking up to the British entrepôt so as to draw upon its equipment and resources were too great to be willingly forgone by any European state.[68]

Unlike the seventeenth-century Dutch world-trading system, which was always a purely mercantile one, the nineteenth-century British world-trading system thus became also an integrated system of mechanized transport and production. Britain was both the chief organizer and the chief beneficiary of this system, within which it performed the double function of central clearinghouse and regulator. While the function of central clearinghouse was inseparable from Britain's role as the workshop of the world, the function of central regulator was inseparable from its role as the leading empire-builder in the non-European world. To return to de la Court's metaphor, unlike Holland, which was and remained a "cat," Britain was and remained a territorial "beast of prey" whose conversion to capitalism only whetted its appetite for territorial expansion. As previously noted, the plunder of India enabled Britain to buy back its national

67 William McNeill, *The Pursuit of Power: Technology, Armed Force, and Society since A.D. 1000* (Chicago, University of Chicago Press, 1982), pp. 211–12. See also Leland H. Jenks, *The Migration of British Capital to 1875* (New York and London, Knopf, 1938), pp. 133–4, and Eric J. Hobsbawm, *Industry and Empire: An Economic History of Britain* since 1750 (London, Weidenfeld & Nicolson, 1968), p. 34.

68 Eric J. Hobsbawm, *The Age of Capital 1848–1875* (New York, New American Library, 1979), pp. 37–9, 50–4.

debt from the Dutch and to start the Napoleonic Wars nearly free from foreign debt. It thereby facilitated the sixfold increase in British public expenditure in 1792–1815 to which McNeill attributes a decisive role in shaping the capital-goods phase of the Industrial Revolution. More important, it initiated the process of conquest of a territorial empire in South Asia that was to become the principal pillar of Britain's global power.

The unfolding of this process of territorial conquest has been detailed elsewhere.[69] Here, I shall simply mention the two main aspects of its relationship to the enlarged reproduction of British power, one demographic and one financial. India's huge demographic resources buttressed British world power both commercially and militarily. Commercially, Indian workers were forcibly transformed from major competitors of European textile industries into major producers of cheap food and raw materials for Europe. Militarily, as already mentioned in Chapter 5, Indian manpower was organized in a European-style colonial army, funded entirely by the Indian taxpayer, and used throughout the nineteenth century in the endless series of wars through which Britain opened up Asia and Africa to Western trade and investment. As for the financial aspect, the devaluation of the Indian currency, the imposition of the infamous Home Charges—through which India was made to pay for the privilege of being pillaged and exploited by Britain—and the Bank of England's control over India's foreign-exchange reserves, jointly turned India into the "pivot" of Britain's world-financial and commercial supremacy.[70]

Under British leadership, the endless accumulation of capital and power thus came to be embedded in a spatial fix of greater scale and scope than in the Genoese–Iberian and Dutch cycles. But, for that very reason, it eventually resulted in a far more massive over-accumulation of capital. As in the earlier cycles, the incumbent center was initially best positioned to take advantage of the intensification of competition that signaled the change of phase from material to financial expan-

---

69 Arrighi and Silver, *Chaos and Governance*, pp. 106–14, 223–46.

70 On these and other aspects of tribute extraction from India, see Michael Barrat Brown, *The Economics of Imperialism* (Harmondsworth, Penguin, 1974), pp. 133–6; B.R. Tomlinson, "India and the British Empire, 1880–1935," *The Indian Economic and Social History Review*, 12, 4 (1975); Marcello de Cecco, *The International Gold Standard: Money and Empire*, 2nd edn (New York, St Martin's Press, 1984), pp. 62–3; David Washbrook, "South Asia, the World System, and World Capitalism," *The Journal of Asian Studies*, 49, 3 (1990), p. 481; Amiya K. Bagchi, *Perilous Passage: Mankind and the Global Ascendancy of Capital* (Lantham, MD, Rowman & Littlefield, 2005), pp. 145–7, 239–43.

sion. The ensuing Edwardian *belle époque*, however, was but a preamble to an escalation of interstate conflicts that once again revolutionized the historical geography of world capitalism. The analogous "revolution" of the late eighteenth and early nineteenth centuries had eliminated from the struggle for capitalist leadership proto-national states like the United Provinces. In the "revolution" of the first half of the twentieth century, it was the turn of the national states themselves to be squeezed out of the struggle unless they controlled integrated agricultural-industrial-military complexes of continental scale.

"Britain's new insecurity and growing militarism and Jingoism [towards the end of the nineteenth century]," notes Andrew Gamble, "arose because the world seemed suddenly filled with industrial powers, whose metropolitan bases in terms of resources and man-power and industrial production were potentially much more power-ful than Britain's."[71] The rapid industrialization of the unified Germany after 1870 was particularly upsetting for the British, because it created the conditions for the rise of a land power in Europe capable of aspiring to continental supremacy and of challenging Britain's maritime rule. During the First World War, Britain and its allies succeeded in containing Germany, and Britain even increased the reach of its overseas territorial empire. But the financial costs of these military-political successes destroyed Britain's capacity to hold the center of world capitalism.

During the war, Britain did continue to function as principal banker and loan-raiser on the world's credit markets, not just for itself, but also by guaranteeing loans to Russia, Italy, and France. This looked like a repetition of Britain's eighteenth-century role as "banker of the coalition." There was nonetheless one critical differ-ence: the huge trade deficit with the United States, which was supplying billions of dollars' worth of munitions and foodstuffs to the Allies but required few goods in return. "Neither the transfer of gold nor the sale of Britain's enormous dollar securities could close this gap; only borrowing on the New York and Chicago money markets, to pay the American munitions suppliers in dollars, would do the trick."[72] When Britain's credit approached exhaustion, the US threw its economic and military weight into the struggle, tilting the balance to its debtors' advantage. Mastery over the European balance of power had shifted decisively from British to US hands. The

---

71 Andrew Gamble, *Britain in Decline* (London, Macmillan, 1985), p. 58.
72 Kennedy, *Rise and Fall of the Great Powers*, p. 268.

insularity that the English Channel no longer provided, the Atlantic still did. More important, as innovations in means of transport and communications continued to overcome spatial barriers, America's remoteness became less of a disadvantage commercially and militarily. "Indeed, as the Pacific began to emerge as a rival economic zone to the Atlantic, the USA's position became central—a continent-sized island with unlimited access to both of the world's major oceans."[73]

This "continent-sized island" had long been in the making. It was the spatial product of the century-long process of territorial seizure and occupation through which the United States had "internalized" imperialism from the very beginning of its history. "American historians who speak complacently of the absence of the settler-type colonialism characteristic of the European powers merely conceal the fact that the whole *internal* history of United States imperialism was one vast process of territorial seizure and occupation. The absence of territorialism 'abroad' was founded on an unprecedented territorialism 'at home.' "[74] As Clyde Barrow points out in summing up Charles Beard's account of this internal imperialism:

> The westward migration brought human carnage and environmental destruction on a massive scale as American settlers moved across successive frontiers like locusts, who stopped only long enough to pillage the land and to remove, kill, or marginalize the native inhabitants. Indeed, on the eve of World War I, Beard lectured student pacifists in his classes that "it was an illusion to think of Americans as a pacific people; they are and always have been one of the most violent peoples in history."[75]

If the continent-sized US "island" was created through massive human and environmental destruction, it was the transport revolution and industrialization of war of the second half of the nineteenth century that turned it into a powerful agricultural-industrial-military complex with decisive competitive and strategic advantages vis-à-vis European

---

73 Joshua S. Goldstein and David P. Rapkin, "After Insularity: Hegemony and the Future World Order," *Futures*, 23 (1991), p. 946.

74 Gareth Stedman Jones, "The History of US Imperialism," in R. Blackburn, ed., *Ideology in Social Science* (New York, Vintage, 1972), pp. 216–17, emphasis in the original. See also John Agnew, *The United States in the World-Economy: A Regional Geography* (Cambridge, Cambridge University Press, 1987).

75 Clyde W. Barrow, "God, Money, and the State: The Spirits of American Empire," Forschungsgruppe Europäische Gemeinschaften, Arbeitspapier 22, Universität Marburg.

states. To be sure, Britain's world-encompassing territorial empire contained even greater resources than the United States. Nevertheless, the global dispersion and weak mutual integration of Britain's colonial domains—in contrast with the regional concentration and strong mutual integration, both political and economic, of the territorial domains of the United States—was a crucial difference in the spatial configuration of the leading capitalist states of the "long" nineteenth and twentieth centuries respectively. As noted earlier, Britain's far-flung empire was an essential ingredient in the formation and con-solidation of the UK-centered system of accumulation. But as soon as interstate competition for "living space" intensified under the impact of the transport revolution and the industrialization of war, the protection costs of Britain's metropolitan and overseas domains began to escalate, and its imperial possessions turned from assets into liabilities. At the same time, the overcoming of spatial barriers brought about by these same two phenomena turned the continental size, compactness, insularity, and direct access to the world's two major oceans of the United States into decisive strategic advantages in the escalating interstate power struggle.[76]

Unsurprisingly, the struggle ended with the arrival of the bipolar world so often forecast in the nineteenth and early twentieth cen-turies: "the international order . . . now moved 'from one system to another.' Only the United States and the USSR counted . . . and of the two, the American 'superpower' was vastly superior."[77] As Thomas McCormick has underscored, US leaders fought the Second World War "not simply to vanquish their enemies, but to create the geopolitical basis for a postwar world order that they would both build and lead." In the pursuit of this ambitious end, awareness of British precedents during the Napoleonic Wars helped. In particular,

> Britain entered the main European theater only when the war had reached its final and decisive stage. Its direct military presence acted to inhibit any other continental power from attempting to take France's place in the continental power structure and rein-forced the legitimacy of Britain's claim to a dominant say in peace negotiations. In parallel fashion, the United States entered the European theater only in the last and determinant phase of World War II. Operation Overlord, its invasion of France in June 1944, and its push eastward into Germany similarly restrained potential

76 Arrighi and Silver, *Chaos and Governance*, pp. 66–84.
77 Kennedy, *Rise and Fall of the Great Powers*, p. 357.

Russian ambitions in the west and assured America's seat at the head of the peace table.[78]

These analogies reflect the fact that, in both transitions, mastery of the balance of power in the interstate system was essential to the empowerment of the rising hegemonic state. But the spatial and organizational fix of the endless accumulation of capital and power that came into being under US hegemony could not be the same as the British. It had to reflect the new historical geography of capitalism that had emerged from the irrevocable destruction of the nineteenth-century British spatial fix. This new historical geography lay at the foundation of the most ambitious political project ever conceived in human history: the creation of a world state. To the rise and demise of this project we now turn.

78 Thomas J. McCormick, *America's Half Century: United States Foreign Policy in the Cold War* (Baltimore, MD, Johns Hopkins University Press, 1989), pp. 35–5.

9

THE WORLD STATE THAT NEVER WAS

Shortly after the end of the Second World War, Ludwig Dehio argued that each round of the European power struggle had created the conditions of a geographical expansion of the European-centered system of sovereign states, of a "migration" of the locus of power further west and east, and of an irreversible mutation in the structure of the expanding system. Indeed, Dehio presented his study of the mechanisms that had reproduced the European balance of power over the preceding five centuries as dealing "with a structure that has ceased to exist . . . in a manner of speaking, as the result of an autopsy."

> The balance of power in the Occident was preserved only because new counterweights from territories beyond its frontiers could again and again be thrown into the scale against forces seeking supremacy. . . . In World War II, the forces that had left Europe in successive emigrations . . . turned back toward the region from which they had come. . . . The old pluralistic system of small states was completely overshadowed by the giant young powers which it had summoned to its aid. . . . Thus the old framework that had encompassed the European scene . . . is breaking up. The narrower stage is losing its overriding importance as a setting for a strong cast of its own, and is being absorbed into the broader proscenium. On both stages the two world giants are taking over the protagonists' role. . . . A divided system of states reverts again and again to a condition of flux. But the old European tendency toward division is now being thrust aside by the new global trend toward unification. And the onrush of this trend may not come to rest until it has asserted itself throughout our planet.[1]

---

1 Ludwig Dehio, *The Precarious Balance: Four Centuries of the European Power Struggle* (New York, Vintage, 1962), pp. 264–6, 269.

Half a century after this was written, the collapse of one of the two "world giants" and the further centralization of global military capabilities in US hands made these remarks sound prophetic. But well before Dehio pointed to the demise of "the old European tendency toward division," Franklin D. Roosevelt had already addressed the issue of what kind of political structure might emerge out of "the new global trend toward unification." Looking back at thirty years of world wars, revolutions, counterrevolutions, and the most serious economic breakdown in capitalist history, he had become convinced that worldwide chaos could be overcome only through a fundamental reorganization of world politics. Central to his vision was the idea that security for the world had to be based on US power exercised through international institutions. "But for such a scheme to have a broad ideological appeal to the suffering peoples of the world, it had to emanate from an institution less esoteric than an international monetary system and less crude than a set of military alliances or bases."[2]

The key body was to be the United Nations, with its appeal to the universal desire for peace and the longing of poor nations for independence and eventual equality with the rich nations. Not without reason, Schurmann finds the political implications of this vision truly revolutionary.

> For the first time in world history, there was a concrete institutionalization of the idea of world government. Whereas the League of Nations was guided by an essentially nineteenth-century spirit of a congress of nations, the United Nations was openly guided by American political ideas. . . . There was nothing revolutionary about the kind of world system Britain created through its empire. . . . Britain's true imperial greatness was economic, not political. The United Nations, however, was and remains a political idea. The American Revolution had proven that nations could be constructed through the conscious and deliberate actions of men. . . . What Roosevelt had the audacity to conceive and implement was the extension of this process of government-building to the world as a whole.[3]

2 Franz Schurmann, *The Logic of World Power: An Inquiry into the Origins, Currents, and Contradictions of World Politics* (New York, Pantheon, 1974), p. 68.

3 Ibid., p. 71.

Roosevelt's vision of world government had both social objectives and fiscal-financial implications. It was a conscious projection on a world scale of the US New Deal.

> The essence of the New Deal was the notion that big government must spend liberally in order to achieve security and progress. Thus postwar security would require liberal outlays by the United States in order to overcome the chaos created by the war. Aid to . . . poor nations would have the same effect as social welfare programs within the United States—it would give them the security to overcome chaos and prevent them from turning into violent revolutionaries. Meanwhile, they would be drawn inextricably into the revived world market system. By being brought into the general system, they would become responsible, just as American unions had during the war. Helping Britain and the remainder of Western Europe would rekindle economic growth, which would stimulate transatlantic trade and, thus, help the American economy in the long run. America had spent enormous sums running up huge deficits in order to sustain the war effort. The result had been astounding and unexpected economic growth. Postwar spending would produce the same effect on a worldwide scale.[4]

And so it did, but only after Roosevelt's "one-worldism"—which included the USSR among the poor nations of the world to be incorporated into the new order for the benefit and security of all—became Truman's "free-worldism," which turned the containment of Soviet power into the main organizing principle of US hegemony. Roosevelt's revolutionary idealism—which saw in institutions of world government the primary instrument through which the New Deal would be extended to the world as a whole—was displaced by the reformist realism of his successors who institutionalized US control over world money and global military power as the primary instruments of US hegemony.[5]

For Roosevelt's project was simply too idealistic for the tastes of Congress and US business. The world was too big and too chaotic a place for the United States to reorganize in its image, particularly if the reorganization had to be achieved through organs of world government within which the US government would have to com-

---

4 Ibid., p. 67.
5 See ibid., pp. 5, 67, 77.

promise with the views and interests of friends and foes alike. Congress and the American business community were far too "rational" in their calculations of the pecuniary costs and benefits of US foreign policy to release the means necessary to carry out such an unrealistic plan. Indeed, as noted in Chapter 7, had Korea not "come along" and given Truman what he needed to "scare hell out of the American people," even the US and European rearmament envisaged in NSC-68 might not have been funded. But Korea did come along and large-scale rearmament during and after the Korean War gave a tremendous boost to the US and world economies.

With the US government acting as a highly permissive world central bank, American military aid to foreign governments and direct military expenditures abroad—both of which grew constantly between 1950 and 1958 and again between 1964 and 1973—pumped US liquidity back into world trade and production, which grew at unprecedented rates.[6] According to McCormick, the twenty-three-year period inaugurated by the Korean War and concluded by the Paris peace accords of 1973, which virtually ended the Vietnam War, was "the most sustained and profitable period of economic growth in the history of world capitalism."[7]

This is the period that many call the Golden Age of Capitalism. Although the rate of expansion of world trade and production in the 1950s and 1960s was indeed exceptional by historical standards, this was hardly the first golden age of capitalism. Just as impressive was Hobsbawm's Age of Capital (1848–75), which late nineteenth-century observers compared to the Age of the Great Discoveries.[8] Like the "age of capital" a hundred years earlier, the golden age of the 1950s and 1960s ended in a long period of financial expansion that culminated in a resurgence of imperialistic practices. The true novelty of the present resurgence in comparison with that of a century ago, I shall argue, is the attempt of the declining hegemonic power to resist decline by turning itself into a world state. Such an attempt is a continuation by other means and under radically different circumstances of Roosevelt's world-government project. Although Roosevelt's one-world, global New Deal vision never materialized,

6 See David Calleo, *The Atlantic Fantasy* (Baltimore, MD, Johns Hopkins University Press, 1970), pp. 86–7; Robert Gilpin, *The Political Economy of International Relations* (Princeton, NJ, Princeton University Press, 1987), pp. 133–4.

7 Thomas J. McCormick, *America's Half Century: United States Foreign Policy in the Cold War* (Baltimore, MD, Johns Hopkins University Press, 1989), p. 99.

8 Eric J. Hobsbawm, *The Age of Capital 1848–1875* (New York, New American Library, 1979), p. 32.

Truman's downsized, militarized, Cold War version resulted in a major expansion of US capital and power. Why then has the neo-conservative project failed so miserably in repeating that experience under conditions of even greater centralization of global military capabilities in US hands?

The Changing Nature of US Protection

Charles Tilly's conceptualization of state activities as complementary facets of the organization and monopolization of violence enables us to provide a simple answer to this question. Whatever else governments might do, argues Tilly, they "stand out from other organizations by their tendency to monopolize the concentrated means of violence." This tendency materializes through four different kinds of activity: protection, state-making, war-making, and extraction. Protection is the most distinctive "product" of governmental activities. As Tilly underscores, "the word 'protection' sounds two contrasting tones." With one tone, it evokes the comforting image of a powerful friend who provides a shelter against danger. With the other, it evokes the sinister image of a racket in which a bully forces merchants to pay tribute in order to avoid a damage that the bully himself tacitly or openly threatens to deliver.

> Which image the word "protection" brings to mind depends mainly on our assessment of the reality and externality of the threat. Someone who produces both the danger and, at a price, the shield against it is a racketeer. Someone who provides a needed shield but has little control over the danger's appearance qualifies as a *legitimate protector*, especially if his price is no higher than his competitors'. Someone who supplies reliable, low-priced shielding from local racketeers and from outside marauders makes the best offer of all.

By this standard, Tilly goes on to argue, the provision of protection by governments often qualifies as racketeering.

> To the extent that the threats against which a given government protects its citizens are imaginary or are consequences of its activities, the government has organized a protection racket. Since governments themselves commonly simulate, or even fabricate threats of external war and the repressive and extractive activities

of governments often constitute the largest current threats to the livelihoods of their own citizens, many governments operate in essentially the same way as *racketeers*. There is, of course, a difference: Racketeers, by the conventional definition, operate without the *sanctity of governments*.[9]

Following Arthur Stinchcombe, Tilly claims that the legitimacy of power-holders depends far less on the assent of those on whom power is exercised than on the assent of other power-holders. To this, Tilly adds that other authorities "are much more likely to confirm the decisions of a challenged authority that controls substantial force; not only fear of retaliation, but also desire to maintain a stable environment recommend that general rule."[10] The credibility of a particular government's claim to provide protection thus increases with its success in monopolizing concentrated means of violence. This involves the elimination or neutralization of rivals both inside its territorial domains (state-making) and outside (war-making). And since protection, state-making, and war-making all require financial and material resources, extraction consists of the activities through which governments procure those resources. If carried out effectively, each of these four activities "generally reinforces the others."[11]

Tilly's model emphasizes the synergy among protection-producing, state-making, war-making, and extraction activities in ensuring governmental success in monopolizing concentrated means of violence *at the national level*. It order to apply the model to the US case of a government that has been trying to organize and monopolize concentrated means of violence *at the global level*, two qualifications are necessary. First, the formation of a world state blurs the distinction between state-making and war-making activities, because the would-be world state claims the entire world as its prospective domain and thus *de facto* rejects the distinction between intra- and interstate domains. Hence the widespread description of the many "wars" that the United States has been waging since the end of the Second World War as police actions rather than wars. Second, since the "sanctity of governments" still belongs to the national states, the would-be world

---

9 Charles Tilly, "War Making and State Making as Organized Crime," in P.B. Evans, D. Rueschemeyer, and T. Skocpol, eds, *Bringing the State Back In* (Cambridge, Cambridge University Press, 1985), pp. 170–1, emphasis added.

10 Arithur L. Stinchcombe, *Constructing Social Theories* (New York, Harcourt, Brace & World, 1968), p. 150; Tilly, "War Making and State Making," p. 171.

11 Tilly, "War Making and State Making," pp. 171, 181.

state faces greater difficulties in presenting itself as the organizer of "legitimate protection" rather than of a "protection racket."

Bearing these qualifications in mind, we can understand the failure of the Bush administration to repeat the achievements of the Truman administration in terms of the difference between a dysfunctional protection racket and legitimate protection. Despite all its limits, the downsized, militarized, world-government project launched by Truman qualified as, and was perceived by a large number of power-holders at the national level to be, legitimate protection. In part, this was due to US reliance throughout the 1950s and 1960s on the United Nations to ensure that at least some of the "sanctity of governments," which still resided at the national level, would be accorded to the world-governmental activities of the United States. The two main reasons why the US Cold War project qualified as legitimate protection, however, were factual rather than institutional.

The first reason, to paraphrase Tilly, was that it offered a needed shield against a danger that the United States had not produced. Although, economically and politically, the United States had been the main beneficiary of the escalating violence of the first half of the twentieth century, the epicenter of the escalation was Europe not the United States. Europe was most in need of the shield because, as Arno Mayer notes in a different context, in both world wars "Europe's blood sacrifice was immeasurably greater and more punishing than America's."[12] But the sacrifice originated in European conflicts. By offering a world order capable of reducing the chances that similar conflicts would recur, the United States thus qualified as a legitimate protector.

The second reason was that the United States offered effective protection at an unbeatable price. Roosevelt and Truman were both proposing to finance the worldwide provision of protection with the surplus capital that had accumulated in the United States during the preceding thirty years of worldwide chaos. No state, let alone any of the newly created international institutions, had the resources necessary to match such a low-priced offer. Indeed, the main problem for the Truman administration was not finding clients for the protection it was offering, but persuading Congress that the investment of US surplus capital in the production of protection on a world scale actually was in the US national interest. It was to this end that Truman artfully inflated the communist threat.

---

12 Arno J. Mayer, "Beyond the Drumbeat: Iraq, Preventive War, 'Old Europe,'" *Monthly Review*, 54, 10 (2003).

This situation began to change with the signal crisis of US hegemony of the late 1960s and early 1970s. The Vietnam War demonstrated that US protection was not as reliable as the United States claimed and its clients expected. In the First and Second World Wars, the United States had grown rich and powerful by letting other countries do most of the actual fighting; by supplying them with credit, food, and weapons; by watching them exhaust one another financially and militarily; and by intervening late in the struggle to ensure an outcome favorable to its national interest. In Vietnam, in contrast, it had to do most of the fighting itself in a socially, culturally, and politically hostile environment, while its European and East Asian clients gathered strength as economic competitors and American multinationals accumulated profits in extraterritorial financial markets, depriving the US government of badly needed tax revenue. As a result of this combination of circumstances, US military might lost credibility and the US gold–dollar standard collapsed. To make matters worse, the United Nations turned into a sounding board for Third World grievances, generating little legitimacy for the US exercise of world-governmental functions.

After a decade of deepening crisis, the Reagan administration initiated the transformation of US legitimate protection into a protection racket. It discarded the United Nations as a source of legitimacy for US hegemony. It began strong-arming Japan—which happened to be both the client most dependent on US protection and the fastest accumulator of surplus capital—into restraining its competition vis-à-vis the United States through "voluntary" export restrictions (a device unheard of in the annals of international trade) and into using its surplus capital to finance the growing US budget and trade deficits. It ratcheted up the balance of terror with the USSR through a major escalation of the armament race. And it engaged a great variety of local bullies (including Saddam Hussein) and religious fundamentalists (including Osama bin Laden) in the rollback of Third World and Soviet power. The United States thus began to charge allies a price for its protection, and at the same time to produce the dangers against which it would later offer protection.[13]

The success of the Reagan administration in undermining Third World and Soviet power created the illusion under George Bush

---

13 On how the US shift under Reagan from direct intervention in the fight against communism to supporting low-level insurgency by private militias bred future terrorists, see Mahmood Mamdani, *Good Muslim, Bad Muslim: America, the Cold War, and the Roots of Terror* (New York, Pantheon, 2004).

Senior that the US "empire of bases" could be made to pay for itself. As Chalmers Johnson has pointed out, such an empire was (and is) far more vulnerable than "the older, self-financing empires" to trade deficits and capital movements. "Occasionally," however, the US empire of bases "makes money because, like gangsters in the 1930s who forced the people and businesses under their sway to pay protection money, the United States pressures foreign governments to pay for its imperial projects." The most prominent among these occasions was the first Iraq War. By bringing the United Nations back to provide legitimacy for the war, the Bush administration managed to extract from its wealthiest and militarily most dependent clients (most notably, Saudi Arabia, Kuwait, the United Arab Emirates, Germany, and especially Japan) financial contributions totaling $54.1 billion, while the US contribution of $7 billion amounted to just over half that of Japan's $13 billion.[14] Moreover, this huge payment was extracted for protection, not against a danger like communism which the United States had not created, but against a danger that could in part be traced to US support of Saddam Hussein's war against Iran.

The shift from legitimate protection to protection racket continued by other means under Clinton. UN mediation as a means of generating legitimacy for US police actions was again discarded, this time in favor of a collective pursuit through NATO of choice "humanitarian" missions. At the same time, the Bretton Woods institutions were refurbished as instruments of US rule over an increasingly integrated global market. The "success" of the Bosnia and Kosovo missions, along with the irresistible rise of the new-economy bubble, gave credence to Secretary of State Albright's representation of the United States as the "indispensable nation." But the foundation of this "indispensability" was not the alleged capacity of the United

---

14 Chalmers Johnson, *The Sorrows of Empire: Militarism, Secrecy, and the End of the Republic* (New York, Metropolitan Books, 2004), pp. 25, 307. According to Johnson, the United States later boasted that it had even made a small net profit from the conflict. See also Eric J. Hobsbawm, *The Age of Extremes: A History of the World, 1914–1991* (New York, Vintage, 1994), p. 242. This was the first and only time that the United States, not just sought to make its clients pay for one of its major wars, but actually succeeded in the endeavor. In itself, the success of the extortion was not a sign of hegemony, because at the height of its hegemony the United States paid in full for its wars and the protection of its clients. Rather, it was a sign that US hegemony had ceased to be hege*money* but was still sufficiently entrenched to enable the United States to make its clients pay for the protection it was providing. The failure of George W. Bush to make US clients pay for the second Iraq War (see below), in contrast, can be taken as a sign that, by then, the United States had lost both hege*money* and hegemony.

States, as Albright claimed, to "see further than other countries into the future."[15] Rather, it was a general fear of the irreparable damage that US policies could inflict on the rest of the world. The dangers against which the United States was now offering protection were dangers that the US itself had created or could create. And the trillions of dollars that foreign governments began pouring into the coffers of the US government showed that US protection was not low priced any more.

Dispensable United States?

The neo-conservatives in the Bush administration thus did not initiate the transformation of the US from legitimate protector into racketeer. When they came to power, the transformation was already at an advanced stage. But by pushing it too far, they unwittingly ended up exposing its limits, both military and economic. As we have seen in Chapter 7, their attempt to demonstrate that American military might could effectively police the world and at the same time ensure the continuing centrality of the United States in the global political economy failed in both respects. We can now trace this double failure to an overstretch of the US worldwide protection racket.

Colin Powell himself once evoked Tilly's sinister image of protection when he said that the United States ought "to be the bully on the block." The rest of the world would happily accept this role, he went on to assert, calling up the comforting image of protection, because the United States "can be trusted not to abuse that power."[16] We do not know on what grounds Powell based this belief. But less than a year after the US invasion of Iraq, reports from around the world showed that the comforting image of US protection had given way to the sinister one of a United States trying to strong-arm everyone onto its own foreign policy agenda. More important, the attempt was not succeeding.

The most compelling piece of evidence was the reluctance of even the most faithful US clients to provide the United States with the resources it needed to extricate itself from the Iraqi quagmire. Despite Colin Powell's attempt to put up a brave front by declaring a success

---

15 Quoted in S. Sestanovich, "Not Much Kinder and Gentler," *New York Times*, February 3, 2005.

16 Quoted in David Harvey, *The New Imperialism* (New York, Oxford University Press, 2003), p. 80.

the "donors conference" convened in Madrid in October 2003, after the UN Security Council had provided the Iraq occupation with some juridical legitimacy, payments fell far short of expectations and, significantly, of the amounts that had been raised for the 1991 Iraq War. Actual donations (that is, grants) were less than one-eighth of the $36 billion target and considerably less than one-fourth of the US $20 billion pledge. In marked contrast with the highly successful extortions of the first Iraq War, this time the United States was left holding the bag. Germany and Saudi Arabia gave virtually nothing. Even Japan's $1.5 billion pledge—by far the largest at Madrid—was meager in comparison with the $13 billion Japan disgorged for the first Iraq conflict, especially given that in real terms US dollars were worth considerably more in 1991 than in 2003.

This sharp decline in the capacity of the United States to extract protection payments from clients can be traced to the perception that its protection had become counterproductive, either because the US squeezed some of its clients dry and then left them exposed to even greater dangers than the ones from which they had been protected; or because US actions threatened to create greater future dangers than the present ones against which it offered protection. Either way, as James Carroll has observed with special reference to West Asia, the "indispensable nation" appeared to be "indispensable only for the spread of chaos."

> Iraqis, Lebanese, Israelis and Palestinians all make violent choices and bear the weight of violent consequences, but the context within which those choices are being made has been overwhelmingly established by violent choices made in Washington.[17]

In part, however, the dramatic reduction of tribute payments can be attributed to a belief that the need for US protection, for what it is worth, is less compelling than it was in 1991. This perception has been far more widespread than the ritualistic respect still paid to US power might suggest. But it is probably most important in the case of US clients in the East Asian region. While, in the past, many states in the region viewed US protection as essential for countering the real or imagined threat that China posed to their security, today China is no

---

17 J. Carroll, "Reject the War," *International Herald Tribune*, December 19, 2006. On US violent choices turning Iraq into a country-size terrorist training ground, see among others Daniel Benjamin and Steven Simon, *The Next Attack: The Failure of the War on Terror and a Strategy for Getting it Right* (New York, Times Books, 2005); and P. Rogers, "The War on Terror: Past, Present, Future," *openDemocracy*, August 24, 2006.

longer seen as a serious threat, and even if such a threat were to re-emerge, US protection is perceived as unreliable. Moreover, the capacity of the United States to extract protection payments from its East Asian clients has been further curtailed by the combination of increasing US dependence on East Asian money and decreasing dependence of East Asian countries on the US market with the consolidation of China as their largest and fastest growing market.

As previously noted, the attraction of China as an economic and strategic partner reaches well beyond the East Asian region. China's ascent is indeed reminiscent of the US ascent during the world wars of the first half of the twentieth century. Just as the United States emerged as the real winner of the Second World War after the USSR had broken the back of the Wehrmacht in 1942–43, so now all the evidence points to China as the real winner of the War on Terror, regardless of whether the US will ever succeed in breaking the back of al Qaeda and the Iraqi insurgency.[18]

In the Epilogue of the book we shall deal with the issue of what kind of new world order (or disorder) may eventually emerge out of this "victory." For now let us simply note that the new imperialism of the Project for a New American Century probably marks the inglorious end of the sixty-year long struggle of the United States to become the organizing center of a world state. The struggle changed the world but even in its most triumphant moments, the US never succeeded in its endeavor. Coming at the end of this long process, all George W. Bush has done is to prove Albright wrong. "The US, it turns out," laments Michael Lind, "is a dispensable nation."

> In recent memory, nothing could be done without the US. Today, however, practically all new international institution-building of any long-term importance in global diplomacy and trade occurs without American participation. . . . Europe, China, Russia, Latin America and other regions and nations are quietly taking measures whose effect . . . will be to cut America down to size.[19]

---

18 In 2004, an Institute of Electrical and Electronic Engineers panelist recalled the old joke that the US fought the Cold War and Japan won. "The new joke," he added, "is that the United States is fighting the war on terror, but China is winning" (J. Kumagi and W. Sweet, "East Asia Rising," *IEEE Spectrum Online*, http://www.spectrum.ieee.org, accessed October 19, 2004). It so happens that the joke captures an important aspect not only of the present but also of the past dynamic of historical capitalism sketched in Chapter 8.

19 M. Lind, "How the U.S. Became the World's Dispensable Nation," *Financial Times*, January 25, 2005.

"To have drastically eroded, in less than four years, the position of respected international leadership built up by the United States over the past hundred years or more"—wrote Brian Urquhart on the eve of the November 2004 elections—"is an extraordinary achievement."[20] In spite of this "extraordinary achievement," and to the amazement of the rest of the world, not only did the elections return President Bush to the White House, but it consolidated the hold of the neo-conservative bloc on all the branches of the US government. Follow-ing the electoral victory, Bush famously declared that he had earned "political capital" which he now intended to spend at his discretion. And yet, if we take the difference between his approval and dis-approval ratings as a rough measure of his political capital, Figure 9.1 shows how also in this respect he was completely out of touch with reality.

What the figure shows is, first, that most of Bush's political capital was not something he had "earned" but a gift he received from bin Laden on September 11; and, second, that despite a sharp but short-lived gain following the invasion of Iraq in March 2003, by the time of his 2004 re-election he had already squandered the gift and was now operating on borrowed time. What had gained him four more years in the White House, besides the lack of ideas among his Democratic challengers on how to clean up the mess he had created, was the famed cunning of his advisor Karl Rove, who concocted the idea that the War on Terrorism was better fought overseas than at home and that, unless the terrorists were routed in Iraq, they would show up in the streets of San Francisco or Des Moines. Effective in once again "scaring hell out of the American people" and getting Bush re-elected, this was hardly a winning argument for the growing majority of Iraqis whose lives were devastated or cut short by US-induced chaos, and indeed for all foreign countries that felt threatened by the combina-tion of ruthlessness and mindlessness with which the US was spread-ing the dangers against which it claimed to be providing protection. But even the American people could not be fooled all the time, nor could the cunning of Karl Rove indefinitely beat the cunning of the underlying historical process, so that—as Figure 9.1 shows—shortly after Bush's second inauguration the depletion of his political capital resumed inexorably.

A major turning point was hurricane Katrina's devastation of Louisiana in September 2005. "If 9/11 is one bookend of the Bush

---

20 K. Anthony Appiah et al., "The Election and America's Future," *New York Review*, November 4, 2004, p. 16.

Figure 9.1   President Bush's approval ratings from February 2001 to
October 2006

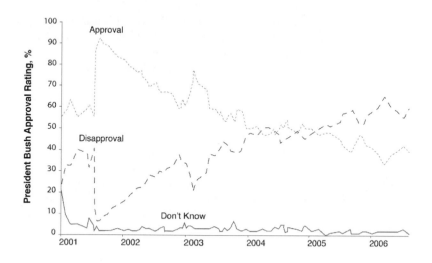

Source: *Washington Post*—ABC News Poll.

administration," wrote Thomas Friedman, "Katrina may be the
other. If 9/11 put the wind at President's Bush's back, Katrina put
the wind in his face."[21] Contrary to Bush's and Rumsfeld's claim that
the tragedy had nothing to do with Iraq, notes Mike Davis, "the
absence of more than a third of the Louisiana National Guard and
much of its heavy equipment crippled rescue and relief operations
from the outset. . . . As an embittered representative from devastated
St Bernard Parish told the *Times-Picayune*: 'Canadian help arrived
before the US Army did.' "[22] And, contrary to Bush's claim that no
one could have predicted the breach in the New Orleans levees,
Katrina was, in Simon Schama's words, "the most anticipated
catastrophe in modern American history."

> In the [2004] election George W. Bush asked Americans to vote for
> him as the man who would best fulfil the most essential obligation
> of government: the impartial and vigilant protection of its citizens.

---

21 "Osama and Katrina," *New York Times*, September 7, 2005.
22 "The Predators of New Orleans," *Le Monde Diplomatique*, English edition,
September 2005. See also R. Scheer, "Finally Fooling None of the People," *Los
Angeles Times*, September 13, 2005.

Now the fraudulence of the claim has come back to haunt him, not in Baghdad but in the drowned counties of Louisiana.[23]

In reality, Iraq and Louisiana were two sides of the same coin of a country that for a quarter of a century had compounded its long-standing belief in the magic of high technology with that of the magic of self-regulating markets. Having gone into Iraq under the slogan "shock and awe," which was "meant to radiate a might never seen on the face of the earth"—writes Polly Toynbee—the United States now faced a different kind of shock.

> It is the shock of discovering that . . . America now looks like some fearsome robotic dinosaur stomping across the landscape, a gigantic Power Ranger toy, all bright gadgets and display but no power and nothing inside. . . . Iraq has shown that smart missiles, heavy-metal techno-tricks and soldiers whose helmets are electronically controlled from Southern Command in Tampa, are virtually useless. The lessons that the Vietcong on bicycles thought they had taught the behemoth are being learned all over again as failure and calamity stare the White House in the face. . . . As the US finds that the power to break nations is useless without the power to make them, shock and awe are over. But it took Hurricane Katrina to expose the real emptiness under the US carapace. No wonder governing Iraq was far beyond the competence of a nation so feebly governed within its own borders. How does a state where half the voters don't believe in government, run anything well? What the great Louisiana catastrophe has revealed is a country that is not a country at all, but atomized, segmented individuals living parallel lives as far apart as possible, with nothing to unite them beyond the idea of a flag.[24]

We are thus back to Arendt's contention that "Hobbes's Commonwealth is a vacillating structure" which "must always provide itself with new props from outside" to avoid the risk of collapsing "overnight into the aimless, senseless chaos of the private interests from which it sprang." But that is precisely why, as memories of Katrina began to fade, the American people's fear of the further damage that

---

23 "Sorry Mr President, Katrina Is Not 9/11," *Guardian*, September 12, 2005.

24 "The Chasm Between Us," *Guardian*, September 9, 2005. For a similar contention, see R. Drayton, "Shock, Awe and Hobbes Have Backfired on America's Neocons," *Guardian*, December 28, 2005.

Bush could inflict on the American flag began to overpower the fear
that terrorists would show up in the streets of San Francisco or Des
Moines, leading to a further erosion of Bush's political capital. In his
starkest admission yet about the costs of the Iraq War to his
presidency, in March 2006 Bush reluctantly admitted: "I'd say I'm
spending [my political] capital on the war."[25] By the November 2006
mid-term elections, he was heavily in the red; the Democrats won
both branches of Congress; all remaining neo-cons in the government,
except Cheney, were dismissed; and all dreams of a new American
century were set aside to concentrate on damage control.

Reprise and Preview

"More graphically than anything else"—Marx wrote to Engels on
September 25, 1857—"the history of the *ARMY* demonstrates the
rightness of our views as to the connection between the productive
forces and social relations."

> Altogether the ARMY is of importance in economic development.
> E.g. it was in the army of Antiquity that the *salaire* [wage system]
> was first developed. . . . Here too the first use of machinery on a
> large scale. Even the special value of metals and their USE as
> money would seem to have been based originally . . . on their
> significance in war. Again, the division of labor *within* a branch
> was first put into practice by armies. All this, moreover, a very
> striking epitome of the whole history of civil societies. If you ever
> have time, you might work the thing out from that point of view.[26]

Had Engels found the time, he might have been able to demonstrate
the rightness of his and Marx's views concerning the connection
between the productive forces and social relations, but only if he
redefined the productive forces to include the production of protection. More important, in all likelihood, he would have felt it necessary
to address the issue of the connection between capitalism, industrialism, and militarism, which was implicitly raised by Smith's ob-

---

25 E. Bumiller, "Bush Concedes Iraq War Erodes Political Status," *New York
Times*, March 22, 2006.

26 Quoted in Russell Johnson, " 'Pre-Conditioning' for Industry: Civil War
Military Service and the Making of an American Working Class," paper presented at
the 25th Annual North American Labor History Conference, Wayne State University,
Detroit, October 16–18, 2003, emphases in the original.

servation that the great expense of modern warfare gives a military advantage to wealthy over poor nations. As we asked in Chapter 3, given the greater role that manufacturing, foreign trade, and navigation played in the European capitalist path—in comparison to Smith's market-based, "natural" path—would not capitalism, industrialism, and militarism reinforce one another in a virtuous circle of enrichment and empowerment at the expense of the rest of the world? And if they did, what are the limits of this enrichment and empowerment?

William McNeill's pathbreaking account of the pursuit of power along the European developmental path, along with the analysis developed in this and the preceding two chapters, suggest several observations which can help in answering these questions. A first observation is that the commercialization of war and an incessant armament race have characterized the Western path of capitalist development from its earliest beginnings in the Italian city-states to its final culmination in the failed US world state. So-called "military Keynesianism"—the practice through which military expenditures boost the incomes of the citizens of the state that has made the expenditures, thereby increasing tax revenues and the capacity to finance new rounds of military expenditures—is no more a novelty of the twentieth century than finance capital and transnational business enterprise. By developing wage-labor relations in war-making and state-making, the Italian city-states were already practicing a kind of small-scale military Keynesianism, which transformed part of their protection costs into revenues and thus appeared to make wars pay for themselves.

> [Enough] money circulated in the richer Italian towns to make it possible for citizens to tax themselves and use the proceeds to buy the services of armed strangers. Then, simply by spending their pay, the hired soldiers put these monies back in circulation. Thereby, they intensified the market exchanges that allowed such towns to commercialize armed violence in the first place. The emergent system thus tended to become self-sustaining.[27]

In reality, the emergent system could become truly self-sustaining only on condition that military expenditures generated revenues greater than the taxes paid to sustain them. This leads us to the second observation that, in the European system, this condition was

---

27 William McNeill, *The Pursuit of Power: Technology, Armed Force, and Society since A.D. 1000* (Chicago, University of Chicago Press, 1982), p. 74.

fulfilled at least for some states through the joint operation of two mechanisms. One was a balance-of-power mechanism that enabled the leading capitalist state of a given epoch to appropriate the benefits of interstate competition—and thus truly make wars pay for themselves. And the other was systematic external expansion, which exercised a double function: it kept alive the competition among European states in devising ever more sophisticated means and techniques of war; and, at the same time, it enabled them to appropriate from the rest of the world the resources needed to expand their trade and tax revenues. As McNeill sums up the process with specific reference to the century and a half *preceding* the Industrial Revolution:

> Within the cockpit of western Europe, one improved modern-style army shouldered hard against its rivals. This led to only local and temporary disturbances of the balance of power, which diplomacy proved able to contain. Towards the margins of the European radius of action, however, the result was systematic expansion— whether in India, Siberia or the Americas. Frontier expansion in turn sustained an expanding trade network, enhanced taxable wealth in Europe, and made support of the armed establishment less onerous than would otherwise have been the case. Europe, in short, launched itself on a self-reinforcing cycle in which its military organization sustained, and was sustained by, economic and political expansion at the expense of other peoples and polities of the earth.[28]

The third observation is that this self-reinforcing cycle was both cause and effect of two different kinds of innovations in the production of protection. A first kind concerned—as Marx suggested in his letter to Engels—the technical division of labor within armies. By rediscovering and bringing to perfection long-forgotten Roman military techniques, in the early seventeenth century Maurice of Nassau reorganized the Dutch army along the lines that Frederick W. Taylor's "scientific management" would reorganize US industry two centuries later. He reorganized siege techniques so as to increase the efficiency of military labor-power, cut costs in terms of casualties, and facilitate the maintenance of discipline in the army's ranks. He standardized marching and the loading and firing of guns and made drilling a regular activity of soldiers. He divided the army into smaller

---

28 Ibid., p. 143.

tactical units, increased the numbers of commissioned and non-commissioned officers, and rationalized lines of command.

> In this way an army became an articulate organism with a central nervous system that allowed sensitive and more or less intelligent response to unforseen circumstances. Every movement attained a new level of exactitude and speed. The individual movements of soldiers when firing and marching as well as the movements of battalions across the battlefield could be controlled and predicted as never before. A well-drilled unit, by making every motion count, could increase the amount of lead projected against the enemy per minute of battle. The dexterity and resolution of individual infantry men scarcely mattered any more. Prowess and personal courage all but disappeared beneath an armor-plated routine. . . . Yet troops drilled in the Maurician fashion automatically exhibited superior effectiveness in battle.[29]

The second kind of innovation corresponds to what Marx refers to as the "use of machinery on a large scale." As noted in Chapter 8, McNeill, among others, attributes a crucial role to military demands on the British economy during the Napoleonic Wars in making the improvement of steam engines and such epoch-making innovations as the iron railway and iron ship possible at a time and under conditions which simply would not have existed without the wartime impetus to iron production. In this sense, the Industrial Revolution in the sectors that really mattered—i.e., the capital-goods industries—was largely a byproduct of the European armament race. Very soon, however, the application of the products and processes of modern industry to war-making activities—what McNeill calls the "industrialization of war"—gave an unprecedented impulse to that race.

The industrialization of war began in earnest in the 1840s when the French navy adopted armored steamships carrying large-caliber shell guns which made wooden warships hopelessly obsolete. As the French navy launched ever more sophisticated armored steamships,

---

29 The diffusion of Maurician "scientific management" to European armies had a double significance. In Europe, it neutralized the advantages of scale enjoyed by Spain and thereby tended to equalize military capabilities and thus reproduce the balance of power. Outside of Europe, it enabled European drillmasters to create miniature armies by recruiting local manpower for the protection of European trading stations on the shores of the Indian Ocean. "By the eighteenth century, such forces, however miniscule, exhibited a clear superiority over the unwieldy armies that local rulers were accustomed to bring into the field" (ibid., pp. 127–39).

the British navy had no choice but to follow suit. As other states did the same, the new armament race acquired a momentum of its own that neither Britain nor France could control.

The Crimean War (1854–56) was a key turning point. Around 1850, craft methods of production were still predominant in the armament industry throughout Europe, as they were in most branches of the capital-goods industry. But, between 1855 and 1870, under the initial impact of the Crimean War, these methods were displaced by what was then called the "American system of manufacture." The key principle was the use of automatic or semiautomatic milling machines to cut interchangeable parts to prescribed shapes. These machines were costly and wasteful of material. "But if a large number of guns were needed, automation paid for itself many times over through the economies of mass production." The British government and Belgian gunmakers were the first to import American machinery but by 1870 they were joined by Austria, France, Prussia, Russia, Spain, Denmark, Sweden, Turkey, and even Egypt. As a result, interstate competition in the procurement of small arms was set free from the shackles of craft production; entire armies could be re-equipped in a matter of years instead of decades; and this speed-up became in itself a factor of incessant innovations in the design of small arms.[30]

At the same time, large-scale private enterprise became a factor in the armament race. The key invention prompted by the Crimean War was the discovery of the Bessemer process for making steel, which made older methods for gun-casting obsolete. Contrary to what had happened in small-gun production—where state arsenals had pioneered changes in the labor process and in product design that enabled them to centralize production in their hands at the expense of private small business—in heavy-artillery production the adoption of new methods and materials was pioneered by big private enterprises, which centralized in their hands activities previously carried out in state arsenals.

A global, industrialized armaments business thus emerged in the 1860s. . . . Even technically proficient government arsenals like the French, British, and Prussian, faced persistent challenge from private manufacturers, who were never loath to point out the ways in which their products surpassed government-made weaponry. Commercial competition thus added its force

---

30 Ibid., pp. 225–7, 233–6.

to national rivalry in forwarding improvements in artillery design.[31]

The Crimean War also added a new momentum to the construction of national railway systems throughout continental Europe. The war demonstrated that steamship technology enhanced the logistical advantages enjoyed by naval powers vis-à-vis land powers. Whereas troops and supplies could be sent from France and England by sea to the Crimea in three weeks, Russian troops and supplies from Moscow sometimes took three months to reach the front. In addition, a British blockade stifled the importation of new weapons into Russia by sea and cut off much of Russia's flow of grain and other exports with which to pay for whatever supplies could be imported overland. The construction of efficient national railway systems thus came to be perceived as an integral aspect of war- and state-making activities, not just in Russia, but in Central and Southern Europe as well, leading to a true mania for railways among European governments. Between 1850 and 1870, 50,000 miles of new line were laid in Europe as against 15,000 in all the years before. The forward and backward linkages of this upsurge in European railway construction, in turn, became the single most important factor in the narrowing of the industrialization gap between Britain and Continental European states.[32]

The industrialization of war gave a new tremendous impulse to the self-reinforcing cycle in which European military organization sustained, and was sustained by, economic and political expansion at the expense of other peoples and polities of the earth. As steamships and railways annihilated natural obstacles of geography and distance, "the drastic discrepancy between European and local organization for

---

31 This was only the beginning of a long process in which business enterprises became protagonists of the armament race, and were in turn transformed by it: "as arms firms became pioneers of one new technology after another—steel metallurgy, industrial chemistry, electrical machinery, radio communications, turbines, diesels, optics, calculators (for fire control), hydraulic machinery, and the like—they evolved into vast bureaucratic structures of a quasi-public character" (ibid., pp. 237, 241, 292).

32 Paul Kennedy, *The Rise and Fall of the Great Powers: Economic Change and Military Conflict from 1500 to 2000* (New York, Random House, 1987), p. 174; William L. McElwee, *The Art of War, Waterloo to Mons* (London, Weidenfeld & Nicolson, 1974), pp. 106–10; David S. Landes, *The Unbound Prometheus: Technological Change and Industrial Development in Western Europe from 1750 to the Present* (Cambridge, Cambridge University Press, 1969), pp. 201–2. According to Clive Trebilcock, the spin-off from public expenditure in arms manufacture between 1890 and 1914 affected European economies almost as much as railroads had done earlier. Quoted in McNeill, *The Pursuit of Power*, p. 292.

war became apparent in one part of the world after another." The newly acquired "near monopoly of strategic communication and transportation, together with a rapidly evolving weaponry that remained always far in advance of anything local fighting men could lay hands on," made imperial expansion "as cheap and easy for Europeans as it was catastrophic to Asians, Africans, and the peoples of Oceania."[33]

A fourth observation concerning the nexus between capitalism, industrialism, and militarism was the importance of control over the world's liquidity in gaining military advantage. In this respect, Schumpeter's capitalists held sway over entrepreneurs. Thus, the abundant liquidity that accumulated in, or passed through, British hands in the nineteenth century was a powerful instrument in the competitive struggle, not just in commodity markets but in the armament race as well. From the mid 1840s through the 1860s, most technological breakthroughs in the design of warships were pioneered by France. And yet, each French breakthrough called forth naval appropriations in Britain that France could not match, so that it was "relatively easy for the Royal Navy to catch up technically and surpass numerically each time the French changed the basis of the competition."[34] This pattern of the nineteenth-century armament race was first and most spectacularly pioneered by the Genoese capitalist diaspora three centuries earlier when, as noted in Chapter 8, it squeezed dry its Iberian partners who had done all the work of opening up to European exploitation new trade routes and continents. But the pattern recurred once again in the competition between the United States and the USSR during the Cold War. The key techno-

---

33 McNeill, *The Pursuit of Power*, pp. 143, 257–8. As previously noted, the ease and cheapness of British imperialism in the Victorian era was due primarily to the forcible extraction from India of pecuniary and military manpower resources. Insofar as India was concerned, the main effect of the industrialization of war was to counteract the increasing sophistication of Indian armed resistance. Whereas in the late eighteenth century British armies could defeat Indian armies six or seven times as large, by the 1840s the British had to use armies equally as large and with superior firepower to defeat Indian armies. See Robert B. Marks, *The Origins of the Modern World: A Global and Ecological Narrative from the Fifteenth to the Twenty-First Century* (Lantham, MD, Rowman & Littlefield, 2007), p. 153, and Philip D. Curtin, *The World and the West: The European Challenge and the Overseas Response in the Age of Empire* (Cambridge, Cambridge University Press, 2000), ch. 2. On some catastrophic aspects of European imperial expansion for the peoples of the future global South, see Mike Davis, *Late Victorian Holocausts: El Niño Famines and the Making of the Third World* (London, Verso, 2001).

34 McNeill, *The Pursuit of Power*, pp. 227–8.

logical innovation of the "war" was the launching of the Soviet *Sputnik* in October 1957; but its achievements were completely overshadowed by the space program that the US launched in 1961 with an abundance of financial means entirely beyond the reach of the USSR.

In short, the interstate struggle for control over the world's resources was an integral dimension of the inter-capitalist competition that drove the endless accumulation of power and capital along the European developmental path. Indeed, the armament race was the primary source of the endless stream of innovations that continually created new spatial configurations of trade and production of increasing scale and scope and destroyed pre-existing ones. What made the European path specifically *capitalist* was the fact that control over the world's financial resources provided the decisive advantage in the struggle over all other resources. Although industrialism was, from the start, an integral component of the path, the Industrial Revolution itself was an "intervening" rather than an "independent" variable: the result of two or three centuries of interaction between finance capitalism, militarism, and imperialism, which then became the most powerful energizer of the mix. Moreover, as soon as industrialization became the key determinant of military might, the virtuous circle of enrichment and empowerment along the European path began to approach its limits. The European struggles over the space considered vital to create and maintain competitive military-industrial complexes spun out of control, creating an opening for the "revolt against the West" of the first half of the twentieth century, which sharply increased the costs and reduced the benefits of overseas territorial expansion. At the same time, it provoked a "migration" of the locus of power further west and east towards the two continent-sized states that had already acquired all the space they needed to create and maintain competitive military-industrial complexes. The result was the irreversible mutation in the structure of the globalized European system sketched by Dehio in the passage quoted at the beginning of this chapter.

Under the new system, global military capabilities became an effective "duopoly" of the United States and the USSR but the armament race continued with a vengeance, driven by a "balance of terror" rather than a balance of power. As McNeill notes, "with the discovery of atomic explosives, human destructive power reached a new, suicidal level, surpassing previous limits to all but unimaginable degree." Unimaginable as it was, this degree was surpassed again when the installation of hundreds of long-range missiles in the decade following 1957 empowered the United States and the USSR to destroy each other's cities in a matter of minutes. The signing of a five-year Strategic Arms Limitation Treaty (SALT) in 1972 consolidated the balance of terror between the two superpowers but did not halt the armament race. It simply shifted it "to other kinds of weapons not mentioned in the treaty for the good reason that they did not yet exist."[35]

In the scientific discovery of new weapons systems—even more than in the industrialization of war—the superpower with greater command over global financial resources could turn the balance of terror to its own advantage by stepping up, or by threatening to step up, its research efforts to levels that the other superpower simply could not afford. This is what the United States did in the 1980s, thereby driving the USSR into bankruptcy and bringing the tendency towards the centralization of global military capabilities to its ultimate consequences. But while the conversion of US wealth into a source of power was relatively easy, the conversion of the ensuing near monopoly of global military capabilities into a source of wealth has been far more problematic.

In dealing with this issue of the relationship between wealth and power, Smith's reduction of the power conferred by wealth to purchasing power is far less useful than Hobbes's original contention, which Smith cites without doing justice to it. Hobbes's remarks on the subject followed the observation that "to have servants, is Power; To have friends, is Power; for they are strengths united," from which he deduced the maxim that: "Also Riches joyned with liberality is Power, because it procureth friends, and servants: Without liberality, not so; because in this case they defend not; but expose men to Envy, as a Prey."[36]

Although these remarks refer to individuals, they are especially useful in capturing the evolving logic of power of capitalist states in the globalizing European system. When the Italian city-states first pioneered the capitalist logic of power through massive accumulations of capital in small territorial containers, they did use some of their wealth to procure "friends" and "servants," but not sufficiently to avoid becoming the prey of the larger territorial states which they mobilized as allies in their mutual struggles. To return to de la Court's metaphor, the same fate befell the "cat of Holland" which,

---

35 Ibid., pp. 360, 368, 372–3.
36 Thomas Hobbes, *Leviathan*, ed. C.B. Macpherson (Harmondsworth, Penguin, 1968), p. 150.

despite its larger territorial domains and its far more extensive networks of trade and accumulation, had an increasingly hard time in keeping at bay the "beasts of prey" of the European jungle. The situation changed when a beast of prey, the "lion" of England, itself became the leading capitalist state and used the resources it extracted from its globe-encircling empire, first and foremost India, to procure allies and clients in the expanding European world, especially in the Americas. As in the case of its predecessors, however, the extraordinary wealth of the English lion exposed it to the envy of other states, which followed in the footsteps of its industrialism and its imperialism, and thereby raised the costs and reduced the benefits of both.

The situation changed even more dramatically when the United States became the leader of the capitalist world, and in an attempt to contain the forces of nationalism and communism, engaged in a project of world government without precedent in the Western system of states. To this end, the United States experimented with the idea that "Riches joyned with liberality is Power, because it procureth friends, and servants." Although US magnanimity was crucial in inflating US power in the early stages of the Cold War, it tended to transform its main beneficiaries (Germany and Japan) into competitors, thereby undermining its own foundations. This does not mean that magnanimity in interstate relations is necessarily self-defeating and short-lived. It simply means that in order to see how Hobbes's maxim could in fact be effective over long periods of time in a different systemic context, and may one day become effective again, we must shift our focus from the European path of capitalist development back to the East Asian path of market-based development—which we now do in Part IV.

Part IV

LINEAGES OF THE NEW ASIAN AGE

10

THE CHALLENGE OF "PEACEFUL ASCENT"

"The storm center of the world has shifted . . . to China. Whoever understands that mighty Empire . . . has a key to world politics for the next five hundred years." Thus, in 1899 US Secretary of State John Hay announced the Open Door policy that demanded for the United States commercial access to China equal to that of other great powers. Quoting Hay more than a century later, former US ambassador to the United Nations Richard Holbrooke has claimed that today "everything is different and nothing has changed." In "very different ways, the United States still seeks an open door; the secretary of the Treasury and an enraged Congress are hammering China to revalue its currency to give U.S. companies a better chance to compete with the world's fastest-growing major economy."[1]

Pace Holbrooke, in this respect the situation today is radically different from a century ago. Under WTO rules, the United States has a commercial access to China equal to that of any other country. What is more, when China joined the WTO in 2001, "it agreed to one of the fastest programs of import duty cuts and market opening ever accepted by a new member"; and despite problems, it has "met the deadlines and passed the laws."[2] The problem in US–Chinese relations at the turn of the twentieth-first century is no longer US commercial access to China. Rather, it is the fact that China has replaced the United States as the world's fastest-growing major economy and is seeking commercial access to the United States equal

---

1 R. Holbrooke, "China Makes its Move," *Washington Post*, May 27, 2005.

2 H. Winn, "Accession Has Brought Changes to China and WTO," *International Herald Tribune*, November 7, 2005. Among other things, China was allowed to join the WTO only after it agreed that other WTO members would be allowed to restrict Chinese textile and apparel exports if these exports surged and disrupted markets. In 2005 both the European Union and the United States took advantage of the agreement to reimpose quotas on Chinese imports. See J. Kanter and K. Bradsher, "A Return to Quotas," *New York Times*, November 9, 2005.

to that of other states. In terms of Hay's metaphor, the problem is not just that the storm center of the world has shifted to China—something that is truer today than a century ago. The problem is the widespread perception in the United States that a China-centered "red storm," as Lou Dobbs put it on the June 27, 2005 edition of his CNN show, "is hitting our shores."

After brewing for years, the issue of how open the US "door" should be to Chinese exports and investment erupted in the panic over the bid of China National Offshore Oil Company (CNOOC) for US oil company Unocal. Although Unocal had already agreed to being taken over by Chevron, as it eventually was, on June 30 the House passed a resolution by a 398-to-15 vote, stating that allowing CNOOC to buy Unocal would "threaten to impair the national security of the United States." Emotions ran high. A director of the Central Intelligence Agency in the Clinton administration called CNOOC the corporate vehicle of "a Communist dictatorship," echoing Dobbs's "red storm" rhetoric. A senior Defense Department official in the Reagan administration described the CNOOC move as a step in providing China with the resources needed "to supplant the United States as the premier economic power in the world and, should it become necessary, defeat us militarily."[3]

Hard as it is to tell where Cold War anti-communism ends and anxiety about a new competitor begins, the 2005 panic over CNOOC's bid for Unocal is reminiscent of late 1980s US anxieties about the "Japanese threat." Back then, Doug Henwood recalls, it was claimed that,

> having destroyed our industrial base through "unfair" competition, the Japanese had moved on to buying up US assets, like Treasury bonds, Rockefeller Center and MCA. The real threat, of course, was that the United States was facing a serious economic competitor. . . . That it was Asian gave the anxious a deep toxic reservoir to draw upon. Then the Japanese bubble burst, and the threat of the yellow peril receded. But it's back again, this time with a Chinese face.[4]

Even observers like Krugman, who fifteen years earlier had urged the US public not to panic about Japanese purchases of US corporations, felt that the "Chinese challenge looks a lot more serious than the

---

3 S. Lohr, "Who's Afraid of China Inc.?" *New York Times*, July 24, 2005.
4 D. Henwood, "Chinese Shark Attack," *The Nation*, July 12, 2005.

Japanese challenge ever did." Krugman found "nothing shocking" about the fact that the Chinese seemed to be no longer "satisfied with the role of passive financiers [of the US foreign debt] and demand the power that comes with ownership." Indeed, the United States should be relieved that the Chinese sought to use their dollars to buy US companies rather than dumping them. Yet, he saw two reasons why Chinese investment differed from Japanese investment fifteen years earlier. One reason is that the Chinese show no inclination to "squander their money [in prestige investments] as badly as the Japanese did." Their investments, therefore, promise to be less of a subsidy to the United States than Japanese investments were. But the more important reason is that "China, unlike Japan, really does seem to be emerging as America's strategic rival and a competitor for scarce resources." This made the Chinese bid for Unocal, an energy company with global reach, "more than just a business proposition."

> Unocal sounds . . . like exactly the kind of company the Chinese government might want to control if it envisions a sort of "great game" in which major economic powers scramble for access to far-flung oil and natural gas reserves. (Buying a company is a lot cheaper, in lives and money, than invading an oil-producing country). . . . If it were up to me, I'd block the Chinese bid for Unocal. But it would be a lot easier to take that position if the United States weren't so dependent on China right now, not just to buy its IOUs, but to help America to deal with North Korea now that the U.S. military is bogged down in Iraq.[5]

All the symptoms of the China syndrome discussed in Chapter 7 are apparent in this diagnosis. The 9/11 attacks had given the neo-conservatives within the Bush administration the golden opportunity they had been waiting for to invade Iraq in the pursuit of the double objective of overcoming the Vietnam syndrome and tightening US control over global energy supplies. Although engagement on the West Asian front involved setting aside the campaign to constrain China long advocated by the neo-conservatives, it was reasonable for them to expect that a quick and easy victory in Iraq would create highly favorable conditions for resuming the campaign more effectively. By the summer of 2004, however, it had become clear that the invasion of Iraq was not going to attain its original objectives and was

---

5 P. Krugman, "The Chinese Challenge," *International Herald Tribune*, June 28, 2005.

instead facilitating the consolidation and further expansion of China's economic and political power in the East Asian region and beyond. A feeling thus began to creep into circles close to the Bush administration that momentum was being lost in the campaign to contain China and that the time had come to devise more realistic alternatives to the failed neo-conservative plan.

The purpose of this chapter is to survey three such alternatives, the problems which they pose, and the reasons why US policies towards China have been characterized by an incoherent mix of the three. All three alternatives have been proposed by conservatives but constitute different logical possibilities that, in one variant or another, can be expected to guide US policies regardless of which party rules the roost in Washington. Which plan will eventually prevail is hard to tell. All we can say for certain is that anti-Chinese rhetoric cuts across party lines and a Democratic administration is unlikely to depart from the repertoire of policies laid out here.

Coming to Terms with China's Ascent

The United States is in the habit of sending to China "bizarrely mixed" signals.

> Play in the capitalist ballpark but not so well that you become one of the big stars. It is a message that, as with the Japan-bashing of the 1980s, is at best paranoid and at worst racist. We in the West can be trusted with enormous economic power, but not the children of a lesser god."[6]

The panic over CNOOC's bid for Unocal sent even more contradictory signals. "We handed China the money they are using to try to buy Unocal," said Clyde V. Prestowitz, a trade official in the Reagan administration. "And now we're telling the Chinese, please keep investing in our bonds but you can't invest what amounts to a sliver of their surplus in an oil company. That's really confused and hypocritical on our part."[7] Worse still, legislators who "authorized the 'preemptive' conquering of the nation with the second-largest oil

---

6 R. Scheer, "On China at Least, Nixon Was Right," *Los Angeles Times*, July 26, 2005.

7 Quoted in Lohr, "Who's Afraid of China Inc.?" *New York Times*, July 24, 2005.

reserves on the planet [are] now challenging China's right to use dollars it earned exporting legal products to buy a U.S.-based multi-national company." While Asians "should [not] feel in the least bit threatened [by] Unocal's ownership of natural gas fields on their continent," Democrats and Republicans alike claim a US right to prevent the Chinese from buying Unocal for reasons of national security, despite the fact that the United States is "the only nation with the military power to implement or prevent a worldwide blockade of [oil] or any other vital resource."[8]

These contradictory signals, and the entire CNOOC event, were integral to a shift of US policy to a more belligerent, anti-Chinese stance. Already at the Republican convention in New York in August 2004, it was proclaimed that "America will help Taiwan defend itself." That same summer, the US Navy carried out "Operation Summer Pulse '04," which involved the simultaneous deployment at sea of seven of the twelve US carrier strike groups. Although only three of the carrier strike groups were sent to the Pacific, the show of force deeply alarmed the Chinese. To calm things down, on October 26 Secretary of State Powell declared to the press in Beijing that "Taiwan is not independent. It does not enjoy sovereignty as a nation, and that remains our policy, our firm policy. . . . We want to see both sides not take unilateral action that would prejudice an eventual outcome, a reunification that all parties are seeking."[9]

Despite Powell's unequivocal statement, after the November election and the transition from Powell's to Rice's State Department, US policy swung conspicuously towards an aggressive anti-Chinese stance. On February 19, 2005 the United States and Japan signed a new military agreement and issued a declaration in which for the first time Japan joined the United States in identifying security in the Taiwan Strait as a "common strategic objective." "Nothing could have been more alarming to China's leaders"—notes Chalmers Johnson—"than the revelation that Japan had decisively ended six decades of official pacifism by claiming a right to intervene in the Taiwan Strait."[10] The official New China News Agency described the joint declaration as "unprecedented" and quoted a senior foreign ministry official as saying that China "resolutely opposes the United States and Japan in issuing any bilateral document concerning

---

8 Scheer, "On China at Least, Nixon Was Right." See also A.M. Jaffe, "China's Oil Thirst: Wasted Energy," *International Herald Tribune*, July 28, 2005.

9 Chalmers Johnson, "No Longer the 'Lone' Superpower: Coming to Terms with China," Japan Policy Research Institute (2005), available at http://www.jpri.org, p. 7.

10 Ibid.

China's Taiwan, which meddles in the internal affairs of China and hurts China's sovereignty."[11]

A few months later, on June 4, Rumsfeld gave a speech at a strategy conference in Singapore in which he observed that China "appears to be expanding its missile forces, allowing them to reach targets in many areas of the world," and is otherwise "improving its ability to project power" in the region. He then went on to ask, "Since no nation threatens China, one must wonder: Why this growing investment? Why these continuing large and expanding arms purchases? Why these continuing robust deployments?" Considering that US planes and warships constantly hover off the Chinese coast; that nuclear-armed US missiles are aimed at China; that US bases encircle China on all sides; and that, over the past ten years, the United States has delivered ever more potent weapons to Taiwan—considering all this, to Beijing, remarks Michael Klare, "these comments must have been astonishing." Astonishing or not, the comments "exhibited a greater degree of belligerence towards China than had been expressed in any official US statements since 9/11, and were widely portrayed as such in the American and Asian press."[12]

A month later, a report on Chinese combat capabilities released by the Pentagon confirmed the belligerent stance. Although the document stressed the weaknesses as well as the strengths of China's military establishment, its main thrust was that China was expanding its capacity to fight wars beyond its own territory and that this constitutes a dangerous challenge to global order. "The pace and scope of China's military build-up are, already, such as to put regional military balances at risk," the report stated. "Current trends in China's military modernization could provide China with a force capable of prosecuting a range of military operations in Asia—well beyond Taiwan—potentially posing a credible threat to modern militaries operating in the region." The Chinese reacted promptly. At a hastily arranged meeting, a senior foreign ministry official told the American ambassador that the report purposefully disseminated the theory of a "China threat." "It crudely interferes in China's internal affairs and is a provocation against China's relations with other countries."[13]

By the time panic over the CNOOC bid for Unocal broke out in

---

11 Quoted in M. Klare, "Revving Up the China Threat: New Stage in US China Policy," *Japan Focus*, October 13, 2005.

12 Klare, "Revving Up the China Threat . . ."

13 Ibid.

Congress and in the media, the Bush administration had thus already resumed its campaign to contain and possibly rollback Chinese power. In this respect, however, distracted as it was by the Iraq War, the administration had fallen behind Congress in anti-Chinese sentiment, especially over the US trade deficit and the allegedly unfair Chinese practices that lay at its roots. Indeed, the administration's resumption of anti-Chinese initiatives in the geopolitical sphere may well be interpreted as aimed at countering pressure in Congress for stepped-up anti-Chinese initiatives in the commercial sphere.

This much is implied in the distinction drawn by the neo-conservative Max Boot between "good China-bashing and bad China-bashing." As he explained,

> bad bashing centers on complaints about Chinese goods flooding our market. The fact is, their success shows a lack of competitiveness in our economy. But the Rumsfeld comments [that China is spending too much on its military budget and not moving fast enough toward "a more open and representative government"] are good bashing, because China's rapid arms build-up . . . [threatens] Taiwan and could ignite an arms race that takes Japan, South Korea and Taiwan nuclear.

In Boot's view, this is why China should refrain in military spending, in spite of US military expenditures five to ten times greater than China's, and accept the Asian status quo with US forces guaranteeing regional security.[14]

Boot's arguments are broadly consistent with the National Security doctrine of September 2002, according to which US forces "will be strong enough to dissuade potential adversaries from pursuing a military buildup in hopes of surpassing, or equaling, the power of the United States." Nevertheless, in the new climate of global sensitivity to American bullying and increasing US economic dependence on China, the Bush administration had to tread more lightly in its attempt to preserve US power. Hence its reluctance to undertake protectionist initiatives that might provoke China into retaliatory measures that would raise US interest rates with unpredictable deflationary consequences on US construction and consumer spending. As the chairman of President Bush's Council of Economic Advisers (now Federal Reserve Chairman), Ben S. Bernanke, put it

---

14 Quoted in R. Cohen, "Shaping China's Future Power," *New York Times*, June 12, 2005.

in July 2005, the US government saw itself as having "little choice except to be patient" as it works to create conditions for a reversal of roles that would make the United States more of a producing nation, even stepping up its exports to Asia, and induce Asia—especially China—to take on more the role of consumer.[15]

In spite of the greater belligerence towards China on geopolitical issues (Boot's "good China-bashing"), difficulties in Iraq called for a more realist posture even in this sphere. The new "realism born in Iraq, an undertaking so costly in terms of American standing and credibility in the world that it has complicated, and may render impracticable, any further exercise of pre-emptive action in the war on terror," soon became evident in "an effort to repair some of the damage of the first [Bush four-year term] by reaching out to allies, listening to them, and attempting cooperative action from Iran to Kossovo."[16] This more realist posture born in Iraq was nonetheless hard to pin down where it matters most—in US–Chinese relations. Moreover, what realism in US–Chinese relations might mean was (and still is) a highly controversial issue even among conservatives. The wide range of variation is best illustrated by the radically contrasting positions of Robert Kaplan, Henry Kissinger, and James Pinkerton.

Towards a New Cold War?

Kaplan's position is an elaboration of Mearsheimer's strategy of containment of Chinese power through a "balancing coalition."[17] Like Mearsheimer, Kaplan contends that the emergence of China as a great power is inevitable and so is the clash of such an emergence with US interests. "Whenever great powers have emerged . . . (Germany and Japan in the early decades of the twentieth century, to cite two recent examples), they have tended to be particularly assertive—and therefore have thrown international affairs into violent turmoil. China will be no exception." Quite legitimately, in Kaplan's view,

the Chinese [have invested] in diesel-powered and nuclear-powered submarines . . . not only to protect their coastal shelves but

---

15 L. Uchitelle, "China and the U.S. Embark on a Perilous Trip," *New York Times*, July 23, 2005.

16 Cohen, "Shaping China's Future Power."

17 Mearsheimer's views were anticipated in Chapter 7 and will be discussed more fully in Chapter 11.

also to . . . safeguard sea lanes for the transport of energy resources from the Middle East and elsewhere. Naturally, they do not trust the United States . . . to do this for them. Given the stakes, and given what history teaches us about the conflicts that emerge when great powers all pursue legitimate interests, the result is likely to be the defining military conflict of the twenty-first century: if not a big war with China, then a series of Cold War-style standoffs that stretch out over years and decades.[18]

In order to win this new Cold War, the United States "must approach power in the most cautious, mechanical, and utilitarian way possible, assessing and reassessing regional balances of power" without being "led astray by the raptures of liberal internationalism and neo-conservative interventionism." As had been the case under moderate Republican presidents like George H.W. Bush, Gerald Ford, and Richard Nixon, the management of risk must again become "a governing ideology." Military adventures like the war on Iraq will have to be carefully avoided.

> Even if Iraq turns out to be a democratic success story, it will surely be a from-the-jaws-of-failure success that no one in the military or the diplomatic establishment will ever want to repeat—especially in Asia, where the economic repercussions of a messy military adventure would be enormous . . . since the United States and China . . . have the capacity to keep fighting even if one or the other lost a big battle or a missile exchange.

In order to avoid such a dangerous course, Kaplan advocates a Bismarckian strategy of containment centered on the US Pacific Command, known as PACOM. Following the German commentator Josef Joffe, he claims that the invasion of Afghanistan exposed a situation in which the United States resembled Bismarck's Prussia. Britain, Russia, and Austria needed Prussia more than they needed one another, thus making them "spokes" to Berlin's "hub." The invasion of Afghanistan showed that the United States could forge different coalitions for different crises, because the world's other powers needed the United States more than they needed one another.

---

18 Robert D. Kaplan, "How We Would Fight China," *Atlantic Monthly* (June 2005), pp. 50–1.

Unfortunately, the United States did not immediately capitalize on this new power arrangement, because President George W. Bush lacked the nuance and attendant self-restraint of Bismarck, who understood that such a system could endure only so long as one didn't overwhelm it. The Bush administration did just that, of course, in the buildup to the invasion of Iraq, which led France, Germany, Russia, and China, along with a host of lesser powers such as Turkey, Mexico, and Chile, to unite against us.[19]

Fortunately, however, a Bismarckian arrangement still prospered in the Pacific, "helped along by the pragmatism of our Hawaii-based military officers, five time zones removed from the ideological hothouse of Washington, D.C." Indeed, claimed Kaplan, PACOM "represents a much purer version of Bismarck's imperial superstructure than anything the Bush administration created prior to invading Iraq." By negotiating bilateral security agreements with countries that have few such arrangements with one another, the US military had formed a Pacific military alliance of sorts, centered on a "a geographic hub of comparative isolation—the Hawaiian Islands—with spokes reaching out to major allies such as Japan, South Korea, Thailand, Singapore, Australia, New Zealand, and India. These countries, in turn, could form secondary hubs to help us manage the Melanesian, Micronesian, and Polynesian archipelagoes, among other places, and also the Indian Ocean."[20]

This "large but nimble construct," unencumbered by a diplomatic bureaucracy, constitutes an "up and running" substitute for the alliance system of the latter half of the twentieth century. "Warfare by committee, as practiced by NATO, has simply become too cumbersome in an age that requires light and lethal strikes." Forging inter-operability with friendly Asian militaries, by constantly moving US troops from one training deployment to another, "would be an improvement over NATO, whose fighting fitness has been hampered by the addition of substandard former-Eastern-bloc militaries." Moreover, "tensions between the United States and Europe currently impede military integration, whereas our Pacific allies, notably Japan and Australia, want more military engagement with the United States, to counter the rise of the Chinese navy." Betting on PACOM does not mean giving up on NATO. On the contrary, "the vitality of NATO itself . . . could be revived by the Cold War in the Pacific—and indeed

---

19 Ibid., p. 50.
20 Ibid., pp. 51, 54–5.

the re-emergence of NATO as an indispensable war-fighting instrument should be America's unswerving aim."

> NATO is ours to lead—unlike the increasingly powerful European Union, whose own defense force, should it become a reality, would inevitably emerge as a competing regional power, one that might align itself with China in order to balance against us. . . . NATO and an autonomous European defense force cannot both prosper. Only one can—and we should want it to be the former, so that Europe is a military asset for us, not a liability, as we confront China.[21]

The idea that the United States "will no longer engage in the 'cynical' game of power politics," in other words, "is illusory." "We will have to continually play various parts of the world off China, just as Richard Nixon played less than morally perfect states off the Soviet Union." The stage will be the Pacific rather than the Atlantic, and the main actor will be PACOM rather than NATO. But the purpose of the game will be pretty much the same: "to dissuade China so subtly that over time the rising behemoth would be drawn into the PACOM alliance system without any large-scale conflagration—the way NATO was ultimately able to neutralize the Soviet Union." Kaplan cautions that US efforts in this direction "will require particular care, because China, unlike the Soviet Union of old (or Russia today, for that matter), boasts soft as well as hard power." By establishing business communities and diplomatic outposts and by negotiating construction and trade agreements all over the globe, "the Chinese are becoming masters of indirect influence." Moreover,

> [b]usiness people love the idea of China. . . . China's mixture of traditional authoritarianism and market economics has broad cultural appeal throughout Asia and other parts of the world. And because China is improving the material well-being of hundreds of millions of its citizens, the plight of its dissidents does not have quite the same market allure as did the plight of the Soviet Union's Sakharovs and Sharanskys.[22]

Kaplan's New Cold War strategy undoubtedly reflects an important current of thought within the Bush administration. For example, according to an Asian security expert and a former defense official,

---

21 Ibid., p. 64.
22 Ibid., p. 54.

"The buzzword in the Pentagon is 'inter-operability' between the US and Taiwan." The cooperation is "really coming close to re-establishing the alliance" that existed between Taiwan and the US before Washington switched its recognition to Beijing. Although neither Japan nor the United States want to admit it, a retired diplomat now at the Heritage Foundation claims that there is "far, far more than meets the eye" in intelligence exchanges between Japanese and Taiwanese forces via the US Pacific command.[23]

More significantly, elements of Kaplan's strategy can be detected in the testimony of Admiral William Fallon, Commander of PACOM, before the Senate Armed Services Committee on March 8, 2005 three months before the publication of Kaplan's article. To counter China's military modernization, Fallon called for improvements in US anti-missile and antisubmarine warfare capabilities, along with a deepening of US military ties with old and new allies in Asia aimed at containing China to its home territory. He described the Theater Security Cooperation Plan for enhanced military cooperation with US allies in the region as "one of the primary means through which we extend US influence, develop access and promote competence among potential coalition partners." The cooperation typically includes the delivery of arms and military assistance, joint military maneuvers, regular consultation among senior military officials, and the expansion or establishment of US military bases. In Japan, for example, PACOM is cooperating in the joint development of a regional ballistic missile defense system; in the Philippines, it is assisting in the reorganization and modernization of national forces; in Singapore—which already plays host to visiting US aircraft carriers—"we are exploring opportunities for expanded access to Singaporean facilities." Fallon also described efforts to woo India into the coalition. "Our relationship with the Indian Integrated Defense Staff and the Indian Armed Services continues to grow," he noted. "US and Indian security interests continue to converge as our military cooperation leads to a stronger strategic partnership."[24]

It would seem from this testimony that Kaplan's New Cold War Strategy is nothing but an elaboration of policies advocated by PACOM itself. And yet, three months after the publication of Kaplan's article, Fallon explicitly rejected the idea that a series of Cold War-style

---

23 M. Dickie, V. Mallet, and D. Sevastopulo, "Washington is turning its attention from the Middle East to contemplate a previously disregarded threat that the Bush administration now sees as more worrying even than North Korea's nuclear weapons programme" (*Financial Times*, April 7, 2005).

24 Klare, "Revving Up the China Threat . . ."

standoffs stretching out over years and decades is likely to be the defining military conflict of the twenty-first century. "Do we have conflict because of the rise of China? I don't believe so," he declared. "As they grow, there's going to be an inevitable push as they take advantage of their economic ability to improve their military capabilities," he said of the Chinese. "We ought to recognize that as a reality. This is not a zero-sum game." In spite of Rumsfeld's remarks questioning China's motives in modernizing its military forces, Fallon went on to claim that he had received a clear mandate from Washington to build a network of contacts with the Chinese government and military through which the power overlap could be managed rather than fought over.[25]

We do not know whether this is just front-stage rhetoric aimed at covering up what is going on back-stage. We do know, however, that Kaplan's is by no means the only route back to the realism of moderate Republican presidents like Nixon, Ford, and Bush the elder. On the contrary, the intellectual father of that realism has been advocating an altogether different route.

Towards Adjustment and Accommodation?

Despite his warnings concerning fundamental differences between the sources of present Chinese and past Soviet power, Kaplan's strategy rests on the premise that China's challenge, like the Soviet, is ultimately military and can be effectively met through the manipulation of a system of military alliances centered on the Pacific rather than the Atlantic. In an article published at about the same time as Kaplan's, Kissinger advanced a radically different realist position. While agreeing that the "center of gravity of world affairs is shifting from the Atlantic . . . to the Pacific," Kissinger questioned the assumption that a strategic confrontation with China is inevitable.

> That assumption is as dangerous as it is wrong. The European system of the 19th century assumed that its major powers would, in the end, vindicate their interests by force. Each nation thought that a war would be short and that, at its end, its strategic position would have improved.[26]

---

25 E. Cody, "Shifts in Pacific Force. U.S. Military to Adapt Thinking," *Washington Post*, September 17, 2005.

26 H.A. Kissinger, "China: Containment Won't Work," *Washington Post*, June 13, 2005.

In a globalized world of nuclear weapons, such calculations make no
sense. "War between major powers would be a catastrophe for all
participants; there would be no winners." Moreover, the kind of
military imperialism that led Germany to challenge Britain with a
naval build-up and to seek to humiliate Russia over Bosnia in 1908
and France in two crises over Morocco in 1905 and 1911, "is not the
Chinese style."

> Clausewitz, the leading Western strategic theoretician, addresses
> the preparation and conduct of a central battle. Sun Tzu, his
> Chinese counterpart, focuses on the psychological weakening of
> the adversary. China seeks its objectives by careful study, patience
> and the accumulation of nuances—only rarely does China risk a
> winner-take-all showdown.[27]

For similar reasons, China is not the Soviet Union. The Soviet Union
was heir to an imperialist tradition that expanded Russia from the
region around Moscow to a territorial empire that stretched from
central Europe to Vladivostok. "The Chinese state in its present
dimensions," in contrast, "has existed substantially for 2,000 years."
More important, China's affirmation of cooperative intentions and
denial of a military challenge express the strategic realities of a
situation in which,

> even at its highest estimate, the Chinese military budget is less than
> 20 percent of America's . . . barely, if at all, ahead of that of Japan
> and . . . much less than the combined military budgets of Japan,
> India and Russia, all bordering China—not to speak of Taiwan's
> military modernization supported by American decisions made in
> 2001. . . . The challenge China poses for the medium-term future
> will, in all likelihood, be political and economic, not military.[28]

It follows that applying to China the policy of military containment of
the Cold War, as Kaplan proposes to do, "is unwise." A Cold War
with the United States can indeed have a "potentially catastrophic
impact . . . on the continued raising of the [Chinese] standard of
living, on which the legitimacy of the government depends." But it
does not follow that a Cold War with China would benefit the United
States. "We would have few followers anywhere in Asia. Asian

---

27 Ibid.
28 Ibid.

countries would continue trading with China. Whatever happens, China will not disappear." The US interest therefore lies in cooperating with China in the pursuit of a stable international system. In such a pursuit, adds Kissinger,

> Attitudes are psychologically important. China needs to be careful about policies seeming to exclude America from Asia and our sensitivities regarding human rights . . . America needs to understand that a hectoring tone evokes in China memories of imperialist condescension and that it is not appropriate in dealing with a country that has managed 4,000 years of uninterrupted self-government.[29]

Kissinger's realist position is remarkably compatible with the Chinese doctrine of *heping jueqi* (literally "emerging precipitously in a peaceful way"). The doctrine was first launched in 2003 at the Boao Forum for Asia—China's attempt to create a Davos-style World Economic Forum for Asia. Based on historical investigations commissioned by the Politburo of past experiences of rising powers and the reactions they triggered, it was advanced as a direct rebuttal of the idea of a "China threat" and as a charm offensive designed to counter the US strategy of encircling China with a system of military bases and security relationships. The central tenet of the doctrine is that China can and will avoid the road of aggression and expansion followed by earlier rising powers. In the words of Zheng Bijian, one of the framers and main advocates of the doctrine, "China will not take the road of Germany in the first world war, or Germany and Japan in the second world war—using violence to pillage resources and seek world hegemony."[30] Rather, as a researcher at a government-affiliated organization put it, "China aims to grow and advance without upsetting existing orders. We are trying to rise in a way that benefits our neighbors."[31]

Since it was first launched, the expression "peaceful rise/emergence" has come under attack from opposite fronts both within and outside the Communist Party. At one pole, there are people who, following Deng Xiaoping's maxim that China should "hide its brightness," feel that speaking at all of a *rise*, even if peaceful, fuels

---

29 Ibid.

30 Quoted in M. Leonard, "China's Long and Winding Road," *Financial Times*, July 9–10, 2005.

31 Quoted in Y. Funabashi, "China Is Preparing a Peaceful Ascendancy," *International Herald Tribune*, December 30, 2003.

ideas of a Chinese threat. At the opposite pole, there are people who feel that speaking of a *peaceful* rise gives the message to the United States and Taiwan that they can impudently push China around. "Between these two poles, the political leadership hedges."[32] Although the expression "peaceful rise" has been quietly dropped in favor of "peaceful development" or "peaceful coexistence," the underlying doctrine has nonetheless remained firmly in place, as witnessed by President Hu Jintao's 2004 proclamation of "four nos" ("no to hegemony, no to force, no to blocs, no to the arms race"), and "four yeses" (to "confidence building, reducing difficulties, developing cooperation, and avoiding confrontation").[33] To Chinese officials, there is no contradiction between their doctrine of "peaceful development" and their determination to develop more capable armed forces, which they see as integral to China's development as well as a natural response to the humiliations from the opium wars of the mid nineteenth century to the brutal Japanese invasion and occupation in 1931–45. "China's national defense policy is one of self-protection," claimed Prime Minister Wen Jiabao, in April 2005. "Over the past 100 years, China has always been bullied by others. China has never sent a single soldier to occupy even an inch of another country's land."[34]

Hu reiterated China's commitment to "peaceful development" during a visit to the United Nations in New York in September 2005, underscoring the challenges entailed in managing and raising the prosperity of a nation of 1.3 billion. According to US officials, both the challenges and the vision impressed Bush.[35] Nevertheless, in a comprehensive statement of the Bush administration's position on China delivered shortly afterwards, Deputy Secretary of State Robert Zoellick described the United States as a "cauldron of anxiety." "Uncertainties about how China will use its power will lead the United States—and others as well—to hedge relations with China. . . . Many countries hope China will pursue a 'peaceful rise,' but

---

32 Leonard, "China's Long and Winding Road."

33 Quoted in M. Bulard, "China: Middle Kingdom, World Centre," *Le Monde Diplomatique*, August 2005.

34 Dickie, Mallet, and Sevastopulo, "Washington is turning its attention from the Middle East . . ." Wen here conveniently glossed over China's invasions of India in the early 1960s and Vietnam in the late 1970s. Nevertheless, as we shall see in Chapter 11, the image of China being bullied by others (especially Japan and the Western powers), fits perfectly well the historical record from the opium wars to the establishment of the PRC.

35 P. Baker and P.P. Pan, "Bush's Asia Trip Meets Low Expectations," *Washington Post*, November 21, 2005.

none will bet their future on it." While accepting that "China does not want a conflict with the United States," he went on to lay down markers by which Chinese behavior will be evaluated. These included an explanation of China's defense spending, intentions, and doctrine; greater opening rather than managing of markets, including currency markets; less tolerance of "rampant theft of intellectual property and counterfeiting"; ensuring North Korea's compliance with an agreement to end its nuclear programs, supporting efforts to end Iran's nuclear programs, and pledging more money to Afghanistan and Iraq; stop attempting to "maneuver toward a prominence of power" in Asia by building separate alliances; speed-up political reforms by considering elections at the county and provincial levels and "stop harassing journalists who point out problems."[36]

The very length of Zoellick's list of markers, many of them impossible to verify or unlikely to materialize, was more indicative of US anxieties than of a coherent agenda. The lack of a coherent agenda was further evinced by the mixed signals that the US government kept sending to China. During a visit to China in October 2005, Treasury Secretary John W. Snow, who had repeatedly criticized China's refusal to allow the yuan to float more freely, praised the Five Year Plan that the CCP had just approved as "beneficial not only for China but good for the world." He especially applauded the plan's objective to reduce the huge divide between city-dwellers and hundreds of millions of mostly rural Chinese, because if the prosperity of rural Chinese improves even marginally, they will probably buy more American goods and the US trade deficit with China will decrease.[37]

Soon after Snow departed, Rumsfeld himself arrived in Beijing. While still criticizing increased Chinese defense spending, he reached an agreement with his Chinese counterparts to "join hands to upgrade Sino-US military ties and make them consistent with overall bilateral relations." Indeed, rumor had it that on this trip Rumsfeld tried to sell US weapons to China, even as he was publicly criticizing its leadership.[38]

At the root of these mixed signals we can detect the difficulties that the loss of credibility of US military power in Iraq created for the

36 G. Kessler, "U.S. Says China Must Address its Intentions," *Washington Post*, September 22, 2005.

37 T. Sakai, "Hu Jintao's Strategy for Handling Chinese Dissent and U.S. Pressure," *Japan Focus*, November 20, 2005.

38 Ibid.

capacity of the United States to keep in check or turn to its own advantage China's "peaceful ascent." Failure in Iraq called for a greater dose of realism in US policies. And yet, it made it more difficult for the United States to mobilize allies in the kind of military-based containment of Chinese power envisaged, for example, in Kaplan's "New Cold War" strategy. Suffice it to mention the case of Singapore, which Kaplan hailed as a model US ally in the PACOM-led coalition he advocated. As the influential dean of the Lee Kuan Yew School of Public Affairs in Singapore, Kishore Mahbuhani, made clear, Singapore's cooperation with PACOM does not imply support for US policies aimed at destabilizing China. On the contrary, as many others in East Asia do, he saw a sudden end of Communist rule in China as the trigger of dangerous nationalist forces that would lead to conflict in the region to no one's benefit.[39]

Not surprisingly, therefore, US attempts to encircle China through a system of military alliances went nowhere. US intelligence and military ties with Vietnam and India improved. But relations between these two countries and China improved even more. At the same time, after years of enmity towards China and a long alliance with the United States, Indonesia concluded a strategic partnership with Beijing that President Hu hailed as inaugurating a "new era" in relations between the two nations. A similar shift has occurred in South Korea. During their visits to the country in November 2005, President Bush was mortified by Seoul's announcement that it would withdraw a third of its troops from Iraq, while President Hu received a standing ovation in the South Korean assembly and declared that relations between South Korea and China had entered the "best era in history."[40] Only Japan moved decisively towards closer military ties with the United States. These closer ties, however, seemed to isolate Japan rather than China. Along with Koizumi's tactless visits to the Yasukumi shrine, they cost Japan the much sought-after permanent seat on the United Nations Security Council, as well as the cancellation in December 2005 of the three-way meeting with China and South Korea that had been held on the sidelines of ASEAN gatherings every year since 1999. This is probably why Koizumi's replacement with Shinzo Abe as Japan's prime minister in 2006 was welcomed not

---

39 M. Vatikiotis, "U.S. Sights Are Back on China," *International Herald Tribune*, June 7, 2005.

40 Cody, "Shifts in Pacific Force . . ."; E. Nakashima, "Vietnam, U.S. to Improve Intelligence, Military Ties," *Washington Post*, June 17, 2005; J. Burton, V. Mallet, and R. McGregor, "A New Sphere of Influence: How Trade Clout Is Winning China Allies yet Stocking Distrust," *Financial Times*, December 9, 2005.

just in Asian capitals but also in Japan as a chance for a shift in direction toward more cooperation between China and Japan.[41]

At the opposite end of the realist spectrum from Kaplan, the mixture of accommodation of Chinese power and reliance on political-economic mechanisms of containment that Kissinger advocated was undoubtedly more acceptable to actual and potential US allies but it was much harder to "sell" to the US electorate. The nearly unanimous opposition to the Chinese bid for Unocal in the House of Representatives was but one of many signs that anti-China sentiment was stronger in Congress across party lines than in the Bush administration.[42] Sino-phobia has a long tradition in US popular culture. But its sudden resurgence at the turn of the twenty-first century was prompted by the realization that China, rather than the United States, was emerging as the main beneficiary of the globalization project that the United States itself had sponsored in the 1980s and 1990s. To expect further economic integration across the Pacific to redress the situation in favor of the United States required a major act of faith in the ultimate competitiveness of the US economy. While most in Congress professed that faith, few behaved accordingly and thus undermined the feasibility of strategies aimed at accommodating China's "peaceful ascent."

A Happy Third?

Considerations of this kind underlies the advocacy of yet another route to greater realism in US policies towards China. Writing in *The*

---

41 B. Wallace, "Japan Looks at Ridding Military of its Shackles," *Los Angeles Times*, November 23, 2005; T. Shanker, "U.S. and Japan Agree to Strengthen Military Ties," *New York Times*, October 30, 2005; Burton, Mallet, and McGregor, "A New Sphere of Influence. . ."; V. Mallet, "Japan's Best Chance to Strike a Deal with China," *Financial Times*, September 28, 2006.

42 G. Dinmore, A. Fifield, and V. Mallet, "The Rivals," *Financial Times*, March 18, 2005. Another sign was the struggle between Congress and the administration over the imposition of tariffs on Chinese imports to force China to let its currency revalue vis-à-vis the dollar. In April 2005, the Republican-controlled Senate voted 67 to 33 for an amendment sponsored by Democratic Senator Charles Schumer and Republican Senator Lindsey Graham aimed at imposing a 27.5 percent tariff on Chinese imports if China failed to change its currency policies. Although the administration managed to convince Schumer and Graham to withdraw the amendment, pressure from Congress forced it to enter into negotiations with China to restrict its exports to the United States. E. Andrews, "Bush's Choice: Anger China or Congress over Currency," *New York Times*, May 17, 2005.

American Conservative, Pinkerton was as critical as Kissinger of strategies of military containment—including Kaplan's PACOM-based strategy.

> A cliché of the era is that China is analogous to Kaiser Wilhelm II's Germany, a rising power looking for its "place in the sun." If so, then it's a question of how the Chinese will be restrained. In the case of Germany, a grand coalition of France, Britain, Russia, and the United States was required—twice—to bring Berlin to heel. It remains to be seen whether the United States could ever assemble an equivalently large coalition to restrain China.[43]

Pinkerton considered this a remote possibility. Worse still, any attempt to assemble such a coalition, in his view, would provoke a disastrous war with China. He was nonetheless even more critical of the alternative strategy of accommodation. Without referring explicitly to Kissinger, he dubbed such a strategy "neo-Angellism" because of its resemblance to Norman Angell's 1910 contention that war had become obsolete. The reasons that Angell—like today's "dogmatic globalists"—gave for this alleged obsolescence were, first, that nations connected to one another other by economics had no choice but to cooperate on politics, and, second, that military and political power no longer gave any commercial advantage. Reassuring as neo-Angellism might be to businesspeople, Pinkerton found it flawed in fundamental ways.

The main flaw is outsourcing. In support of the view that outsourcing is essential to US competitiveness, Pinkerton quoted the executive of a large American multinational company who told him "You show me a company that doesn't do its manufacturing in China, and I'll show you a company that can be beaten, competitively." At the same time, however, he underscored how outsourcing creates a substantial backlash in the United States, as workers fear losing their jobs, and especially how it jeopardizes US national security:

> a totally post-industrial America would be unable to produce the necessary implements of war, should they be needed. Indeed, the Pentagon is struggling to maintain some sort of domestic industrial base for the U.S. . . . [I]f present trends continue, the Chinese will

---

43 James P. Pinkerton, "Superpower Showdown," *The American Conservative*, November 7, 2005, p. 5 available at http://www.amconmag.com.

soon be able simply to pull the plug on our economy—and so we won't be able to fight China even if we want to, or have to, which might make war all the more tempting to the Chinese.

He then went on to cite the British Conservative politician Leo Amery, "who had regularly argued against Angell, as well as other dogmatic globalists."

> Amery warned that Germany's mercantilist neighbor-beggaring economic strategy, the opposite of Britain's Angellist approach, was giving the Kaiser a dangerous war-production advantage. "The successful powers will be those who have the greatest industrial base," Amery prophesied, adding that those holding "the industrial power and the power of invention and science will be able to defeat all others." As Winston Churchill, whom Amery served in Britain's World War II cabinet, once observed, a country engaged in war needs the tools to finish the job.[44]

A second flaw is that Angellism "will not prove politically acceptable to hawkishly Beijing-bashing Americans." To be sure, "most of the Fortune 500 will engage lobbyists to keep the trade routes open to the east." And yet, "all the lobbyists on K Street could not tamp down the wildfire of anti-Chinese feeling that erupted over the failed bid by the China National Overseas Oil Company to buy . . . Unocal."

> If issues of status and primacy are at stake, it seems as though lizard brains take over, diminishing rational thinking—as nationalism, xenophobia, and more primitive reflexes rise up in a sanguinary primordialism. The outcome is predictable: as with Angell 90 years ago, the neo-Angells will be overwhelmed yet again.[45]

In short, while a military strategy of containment would lead to a disastrous war with China, because "if you fake something long enough, you will make it happen," neo-Angellism "would lose its D.C. policy struggle to the [nationalist-militarist] camp—which then would go back to fighting its disastrous war with China." So, asks Pinkerton, what is to be done? "Are America's only choices militaristic jingoism or naive Angellism?"[46] The better choice, he claimed, is

---

44 Ibid., p. 8.
45 Ibid., pp. 8–9.
46 Ibid., pp. 6–7, 9.

a two-pronged strategy. Following Michael Lind, on the geopolitical front he advocated the containment of China through a balance-of-power strategy.

> For centuries, [Britain] juggled European rivals against each other, and it worked well for the Empire. So if the British could play off the likes of the Bourbons, Hapsburgs, Hohenzollerns, and Romanovs, perhaps the U.S. can play off the inevitable rivalry of the Asian powers. It's the good fortune of Americans, after all, that we are unchallenged in our own hemisphere and likely to remain so for a long time to come. And by our further good fortune, three enormous powers—China, India, and Japan—are all next to each other, just like Spain, France, Holland, and Germany in times past.[47]

Instead of confronting directly the rising Asian powers, the United States should play them off each other. As the Latin expression *tertium gaudens*—the happy third—reminds us, rather than getting in the middle of every fight, sometimes it is better "to hold the coats of those who do." For the US national interest, "a better Asia would be one in which China, India, Japan, and possibly another 'tiger' or two contend with each other for power while we enjoy the happy luxury of third-party by-standing."[48]

A prerequisite of success in the pursuit of this strategy is a realist solution of the Taiwanese problem. Barring a general war, just as the US North reunified with the South after the Civil War, so China will reunify with Taiwan. "The federal government in Washington . . . would not have looked kindly on any foreign power that sought to assure the secession of Richmond. . . . Using honest realpolitik, the U.S. should tell Taipei that its optimal course is a peaceful Hong Kong/Macau-like return to the motherland." Freed from the Taiwan issue, the United States would be in a position to reap the benefits rather than bear the costs of conflicts among the three great powers of Asia. "So if Japan, for instance, marched down the nuclear road . . . other Asian powers would resist such Japanese rearmament, but that should be their problem, not ours. It's better to be the happy third in any such Asian struggle—not an unhappy primary participant."[49]

In order to become the "happy third" on the geopolitical front,

---

47 Ibid., p. 9.
48 Ibid., p. 1.
49 Ibid., p. 10.

however, action is needed also on the home front. "Americans should keep from kidding themselves that our currently booming domestic real-estate market . . . will assure our long-term geopolitical primacy." Such a primacy can only be attained through a "21st-century equivalent of Alexander Hamilton's 18th-century 'Report on Manufactures' "; that is, a decision of what industries are essential to national security, and "a conscious techno-industrial policy to make sure that those vital industries remain onshore." Although this neo-Hamiltonian policy would increase the price of consumer goods, raise interest rates, and perhaps lower the stock market, these "are a small price to pay for true national security." Pinkerton acknowledged that this two-pronged strategy was beyond the current horizon of US polity and society. He nonetheless hoped "that the dire wake-up call, when it comes, will not be too damaging. Bad policies can be reversed, although, unfortunately, it usually takes a defeat to get the attention of policymakers and the public."[50]

This happy-third strategy has far more important precedents in US history than Pinkerton acknowledged. In his view, only in 1901–09—mostly during the presidency of Theodore Roosevelt—did the United States practice such a strategy.[51] In reality, as we have seen in Chapter 8, throughout the nineteenth century, and especially in the first half of the twentieth century, the United States benefited immensely from the conflicts that set the European powers against one another. And its capacity to turn the world wars of the early twentieth century to its own advantage was due as much to the self-sufficiency and technical proficiency of its military-industrial complex, as it was to relative continental isolation.

Whether avowed or not, in the wake of defeat in Iraq, the United States may well attempt to fall back on this tradition. Nevertheless, the Asian elements of the balancing-power mode that Pinkerton advocates can already be detected in present US policies. Koizumi might indeed have believed that his repudiation of six decades of Japan's official pacifism "to supplant Australia as Washington's 'deputy sheriff' in the Asia–Pacific region" would strengthen the sheriff's ultimate commitment to the protection of Japan in the eventuality of a conflict with China.[52] But it is also possible that past and future US encouragement of Japanese involvement in the

---

50 Ibid., p. 11.
51 Ibid.
52 S. Tisdall, "Japan Emerges as America's Deputy Sheriff in the Pacific," *Guardian*, April 19, 2005.

Taiwanese dispute are inscribed, not in a Kaplan-type coalition-building strategy, but in a Pinkerton-type balancing-power strategy. That is to say, US encouragement of Japan's emergence from its recent pacifist past to become again a military power of regional significance may turn out to be a way of facilitating US military disengagement from East Asia through the creation within Asia of military counterweights to China.

This eventuality, of course, does not need to be, and probably is not, the undeclared objective of present US policies. But it may well be the fallback (or "plan B") to which the United States can advantageously resort should the attempt to build a PACOM-led anti-Chinese coalition fail to materialize or become too risky. Indeed, the possibility that failure in Iraq may result in a military disengagement of the United States from the East Asian region has not escaped Taiwanese observers. Thus, in October 2005, Taiwan's former minister of foreign affairs, T'ien Hung-mao, stated in an interview with local media:

> If the United States pulls out of Iraq, America will be swept by isolationism and not want to become involved overseas, and the spread of Chinese hegemony will pick up speed. As America's desire for a fight falls, the likelihood of a military conflict in the Taiwan Straits will decrease. The Taiwanese government should face up to this scenario, and make realistic plans about how it will deal with such a situation.[53]

The Taiwanese government may not be inclined to face up to this scenario. Significantly, however, its indecision at the end of 2005 on whether to finance an arms-procurement package on offer from Washington for more than four years caused indignation in the US Congress. After noting that Taiwan had accumulated tens of billions of dollars of foreign-exchange reserves, Tom Lantos, at the time the senior Democrat on the Foreign Affairs Committee of the House of Representatives, ominously declared: "If you expect us to come to your aid, to quibble over an 18 billion-dollar package is an outrage."[54]

Outrageous or not, the Taiwanese indecision does not just betray the suspicion that the protection offered by a US-sponsored anti-

---

53 Quoted in Sakai, "Hu Jintao's Strategy. . ."
54 Quoted in Dickie, Mallet, and Sevastopulo, "Washington is turning its attention from the Middle East . . ." See also Cody, "Shifts in Pacific Force . . ."

Chinese coalition may not be all that reliable. It points also to a basic contradiction of the happy-third strategy. If the United States disengaged militarily from the region, why should the Asian powers escalate their mutual conflicts to the benefit of the United States, rather than seek mutual accommodation to their own benefit? The capacity of the United States to be the *tertium gaudens* of the intra-European power struggles of the early twentieth century depended critically on an intensity and inner momentum of those struggles that have no equivalent in contemporary Asia. Indeed, as noted in previous chapters, East Asia has been the true "happy third" of the late twentieth and early twenty-first centuries. In the 1980s, Japan and the four "little tigers" were the main beneficiaries of the escalation of the Cold War between the United States and the USSR, and lately China has been emerging as the real winner of the US War on Terror. Miscalculations, of course, are always possible. *Pace* Latos, however, it is unclear why all of a sudden the Asian states would engage in an armament race that would benefit the US armament industries and economy but would seriously undermine the creditor position that constitutes the main source of the Asian states' power.

Indeed, the first East Asian summit held in Kuala Lampur in December 2005 already showed how difficult it would be for the United States to play Asian states off one another. Washington had always opposed the very idea of such a summit and had promoted the far more inclusive APEC as an alternative forum in which the United States would be the most influential participant. In recent years, however, while US influence relative to China within APEC has declined, the importance of an expanding ASEAN that excludes the United States and includes China in decisions affecting East Asia has been steadily rising.[55] "While China and America spar over geopolitical preeminence, the rest of East Asia just want a more efficient trading area and access to a larger market. And right now, the biggest market is China." As a result, at the ASEAN summit meeting held in the Philippines in January 2007, China took center-stage, signing a

---

55 ASEAN first expanded to include China, Japan, and South Korea into the so-called ASEAN+3 in the wake of the 1997–8 East Asian financial crisis. This was a move explicitly aimed at reducing the influence of the United States, which was widely perceived as being responsible for the seriousness of the crisis. The further expansion of the ASEAN+3 into the ASEAN+3+3, to include India, Australia, and New Zealand as full participants at the first East Asian summit, in contrast, was seen primarily as a move to balance China in the absence of the United States. See S. Mydans, "New Group for 'Asian Century' Shuns U.S," *International Herald Tribune*, December 12, 2005; Burton, Mallet, and McGregor, "A New Sphere of Influence . . ."

new trade-in-services agreement and, more important, fully participating in various agreements aimed at steering the association towards an EU-style charter.[56]

The Great Wall of Unknowns

In July 2004, a commentary published in the *International Herald
Tribune* lamented the lack of a US China strategy.

> Our actions defy coherent categorization. Do we treat China as a
> full partner? Rarely. Do we treat China as a competitor? Some-
> times. Are we confident about how we act? Almost never. Not
> much of a policy. The U.S. has been lucky that more crises,
> economic or political, have not materialized while it has been
> occupied with Iraq.[57]

Two and a half years later, the United States still has no China
strategy to speak of. The realization that US difficulties in Iraq have
consolidated China's empowerment has led to a stepping-up of anti-
Chinese initiatives and simultaneously to a greater dose of realism in
US policies. But the resulting combination continues to defy coherent
categorization.

We can detect at least three main reasons for this continuing lack of
a coherent US China policy. One is that for the Bush administration
the decisive battle to contain the rising power of China is still being
fought in Iraq. Earlier dreams of an easy victory that would have
enabled the United States to deal with China from a position of
strength have given way to the objective of withdrawing from Iraq
with minimal losses to US credibility. Under these circumstances,
anti-Chinese rhetoric and attempts to empower the Australian and
especially Japanese "deputy sheriffs" in East Asia have been stepped
up. But until the United States has disentangled itself from the Iraqi
quagmire, it has to continue to engage China. From this standpoint,
there has been no incoherence in the US China policy: just a tactical
adaptation to the necessity of rescuing what can be rescued of US
credibility vis-à-vis China and the world at large. Even critics of the

---

56 M. Vatikiotis, "East Asia Club Leaves U.S. Feeling Left Out," *International
Herald Tribune*, April 6, 2005; C.H. Conde, "China and Asean Sign Broad Trade
Accord," *International Herald Tribune*, January 15, 2007.

57 T. Manning, "America Needs a China Strategy," *International Herald
Tribune*, July 22, 2004.

administration in Congress agree on this. An early complaint among Democrats about the invasion of Iraq was that it distracted the United States from the task of confronting China. But once the Iraqi adventure went sour, Democrats themselves became deeply divided on what ought to be done to cut losses. The debate thus shifted to the issue of whether and how to withdraw from Iraq, overshadowing concerns over the "Chinese threat."

A second reason for the continuing lack of a coherent China policy is conflicting visions of what constitutes national interest. There is a fairly general agreement among observers that a strategy of adjustment and accommodation suits the interests of US business, especially big business.[58] US big business has indeed embraced Chinese economic expansion far more enthusiastically than it embraced Japanese economic expansion in the 1980s, in spite of the greater long-term challenge that China poses to US preeminence.

> The welcome that China is offering to multinational companies and foreign investment has left many Western business executives, so critical of a closed Japan more than a decade ago, enthusiastically embracing China, its cheap work force and its huge markets. . . . Japan rapidly caught up with the West by licensing technology. . . . But China has both licensed technology and used the attraction of its potentially huge market to lure foreign investment. That has not only brought further investment but . . . has also helped to insulate China from trade clashes. Many of the same multinationals that once fought with the Japanese, like the Detroit automakers, are now big investors in China—investors that oppose trade restrictions on it.[59]

At the same time, however, the old saying that what is good for General Motors is good for America no longer goes unchallenged, quite apart from the fact that China's best customer, Wal-Mart, has displaced General Motors as America's largest corporation. Voicing a widely held view, Fishman asserted that "China's promise looks so magnificent to big U.S. corporations and the super-rich that the U.S. national interest and the long-term health of the economy count

---

58 As the previously quoted passages show, Kaplan and Pinkerton are in agreement on this. Although Kissinger does not say anything explicit about the interests of big business, he nonetheless felt obliged in the previously quoted article to acknowledge that his consulting firm advises corporations doing business with China.

59 K. Bradsher, "Like Japan in the 1980's, China Poses Big Economic Challenge," *New York Times*, March 2, 2004.

little."[60] In support of this view, it is often noted that nearly half of US exports and imports are traded within multinational corporations, which move materials and components back and forth among their far-flung factories and relocate production across national boundaries to cut costs, especially wage costs. While corporations and investors benefit greatly from this kind of operation, it is claimed, the nations themselves, including the United States, do not.[61]

Granted the possibility of a conflict between the interests of US corporations and the US national interest, there is no agreement on whether closer US–Chinese economic integration advance the national interest. Conservatives like Pinkerton emphasize the threat that outsourcing poses to national security. But even leading exponents of the military–industrial complex doubt whether US military preeminence can be maintained without some outsourcing, which in any event involves China marginally or not at all.[62] Democrats and organized labor emphasize jobs lost to China through trade and outsourcing, and call for protective measures and government action to force China to revalue its currency. But others emphasize the even greater danger of a rapidly depreciating US dollar, which might "risk America's global political clout" and plunge the United States "into the debt trap long suffered . . . by Latin America."[63] And some point to the benefits that the flood of cheap Chinese credit and commodities bring not just to the super-rich but also to the lower strata of US society.

> The United States is awash in debt. . . . Much of the debt is held by
> workers ramping up their loans on one credit card after another, or

---

60 T. Fishman, "Betting on China," *USA Today*, February 16, 2005.

61 See, among others, W. Greider, "Trade Truth that the Public Won't Hear," *International Herald Tribune*, July 19, 2005; and J. Petras, "Statism or Free Markets: China Bashing and the Loss of US Competitiveness," *CounterPunch*, October 22, 2005.

62 A recent Pentagon study identified seventy-three mostly Western European foreign suppliers who provided parts to twelve of the most important US weapon systems. "Our job is to get the best for the war fighter," said the Pentagon's chief weapons buyer. "Innovation is not always bounded by borders. We want the best capability at the most cost-effective price and from the best suppliers we can find." A senior vice-president at Lockheed Martin, the largest US military contractor, for his part declared that the United States could not have all its military supplies made within the country even if it wanted to. US industrial partners are always sought out first, but in some cases there is no choice but to look overseas. See L. Wayne, "U.S. Weapons, Foreign Flavor," *New York Times*, September 27, 2005.

63 Fishman, "Betting on China."

obtaining dubious mortgages in a bid to secure some fraction of the heady lifestyle of an upper class that keeps getting richer. . . . The spread of debt is one of the more significant social phenomena in the United States today, allowing the less well-off to spend more than they have and so assuage feelings of being left behind by the conspicuous rich. As long as interest rates do not rise steeply, this social process will continue to function. Hence Hu [Jintao]'s heft on Main Street.[64]

In short, as Krugman put it, the United States has "developed an addiction to Chinese dollar purchases"—and we may add, to cheap Chinese products—"and will suffer painful withdrawal symptoms when they come to an end." Breaking the addiction might eventually make US industries more competitive, but the painful withdrawal symptoms will come first.[65] The more things went sour in Iraq, the more dependent did the Bush administration become on this addiction in order to prevent things from going sour also on the economic and social front at home. Hence the administration's reluctance to press China too hard on the appreciation of the yuan, its praise for the CCP's 2005 Five Year Plan, and more generally its greater restraint than Congress in complaining about Chinese goods flooding the US market and US jobs being lost to China.

Stepped-up anti-Chinese rhetoric and initiatives on the geopolitical front—Boot's "good China-bashing"—have not been mere cover for this greater restraint in bashing China on economic issues—Boot's "bad China-bashing." Nor have they been mere chest-thumping to reassure client states (and to warn potential competitors) in East Asia and elsewhere that difficulties in Iraq have not reduced US resolve to preserve its regional and global military predominance. It has also been the expression of the national interest as understood by the core electoral base of the Republican Party under neo-conservative hegemony.

As Thomas Frank has argued, one of the most significant US political phenomena of the past two decades has been the rise of what he calls "backlash conservatives." These are mostly white working-class and middle-class Americans who have reacted to their loss of status and relative income by identifying themselves more with God, the armed forces, and the Republican Party, than with their class

64 R. Cohen, "China and the Politics of a U.S. Awash in Debt," *International Herald Tribune*, May 21, 2005.

65 P. Krugman, "The Chinese Connection," *New York Times*, May 20, 2005.

interests, working-class organizations, and the Democratic Party. The neo-conservatives skillfully exploited this disposition to win the popular vote and, once in power, to carry out policies that benefited the rich while indirectly reproducing the frustrations that led their popular base to identify itself with God, the armed forces, and the Republican Party.[66]

From this perspective, though not from the perspective of more traditional conservatives within and outside the Republican Party, it did not matter that the US government and consumer became ever more addicted to cheap Chinese credit and products. What mattered most was that the US President be seen "as rooted, patriotic, a real man, and, for some, a divine agent in the White House."[67] This meant that restraint in "bad" China-bashing had to be accompanied by stepped-up "good" China-bashing, warning the Chinese Communist leadership not to dare to challenge the supremacy of the US armed forces and instead to embrace American freedoms and values. And the greater the troubles of the US armed forces in Iraq, the louder the warning had to become. In short, a second reason for the continuing lack of a coherent US China policy has been the dual allegiance of the Bush administration to big business and moneyed interests on the one side, and to "backlash conservatives" on the other. From this standpoint, the incoherence of US China policies has been an expression of the need of the Bush administration to accommodate the inclination of US capital to profit from the Chinese economic expansion, and simultaneously pander to the nationalist-militarist dispositions of its electoral base.

A third and, for present purposes, last reason for the continuing lack of a coherent US China policy has been the difficulty of figuring out present and future trends of the Chinese political economy. In this regard, US observers and politicians have faced "a great wall of

---

66 Thomas Frank, *What's the Matter with Kansas? How Conservatives Won the Heart of America* (New York, Owl Books, 2005).

67 Cohen, "China and the Politics of a U.S. Awash in Debt." As Cohen notes, "there is nothing very new in people confronted by economic difficulties turning to God, patriotism and the armed forces." Indeed, there are some similarities between early twenty-first-century militaristic jingoism in the United States and jingoism in Britain a century earlier. The main difference is the far greater emphasis on God rather than Empire in the US brand of jingoism—an emphasis deeply rooted in the religious tradition of US expansionism. On the religious tradition of US expansionism, see Clyde W. Barrow, "God, Money, and the State: The Spirits of American Empire," Forschungsgruppe Europäische Gemeinschaften (FEG), Arbeitspapier 22, Universität Marburg.

unknowns." There has been a growing realization that "the very magnitude and speed of China's growth . . . made it an unpredictable X factor in the world [political] economy. Good and bad surprises will multiply—unprecedented gains, losses, threats and opportunities." But there has been little understanding of what these surprises might be.

> All we know for certain is that we really don't know. With a country as big as China undergoing so much dramatic change— moving from a "command and control" economy to a market system—the chances that anyone has a complete picture of what's going on are slim or nonexistent. In a smaller country, our ignorance wouldn't matter much. But in China, it's slightly terrifying.[68]

What is most terrifying, of course, is that this ignorance has informed the policies of a country, the United States, that has the capacity to unleash the Armageddon that the most fanatic groups among backlash conservatives are gleefully waiting for. The problem is not just that using knowledge of the present and past to forecast the future is always a difficult and risky endeavor. The main problem lies rather in the kind of knowledge that is being mobilized for this purpose. "Chinese history," Lyric Hughes Hale notes "is barely studied in the United States." Many who talk about China "sprinkle a few facts on a well-worn agenda," while conveniently ignoring facts that do not fit into the agenda.[69] Worse still, such a sprinkling of a few facts on a well-worn agenda is evident also in the assumptions that underlay US policies towards China and the proposed alternative realist strategies discussed in this chapter. With the exception of Kissinger's, they all ignore completely Chinese history and rely on a very reductive reading of Western history. Some selective reading of the past is, of course,

---

68 R.J. Samuelson, "Great Wall of Unknowns," *Washington Post*, May 26, 2004.

69 For example, those who complain about the United States losing 2 million manufacturing jobs mostly to China are silent on the "many millions more Chinese [who]have lost theirs over the same period of time, mostly because of restructuring of state-owned enterprises." And those who complain about intellectual property violations in China conveniently forget that similar laws were flouted in Japan, until Japanese companies themselves needed the same protection. L.H. Hale, "It's a Juggernaut . . . Not!: The China of our Imagination Bears No Resemblance to Reality," *Los Angeles Times*, May 22, 2005.

necessary in order to pierce through the great wall of unknowns that surrounds the prospective consequences of China's ascent. But which particular selective reading is most useful to foresee what to expect or not to expect is a question that has no easy answer. This is the question to which we now turn.

11

STATES, MARKETS, AND CAPITALISM, EAST AND WEST

In a recent exchange with Mearsheimer, Zbigniew Brzezinski gave an assessment of China's "peaceful ascent" that closely resembles Kissinger's. "China is clearly assimilating into the international system. Its leadership appears to realize that attempting to dislodge the United States would be futile, and that the cautious spread of Chinese influence is the surest path to global preeminence." Against this assessment, Mearsheimer reiterated the view that "China cannot rise peacefully." If its dramatic economic growth continues over the next few decades, "the United States and China are likely to engage in an intense security competition with considerable potential for war. Most of China's neighbors, including India, Japan, Singapore, South Korea, Russia, and Vietnam, will likely join with the United States to contain China's power."[1]

Mearsheimer and Brzezinski see their contrasting views as being rooted in a difference of method. Mearsheimer privileges theory over political reality, because "we cannot know what political reality is going to look like in the year 2025." A theory of the rise of great powers, in contrast, can tell us what to expect "when China has a much larger gross national product and a much more formidable military than it has today." His theory has "a straightforward answer" on what to expect: China will "try to push the United States out of Asia, much the way the United States pushed the European great powers out of the Western Hemisphere"; and the United States "will seek to contain China and ultimately weaken it to the point where it is no longer capable of dominating Asia . . . [behaving] toward China much the way it behaved toward the Soviet Union during the Cold War."[2]

---

1 Zbigniew Brzezinski and John L. Mearsheimer, "Clash of the Titans," *Foreign Policy* (January–February, 2005), p. 2.

2 Ibid., pp. 2–3.

Brzezinski, in contrast, privileges political reality over theory, because "theory—at least in international relations—is essentially retrospective. When something happens that does not fit the theory, it gets revised." He suspects that this will be the case with the US–China relationship. For one thing, nuclear weapons have altered power politics. The avoidance of direct conflict in the US–Soviet standoff "owed much to weaponry that makes the total elimination of societies part of the escalating dynamic of war. It tells you something that the Chinese are not trying to acquire the military capabilities to take on the United States." Moreover, how great powers behave is not predetermined. "If the Germans and the Japanese had not conducted themselves the way they did, their regimes might not have been destroyed." In this respect, "the Chinese leadership appears much more flexible and sophisticated than many previous aspirants to great power status."[3]

There is much to be said for both methods. What happens in the "short-run" of a decade or two is determined by a host of contingent and random events that in a longer perspective, as Mearsheimer put it, "get washed out of the equation" by more durable underlying trends. Unless we have a theory capable of identifying and explaining these more durable trends, we will be at a loss in figuring out what will happen when the "dust" of contingent and random events settles. However, durable underlying trends are neither unchanging nor ineluctable; nor are contingent and random events mere "dust." Ideally, a theory of world politics and society must be able to account for change, as well as continuity, in the behavior and mutual inter-actions of key actors; it must allow for learning, if not from the theory itself, at least from the historical experiences that the theory attempts to describe and explain; and it must specify the conditions under which contingent and random events, instead of being "washed away," can destabilize established trends and facilitate the emergence of new ones. This is no easy task. But to be of any use, a theory of the relationship between incumbent and emergent great powers must fulfill at least two requirements: it must be grounded in the historical experiences that are most germane to the problem at hand; and it must leave open the possibility of breaks with underlying trends. If the problem with Brzezinski's views is that they have no theoretical foundation, the problem with Mearsheimer's views is that they rule out any deviation from the predicted outcome (i.e., a military confrontation) and are built on wholly inappropriate historical foundations.

---

3 Ibid., p. 3.

Mearsheimer downplays the role that markets and capital have played historically as instruments of power in their own right. He does see the continuing economic growth of China as a condition of its eventual transformation into a great power capable of challenging the United States militarily. But, in his scheme of things, only the conversion of economic power into the kind of military power that is now concentrated in the hands of the United States can transform China into a truly great power.

> If the Chinese are smart, they will . . . concentrate on building their economy to the point where it is bigger than the U.S. economy. Then they can translate that economic strength into military might and create a situation where they are in a position to dictate terms to states in the region and to give the United States all sorts of trouble. . . . The great advantage the United States has at the moment is that no state in the Western Hemisphere can threaten its survival or security interests. So the United States is free to roam the world causing trouble in other people's backyards. Other states, including China of course, have a vested interest in causing trouble in the United States' backyard to keep it focused there.[4]

The possibility that it might be "smarter" on the part of the Chinese to continue to use their rapidly expanding domestic market and national wealth as instruments of regional and global power (as they are already doing, while the allegedly all-powerful US military apparatus is bogged down in Iraq) is ruled out on specious historical grounds. In dismissing Brzezinski's contention that China's desire for continued economic growth makes conflict with the United States unlikely, Mearsheimer argues that "that logic should have applied to Germany before World War I and to Germany and Japan before World War II." And yet, despite their "impressive economic growth," Germany started both world wars and Japan started conflict in Asia.[5] In reality, neither Germany before the First World War, nor Germany and Japan before the Second World War were all that successful *economically*. They were very successful *industrially*, but in terms of national wealth they were barely narrowing the per capita income gap that separated them from Britain, and were falling behind the United

---

4 Ibid., p. 4.
5 Ibid., p. 3.

States.[6] Their resort to war can in fact be interpreted as an attempt to attain by military means the power they could not attain by economic means.

The United States, in contrast, had no need to challenge Britain militarily in order to consolidate its growing economic power. As we saw in Chapter 8, all it had to do was, one, let Britain and its challengers exhaust one another militarily and financially; two, enrich itself by supplying goods and credit to the wealthier contestant; and, three, intervene in the war at a late stage so as to be in a position to dictate terms of the peace that facilitated the exercise of its own economic power on the largest possible geographical scale. Today there are no emergent military powers with the inclination or the capacity to challenge the dominant power. Nevertheless, the dominant power is involved in an open-ended war aimed at demonstrating what evidently it cannot demonstrate, namely, that it can impose on the world its interests and values on the basis of the destructive powers of its armed forces. Under these circumstances, could not China's optimal power strategy vis-à-vis the United States be a variant of the earlier US strategy vis-à-vis Britain? Would it not be in China's best interest, one, to let the United States exhaust itself militarily and financially in an endless war on terror; two, to enrich itself by supplying goods and credit to the increasingly incoherent US superpower; and, three, use its expanding national market and wealth to win over allies (including some US corporations) in the creation of a new world order centered on China, but not necessarily dominated militarily by China?

Mearsheimer's failure even to consider this possibility is related to a general tendency on the part of US analysts to focus exclusively on instances of competitive rather than cooperative relations between incumbent and emerging great powers. Thus, the contemporary US–China relation is usually compared with Germany's relation to Britain in the late nineteenth and early twentieth centuries, or Japan's relation to the United States in the inter-war period, or US–Soviet relations after the Second World War. Surprisingly, most US observers disregard what seems to be the most relevant comparison— the comparison, that is, between today's US–Chinese relations and relations between the incumbent hegemonic power of the late nine-

---

6 David Landes, *The Unbound Prometheus: Technological Change and Industrial Development in Western Europe from 1750 to the Present* (Cambridge, Cambridge University Press, 1969), p. 239; Giovanni Arrighi, *The Long Twentieth Century: Money, Power and the Origins of our Times* (London, Verso, 1994), p. 334.

teenth and early twentieth centuries (the United Kingdom) and the economically most successful emergent power of the epoch (the United States). This was a relationship that evolved from deep mutual hostility to increasingly close cooperation, precisely when the United States began challenging British hegemony both regionally and globally.[7] If this has happened before, why can it not happen again? A theory that provides no answer to this question, and predicts that the United States and China are inevitably headed towards a military confrontation two or three decades down the line, may well be worse than no theory at all.

This assessment is especially warranted in view of the fact that Mearsheimer's theory (as well as Kaplan's and Pinkerton's positions discussed in Chapter 10) completely disregards the historical experience of the indigenous East Asian interstate system. The main purpose of this chapter is to show that, not just China (as Kissinger has noted), but the entire East Asian system of interstate relations has been characterized by a long-term dynamic that contrasts sharply with the Western dynamic on which Mearsheimer's theory is based. This different dynamic resulted in a widely recognized Chinese primacy in state- and national economy-making through the eighteenth and early nineteenth centuries. But it created also the conditions for the subsequent subordinate incorporation of the East Asian system within the structures of the globalizing European system. This subordinate incorporation transformed but did not destroy the pre-existing regional system of international relations. More important, it also contributed to the ongoing transformation of the incorporating Western system itself. The result was a hybrid political-economic formation that has provided a particularly favorable environment for the East Asian economic renaissance and the consequent transformation of the world beyond the capacity of theories based on the Western experience to comprehend what is going on.

---

7 As Brad DeLong has noted with specific reference to possible future developments of current US–Chinese relations, as late as the 1840s the United States and Britain came close to war over territorial disputes in the Pacific Northwest and the lucrative fur trade there. But, in subsequent decades, Britain chose to accommodate rather than suppress the United States, developing increasingly close economic and political ties. Quoted in G. Ip and N. King, "Is China's Rapid Economic Development Good for U.S.?" *Wall Street Journal*, June 27, 2005.

The Five Hundred Years' Peace

One of the great myths of Western social science is that national states and their organization in an interstate system are European inventions. In reality, except for a few states that were the creation of European colonial powers (most notably, Indonesia, Malaysia, and the Philippines), the most important states of East Asia—from Japan, Korea, and China to Vietnam, Laos, Thailand, and Kampuchea—were national states long before any of their European counterparts. What is more, they had all been linked to one another, directly or through the Chinese center, by trade and diplomatic relations and held together by a shared understanding of the principles, norms, and rules that regulated their mutual interactions as a world among other worlds. As Japanese scholars specializing in the China-centered tribute trade system have shown, this system presented sufficient similarities with the European interstate system to make their comparison analytically meaningful.[8]

Both systems consisted of a multiplicity of political jurisdictions that appealed to a common cultural heritage and traded extensively within their region. Although cross-border trade was more publicly regulated in East Asia than in Europe, since Song times (960–1276) private overseas trade had flourished and transformed the nature of tribute trade, the main purpose of which, in Takeshi Hamashita's words, "came to be the pursuit of profits through the unofficial trade that was ancillary to the official system." Analogies can also be detected in the interstate competition that characterized the two systems. The separate domains that were held together by the tribute trade system centered on China were "close enough to influence one another, but . . . too far apart to assimilate and be assimilated." The tribute trade system provided them with a symbolic framework of mutual political-economic interaction that nonetheless was loose enough to endow its peripheral components with considerable auton-

---

8 See Satoshi Ikeda, "The History of the Capitalist World-System vs. The History of East-Southeast Asia," *Review*, 19, 1 (1996) for an overview of the contribution of these scholars. The Japanese school builds upon, and critically departs from, the earlier conceptualization of the China-centered system by Fairbank and his students (John K. Fairbank, ed., *The Chinese World Order* [Cambridge, MA, Harvard University Press, 1968]). On the relationship between the two conceptualizations, see Peter C. Perdue, "A Frontier View of Chineseness," in G. Arrighi, T. Hamashita, and M. Selden, eds, *The Resurgence of East Asia: 500, 150 and 50 Year Perspectives* (London and New York, Routledge, 2003).

omy vis-à-vis the Chinese center. Thus Japan and Vietnam were peripheral members of the system but also competitors with China in the exercise of the imperial title-awarding function, Japan establishing a tributary-type relationship with the Ryukyu Kingdom, and Vietnam with Laos.[9] Sugihara explicitly maintains that the diffusion of the best technology and organizational know-how within East Asia makes it "possible to think of the presence of an East Asian multi-centered political system . . . with many features analogous to the interstate system in Europe."[10]

These similarities make a comparison of the two systems analytically meaningful. But, once we compare their dynamics, two fundamental differences become immediately evident. First, as argued in previous chapters, the dynamic of the European system was characterized by an incessant military competition among its national components and by a tendency towards the geographical expansion both of the system and of its shifting center. Long periods of peace among European powers were the exception rather than the rule. Thus, the "hundred years' peace" (1815–1914) that followed the Napoleonic Wars was "a phenomenon unheard of in the annals of Western civilization."[11] Moreover, even during this hundred years' peace European states were involved in countless wars of conquest in the non-European world and in the escalating armament race that culminated in the industrialization of war. While the initial result of these involvements was a new wave of geographical expansion which dampened conflicts within the European system, their eventual result was a new round of wars among European powers (1914–45) of unprecedented destructiveness.[12]

In sharp contrast to this dynamic, the East Asian system of national

---

9 Takeshi Hamashita, "The Tribute Trade System of Modern Asia," *The Memoirs of the Toyo Bunko*, XLVI (1988), pp. 75–6; Takeshi Hamashita, "The Tribute Trade System and Modern Asia," in A.J.H. Latham and H. Kawakatsu, eds, *Japanese Industrialization and the Asian Economy* (London and New York, Routledge, 1994), p. 92; Takeshi Hamashita, "The Intra-Regional System in East Asia in Modern Times," in Peter J. Katzenstein and T. Shiraishi, eds, *Network Power: Japan and Asia* (Ithaca, NY, Cornell University Press, 1997), pp. 114–24.

10 Kaoru Sugihara, "The Economic Miracle and the East Asian Miracle: Towards a New Global Economic History," *Sangyo to Keizai*, XL, 12 (1996), p. 38.

11 While between 1815 and 1914 there were wars among the European powers for a mere three and a half years (including the Crimean War), in each of the two centuries preceding 1815 European powers were at war with one another for an average of sixty to seventy years. See Karl Polanyi, *The Great Transformation: The Political and Economic Origins of our Time* (Boston, MA, Beacon Press, 1957), p. 5.

12 See Chapters 5 and 8, above.

states stood out for the near absence of intra-systemic military competition and extra-systemic geographical expansion. Thus, with the exception of China's frontier wars to be discussed presently, prior to their subordinate incorporation in the European system the national states of the East Asian system were almost uninterruptedly at peace with one another, not for one hundred, but for three hundred years. This three hundred years' peace was bracketed by two Japanese invasions of Korea, both of which precipitated a war with China—the Sino-Japanese wars of 1592–98 and 1894–95. Between 1598 and 1894 there were only three brief wars that involved China—the 1659–60 and the 1767–71 wars with Burma, and the 1788–89 war with Vietnam, and two wars that did not involve China—the Siamese-Burmese wars of 1607–18 and of 1660–62. Indeed, insofar as China is concerned, we should speak of a five hundred years' peace, since in the two hundred years preceding the 1592 Japanese invasion of Korea China was at war with other East Asian states only during the invasion of Vietnam in 1406–28 to restore the Tran dynasty.[13]

The infrequency of wars among East Asian states was associated with a second crucial difference between the East Asian and European systems: the absence of any tendency among East Asian states to build *overseas* empires in competition with one another and to engage in an armament race in any way comparable to the European. East Asian states did compete with one another. Sugihara, for example, detects a competitive relation in two complementary tendencies typical of Tokugawa Japan (1600–1868): its attempt to create a tribute trade system centered on Japan instead of China, and its extensive absorption of technological and organizational know-how in agriculture, mining, and manufacturing from Korea and China. Through these tendencies, as Heita Kawakatsu put it, "Japan was trying to become a mini-China both ideologically and materially."[14] This kind of com-

---

13 Based on information contained in Jaques Gernet, *A History of Chinese Civilization* (New York, Cambridge University Press, 1982); G.S.P. Freeman-Grenville, *History Atlas of Islam* (New York, Continuum, 2002); "Ancient Battles and Wars of Siam and Thailand," in *Siamese and Thai History and Culture*, available at http://www.usmta.com/Thai-History-Frame.htm (1999); "China, 1400–1900 A.D.," in *Timeline of Art History*, the Metropolitan Museum of Art, New York, October 2004, at http://www.metmuseum.org/toah/ht/10/eac/ht10eac.htm, and "Southeast Asia, 1400–1900 A.D," in *Timeline of Art History*, the Metropolitan Museum of Art, New York, October 2001, at http://www.metmuseum.org/toah/ht/08/sse/ht08sse.htm.

14 Sugihara, "The Economic Miracle and the East Asian Miracle, " pp. 37–8; Heita Kawakatsu, "Historical Background," in A.J.H. Latham and H. Kawakatsu, eds, *Japanese Industrialization and the Asian Economy* (London and New York, Routledge, 1994), pp. 6–7.

petition, however, drove the East Asian developmental path towards state- and national economy-making rather than war-making and territorial expansion—that is, in the opposite direction of the European path.

This contention may seem to be at odds with the long series of wars that China fought on its frontiers during the closing years of Ming rule and in the first 150 years of Qing rule. As Peter Perdue has noted, the history of the China-centered system appears in a different light when seen from a "frontier perspective." The presence of nomadic horsemen who raided the borders and sometimes conquered the Chinese capital made military activity particularly prominent in the history of China's north and northwest frontier. Military activity became more prominent when northern conquerors in 1644 established the Qing dynasty and set out to ensure that other northern invaders would not do to them what they had done to the Ming.

> In the north and northwest, China faced much more powerful and more sharply distinctive peoples than on other frontiers. Here it was very clear that the threat of force undergirded the trading-ritual order. The Qing could only seriously claim to be the uncontested central pole of a tribute system focused on Beijing after they had created military alliances with the Eastern Mongols, exterminated the rival Western Mongols, conquered Xinjiang, and secured formal suzerainty over Tibet.[15]

The territorial expansion that ensued, and the military activities that sustained it, fixed the boundaries that all subsequent Chinese regimes would struggle to preserve. Their main purpose was the transformation of a hard-to-defend frontier into a pacified periphery and a buffer against raiders and conquerors from Inner Asia. Once the objective had been attained, as it was by the 1760s, territorial expansion ceased and military activities turned into police activities aimed at consolidating the monopoly of the Chinese state over the use of violence within the newly established boundaries. Although quite substantial, this territorial expansion paled in comparison with the successive waves of European expansion—the earlier Iberian expansion in the Americas and Southeast Asia; the contemporary Russian expansion in North Asia, and Dutch expansion in Southeast Asia; not to speak of

---

15 Perdue, "A Frontier View of Chineseness," pp. 60, 65.

the later expansion of Britain in South Asia and Africa and of its offsprings in North America and Australia. Unlike these successive waves, the Qing expansion was strictly limited in space and time by its boundary-drawing objectives, rather than a link in an "endless" chain of connected expansions.

The difference was not just quantitative but qualitative as well. China's territorial expansion under the Qing was not embedded in the kind of "self-reinforcing cycle," discussed in Chapter 8, whereby the competing military apparatuses of European states sustained, and were sustained by, expansion at the expense of other peoples and polities of the earth. No self-reinforcing cycle of this kind could be observed in East Asia. Qing China's territorial expansion was neither driven by, nor did it result in, competition with other states in extracting resources from overseas peripheries. The logic of political economy associated with this latter kind of competition had little in common with China's practices. "Rather than extract resources from peripheries, the Chinese state was more likely to invest in them. Political expansion to incorporate new frontiers committed the government to a shift of resources to the peripheries, not extraction from them."[16]

These different dynamics of the European and East Asian systems were closely related to, and in key respects determined by, two other differences—a difference in the distribution of power among the systems' units, and a difference in the degree to which the primary source of power was internal or external to the system. Even before the "extended" sixteenth century in European history (1350–1650) and the Ming era in East Asian history (1368–1643), political, economic, and cultural power in East Asia was far more concentrated in its center (China) than in Europe, where a center proper was much harder to identify. But the difference became sharper with the defeat in 1592–98 of Japan's attempt to challenge militarily Chinese centrality and the institutionalization of the European balance of power by the treaties of Westphalia in 1648.

The balanced power structure of the European system in itself contributed to the disposition of European states to wage war on one another. As Polanyi has underscored, balance-of-power mechanisms—the mechanisms, that is, whereby "three or more units capable of exerting power . . . behave in such a way as to combine the power

---

16 R. Bin Wong, *China Transformed: Historical Change and the Limits of European Experience* (Ithaca, NY, Cornell University Press, 1997), p. 148.

of the weaker units against any increase in power of the strongest"—
were a key ingredient in the organization of the nineteenth-century
hundred years' peace. Historically, however, balance-of-power mechanisms had always attained the objective of maintaining the
independence of the participating units "only by continuous war
between changing partners."[17] The main reason why in the nineteenth century those same mechanisms resulted in peace rather than
war is that political and economic power came to be so concentrated
in the hands of Britain as to enable it to transform the balance of
power, from a mechanism that no individual state controlled and
functioned through wars, into an instrument of informal British rule
that promoted peace.[18]

The nineteenth-century association between an increase in the
imbalance of power and a decrease in the frequency of war within
the European system suggests that the imbalance of power typical of
the East Asian system was a reason for the infrequency of wars among
East Asian states. However, the fact that the nineteenth-century
concentration of power in British hands was accompanied by an
escalation of interstate competition both in the production of ever
more destructive means of war and in the use of these means to gain
access to extra-systemic resources, suggests that a greater imbalance
of power cannot in itself explain the virtual absence of these two
kinds of competition in the East Asian system. Some other ingredient
had to be present in the European and absent in the East Asian "mix"
to produce this divergent pattern of interstate competition. The most
plausible candidate is the greater extroversion of the European
developmental path in comparison with, and in relation to, the East
Asian path.

Although trade within, between, and across political jurisdictions
was essential to the operations of both systems, the economic and
political weight of long-distance trade relative to short-distance trade
was far greater in the European than in the East Asian system. East–
West trade in particular was a far more important source of wealth
and power for European than for East Asian states, especially China.
It was this fundamental asymmetry that had made the fortunes of
Venice and induced the Iberian states, instigated and assisted by
Venice's Genoese rivals, to seek a direct link with the markets of the

---

17 Polanyi, *Great Transformation*, pp. 5–7.

18 On the British transformation of the balance of power into an instrument of
informal rule, see Giovanni Arrighi and Beverly J. Silver, *Chaos and Governance in
the Modern World System* (Minneapolis, MN, University of Minnesota Press, 1999),
pp. 59–64.

East.[19] It was this same asymmetry, as we shall see, that underlay the low returns, relative to costs, of Zheng He's fifteenth-century expeditions in the Indian Ocean. Were it not for this asymmetry, Zheng He might very well have sailed "around Africa and 'discover[ed]' Portugal several decades before Henry the Navigator's expeditions began earnestly to push south of Ceuta."[20] Columbus's accidental "discovery" of the Americas, while seeking a shorter route to the wealth of Asia, changed the terms of the asymmetry by providing European states with new means to seek entry in Asian markets, as well as with a new source of wealth and power in the Atlantic. But even two centuries after the discovery, Charles Davenant still claimed that whoever controlled the Asian trade was in a position to "give law to all the commercial world."[21]

In Chapter 8, we argued that this extroversion of the European power struggle was a major determinant of the peculiar combination of capitalism, militarism, and territorialism that propelled the globalization of the European system. The opposite dynamic of the East Asian system—in which a growing introversion of the power struggle generated a combination of political and economic forces that had no tendency towards "endless" territorial expansion—can now be taken as counterfactual evidence in support of that contention. But, just as the emergence of the extroverted European path could only be understood in light of the diffusion of the strategies of power pioneered by the Italian city-states, so the emergence of the introverted East Asian path can only

---

19 Arrighi, *Long Twentieth Century*, ch. 2. The East–West asymmetry has a long history, which antedates the "extended" sixteenth century and the Ming era. See Archibald Lewis, *The Islamic World and the West, A.D. 622–1492* (New York, Wiley, 1970), p. vii; Carlo Cipolla, (*Before the Industrial Revolution: European Society and Economy, 1000–1700* (New York, Norton, 1976), p. 206; Janet Abu-Lughod, *Before European Hegemony: The World System A.D. 1250–1350* (New York, Oxford University Press, 1989), pp. 106–7. In this study, however, we are only concerned with the particular East–West asymmetry that shaped, and was itself transformed by, developments in Europe during the "extended" sixteenth century and in East Asia during the Ming era.

20 Paul Kennedy, *The Rise and Fall of the Great Powers: Economic Change and Military Conflict from 1500 to 2000* (New York, Random House, 1987), p. 7. Alternatively, as McNeill put it, "it is easy to suppose that if the Chinese had chosen to continue sending exploratory voyages overseas, a Chinese admiral, riding the Japan current, might have sailed into San Francisco Bay several decades before Columbus blundered into the Caribbean islands" (William McNeill, "World History and the Rise and Fall of the West," *Journal of World History*, 9, 2 [1998], p. 229). With ships that probably displaced 1,500 tons, compared to the 300-ton flagship of Vasco da Gama, China's seaborne capacity at this time had no peer. See William McNeill, *The Pursuit of Power: Technology, Armed Force, and Society since A.D. 1000* (Chicago, University of Chicago Press, 1982), p. 44.

21 Quoted in Eric Wolf, *Europe and the People without History* (Berkeley, CA, University of California Press, 1982), p. 125.

be understood in light of the success of Ming and Qing policies in developing by far the largest market economy of their times.

Market Economy and China's "Natural" Path to Opulence

National markets are no more a Western invention than national states and interstate systems. As we saw in Part I, Adam Smith knew very well what Western social science later forgot—namely, that through the eighteenth century by far the largest national market was to be found not in Europe but in China. This national market had been long in the making, but its eighteenth-century configuration originated in the state-making activities of the Ming and early Qing.

During the Southern Song period (1127–1276), the heavy military expenditures and reparations involved in the wars with Mongol and Tungusic peoples on China's northern frontiers, along with the loss of control over the silk route, and the weakening of such profitable government monopolies as salt, iron, and wine production, induced the Song court to encourage private sea trade as a source of revenue. Particularly significant was the encouragement of navigation technology through the provision of financial and technical support to shipbuilders. Having pioneered the use of the compass in navigation, the sharp-head, flat-rear and sharp-base design of Chinese junks enabled them to navigate at high speed in turbulent seas like no other vessel in the world. Military pressure and territorial losses in the north provoked also massive migrations towards southern regions, which were especially suitable for high-yielding wet-rice cultivation. Since under this kind of cultivation additional inputs of labor could increase significantly the productivity of land, the population of these regions grew rapidly, achieving densities far higher than in Europe. Moreover, the efficiency of wet-rice cultivation in guaranteeing surpluses of food above subsistence enabled farmers to increase the quantity and variety of products cultivated and marketed and to engage in non-agricultural activities.[22]

---

22 Giovanni Arrighi et al., "Historical Capitalism, East and West," in Giovanni Arrighi, Po-keung Hui, Ho-fung Hung, and Mark Selden, eds, The Resurgence of East Asia: 500, 150 and 50 Year Perspectives (London and New York, Routledge, 2003), pp. 269–70; Jung-pang Lo, "Maritime Commerce and its Relation to the Sung Navy," Journal of the Economic and Social History of the Orient, XII (1969), pp. 77–91; Francesca Bray, The Rice Economies: Technology and Development in Asian Societies (Berkeley, CA, University of California Press, 1986), p. 119; Mark Elvin, The Pattern of the Chinese Past (Stanford, CA, Stanford University Press, 1973), ch. 9; Ravi A. Palat, "Historical Transformations in Agrarian Systems Based on Wet-Rice Cultivation: Toward an Alternative Model of Social Change," in P. McMichael, ed., Food and Agrarian Orders in the World-Economy (Westport, CT, Praeger, 1995), p. 59.

Under the joint impact of maritime trade and the development of wet-rice cultivation, the coastal regions experienced a long economic upswing based on advances in navigation technology, the consolidation of the "sea silk route," and the flourishing of Guangzhou, Quanzhou, and smaller port cities on the southeastern coast as centers of tributary trade. At the same time, Chinese settlements throughout insular Southeast Asia boosted private sea trade, which surpassed official tributary trade as the main form of economic exchange between China and maritime Asia.[23] Continuing state support for private sea trade and migration to southeast Asia under the Yuan (1277–1368) led to the formation of overseas Chinese trading networks across the Southern Seas and the Indian Ocean as extensive as any contemporaneous European network. Under the Song and the Yuan, tendencies which would later become typical of the European developmental path were thus already present in East Asia.[24]

In East Asia, however, these tendencies did not lead to interstate competition in building overseas commercial and territorial empires as they did in Europe. On the contrary, under the Ming, they were brought under control through policies that prioritized domestic trade and, at times, proscribed foreign trade. The shift of the capital from Nanjing to Beijing, to protect more effectively the northern frontier from Mongolian invasions, extended to the north the circuits of market exchange that had formed in the south. Moreover, in order to guarantee the supply of food to the capital and surrounding region, the Ming repaired and extended the canal system that connected the rice-growing southern regions to the northern political center, thereby promoting the further growth of the market economy and "canal cities" in the lower Yangzi region. Also important was the early Mings' promotion of cotton-growing in the north. The ensuing specialization of the north in the production of raw cotton and of the lower Yangzi in the manufacturing of cotton textiles further

23 Lo, "Maritime Commerce and its Relation to the Sung Navy," pp. 57–8; Po-keung Hui, "Overseas Chinese Business Networks: East Asian Economic Development in Historical Perspective," PhD Thesis, 1995, Department of Sociology, State University of New York at Binghamton, pp.29–30.

24 Lien-Shen Yang, *Money and Credit in China: A Short History* (Cambridge, MA, Harvard University Press, 1952); Elvin, *The Pattern of the Chinese Past*, ch. 14; Yoshinobu Shiba, "Sung Foreign Trade: Its Scope and Organization," in M. Rossabi, ed., *China among Equals: The Middle Kingdom and its Neighbors, 10th–14th Centuries* (Berkeley, CA, University of California Press, 1983), pp. 106–7; Luquan Guan, *Songdai Guangzhou de haiwai maoyi* (The Guangzhou Sea Trade in the Song Dynasty) (Guangzhou, Guangdong renmin chubanshe, 1994), pp. 57–60.

expanded the national market by fostering north–south trade along the grand canal.[25]

While promoting the formation and expansion of a national market, the Ming sought to centralize control over revenues, by imposing administrative restrictions on sea trade and on Chinese migration to southeast Asia. Admiral Zheng He's seven great voyages to southeast Asia and across the Indian Ocean between 1405 and 1433 were also meant to extend state control over foreign trade. The expeditions, however, turned out to be exceedingly expensive; and as the Ming became more preoccupied with immediate military threats on the northern frontiers, they were discontinued. For more than a century after that the Ming regime turned inward: it continued to promote internal trade but circumscribed private maritime commerce, cracked down on unauthorized external trade with maritime Asia, restricted the number of tributary missions, and even banned the building of seagoing ships.[26]

Janet Abu-Lughod claims that Ming China's withdrawal from the Indian Ocean "has perplexed—indeed caused despair among—serious scholars for at least the past one hundred years." More specifically,

> Close to exercising domination over a significant portion of the globe and enjoying a technological advantage not only in peaceful production but in naval and military might as well . . . why did [China] turn her back, withdraw her fleet, and thus leave an enormous vacuum of power that Muslim merchantmen, unbacked by state sea power, were totally unprepared to fill, but which their European counterparts would be more than willing and able to— after a hiatus of some 70 years?[27]

The previously noted asymmetry between the pursuit of wealth and power in the East Asian and European contexts provides a simple

---

25 Arrighi et al., "Historical Capitalism, East and West," p. 271; Ho-fung Hung, "Imperial China and Capitalist Europe in the Eighteenth-Century Global Economy," *Review* (Fernand Braudel Center), 24, 4 (2001), pp. 491–7.

26 Gungwu Wang, "Ming Foreign Relations: Southeast Asia," in Denis Twitchett and Frederick Mote, eds, *The Cambridge History of China, Vol. 8 (2): The Ming Dynasty* (Cambridge, Cambridge University Press, 1998), pp. 316–23; William McNeill, *The Pursuit of Power: Technology, Armed Force, and Society since A.D. 1000* (Chicago, University of Chicago Press, 1982), p. 47; Binchuan Zhang, "Mingqing haishang maoyi zhengce: biguanzishou?" (The Sea Trade Policy of Ming and Qing: Closed Door and Conservative?), *Selected Essays in Chinese Maritime History*, IV (Taipei: Academia Sinica, 1991), pp. 49–51; Hui, "Overseas Chinese Business Networks," pp. 34–8, 53.

27 Abu-Lughod, *Before European Hegemony*, pp. 321–2.

answer to this question. European states fought endless wars to establish an exclusive control over sea lanes linking West to East, because control over trade with the East was a critical resource in their pursuit of wealth and power. For the rulers of China, in contrast, control over these trade routes was far less important than peaceful relations with neighboring states and the integration of their populous domains into an agriculturally based national economy. It was therefore eminently reasonable for the Ming not to waste resources in trying to control East–West sea lanes and concentrate instead on developing the national market, opening up what Smith later took as the exemplar of his "natural" path to opulence.

Indeed, even China's "tribute trade"—the scope of which Zheng He's expeditions sought to expand and the Ming subsequently curtailed—had greater economic costs than benefits. Ever since the establishment of a unified taxation system under the Qin and Han dynasties more than a thousand years earlier, tributary relations between the Chinese imperial court and vassal states did not involve the collection of a tax. On the contrary, especially after the Tang dynasty, and with the sole exception of the Yuan dynasty, vassal states offered the Chinese imperial court only symbolic gifts and received in return much more valuable gifts. Thus, what was nominally "tribute" was in fact a two-way transaction which enabled the Middle Kingdom to "buy" the allegiance of vassal states, and at the same time to control flows of people and commodities across its far-flung frontiers.[28]

The sustainability and efficacy of this practice—which, world-historically, provides the most important illustration of the validity of Hobbes's dictum that "Riches joyned with liberality is Power, because it procureth friends, and servants"—depended on several conditions. The Chinese economy had to generate the resources necessary to buy the allegiance of the vassal states; the Chinese state had to be in a position to command these resources; and surrounding states had to be persuaded that attempts to seize resources from the Chinese state and economy by means that challenged the authority of the Chinese government (such as raids, conquest, war, or just illegal trade) would not pay off. Despite, or possibly because of, their success in consolidating and expanding the national economy, by the early sixteenth century the inward-looking policies of the Ming faced

---

28 Cf. Weinong Gao, *Zou xiang jinshi de Zhongquo yu "chaogong" guo guanxi* (The Relation between China and its Tributary States in Modern Times) (Guangdong, Guangdong gaodeng jiaoyu chubanshe, 1993), pp. 1–78.

increasing difficulties in reproducing these conditions. Widespread corruption, mounting inflation, and increasing fiscal shortfalls on the domestic front, were accompanied by growing external pressures, from the expansion of the Jurchens in the north, and from the expansion of illegal trade that bypassed Ming tax collectors along the southeastern coast. Carried out by armed Chinese and Japanese traders, the illegal trade was actively encouraged by Japanese warlords, who sought to use the profitable trade in Chinese products to finance their mutual struggles. With the financially strapped Ming cutting back on the costly tributary trade, and unable to exercise effective military control over southern coastal areas, private trade became once again the main form of economic exchange in the region.[29]

Internal degradation and external pressures reinforced one another leading to explosive social disturbances. Faced with the growing ungovernability of the empire, the Ming sought to solve the crisis by easing peasants' grievances through tax reforms and the exploitation of the flourishing private trade. Corvée labor and taxation in kind—two of the main causes of peasant hardship and unrest—were largely replaced by a single tax payable in silver. The crippled paper currency was abandoned in favor of a silver standard, and in order to expand the silver influx from overseas, in the 1560s restrictions on trade with Southeast Asia were relaxed and licensed seafaring merchants were taxed.[30]

---

29 W. James Tong, *Disorder under Heaven: Collective Violence in the Ming Dynasty* (Stanford, CA, Stanford University Press, 1991), pp. 115–29; Frederic Wakeman, *The Great Enterprise: The Manchu Reconstruction of Imperial Order in Seventeenth-Century China* (Berkeley, CA, University of California Press, 1985), ch.1; Ray Huang, "Fiscal Administration during the Ming Dynasty," in Charles O. Hucker, ed., *Chinese Government in Ming Times* (New York, Columbia University Press, 1969), pp. 105–23; Ho-fung Hung, "Maritime Capitalism in Seventeenth-Century China: The Rise and Fall of Koxinga in Comparative Perspective," unpublished manuscript, Department of Sociology, Johns Hopkins University, pp. 12–18; John E. Wills, Jr, "Maritime China from Wang Chih to Shih Lang: Themes in Peripheral History," in Jonathan D. Spence and John E. Wills, Jr, eds, *Conquest, Region, and Continuity in Seventeenth-Century China* (New Haven, CT, and London, Yale University Press, 1979), pp. 210–11.

30 Tong, *Disorder under Heaven*; William S. Atwell, "Some Observations on the 'Seventeenth-Century Crisis' in China and Japan," *Journal of Asian Studies*, XLV (1986); Dennis O. Flynn and Arturo Giraldez, "Born with 'Silver Spoon': The Origin of World Trade in 1571," *Journal of World History*, 6, 2 (1995); Wills, "Maritime China from Wang Chih to Shih Lang," p. 211; Jurgis Elisonas, "The Inseparable Trinity: Japan's Relations with China and Korea," in John Hall, ed., *The Cambridge History of Japan, Vol. 4, Early Modern Japan* (Cambridge, Cambridge University Press, 1991), pp. 261–2. Hung, "Imperial China and Capitalist Europe," pp. 498–500.

This shift in fiscal, monetary and trade policies was made possible and encouraged by the massive silver influx from overseas trade, initially with Japan (the major silver supplier in the region) and subsequently with Europe and the Americas.[31] Although Spanish shipments of much of their American silver to China via Manila eased the fiscal and social crisis, Ming financial difficulties sky-rocketed owing to the costly war with Japan in the 1590s, the outbreak of full-fledged warfare with the Manchus in the 1610s, and mounting corruption at court and throughout the administration. Japan's imposition of restrictive trade policies in the 1630s, combined with a sharp decline in European silver supplies in the 1630s and 1640s, was the straw that broke the camel's back: by driving up the price of silver, it increased the burden of taxation on the peasantry and led to the resurgence of empire-wide unrest that culminated in the collapse of the Ming in 1644.[32]

With the consolidation of Qing rule, the early Ming's policy privileging domestic over foreign trade resumed with greater vigor. Between 1661 and 1683, the Qing reimposed the ban on private sea traffic and pursued a scorched-earth policy that transformed China's southeast coast from a crucial link connecting the Chinese and the world markets into a no-man's-land that kept the two apart. The sea ban was lifted in 1683, but strict regulations were imposed on the shipbuilding industry, restricting the size and weight of all trading junks, and firearms on board were outlawed. A new era was thus inaugurated in which trade was legal, but maritime China lost its fragile autonomy. Moreover, in 1717 Chinese subjects were once again forbidden to go privately overseas, and in 1757 the designation of Guangzhou as the sole legal port for foreign trade sealed the fate of the whole southeast coast region for nearly a century.[33]

While foreign trade was discouraged, the incorporation of border-lands on all sides did not just increase the scale of the national market; it also reduced protection costs throughout the empire—a reduction that Qing rulers passed on to their subjects in the form of low and

---

31 William S. Atwell, "Ming China and the Emerging World Economy, c. 1470–1650," in Denis Twitchett and Frederick Mote, eds, *The Cambridge History of China, Vol. 8 (2), The Ming Dynasty* (Cambridge: Cambridge University Press, 1998), pp. 403–16; Timothy Brooks, *The Confusions of Pleasure: Commerce and Culture in Ming China* (Berkeley, CA, University of California Press, 1998), p. 205.

32 Atwell, "Some Observations on the 'Seventeenth-Century Crisis'" and "Ming China and the Emerging World Economy," pp. 408–15.

33 W.G. Skinner, "The Structure of Chinese History," *Journal of Asian Studies*, 44, 2 (1985), pp. 278–9; Wills, "Maritime China from Wang Chih to Shih Lang."

stable taxes. Low and stable taxation was accompanied by vigorous state action aimed at stamping out bureaucratic corruption and tax evasion, through empire-wide land surveys, fiscal reforms, and more effective information-gathering systems. Equally important was the promotion of land redistribution and reclamation. In order to consolidate their power vis-à-vis Han landlords, the early Qing encouraged the ongoing partition of large estates into small plots and the conversion of indentured labor into tenants. At the same time, they launched a wide variety of land-reclamation programs aimed at re-establishing the fiscal base without raising taxes.[34]

The double "democratization" of land tenure—through the break-up of large estates and through land reclamation—called forth massive state action in maintaining and expanding the hydraulic infrastructure. As the highly influential official Chen Hongmou put it,

> When poor people bring new land under cultivation, it is up to the administration to provide timely assistance in development of local irrigation systems. If the cost is too high for the local society to bear, funds should be provided out of official accounts. If decisions on what waterworks to build are made solely on the basis of what the people themselves can afford, then very little indeed will be accomplished.[35]

Government involvement in agricultural improvement, irrigation and waterborne transportation was integral to Qing action in countering the spatial and temporal unevenness of economic development. As previously noted, spatial unevenness was countered through policies

---

34 Yeh-chien Wang, *Land Taxation in Imperial China, 1750–1911* (Cambridge, MA, Harvard University Press, 1973); Peter C. Perdue, *Exhausting the Earth: State and Peasant in Hunan, 1500–1850* (Cambridge, MA, Harvard University Press, 1987), pp. 78–9; Ho-fung Hung, "Early Modernities and Contentious Politics in Mid-Qing China, c. 1740–1839," *International Sociology*, 19, 4 (2004), pp. 482–3; Beatrice S. Bartlett, *Monarchs and Ministers: The Grand Council in Mid-Ch'ing China, 1723–1820* (Berkeley, CA, University of California Press, 1991); Philip C.C. Huang, *The Peasant Economy and Social Change in North China* (Stanford, CA, Stanford University Press, 1985), pp. 97–105; Junjian Jing, "Hierarchy in the Qing Dynasty," *Social Science in China: A Quarterly Journal*, 3, 1 (1982), pp. 169–81. As Qing policies resulted in explosive demographic growth, the purpose of land reclamation shifted from the re-establishment of the central government's fiscal base to the search of new sources of food to maintain the rapidly expanding population. See William Rowe, *Saving the World: Chen Hongmou and Elite Consciousness in Eigteenth-Century China* (Stanford, CA, Stanford University Press, 2001), pp. 56–7.

35 Quoted in Rowe, *Saving the World*, p. 223.

that encouraged market tendencies towards the economic uplifting of internal peripheries. These included the encouragement of migration towards less populated areas through the provision of information, infrastructure, and loans; efforts to spread new crop varieties and craft skills; heavy infrastructural investments to secure subsistence in ecologically marginal areas; and land-tax policies that favored poorer areas.[36]

As for temporal unevenness, the centerpiece of Qing action was a major expansion and unprecedented coordination of the "ever-normal granaries" practice. The Qing government relied on market mechanisms to feed China's huge and expanding population no less, and probably more, than any of its predecessors. It nonetheless surpassed them all in protecting the population from the vicissitudes of the grain market through a system of granaries that enabled it to buy and store grain at times of abundance and low prices, and to sell the grain back at sub-market prices at times of scarcity and unusually high prices. Moreover, high-level officials coordinated flows of grain among local granaries to ensure that each and every one of them could promptly and effectively counter excessive cyclical fluctuations in prices.[37]

The joint outcome of these policies was the remarkable peace, prosperity, and demographic growth which made eighteenth-century China the exemplar of Smith's "natural" path to opulence, as well as a source of inspiration for European advocates of benevolent absolutism, meritocracy, and an agriculturally based national economy. Although no eighteenth-century Chinese thinker theorized the contribution of self-interested enterprise to the national economy, notes Rowe, the previously quoted Chen Hongmou esteemed the market as an instrument of rule no less than Smith, Hobbes, Locke or Montesquieu.

> Chen has no hesitation whatsoever in appealing to the profit motive to get local populations to fall in line with his various development projects such as building new roads, introducing new commodities for regional export, founding community granaries,

36 Kenneth Pomeranz, *The Great Divergence: Europe, China, and the Making of the Modern World Economy* (Princeton, NJ, Princeton University Press, 2000), p. 250; Susan Mann, "Household Handicrafts and State Policy in Qing Times," in J.K. Leonard and J. Watt, eds, *To Achieve Security and Wealth: The Qing State and the Economy* (Ithaca, NY, Cornell University Press, 1992), p. 86; Wong, *China Transformed*, p. 148.

37 Pierre-Etienne Will and R. Bin Wong, *Nourish the People: The State Civilian Granary System in China, 1650–1850* (Ann Arbor, University of Michigan Press, 1991); Rowe, *Saving the World*, pp. 155–85.

and so on. In a formulation not too distant from Adam Smith's "invisible hand" Chen contends that such projects will bring profit to all . . . precisely to the extent they bring profit to oneself.[38]

Neither Chen, nor any of his Chinese contemporaries, however, "rejected the Confucian ideal of social harmony in favor of a view of unfettered struggle in the market place . . . and a blanket policy of laissez-faire."[39] Although Smith was no Confucian, as we have seen in Chapter 2, the idea of jeopardizing social peace and national security through a blanket policy of laissez-faire was as alien to him as it was to Chen. Had he been in Chen's shoes, it is hard to see what he would have done differently. True, he thought that greater involvement in foreign trade, especially if carried out on Chinese ships, would have further increased China's national wealth. But the developmental priority that the Qing government assigned to agricultural improvement, land redistribution and reclamation, and the consolidation and expansion of the domestic market, is precisely what Smith advocated in *The Wealth of Nations*.

The problem with Chen's and the Qing's conception of development is not the rejection of a blanket policy of laissez-faire but its blindness to the gathering storm that was about to hit the Chinese shores. Like Smith, they failed to see that the seemingly "unnatural" European path to opulence was remaking the world through a process of creative destruction that had no precedent in world history. "European ships"—in McNeill's words—"had in effect turned Eurasia inside out. The sea frontier had superseded the steppe frontier as the critical meeting point with strangers, and the autonomy of Asian states and peoples began to crumble."[40] If Smith—who was sitting at the epicenter of the storm—did not see it coming, we may excuse Chen and the Qing for not seeing it either. What they all missed, as many of our contemporaries still do, is the fundamental difference between capitalist and non-capitalist market-based development.

Capitalists in a Non-Capitalist Market Economy

In concluding his classic study of the formation of "the world's largest enduring state," Elvin suggests that China's entrapment in a high-

---

38 Rowe, *Saving the World*, pp. 201–2.
39 Ibid., p. 204.
40 McNeill, "World History and the Rise and Fall of the West," p. 231.

level equilibrium was a result of its very success in developing a huge national market. Rapid growth of production and population made all resources *except labor* scarce and this, in turn, made profitable innovations increasingly problematic.

> With falling surplus in agriculture, and so falling per capita income and per capita demand, with cheapening labor but increasingly expensive resources and capital, with farming and transport technologies so good that no simple improvements could be made, rational strategy for peasant and merchant alike tended in the direction not so much of labor saving machinery as of economizing on resources and fixed capital. Huge but nearly static markets created no bottlenecks in the production system that might have prompted creativity. When temporary shortages arose, mercantile versatility, based on cheap transport, was a faster and surer remedy than the contrivance of machines. This situation may be described as a "high-level equilibrium trap."[41]

There is some ambiguity in this account as to when, exactly, China was caught in this high-level equilibrium trap. Elvin nonetheless makes two claims that help, not just in resolving the ambiguity, but in identifying the nature of market-based development under the Ming and early Qing. The first claim is that the disappearance of serfdom and serf-like tenancy under the Qing led to "the rise of an essentially new type of rural society." And the second is that "technological innovations and inventions during the period 800 to 1300 produced changes so great that the result can only reasonably be described as a 'revolution,' and that Chinese growth thereafter slowed down not only relative to an accelerating Europe but also to its own earlier performance."[42]

Chinese development before 1300 falls beyond the scope of our investigation. For our purposes, suffice to say that available evidence, including Elvin's, gives credibility to Christopher Chase-Dunn's and Thomas Hall's contention that capitalism "nearly occurred first" in Song China.[43] We ourselves noted earlier in this chapter that tendencies that became typical of the European capitalist path in the "extended" sixteenth century were already present in China under the

---

41 Elvin, *The Pattern of the Chinese Past*, p. 314.

42 Ibid., p. 318.

43 Christopher Chase-Dunn and Thomas Hall, *Rise and Demise: Comparing World-Systems* (Boulder, CO, Westview Press, 1997), p. 47.

Song and the Yuan. Be that as it may, the slowdown in Chinese growth after 1300 can be interpreted as a first entrapment in a high-level equilibrium—as Smith himself appears to do when he claims that China "had perhaps, even long before [Marco Polo's] time, acquired that full complement of riches which the nature of its laws and institutions permits it to acquire."[44]

This interpretation, however, clashes with the remarkable economic growth which Sugihara calls the "Chinese miracle" of the eighteenth century and which, as Figure 1.1 shows, enabled the East Asian share of world GDP to increase further for almost half a century after the beginning of the British Industrial Revolution. If China had entered a stationary state *circa* 1300 or earlier, what accounts for this new upswing of economic growth? Did the state- and national economy-making activities of the Ming and early Qing, and the rise under the latter of "an essentially new type of rural society," not help at all in freeing China from the high-level equilibrium trap? Bearing in mind the distinction drawn in Chapter 3 between capitalist and non-capitalist market-based development, we may answer as follows.

First, the tendency of Smithian growth to get stuck in a high-level equilibrium trap does not rule out the existence of even higher equilibria, attainable through suitable changes in the geographical and institutional environment in which the economy is embedded. Second, the eighteenth-century Chinese economic "miracle" can best be interpreted as a shift of the economy from a high to an even higher equilibrium, due primarily to the changes in the institutional and geographical environment brought about by Ming and Qing policies. Third, despite this upward shift, market-based development in China moved in a different direction than in Europe, because it became less, rather than more, capitalist in orientation.[45]

As argued in Chapters 3 and 8, the capitalist character of market-based development is not determined by the presence of capitalist institutions and dispositions but by the relation of state power to

----

44 Smith immediately qualifies this statement with another, which betrays an ambiguity similar to Elvin's in dating China's entrapment in a stationary state: "China, however, though it may perhaps stand still, does not seem to go backward" (Adam Smith, *An Inquiry into the Nature and Causes of the Wealth of Nations*, 2 vols [London, Methuen, 1961], vol. 1, pp. 80–1).

45 In terms of the diagrammatic representation of Figure 3.1, the second proposition says that the eighteenth-century Chinese economic "miracle" is best represented by an upward shift to the right of the curve dy/y. The third proposition says that, in spite of such an upward shift, market-based development in China showed no tendency towards the kind of recurrent financial expansions and "spatial fixes" of increasing scale discussed in Chapter 8.

capital. Add as many capitalists as you like to a market economy, but unless the state has been subordinated to their class interest, the market economy remains non-capitalist. Braudel himself takes imperial China as the example that "most opportunely supports [his] insistence on separating the *market economy* and *capitalism*." Not only did China "have a solidly-established market economy . . . with its chains of local markets, its swarming population of small artisans and itinerant merchants, its busy shopping streets and urban centers," in addition, the merchants and bankers of Shanxi province and the overseas Chinese originating from Fujian and other southern coastal provinces closely resembled the business communities that constituted the preeminent capitalist organizations of sixteenth-century Europe. And yet, the state's "unmistakable hostility to any individual making himself 'abnormally' rich" meant that "there could be no capitalism, except within certain clearly-defined groups, backed by the state, supervised by the state and always more or less at its mercy."[46]

Braudel exaggerates the extent to which under the Ming and the Qing—not to speak of earlier dynasties—capitalists were at the mercy of a hostile state. It remains nonetheless true that there is no parallel in East Asia for the sequence of ever more powerful states that identified themselves with capitalism in Europe—from the Italian city-states, through the Dutch proto-nation-state, to a national state, Britain, in the process of becoming the center of a world-encircling maritime and territorial empire. As argued in previous chapters, this sequence more than anything else marks the European developmental path as capitalist. And conversely, the absence of anything comparable to this sequence is the clearest sign that in the Ming and early Qing eras market-based development in East Asia remained non-capitalist. Closely related to this was the absence of anything remotely resembling the incessant armament race and overseas territorial expansion typical of European states. As Wong put it,

> Much European commercial wealth was tapped by needy governments anxious to expand their revenue bases to meet ever-escalating expenses of war. . . . Both European merchants and their governments benefitted from their complex relationship, the former gaining fabulous profits, the latter securing much-needed

---

46 Fernand Braudel, *Civilization and Capitalism, 15th–18th Century, Volume II: The Wheels of Commerce* (New York, Harper & Row, 1982), pp. 153, 588–9, emphasis in the original.

revenues. The late imperial Chinese state did not develop the same kind of mutual dependence on rich merchants. Lacking the scale of financial difficulties encountered in Europe between the sixteenth and eighteenth centuries, Chinese officials had less reasons to imagine new forms of finance, huge merchant loans, and the concept of public as well as private debt.[47]

Capitalism in East Asia did not thereby wither away. Within China, large business organizations controlling extensive networks of commercial intermediaries and subcontractors developed as integral components of the national economy. But entry even in trade over long distances was far more open and accessible to people from all over the country than in Europe.[48] As a result, capitalists remained a subordinate social group with no capacity to subject the general interest to their own class interest. Indeed, the best chances for capitalism to develop in East Asia was not close to the centers, but interstitially, on the outer rims of the system's states. The most prominent embodiment of this development was the overseas Chinese diaspora, whose resilience and enduring economic importance has few parallels in world history. Despite Ming restrictions, periodic reverses and challenges from Muslims and other competitors, the overseas Chinese diaspora made extraordinary profits and provided a steady flow of revenue for local governments and of remittances to China's coastal regions.[49]

The seventeenth-century transition from Ming to Qing rule even created the conditions for a development that resembled what was going on in Europe: the establishment by the Zheng family of a commercial empire comparable to the Dutch. By deploying European-style warships and firearms, the Zhengs eliminated Portuguese competition, successfully defied Ming tax collectors and naval forces, monopolized the silk and ceramics trade, and built a sphere of influence that stretched from Guangdong and Fujian to Japan,

---

47 Wong, *China Transformed*, p. 146.

48 Gary G. Hamilton and Wei-an Chang, "The Importance of Commerce in the Organization of China's Late Imperial Economy," in Giovanni Arrighi, T. Hamashita, and M. Selden, eds, *The Resurgence of East Asia: 500, 150 and 50 Year Perspectives* (London and New York, Routledge, 2003); R. Bin Wong, "The Role of the Chinese State in Long-Distance Commerce," Working Paper no. 05/04, Global Economic History Network, Department of Economic History, London School of Economics.

49 Hui, "Overseas Chinese Business Networks," pp. 35–6; Wills, "Relations With Maritime Europeans," p. 333; Gungwu Wang, *China and the Chinese Overseas* (Singapore, Times Academic Press, 1991), pp. 85–6, and "Ming Foreign Relations," pp. 320–3.

Taiwan, and Southeast Asia. By 1650, they had also created a rebel
state on the southeast coast of China. Having failed to defeat the
Manchus on the mainland, in 1662 they retreated to Taiwan, expelled
the Dutch, and founded their own kingdom. So impressed was a
former Dutch governor of Taiwan by these achievements that in 1675
he compared the rise of the Zhengs as a seaborne power to the rise of
the Dutch in Europe a century earlier. This comparison is a bit far-
fetched but Chumei Ho is on firmer grounds in claiming that "[t]he
Zheng networks of commercial and political intelligence must have
been at least as effective as those of either of its main enemies, the
Manchus and the Dutch. . . . Arguably, the Zheng organization had
some of the same traits as the VOC."[50]

Equally important, the Zhengs were not insignificant players in the
dynastic transition. A respected ally of the Ming in the early stages of
the struggle—when many members of the Zheng family became
officers and generals of the Ming army—after the Qing army entered
Fujian in 1647, Zheng Zhilong attempted to switch sides. The attempt
failed, as the Qing responded to Zheng Zhilong's overtures by jailing
and eventually executing him. And yet, under Zheng Chenggong, the
power of the Zhengs reached new heights. Through the 1660s and
1670s, their regime in Taiwan remained a *de facto* independent
kingdom, exacting tribute and conducting trade with the Spanish
Philippines, the Ryukyus, and various kingdoms of Southeast Asia.
Zheng Chenggong's successor, Zheng Jing, repeatedly rejected Qing
offers of a semi-autonomous status, proposing instead recognition as
a tribute vassal of the Qing based on Korean and Ryukyu precedents.
The Kangxi emperor, however, insisted that "the thieves in Taiwan
are Fujianese, Taiwan is not comparable to Korea and Ryukyu."
Having asked too much, in the end the Zhengs got nothing, their
regime being terminated by military defeat in 1683.[51]

The very comparability of the Zheng and the Dutch commercial
empires makes their opposite fates especially instructive. In the
European context, the Dutch became the leaders of the institutiona-

---

50 Wills, "Maritime China from Wang Chih to Shih Lang" and "Relations with
Maritime Europeans"; Young-tsu Wong, "Security and Warfare on the China Coast:
The Taiwan Question in the Seventeenth Century," *Monumenta Serica*, XXXV
(1983); Frederick Coyett, *Verwaerloosde Formosa* (1675), in William Campbell, ed.,
Formosa under the Dutch: Described from Contemporary Records (London, Kegan
Paul, Trench & Trubner, 1903); Chumei Ho, "The Ceramic Trade in Asia, 1602–82,"
in A.J.H. Latham and H. Kawakatsu, eds, *Japanese Industrialization and the Asian
Economy* (London and New York, Routledge, 1994).

51 Hung, "Maritime Capitalism in Seventeenth-Century China," pp. 33–7.

lization of the balance of power among European states; of the empowerment of capitalist strata within these states; and of the intensification of interstate competition in building overseas empires. In East Asia, in contrast, the downfall of the Zheng empire cleared the way for the demilitarization of the Chinese merchants, the consolidation of national economy-making, both in Qing China and Tokugawa Japan, and the precipitous decline of the power of the overseas Chinese vis-à-vis the region's territorial states. As Pomeranz notes, the Zheng empire "stands as an illuminating example of a kind of activity that successfully paralleled European armed trading and colonization but was not a normal part of the Chinese state system."[52]

Despite their success in promoting the East Asian Industrious Revolution and a further increase in the East Asian share of world production, the inward-looking policies of Qing China and Tokugawa Japan—as Sugihara himself acknowledges—resulted in a sharp contraction of trade among Asian countries from the early eighteenth century.[53] Worse still, they left a political void in maritime East Asia, which the demilitarized Chinese merchants were ill-equipped to fill. Gradually, the void was filled by European states, companies, and merchants whose capacity to dominate maritime East Asia increased rapidly at the turn of the eighteenth and nineteenth centuries. Critical in this respect was the continuing decline of Chinese shipbuilding industries and navigation technologies at a time of rapid European advances in both.[54]

In this respect, Smith's previously quoted assessment that a more extensive foreign trade would have been in China's national interest ("especially if any considerable part of [it] was carried on in Chinese ships") had some validity, not so much on strictly economic grounds, but on grounds of national security—that is, of China's capacity to monitor and meet the growing naval challenge posed by the Europeans. For at least a century, however, the chief security problem for the Qing was on the northwestern frontier and within Han China, where the legitimacy of their rule as foreign conquerors remained precarious. Under these circumstances, pouring resources into shipbuilding, navigation, and the carrying trade necessarily appeared as a

---

52 Pomeranz, *The Great Divergence*, p. 204.

53 Sugihara, "The European Miracle and the East Asian Miracle," pp. 38–9.

54 Jennifer Wayne Cushman, *Fields from the Sea: Chinese Junk Trade with Siam during the Late Eighteenth and Early Nineteenth Centuries*, Studies on Southeast Asia, Southeast Asia Program, Cornell University, p. 136; Hui, "Overseas Chinese Business Networks," pp. 79–80.

luxury at best, and the surest road to imperial overstretch at worst. Moreover, why risk such an overstretch when Europeans fiercely competed with one another in pouring silver into China in exchange for Chinese commodities? As a result of China's highly competitive exports of silk, porcelain, and tea, and a Chinese demand for silver that drove silver prices to levels twice those prevailing in other parts of the world, from the sixteenth until well into the eighteenth century, fully three-fourths of "new world" silver found its way to China.[55] It is indeed hard to imagine how the success of China's self-centered development—which so much impressed even Europeans—could not blind the Qing to the new power that the aggressive seaborne "barbarians" were bringing to the region.

In short, the synergy typical of the European developmental path between militarism, industrialism, and capitalism, which propelled, and was in turn sustained by, ceaseless overseas territorial expansion, was absent in East Asia. As a result, East Asian states experienced much longer periods of peace than European states, and China could consolidate its position as the world's largest market economy. And yet, lack of involvement in overseas expansion and in an armament race, European-style, made China and the entire East Asian system vulnerable to the military onslaught of the expanding European powers. When the onslaught came, the subordinate incorporation of East Asia within the globalizing European system was a foregone conclusion.

Incorporation and Hybridization

The subordinate incorporation of East Asia within the European system, and the eclipse of the region in world production shown in Figure 1.1, were not due primarily to the competitive edge of Western vis-à-vis East Asian, especially Chinese, economic enterprise. As anticipated in Chapter 3, contrary to Marx's and Engels's claim that cheap commodities were the "heavy artillery" with which the European bourgeoisie "batter[ed] down all Chinese Walls," even after British gunboats had battered down the wall of governmental regulations that enclosed the Chinese domestic

---

55 Dennis O. Flynn and Arturo Giraldez, "Spanish Profitability in the Pacific: The Philippines in the Sixteenth and Seventeenth Centuries," in Dennis O. Flynn, Lionel Frost, and A.J.H. Latham, eds, *Pacific Centuries: Pacific and Pacific Rim History since the Sixteenth Century* (London, Routledge, 1999), pp. 23–4.

economy, British merchants and producers had a hard time in out-
competing their Chinese counterparts. From the 1830s, imports of
British cotton textiles did devastate some sectors and regions of the
Chinese economy. Yet British cotton cloth was never able to
compete in rural markets with stronger Chinese cloth. Moreover,
as foreign imports displaced handicraft spinning of cotton yarn, the
use of cheaper, machine-produced yarn gave new impetus to the
domestic weaving industry, which managed to hold its own and
even expand.[56] Western firms that set up production facilities in
China could never penetrate effectively the vast interior of the
country, and had to rely on Chinese traders in the procurement of
raw materials and the marketing of their products. Western products and businesses did triumph in a few industries. But outside of
railways and mines, the China market generally spelled frustration
for foreign merchants.[57]

Far from destroying indigenous forms of capitalism, the incorporation of China within the structures of the UK-centered capitalist
economy led to a renewed expansion of the Chinese merchant
communities which had developed in the interstices of the China-
centered tribute trade system. As the opium wars and domestic
rebellions shattered the capacity of the Qing court to regulate flows
of goods and people across China's borders, profitable opportunities
for these communities proliferated. The opium trade was a major
source of such opportunities; but the greatest opportunities arose in
the "coolie trade"—in the procurement and transshipment overseas
of indentured labor and in the financial transactions associated with
remittances back to China. The coolie trade made the fortunes, not
just of individual merchants, but of the port-cities of Singapore,
Hong Kong, Penang, and Macao, which became privileged "containers" of the wealth of the Chinese business diaspora. It also increased

---

56 Linda Cooke Johnson, "Shanghai: An Emerging Jiangnan Port, 1638–1840,"
in Linda Cooke Johnson, ed., *Cities of Jiangnan in Late Imperial China* (Albany, State
University of New York Press, 1993), pp. 171–4; Albert Feuerwerker, "Handicraft and
Manufactured Cotton Textiles 1871–1910," *Journal of Economic History*, 30, 2
(1970), pp. 371–5; Hamilton and Chang, "The Importance of Commerce."

57 Resat Kasaba, "Treaties and Friendships: British Imperialism, the Ottoman
Empire, and China in the Nineteenth Century," *Journal of World History*, 4, 2 (1993);
Ciyu Chen, "On the Foreign Trade of China in the 19th Century and the China–
India–Britain Triangular Trade," in *Essays in Chinese Maritime History* (Taipei, Sun
Yat-sen Institute for Social Sciences and Philosophy, Academia Sinica, 1984), pp. 58–
61; Alvin Y. So, *The South China Silk District* (Albany, State University of New York
Press, 1986), pp. 103–16; Andrew J. Nathan, "Imperialism's Effects on China,"
Bulletin of Concerned Asian Scholars, 4, 4 (1972), p. 5.

Chinese settlement throughout Southeast Asia, thereby strengthening the capacity of overseas Chinese capital to profit from commercial and financial intermediation within and across jurisdictions in the region.[58]

The fiscal and financial pressures engendered by wars, rebellions, worsening trade conditions, and natural disasters forced the Qing court, not only to relax controls on the activities of the overseas Chinese, but to seek their financial assistance. In exchange for the assistance, the Qing court granted them offices, titles, protection for their properties and connections in China, as well as access to the highly profitable arms trade and government loan business. This "political exchange" did not save the Qing but, up to their final collapse in 1911, was a major source of enrichment for overseas Chinese capitalists.[59]

As noted in Chapter 3, Marx himself was not so sure about the role that the metaphorical artillery of cheap commodities actually played in remaking the world to suit the interests of the European bourgeoisie; and he explicitly mentioned the opium wars as an instance of the continuing importance of military force as the "midwife" of that transformation. Military force was indeed the key to the subjection of East Asia to the West. What is more, its use was a direct result of the incapability of British merchants to penetrate the Chinese market by legal means.

Throughout the first half of the nineteenth century—notes Joseph Esherick—opium was "the West's only feasible entree into the China market."[60] In Britain's case it was much more than that, because British sales of Indian opium to China were crucial in the transfer of tribute from India to London. As the head of the statistical department at the East India House explained,

India, by exporting opium, assists in supplying England with tea. China by consuming opium, facilitates the revenue operations

---

58 Hui, "Overseas Business Networks," ch. 3; David Northup, *Indentured Labor in the Age of Imperialism, 1834–1922* (Cambridge, Cambridge University Press, 1995); Daniel R. Headrick, *The Tentacles of Progress: Technology Transfer in the Age of Imperialism, 1850–1940* (London, Oxford University Press, 1988), pp. 259–303.

59 Jung-fang Tsai, *Hong Kong in Chinese History: Community and Social Unrest in the British Colony, 1842–1913* (New York, Columbia University Press, 1993), p. 63; Hui, "Overseas Business Networks," ch. 3.

60 Joseph Esherick, "Harvard on China: The Apologetics of Imperialism," *Bulletin of Concerned Asian Scholars*, IV, 4 (1972), p. 10.

between India and England. England by consuming tea contributes
to increase the demand for the opium of India.[61]

The need to expand the India–China trade in order to facilitate the
"revenue operations" between India and England had been from the
start the main stimulus behind the expansion of the opium trade. As
early as 1786, Lord Cornwallis, then Governor General of India,
pointed out that the expansion of the India–China trade was
essential to paying at least in part for Chinese exports of tea
and silk to Britain and other European countries and, above all,
to transfer the vast tribute of Bengal to England *without heavy
losses through exchange depreciation.*[62] After the India trade monopoly of the East India Company was abrogated in 1813, the
Company redoubled its efforts in promoting opium-smuggling into
China. Shipments expanded rapidly—more than threefold between
1803–13 and 1823–33—and the soundness of Cornwallis's argument
was vindicated. In the words of a contemporary account, from the
opium trade

> The Honourable Company has derived for years an immense
> revenue and through them the British Government and nation
> have also reaped an incalculable amount of political and financial
> advantage. The turn of the balance of trade between Great Britain
> and China in favour of the former has enabled India to increase
> tenfold her consumption of British manufacture; contributed
> directly to support the vast fabric of British dominion in the East,
> to defray the expenses of His Majesty's establishment in India, and
> by the operation of exchanges and remittances in teas, to pour an
> abundant revenue into the British Exchequer and benefit the nation
> to an extent of £6 million yearly.[63]

The abrogation of the East India Company's China monopoly in
1833 intensified competition in this lucrative branch of British
commerce and emboldened British merchants to agitate for "the
strong arm of England" to bring down the restrictions that the

---

61 Edward Thornton, *India, its State and Prospects* (London, Parbury, Allen &
Co., 1835), p. 89.

62 Amiya K. Bagchi, *The Political Economy of Underdevelopment* (Cambridge, Cambridge University Press, 1982), p. 96; Michael Greenberg, *British Trade
and the Opening of China, 1800–1842* (Cambridge, Cambridge University Press,
1951), ch. 2.

63 Quoted in Greenberg, *British Trade and the Opening of China*, pp. 106–7.

Chinese government imposed on the opium trade. Far from yielding
to British pressures, the Chinese government moved swiftly to
suppress a trade which was as baneful for China as it was beneficial
for Britain. Beyond the deleterious impact on the social fabric of a
growing number of addicts, the trade had highly disruptive effects
on the Chinese political economy. The proceeds of opium-smuggling
trickled down to Chinese officials, whose corruption impaired the
execution of official policy in all spheres and, directly and indirectly,
fed social unrest. At the same time, the trade caused a massive drain
of silver from China to India, which grew from 1.6 million taels a
year in 1814–24 to 5.6 million taels a year in the two years preceding
the first Opium War.[64] As the imperial edict of 1838 emphasized in
announcing the decision to destroy the trade, the effects of the drain
on the financial and fiscal integrity of the Chinese state were
devastating. "If steps not be taken for our defence," declared the
edict, "the useful wealth of China will be poured into the fathom-
less abyss of transmarine regions."[65]

In putting the vigorous and incorruptible Lin Zexu in charge of the
suppression of opium-smuggling, the Chinese government had no
intention of thwarting commercial opportunities in other branches of
foreign trade, such as silk, tea, and cotton goods, which it continued
to promote. Lin himself was careful in drawing a distinction between
the illegal opium trade—which he was determined to suppress with or
without the cooperation of the British government—and legal forms
of trade, which he asked the British government to encourage as a
substitute for the illegal trade.[66] Having failed to persuade Britain to
cooperate in the suppression of the traffic in the name of international
law and common morality, he proceeded to confiscate and destroy
smuggled opium and to incarcerate some smugglers. This police
operation on Chinese territory was denounced in the British Parlia-
ment as "a grievous sin—a wicked offence—an atrocious violation of
justice, for which England had the right, a strict and undeniable

64 Zhongping Yen et al., *Zhongguo jindai jingjishi tongji* (Collections of
Statistical Data of Modern Chinese Economic History) (Beijing, Scientific Publishers,
1957), p. 34; Manhong Lin, "The Silver Drain of China and the Reduction in World
Silver and Gold Production (1814–1850)," in *Essays in Chinese Maritime History IV*
(Taipei, Sun Yat-sen Institute for Social Sciences and Philosophy, Academia Sinica,
1991), p. 11.
65 Quoted in Greenberg, *British Trade and the Opening of China*, p. 143.
66 Arthur Waley, *The Opium War through Chinese Eyes* (London, Allen &
Unwin, 1958), pp. 18, 28–31, 46, 123; Yen-p'ing Hao, *The Commercial Revolution in
Nineteenth-Century China* (Berkeley, CA, California University Press, 1986), pp. 113–
15.

right," by "the law of God and man," "to demand reparation by force if refused peaceable applications."[67]

Evidently, two quite different views of international law and common morality held sway in Britain and China. But while the Chinese view claimed a right to lay down and enforce the law only at home, the British view claimed a right to lay down and enforce the law not just at home but in China as well. To paraphrase Marx, between equal rights force decides, and Britain had all the firepower it needed to make its view of right and wrong prevail over the Chinese. China had no answer to the steam-powered warship that in a single day in February 1841 destroyed nine war junks, five forts, two military stations, and one shore battery.[68] After a disastrous war, an explosion of major rebellions, and a second, equally disastrous war with Britain (now joined by France), China virtually ceased to be the center of a relatively self-contained East Asian interstate system. For about a century, it became instead a subordinate, and increasingly peripheral, member of the global capitalist system. This increasing peripherality was not merely the result of the subordinate incorporation of East Asia within the European system. Equally important was the radical change in interstate relations within East Asia precipitated by Chinese and Japanese attempts to follow in the footsteps of the European developmental path.

As Kawakatsu and Hamashita have underscored, Japan's modernization and territorial expansion of the late nineteenth and early twentieth centuries were a continuation by new means of centuries-long Japanese endeavors to recenter upon itself the East Asian tribute trade system.[69] Nevertheless, the change in systemic context transformed radically the nature of the interstate competition that had characterized the East Asian system since the consolidation of the Tokugawa and Qing regimes. In the new context, interstate competition within East Asia became inseparable from attempts to catch up

---

67 Quoted in Bernard Semmel, *The Rise of Free Trade Imperialism* (Cambridge, Cambridge University Press, 1970), p. 153; see also D.E. Owen, *British Opium Policy in China and India* (New Haven, CT, Yale University Press, 1934).

68 Geoffrey Parker, "Taking Up the Gun," *MHQ: The Quarterly Journal of Military History*, 1, 4 (1989), p. 96. As K.N. Chauduri put it, "When after a disastrous war (1839–42) the Chinese government agreed to open its ports to British opium traders, it did not do so choosing between right and wrong: the choice was between survival and destruction" (*Asia before Europe: Economy and Civilization of the Indian Ocean from the Rise of Islam to 1750* [Cambridge, Cambridge University Press, 1990], p. 99).

69 Kawakatsu, "Historical Background," pp. 6–7; Hamashita, "The Tribute Trade System," p. 20.

with Western proficiency in the capital-goods industries, whose modernization (in East Asia no less than in Europe) was intimately associated with the enhancement of military capabilities. The armament race which had long been a feature of the European system was thus "internalized" by the East Asian system.[70]

For about twenty-five years after they were launched, industrialization efforts yielded similar economic results in China and Japan. On the eve of the Sino-Japanese War of 1894, "the disparity between the degree of modern economic development in the two countries was not yet flagrant."[71] Nevertheless, Japan's victory in the war was symptomatic of a fundamental difference between the industrialization drive of the two countries. In China, the main agency of the drive were provincial authorities, whose power vis-à-vis the central government had increased considerably during the repression of the rebellions of the 1850s, and who used industrialization to consolidate their autonomy. In Japan, in contrast, the industrialization drive was integral to the Meiji Restoration, which centralized power in the hands of the national government at the expense of provincial authorities.[72]

The outcome of the Sino-Japanese war, in turn, deepened the underlying divergence in the trajectories of Japanese and Chinese industrialization. China's defeat weakened national cohesion, initiating half a century of political chaos, marked by further restrictions on sovereignty, crushing war indemnities, the final collapse of the Qing regime and the growing autonomy of semi-sovereign warlords, followed by Japanese invasion, and recurrent civil wars between the forces of nationalism and communism. This catastrophic state break-

---

70 By revealing brutally the full implications of Western military superiority, the opium wars awoke the ruling groups of China and Japan to the imperatives of accelerated military modernization. The awakening led the Chinese scholar-official Wei Yuan to develop the old idea of using the barbarians to control the barbarians into the new idea of using barbarian *armaments* (and the means to produce them) to control the barbarians. In China the idea became central to the Self-Strengthening Movement that took off after the second Opium War. A few years later the Meiji Restoration also embraced the idea and propelled Japan along the same path of rapid modernization. See Ting-fu Tsiang, "The English and the Opium Trade," in F. Schurmann and O. Schell, eds, *Imperial China* (New York, Vintage, 1967), p. 144; John K. Fairbank, *The United States and China* (Cambridge, MA, Harvard University Press, 1983), pp. 197–8; Alvin Y. So and Stephen W.K. Chiu, *East Asia and the World-Economy* (Newbury Park, CA, Sage, 1995), pp. 49–50.

71 Albert Feuerwerker, *China's Early Industrialization: Sheng Hsuan-Huai 1844–1916 and Mandarin Enterprise* (Cambridge, MA, Harvard University Press, 1958), p. 53.

72 So and Chiu, *East Asia and the World-Economy*, pp. 53, 68–72.

down is probably the single most important reason—to answer O'Brien's question quoted in Chapter 1—why it took such a long time for China to regain the economic rank and status it held globally in the mid eighteenth century.

Victory over China in 1894, followed by victory over Russia in the war of 1904–05, in contrast, established Japan—to paraphrase Akira Iriye—as "a respectable participant in the game of imperialist politics."[73] The acquisition of Chinese territory—most notably, Taiwan in 1895, followed by the Liaodong peninsula and the securing of all Russian rights and privileges in South Manchuria in 1905, and culminating in China's recognition of Japanese suzerainty over Korea, annexed as a colony in 1910—provided Japan with valuable outposts from which to launch future attacks on China, as well as with secure overseas supplies of cheap food, raw materials and markets. At the same time, Chinese indemnities amounting to more than one-third of Japan's national income helped Japan to finance the expansion of heavy industry and to put its currency on the gold standard. This, in turn, improved Japan's credit rating in London and its capacity to tap additional funds for industrial expansion at home and imperialist expansion overseas.[74]

This bifurcation of the Japanese and Chinese developmental paths culminated in the 1930s in the eclipsing of Britain by Japan as the dominant power in the region. With the Japanese seizure of Manchuria in 1931, followed by the occupation of North China in 1935, full-scale invasion of China from 1937, and the subsequent conquest of parts of Inner Asia and much of Southeast Asia, Japan seemed to be finally succeeding in recentering upon itself the East Asian region. The Japanese bid for regional supremacy, however, could not be sustained. As the massive destruction inflicted on Japan by the US strategic bombing campaign in the final months of the war demonstrated even before Hiroshima and Nagasaki, Japanese advances in Western military technology could not keep up with US advances. But the Japanese bid collapsed also because it called forth in China

---

73 Akira Iriye, "Imperialism in East Asia," in J. Crowley, ed., *Modern East Asia* (New York, Harcourt, 1970), p. 552.

74 Mark Peattie, "Introduction," to Ramon Myers and Mark Peattie, eds, *The Japanese Colonial Empire, 1895–1945* (Princeton, NJ, Princeton University Press, 1984), pp. 16–18; Peter Duus, "Economic Dimensions of Meiji Imperialism: The Case of Korea, 1895–1910," in R.H. Myers and M.R. Peattie, eds, *The Japanese Colonial Empire, 1895–1945* (Princeton, NJ, Princeton University Press, 1984), pp. 143, 161–2; Herbert Feis, *Europe: The World's Banker, 1870–1914* (New York, Norton, 1965), pp. 422–3.

countervailing forces as firmly opposed to Japanese as to Western domination. Once Japan had been defeated, the formation of the People's Republic of China would contest Western hegemonic drives in a struggle for centrality in East Asia that has shaped trends and events in the region ever since.

US Hegemony and the Japanese Ascent

The hybridization of the Western and East Asian developmental paths has been a two-way process. If in the late nineteenth and early twentieth centuries, convergence was primarily from the East Asian towards the Western path—with disastrous consequences for every East Asian state, including Japan, whose initial success in the game of imperialist politics ended in the nuclear holocaust of Hiroshima and Nagasaki—in the second half of the twentieth century it was the turn of the Western path to converge towards the East Asian. This little-noticed convergence began with the establishment of the US Cold War regime.

The US military occupation of Japan in 1945 and the division of the region in the aftermath of the Korean War into two antagonistic blocs created, in Cumings's words, a US "vertical regime solidified through bilateral defense treaties (with Japan, South Korea, Taiwan, and the Philippines) and conducted by a State Department that towered over the foreign ministries of these four countries."

> All became semisovereign states, deeply penetrated by U.S. military structures (operational control of the South Korean armed forces, Seventh Fleet patrolling of the Taiwan Straits, defense dependencies for all four countries, military bases on their territories) and incapable of independent foreign policy or defense initiatives. . . . There were minor demarches through the military curtain beginning in the mid-1950s. . . . But the dominant tendency until the 1970s was a unilateral U.S. regime heavily biased toward military forms of communication.[75]

The militaristic nature of this unilateral US regime had no precedent in East Asia, with the partial exception of the Yuan regime in the late

---

75 Bruce Cumings, "Japan and Northeast Asia into the Twenty-First Century," in P.J. Katzenstein and T. Shiraishi, eds, *Network Power: Japan and Asia* (Ithaca, NY, Cornell University Press, 1997), p. 155.

thirteenth and early fourteenth centuries and the aborted Japan-centered regime of the early twentieth century. Nevertheless, the US regime presented three important similarities with the China-centered tribute trade system. First, the domestic market of the central state was incomparably larger than that of the vassal states. Second, in order to receive regime legitimation and to gain access to the central state's domestic market, vassal states had to accept a relationship of political subordination to the central state. And, third, in exchange for political subordination, vassal states were granted "gifts" and highly advantageous trade relations with the central state. This was the "magnanimous" early postwar trade and aid regime of Pax Americana to which both Ozawa and Sugihara trace the origins of the East Asian renaissance.[76]

In light of these similarities, we may say that US supremacy in East Asia after the Second World War was realized through the transformation of the periphery of the former China-centered tribute trade system into the periphery of a US-centered tribute trade system. There were nonetheless two important differences between the two systems. The first was that the US-centered system was not only far more militaristic in structure and orientation than its China-centered predecessors; it also fostered a functional specialization between the imperial and the vassal states that had no precedent in the old China-centered system. As in the Iberian–Genoese relationship of political exchange of sixteenth-century Europe noted in Chapter 8, the United States specialized in the provision of protection and the pursuit of political power regionally and globally, while its East Asian vassal states specialized in trade and the pursuit of profit. This relationship of political exchange played a decisive role in promoting the spectacular Japanese economic expansion that initiated the regional renaissance. As Schurmann wrote at an early stage of the expansion, "Freed from the burden of defense spending, Japanese governments . . . funneled all their resources and energies into an economic expansionism that has brought affluence to Japan and taken its business to the farthest reaches of the globe."[77]

The second difference is that the US-centered Cold War regime in the region, unlike the earlier China-centered regimes, was highly

---

76 Terutomo Ozawa, "Foreign Direct Investment and Structural Transformation: Japan as a Recycler of Market and Industry," *Business and the Contemporary World*, 5, 2 (1993), p. 130; Sugihara, "The East Asian Path of Economic Development," p. 81.

77 Franz Schurmann, *The Logic of World Power: An Inquiry into the Origins, Currents, and Contradictions of World Politics* (New York, Pantheon, 1974), p. 143.

unstable: it started breaking down soon after it was established. The Korean War had instituted the US-centric East Asian regime by excluding the PRC from normal commercial and diplomatic inter-course with the non-Communist part of the region, through blockade and war threats backed by "an archipelago of American military installations."[78] Defeat in the Vietnam War, in contrast, forced the United States to readmit China to normal commercial and diplomatic intercourse with the rest of East Asia. The scope of the region's economic integration and expansion was thereby broadened consid-erably but the capacity of the United States to control the process was reduced correspondingly.[79]

The crisis of the US militaristic regime and the contemporaneous expansion of the Japanese national market and business networks in the region, marked the re-emergence of a pattern of interstate relations that resembled more closely the indigenous (East Asian) pattern—in which centrality was determined primarily by the relative size and sophistication of the system's national economies—than the transplanted (Western) pattern—in which centrality had come to be determined primarily by the relative strength of the system's military-industrial complexes. While the defeat of the United States in Vietnam laid bare the limits of industrial militarism as a source of power, Japan's growing influence in world politics in the 1980s demonstrated the increasing effectiveness of economic relative to military sources of power. It was not its mighty military apparatus, but cheap Japanese credit and commodities which made it possible for the United States to reverse in the 1980s the precipitous decline of its power of the 1970s. The previous relationship of Japanese political and economic dependence on the United States was thus transformed into a relation-ship of mutual dependence: Japan remained dependent on US military protection, but the reproduction of the US protection-producing apparatus came to depend critically on Japanese finance and industry.

Japan's growing economic power in the 1980s was not based on any major technological breakthrough. Its main foundation was organizational. As argued in Chapter 6, the worldwide proliferation of vertically integrated, multinational corporations intensified their mutual competition, forcing them to subcontract to small businesses

---

78 Cumings, "Japan and Northeast Asia," pp. 154–5.

79 Giovanni Arrighi, "The Rise of East Asia: World-Systemic and Regional Aspects," *International Journal of Sociology and Social Policy*, 16, 7 (1996); Mark Selden, "China, Japan and the Regional Political Economy of East Asia 1945–1995," in P. Katzenstein and T. Shiraishi, eds, *Network Power: Japan and Asia* (Ithaca, NY, Cornell University Press, 1997).

activities previously carried out within their own organizations. The tendency towards the vertical integration and bureaucratization of business—which had made the fortunes of US capital since the 1870s—thus began to be superseded by a tendency towards informal networking and the subordinate revitalization of small business. This new tendency has been in evidence everywhere but nowhere has it been pursued more successfully than in East Asia. According to Japan's External Trade Organization, without the assistance of multiple layers of formally independent subcontractors "Japanese big business would flounder and sink." Starting in the early 1970s, the scale and scope of this multilayered subcontracting system increased rapidly through a spillover into a growing number of East Asian states.[80]

Although Japanese capital was its leading agency, the spillover relied heavily on the business networks of the overseas Chinese, who were from the start the main intermediaries between Japanese and local business, not just in Singapore, Hong Kong, and Taiwan, but in most southeast Asian countries, where the ethnic Chinese minority occupied a commanding position in local business networks. The region-wide expansion of the Japanese multilayered subcontracting system was thus supported, not just by US political patronage from above, but also by Chinese commercial and financial patronage from below.[81]

Over time, however, patronage from above and below began to constrain the capacity of Japanese business to lead the process of regional economic integration and expansion. As a representative of Japanese big business lamented in the early 1990s,

> We don't have military power. There is no way for Japanese businessmen to influence policy decisions of other countries. . . . This is a difference with American business and it is something Japanese businessmen have to think about.[82]

80 Daniel I. Okimoto and Thomas P. Rohlen, *Inside the Japanese System: Readings on Contemporary Society and Political Economy* (Stanford, CA, Stanford University Press, 1988), pp. 83–8; Giovanni Arrighi, Satoshi Ikeda, and Alex Irwan, "The Rise of East Asia: One Miracle or Many?" in R. Palat, ed., *Pacific Asia and the Future of the World-Economy* (Westport, CT, Greenwood Press, 1993), pp. 55ff.

81 Hui, "Overseas Business Networks"; Alex Irwan, "Japanese and Ethnic Chinese Business Networks in Indonesia and Malaysia," PhD diss. (1995), Department of Sociology, State University of New York at Binghamton.

82 J. Friedland, "The Regional Challenge," *Far Eastern Economic Review*, June 9, 1994.

This difference did not just mean that Japan could not match the capacity of the United States to influence the policies of third countries. It meant also that Japan's own policies were far more susceptible to being shaped by US interests than vice versa. This asymmetry was not a problem as long as the "magnanimous" postwar US trade and aid regime was in place. As argued in Chapter 9, however, by the 1980s and early 1990s that regime was being replaced by a veritable protection racket, which extorted from Japan trade concessions, such as a massive revaluation of the yen and Voluntary Export Restrictions, as well as outright protection payments, such as those extracted to pay for the Gulf War. Under these circumstances, the profitability of Japan's relation of political exchange with the United States began to wane.

Worse still, US business began restructuring itself to compete more effectively with Japanese business in the exploitation of East Asia's rich endowment of labor and entrepreneurial resources, not just through direct investment, but also and especially through all kinds of subcontracting arrangements in loosely integrated organizational structures. As noted in Chapter 10, this tendency led to the displacement of vertically integrated corporations, such as General Motors, by subcontracting corporations, such as Wal-Mart, as the leading US business organization. As Gary Hamilton and Chang Wei-An have shown, "buyer-driven" subcontracting arrangements, like Wal-Mart's, were a distinctive feature of big business in late imperial China, and remained the dominant form of business organization in Taiwan and Hong Kong up to the present.[83] We may therefore interpret the formation and expansion of US subcontracting networks as another instance of Western convergence towards East Asian patterns. Despite this convergence, the main beneficiary of the mobilization of East Asian subcontracting networks in the intensifying competitive struggle among the world's leading capitalist organizations was neither Japanese nor US capital. Rather, it was another legacy of the East Asian developmental path: the overseas Chinese capitalist diaspora.

As previously noted, the greatest opportunities for the growth of the overseas Chinese diaspora—which for centuries had been the primary locus of the seeds of capitalism that sprouted in the interstices of the China-centered tribute trade system—came with the subordinate incorporation of East Asia within the structures of the globalizing UK-centered system. In the early twentieth century,

---

83 Hamilton and Chang, "The Importance of Commerce."

elements of the diaspora attempted to transform their growing economic power into political influence over mainland China, by supporting the 1911 revolution and the Guomindang (GMD) in the warlord era. But the attempt failed, owing to escalating political chaos, the takeover of China's coastal regions by Japan, and the eventual defeat of the GMD by the Chinese Communist Party (CCP).[84]

By generating a new spurt of Chinese migration to southeast Asia, especially Hong Kong and Taiwan, and to the United States, the Communist victory replenished the entrepreneurial ranks of the diaspora. Shortly afterwards, the Korean War revived the flow of interregional trade and created new business opportunities for the overseas Chinese; and so did the withdrawal of the European and US colonial-era large-scale enterprises and the arrival of new multi-national corporations seeking capable joint-venture partners.[85] Under the US unilateral regime that emerged out of the Korean War, however, the role of the overseas Chinese as commercial intermediaries between mainland China and the surrounding maritime region, was stifled as much by the US embargo on trade with the PRC as by the PRC's restrictions on trade. Moreover, in the 1950s and 1960s the expansion of overseas Chinese capital was held in check by the spread of nationalism and national development ideologies and practices in southeast Asia. In spite of this unfavorable environment, overseas Chinese business networks managed to consolidate their hold on the commanding heights of most Southeast Asian economies.[86]

Overseas Chinese capital was thus eminently well positioned to profit from the trans-border expansion of Japan's multilayered

---

84 On the relationship between the overseas Chinese diaspora and Chinese nationalism, see Prasenjit Duara, "Nationalists Among Transnationals: Overseas Chinese and the Idea of China, 1900–1911," in A. Ong and D.M. Nonini, eds, *Ungrounded Empires: The Cultural Politics of Modern Chinese Transnationalism* (New York, Routledge, 1997).

85 Siu-lun Wong, *Emigrant Entrepreneurs* (Hong Kong, Oxford University Press, 1988); Jamie Mackie, "Business Success among Southeast Asian Chinese— The Role of Culture, Values, and Social Structures," in R.W. Hefner, ed., *Market Cultures: Society and Morality in New Asian Capitalism* (Boulder, CO, Westview Press, 1998), p. 142.

86 Christopher Baker, "Economic Reorganization and the Slump in Southeast Asia," *Comparative Studies in Society and History*, 23, 3 (1981), pp. 344–5; Yuan-li Wu and Chun-hsi Wu, *Economic Development in Southeast Asia: The Chinese Dimension* (Stanford, CA, Hoover Institution Press, 1980), pp. 30–4; Jamie Mackie, "Changing Patterns of Chinese Big Business," in R. McVey, ed., *Southeast Asian Capitalists* (Southeast Asian Program, Cornell University, 1992), p. 165; Hui, "Overseas Business Networks," pp. 184–5.

subcontracting system and the growing demand by US corporations for business partners in the region. The more intense competition over East Asian low-cost and high-quality human resources became, the more the overseas Chinese emerged as one of the most powerful capitalist networks in the region, in many ways overshadowing the networks of US and Japanese multinationals.[87] But the greatest opportunities for their enrichment and empowerment came with the reintegration of mainland China in regional and global markets in the 1980s. Crucial in this respect was the opening of the PRC to foreign trade and investment, whose success inaugurated an entirely new stage of the East Asian renaissance—the stage of the recentering of the regional economy on China. It is this new stage that we shall now examine.

87 Arrighi et al., "Historical Capitalism, East and West," p. 316; Aihwa Ong and Donald M. Nonini, eds, *Ungrounded Empires: The Cultural Politics of Modern Chinese Transnationalism* (New York, Routledge, 1997).

12

ORIGINS AND DYNAMIC
OF THE CHINESE ASCENT

Contrary to widespread belief, the main attraction of the PRC for foreign capital has not been its huge and low-priced reserves of labor as such—there are plenty of such reserves around the world but nowhere have they attracted capital to the extent that they have in China. The main attraction, we shall argue, has been the high quality of those reserves—in terms of health, education, and capacity for self-management—in combination with the rapid expansion of the supply and demand conditions for the productive mobilization of these reserves within China itself. Moreover, this combination was not created by foreign capital but by a process of development based on indigenous traditions—including the revolutionary tradition that gave birth to the PRC. Foreign capital intervened late in the process, sustaining it in some directions but undermining it in others.

The "matchmaker" that facilitated the encounter of foreign capital and Chinese labor, entrepreneurs, and government officials was Chinese diaspora capital.[1] This role of matchmaker was made possible by the determination with which the PRC under Deng sought the assistance of the overseas Chinese in opening China to foreign trade and investment and in seeking the recovery of Hong Kong, Macau, and—eventually—Taiwan in accordance with the "One Nation, Two Systems" model. This alliance proved far more fruitful for the Chinese government than its open-door policy towards US, European, and Japanese corporations. Bothered by the regulations that restricted their freedom to hire and fire labor, to buy and sell commodities, and to remit profits out of China, these corpora-

---

1 On Chinese diaspora capital as "matchmaker," see among others Nicholas R. Lardy, *Foreign Trade and Economic Reform in China, 1978–1990* (Cambridge, Cambridge University Press, 1992), pp. 37–82; Kichiro Fukasuku and David Wall, *China's Long March to an Open Economy* (Paris, OECD, 1994), pp. 26–42; Louis Kraar, "The New Power in Asia," *Fortune*, October 31, 1993, p. 40. On the origins of Chinese diaspora capital, see Chapter 11.

tions tended to keep their investments to the bare minimum needed to keep a foothold in the PRC. The overseas Chinese, in contrast, could bypass most regulations, thanks to familiarity with local customs, habits, and language, to the manipulation of kinship and community ties—which they strengthened through generous donations to local institutions—and to the preferential treatment that they received from CCP officials. Thus, while foreign corporations kept complaining about the "investment climate," Chinese entrepreneurs began moving from Hong Kong into Guandong almost as fast as (and far more massively than) they had moved from Shanghai to Hong Kong forty years earlier. Encouraged by the success, in 1988 the Chinese government redoubled its efforts to win the confidence and assistance of overseas Chinese capital by extending to Taiwan's residents many of the privileges previously granted to Hong Kong's residents.[2]

Well before the Tienanmen crackdown, a political alliance was thus established between the CCP and overseas Chinese business. The cooling of US–Chinese relations after Tienanmen dampened further Western enthusiasm for investment in China. Although the Chinese share of Japan's total direct investment in East Asia increased rapidly—from 5 percent in 1990, to 24 percent in 1993—the increase did not re-establish the position of leadership in the process of regional economic integration and expansion that Japan held in the 1970s and 1980s (see Chapter 11). Rather, it reflected the attempt of Japanese business to catch up with the overseas Chinese in reaping the profitable opportunities opened up by economic reforms in the PRC. By 1990, when Japanese investment took off, the combined investments of US\$ 12 billion from Hong Kong and Taiwan accounted for 75 percent of all foreign investment in China, almost thirty-five times the Japanese share. No matter how fast Japanese investment grew thereafter, it followed rather than led the boom of foreign investment in China.[3] As the Chinese ascent gained momentum under its own steam in the 1990s, Japanese, US, and European capital flocked ever more massively to China. Foreign direct invest-

---

2 Alvin Y. So and Stephen W.K. Chiu, *East Asia and the World Economy* (Newbury Park, CA, Sage, 1995), ch. 11.

3 Giovanni Arrighi et al., "Historical Capitalism, East and West," in G. Arrighi, T. Hamashita, and M. Selden, eds, *The Resurgence of East Asia: 500, 150 and 50 Year Perspectives* (London and New York, Routledge, 2003), pp. 316–17. Despite the boom in foreign direct investment of the 1990s and early 2000s, overseas Chinese still provide more than half of the foreign money spent to set up businesses in China. See Ted C. Fishman, *China, INC: How the Rise of the Next Superpower Challenges America and the World* (New York, Scribner, 2005), p. 27.

ment, which had totaled only $20 billion for the whole decade of the 1980s, soared to $200 billion by 2000 and then more than doubled to $450 billion in the next three years. "But if the foreigners were investing," comments Clyde Prestowitz, "it was only because the Chinese were investing more."[4]

Foreign capital, in other words, jumped on the bandwagon of an economic expansion which it neither started nor led. Foreign direct investment did play a major role in boosting Chinese exports. As Figure 5.1. shows, however, the boom in Chinese exports was a late episode of the Chinese ascent. In any event, even then foreign (especially US) capital needed China far more than China needed foreign capital. US companies from Intel to General Motors, "face a simple imperative: invest in China to take advantage of the country's cheap labor and its fast-growing economy or lose out to rivals." Once just a manufacturing center, China has become the place to develop and sell high-tech goods. "Everybody and their brother wants to go to China. There are 1.2 billion consumers over there," says the head of US tech trade group AEA. The vice-president of tech component maker Corning agrees: "There are few other countries that look like they could become this significant."[5]

But how did China become this significant? To what combination of actions and circumstances can we trace its extraordinary economic transformation, "probably the most remarkable . . . in history," according to Stiglitz?[6] And how does the present economic renaissance relate to earlier traditions of non-capitalist market-based development, to the hundred-year eclipse that followed the opium wars, and the revolutionary tradition that gave birth to the PRC? In seeking answers to these questions, let us begin by disposing of the myth that the Chinese ascent can be attributed to an alleged adherence to the neo-liberal creed.

The China Opening: Smith versus Friedman

It is often observed that China's economic expansion differs from the earlier Japanese expansion by being more open to foreign trade and

---

4 Clyde Prestowitz, *Three Billion New Capitalists: The Great Shift of Wealth and Power to the East* (New York, Basic Books, 2005), p. 61.

5 "Is the Job Drain China's Fault?" *Business Week Online*, October 13, 2003; M. Kessler, "U.S. Firms: Doing Business in China Tough, but Critical," *USA Today*, August 17, 2004, pp. 1–2.

6 J. Stiglitz, "Development in Defiance of the Washington Consensus," *Guardian*, April 13, 2006.

investment. The observation is correct, but not the inference that China has thereby adhered to the neo-liberal prescriptions of the Washington Consensus. The inference has been as common among left intellectuals as among the promoters of the Consensus. Deng Xiaoping, for example, figures prominently, along with Reagan, Pinochet, and Thatcher, on the front cover of Harvey's *A Brief History of Neoliberalism*, and a whole chapter of the book is dedicated to "Neoliberalism 'with Chinese characteristics.' "[7] Likewise, Peter Kwong argues that both Reagan and Deng "were great fans of the neo-liberal guru Milton Friedman."

> It is intriguing how early the Chinese had searched out Friedman for guidance—only one year after Thatcher began her brutal "there is no other alternative" reforms. So just as Ronald Reagan started his "revolution" in America by stripping away social and welfare safety nets that had been in place since the FDR era, Deng and his supporters followed Friedman's recipe to "get the government off the people's back," ushering China into the neo-liberal universe.[8]

At the opposite end of the ideological spectrum, the institutional promoters of the Washington Consensus—the World Bank, the IMF, the US and UK Treasuries, backed by opinion-shaping media such as the *Financial Times* and *The Economist*—have boasted that the reduction in world income inequality and poverty, which has accompanied China's economic growth since 1980, can be traced to Chinese adherence to their policy prescriptions.[9] The claim is contradicted by the long series of economic disasters that actual adherence to these prescriptions have provoked in Sub-Saharan Africa, Latin America, and the former USSR. In light of this experience, James Galbraith wonders whether we should continue to consider the 1990s a "golden age of capitalism" rather than "something closer to a golden age of reformed socialism in two places (China and India)—alongside an age of disasters for those who followed the prescriptions favored by *The Economist*."

---

7 David Harvey, *A Brief History of Neoliberalism* (New York, Oxford University Press, 2005).

8 Peter Kwong, "China and the US Are Joined at the Hip: The Chinese Face of Neoliberalism," *Counterpunch*, October 7–8, 2006, pp. 1–2.

9 For a critical survey of these claims, see Robert Wade, "Is Globalization Reducing Poverty and Inequality?" *World Development*, 32, 4 (2004).

Both China and India steered free from Western banks in the 1970s, and spared themselves the debt crisis. Both continue to maintain capital controls to this day, so that hot money cannot flow freely in and out. Both continue to have large state sectors in heavy industry to this day. . . . Yes, China and India have done well, on the whole. But is this due to their reforms or to the regulations they continued to impose? No doubt, the right answer is: Partly to both."[10]

Focusing exclusively on China, and leaving aside for now the question of whether it has been practicing "reformed socialism" rather than some variant of capitalism, Galbraith's claim that China's reforms have not followed neo-liberal prescriptions finds support in Stiglitz's contention, quoted in Chapter 1, that the success of Chinese reforms can be traced to *not* having given up gradualism in favor of the shock therapies advocated by the Washington Consensus; to having recognized that social stability can only be maintained if job creation goes in tandem with restructuring; and to having sought to ensure the fruitful redeployment of resources displaced by intensifying competition. Although China welcomed the World Bank's advice and assistance from the start of the reforms, it always did so on terms and at conditions that served the Chinese "national interest," rather than the interests of the US Treasury and Western capital. As Ramgopal Agarwala recalls from his own experience in Beijing as a senior World Bank official,

China is perhaps the best example of a country that has listened to foreign advice but has made decisions in the light of its own social, political, and economic circumstances. . . . Whatever else may be the basis for China's success, it was definitely not a blind adoption of the policies of the Washington [Consensus]. Reform with "Chinese characteristics" was the defining feature of China's reform process.[11]

The Chinese government also welcomed foreign direct investment, but again only if they saw it as serving China's national interest. Thus, in the early 1990s Toshiba and other Japanese big companies

---

10 J.K. Galbraith, "Debunking *The Economist* Again," available at http://www.salon.com/opinion/feature/2004/03/22/economist/print.html.

11 Ramgopal Agarwala, *The Rise of China: Threat or Opportunity?* (New Delhi, Bookwell, 2002), pp. 86–9.

were told rather unceremoniously that, unless they brought along their parts makers, they should not bother to come at all.[12] More recently, Chinese automotive companies have been in the enviable position of having simultaneous joint-venture agreements with rival foreign competitors, such as Guangzhou Automotive's with Honda and Toyota, something Toyota never agreed to do anywhere else. This arrangement has enabled the Chinese partner to learn best practices from both competitors and be the only one in the three-player network to have access to all others.[13]

More generally, deregulation and privatization have been far more selective, and have proceeded at a far slower pace, than in countries that have followed neo-liberal prescriptions. Indeed, the key reform has not been privatization but the exposure of state-owned enterprises (SOEs) to competition with one another, with foreign corporations, and, above all, with a mixed bag of newly created private, semi-private, and community-owned enterprises. The competition did result in a sharp decline in the share of SOEs in employment and production in comparison with the period 1949–79; but as we shall see presently, the role of the Chinese government in promoting development did not subside. On the contrary, it poured huge sums of money in the development of new industries, in the establishment of new Export Processing Zones (EPZs), in expanding and modernizing higher education, and in major infrastructure projects, to an extent without precedent in any country at comparable levels of per capita income.

Thanks to the continental size and huge population of the country, these policies have enabled the Chinese government to combine the advantages of export-oriented industrialization, largely driven by foreign investment, with the advantages of a self-centered national economy informally protected by language, customs, institutions, and networks accessible to outsiders only through local intermediaries. A good illustration of this combination are the huge EPZs that the Chinese government built from scratch and now house two-thirds of the world's total numbers of EPZs workers. Sheer size has enabled China to build three basic manufacturing clusters, each with its own specialization: the Pearl River Delta, specializing in labor-intensive manufacturing, production of spare parts, and their assembly; the Yangtze River Delta, specializing in capital-intensive industry and the

---

12 *Far Eastern Economic Review*, September 6, 1994, p. 45.

13 Oded Shenkar, *The Chinese Century* (Upper Saddle River, NJ, Wharton School Publishing, 2006), p. 66; Fishman, *China, INC*, pp. 208–10.

production of cars, semi-conductors, mobile phones, and computers; and Zhongguan Cun, Bejing, China's Silicon Valley. More than elsewhere, here the government intervenes directly to foster the collaboration of universities, enterprises, and state banks in the development of information technology.[14]

The division of labor among EPZs illustrates also the Chinese government's strategy of promoting the development of knowledge-intensive industries without abandoning labor-intensive industries. In the pursuit of this strategy, which has transformed several Chinese cities into hotbeds of high-tech research, the Chinese government has modernized and expanded the educational system at a pace and on a scale without precedent even in East Asia. Building on the exceptional achievements of the Mao era in primary education, it increased the average length of schooling to about eight years and the student population to 340 million. As a result, China's state colleges produce graduates in absolute numbers comparable to much wealthier countries. In 2002, for example, China had 590,000 college graduates majoring in science and technology, in comparison to Japan's 690,000 only one or two years earlier. Moreover, Chinese institutions of higher education are showing greater openness to outside influences than their Japanese and Korean counterparts. Not only are its top universities upgrading their infrastructure and academic personnel; in addition, China has the largest contingent of foreign students in the United States, and rapidly growing contingents in Europe, Australia, Japan, and elsewhere. While the Chinese government has been offering all kinds of incentives to entice Chinese students abroad to return on completion of their degrees, many of them, including

---

14 Loong-yu Au, "The Post MFA Era and the Rise of China," *Asian Labour Update*, 56 (Fall 2005), pp. 10–13. In addition to these and other EPZs, industrial clusters of all kinds have proliferated all over the country. "Although manufacturing clusters aren't new, with Italy especially known for them, the Chinese have taken it to a new scale," creating giant industrial districts each "built to specialize in making just one thing, including some of the most pedestrian of goods: cigarettes, lighters, badges, neckties, fasteners." In the Datang area, more than 10,000 households in 120 villages make their living off socks. In 2004 they made 9 billion pairs of socks, while the Appalachian town of Fort Payne—which once declared itself "Sock Capital of the World"—made less than 1 billion. Datang's sock-related businesses include about 1,000 textile material processors, 400 yarn dealers, 300 sewing firms, 100 pressing operations, 300 packagers and 100 forwarders, as well as thousands of sewing shops, with an average of 8 knitting machines each. D. Lee, "China's Strategy Gives it the Edge in the Battle of Two Sock Capitals," *Los Angeles Times*, April 10, 2005.

practicing scientists and executives, are lured back by the opportunities afforded by a fast-growing economy.[15]

In short, the relative gradualism with which economic reforms have been carried out, and the countervailing actions with which the government has sought to promote the synergy between an expanding national market and new social divisions of labor, show that the utopian belief of the neo-liberal creed in the benefits of shock therapies, minimalist governments, and self-regulating markets has been as alien to Chinese reformers as it was to Smith. In Smith's conception of market-based development sketched in Chapter 2, governments use markets as instruments of rule and, in liberalizing trade, do so gradually not to upset "public tranquility." They make capitalists, rather than workers, compete with one another, so that profits are driven to a minimum tolerable level. They encourage division of labor among, rather than within, production units and communities, and invest in education to counter the negative effects of the division of labor on the intellectual qualities of the population. They assign priority to the formation of a domestic market and to agricultural development as the main foundation of industrialization and, over time, of foreign trade and investment as well. However, if and when this priority clashes with "the first duty of the sovereign"— "protecting the society from the violence and invasion of other independent societies"—Smith admits that priority should be given to industry and foreign trade.

Most features of China's return to a market economy fit this conception of market-based development better than Marx's conception of capitalist development—a conception according to which governments play the role of committees for managing the common affairs of the bourgeoisie and, as such, facilitate the separation of the direct producers from the means of production and the tendency of capitalist accumulators to shift competitive pressures from their

---

15 Yugui Guo, *Asia's Educational Edge: Current Achievements in Japan, Korea, Taiwan, China, and India* (Oxford, Lexington, 2005), pp. 154–5; Au, "The Post MFA Era"; Shenkar, *The Chinese Century*, pp. 4–5; P. Aiyar, "Excellence in Education: The Chinese Way," *The Hindu*, February 17, 2006; H.W. French, "China Luring Scholars to Make Universities Great," *New York Times*, October 24, 2005; C. Buckley, "Let a Thousand Ideas Flower: China Is a New Hotbed of Research," *New York Times*, September 13, 2004. According to *People's Daily* (November 17, 2003) and statistics of the Ministry of Education, more than 580,000 Chinese students have gone abroad to pursue advanced studies since the beginning of the reforms in 1978, and 150,000 of them have returned to China. Among other things, returned students have started up to 5,000 businesses across the country, generating revenues exceeding 10 billion yuan.

midst onto workers. To be sure, in promoting exports and the import of technological know-how, the Chinese government has sought the assistance of foreign and Chinese diaspora capitalist interests to a far greater extent than the governments of Ming and pre-opium wars Qing China, not to speak of the PRC under Mao, ever did. Indeed, its relation with Chinese diaspora capital closely resembles the relation of political exchange that sixteenth-century Spain and Portugal entertained with the Genoese capitalist diaspora. However, as noted above, in these relations the Chinese government has retained the upper hand, itself becoming one of the main creditors of the dominant capitalist state (the US) and accepting assistance on terms and at conditions that suit China's national interest. By no stretch of the imagination can it be characterized as the servant of foreign and Chinese diaspora capitalist interests.[16]

More difficult to assess is whether the Chinese government is in the process of becoming a committee for managing the common affairs of the national bourgeoisie that is emerging within mainland China itself. We shall later return to this issue, but for now another Smithian feature of China's transition to a market economy suggests caution in characterizing it as a transition to capitalism. This other feature is the government's active encouragement of competition, not just among foreign capitals, but among all capitals, whether foreign or domestic, private or public. Indeed, the reforms put greater emphasis on the intensification of competition through the breakup of national monopolies and the elimination of barriers, than on privatization.[17] The result has been a constant over-accumulation of capital and downward pressure on rates of profits, which has been characterized as "China's jungle capitalism" but looks more like a Smithian world of capitalists driven by relentless competition to work in the national interest.

A new product is introduced, often by a foreign company, and within months a throng of manufacturers, many of them private

---

16 The latest proof of this is the spate of new hurdles that in 2006 the Chinese government has created for foreign investors—including increased scrutiny of foreign-backed mergers and proposed restrictions in areas from banking to retailing to manufacturing—which foreign companies found particularly alarming because they stem from the government's growing preoccupation with helping China's expanding universe of domestic companies and pressing social issues such as poverty and income inequality. A. Batson and M. Fong, "In Strategic Shift, China Hits Foreign Investors with New Hurdles," Wall Street Journal, August 30, 2006, A1.

17 Thomas G. Rawski, "Reforming China's Economy: What Have We Learned?" The China Journal, 41 (1999), pp. 142, 145; Agarwala, The Rise of China, pp. 103–6.

Chinese companies, start cracking them out. Raging competition sets in, sending prices sliding. And before long producers look to new markets, increasingly overseas. Driving all this is a jumble of forces that have spawned one of the world's most competitive markets. A tidal wave of foreign investment . . . has taught the country some of the most modern manufacturing techniques. A ferocious appetite for foreign technology has powered productivity gains across the economy, while nationwide entrepreneurial zeal has sprouted from the shambles of its once centrally planned system.[18]

Cut-throat competition among public and private enterprises did, of course, result in major disruptions in the security of employment enjoyed by urban workers in the Mao era, as well as in countless episodes of super-exploitation, especially of migrant workers.[19] As we shall see in the chapter's concluding section, the hardships suffered by laid-off urban workers and the super-exploitation of migrant workers have been among the main causes of the escalation of labor unrest and social conflict of the late 1990s and early 2000s. Nevertheless, workers' hardships and rebellions must be put in the context of government policies that, also in this respect, did not embrace the key neo-liberal prescription of sacrificing workers' welfare to boost profitability. Not only have medical, pension, and other "mandatory benefits" for workers in joint ventures remained more generous, and the firing of workers more difficult, in China's formal sector than in countries at comparable or even higher levels of per capita income; more important, the expansion of higher education, the rapid increase in alternative employment opportunities in new industries, and rural tax relief and other reforms, which are encouraging villagers to put more labor into the rural economy, have combined in creating labor shortages that are

18 K. Leggett and P. Wonacott, "Burying the Competition," *Far Eastern Economic Review*, October 17, 2002. For similar accounts see, among others, James Kynge, *China Shakes the World* (Boston, MA, Houghton Mifflin, 2006), and S. Kotkin, "Living in China's World," *New York Times*, November 5, 2006.

19 See, among others, Anita Chan, "Globalization, China's Free (Read Bounded) Labor Market, and the Trade Union," *Asia Pacific Business Review*, 6, 3–4 (2000); Jun Tang, "Selection from Report on Poverty and Anti-Poverty in Urban China," *Chinese Sociology and Anthropology*, 36, 2–3 (2003–04); Ching Kwan Lee and Mark Selden, "Durable Inequality: The Legacies of China's Revolutions and the Pitfalls of Reforms," in J. Foran, D. Lane, and A. Zivkovic, eds, *Revolution in the Making of the Modern World: Social Identities, Globalization, and Modernity* (London, Routledge, 2007).

undermining the foundations of the super-exploitation of migrant labor. "We're seeing the end of the golden period of extremely low-cost labor in China," declares a Goldman Sachs economist. "There are plenty of workers, but the supply of uneducated workers is shrinking. . . . Chinese workers . . . are moving up the value chain faster than people expected."[20]

The Smithian features of China's reforms thus far examined—the gradualism of reforms and state action aimed at expanding and upgrading the social division of labor; the huge expansion of education; the subordination of capitalist interests to the national interest; and the active encouragement of inter-capitalist competition—have all contributed to this emerging shortage. But the most critical factor has probably been another Smithian feature of China's reforms: the leading role which they assigned to the formation of the domestic market and the improvement of living conditions in rural areas. To this most crucial factor we now turn.

Accumulation without Dispossession

As Smith would have advised, Deng's reforms targeted the domestic economy and agriculture first. The key reform was the introduction in 1978–83 of the Household Responsibility System, which returned decision-making and control over agricultural surpluses from communes to rural households. In addition, in 1979 and again in 1983 agricultural procurement prices were increased substantially. As a result, farm productivity and returns to farm activity increased dramatically, strengthening the earlier tendency of commune and brigade enterprises to produce non-agricultural goods. Through various institutional barriers to spatial mobility, the government encouraged rural labor to "leave the land without leaving the village." In 1983, it nonetheless gave permission to rural residents to engage in long-distance transport and marketing to seek outlets for their products. This was the first time in a generation that Chinese farmers were given the right to conduct business outside their home villages. In 1984, regulations were further relaxed to allow farmers to work in nearby towns in the

---

20 D. Barboza, "Labor Shortage in China May Lead to Trade Shift," *New York Times*, April 3, 2006; T. Fuller, "Worker Shortage in China: Are Higher Prices Ahead?" *Herald Tribune Online*, April 20, 2005; S. Montlake, "China's Factories Hit an Unlikely Shortage: Labor," *Christian Science Monitor*, May 1, 2006; "China's People Problem," *The Economist*, April 14, 2005.

emerging collectively owned Township and Village Enterprises (TVEs).[21]

The emergence of TVEs was prompted by two other reforms: fiscal decentralization, which granted autonomy to local governments in the promotion of economic growth and in the use of fiscal residuals for bonuses; and a switch to the evaluation of cadres on the basis of the economic performance of their localities, which provided local governments with strong incentives to support economic growth. TVEs thus became the primary loci of the reorientation of the entrepreneurial energies of party cadres and government officials towards developmental objectives. Mostly self-reliant financially, they also became the main agency of the re-allocation of agricultural surpluses to the undertaking of labor-intensive industrial activities capable of absorbing rural surplus labor productively.[22]

The result was an explosive growth of the rural labor force engaged in non-agricultural activities, from 28 million in 1978 to 176 million in 2003, most of the increase occurring in TVEs. Between 1980 and 2004 TVEs added almost four times as many jobs as were lost in state and collective urban employment. Although between 1995 and 2004 the increase of jobs in TVEs fell far short of the decrease in state and collective urban employment, by the end of the period TVEs still employed more than twice as many workers as all foreign, private and jointly owned urban enterprises combined.

---

21 Fang Cai, Albert Park, and Yaohui Zhao, "The Chinese Labor Market," paper presented at the Second Conference on China's Economic Transition: Origins, Mechanisms, and Consequences, University of Pittsburgh, November 5–7, 2004; Jonathan Unger, *The Transformation of Rural China* (Armonk, NY, M.E. Sharpe, 2002).

22 Jean Oi, *Rural China Takes Off: Institutional Foundations of Economic Reform* (Berkeley, CA, University of California Press, 1999); Nan Lin, "Local Market Socialism: Local Corporatism in Action in Rural China," *Theory and Society*, 24 (1995); Andrew Walder, "Local Governments as Industrial Firms: An Organizational Analysis of China's Transitional Economy," *American Journal of Sociology*, 10, 2 (1995); Susan H. Whiting, *Power and Wealth in Rural China: The Political Economy of Institutional Change* (Cambridge, Cambridge University Press, 2001); Juan Wang, "Going Beyond Township and Village Enterprises in Rural China," *Journal of Contemporary China*, 14, 42 (2005), p. 179; Kellee S. Tsai, "Off Balance: The Unintended Consequences of Fiscal Federalism in China," *Journal of Chinese Political Science*, 9, 2 (2004); Justin Yifu Lin and Yang Yao, "Chinese Rural Industrialization in the Context of the East Asian Miracle," China Center for Economic Research, Beijing University (n.d.).

The dynamism of rural enterprises took Chinese leaders by surprise. The development of the TVEs—acknowledged Deng Xiaoping in 1993—"was totally out of our expectations." By then the government had stepped in to legalize and regulate TVEs. In 1990 collective ownership of the TVEs was assigned to all inhabitants of the town or village. Local governments, however, were given authority to appoint and fire managers or to delegate this authority to a governmental agency. The allocation of TVE profits was also regulated, mandating the reinvestment of more than half within the enterprise, to modernize and expand production and to increase welfare and bonus funds, and the remittance of most of what was left to the construction of agricultural infrastructure, technology services, public welfare, and investment in new enterprises. In the late 1990s, attempts were made to transform vaguely defined property rights into some form of shareholding or purely private ownership. All regulations—including those mandating the allocation of profits—were nonetheless hard to enforce, so that TVEs came to be characterized by such a variety of local arrangements and practices that makes their categorization extremely difficult.[23]

And yet despite, or perhaps because of, their organizational variety, in retrospect TVEs may well turn out to have played as crucial a role in the Chinese economic ascent as vertically integrated, bureaucratically managed corporations did in the US ascent a century earlier. Their contributions to the success of the reforms are manifold. First, their labor-intensive orientation enabled them to absorb rural surplus labor and raise rural incomes without a massive increase in migration to urban areas. Indeed, most labor mobility in the 1980s was the movement of farmers out of farming to work in rural collective enterprises. Second, since TVEs were relatively unregulated, their entry into numerous markets increased competitive pressure across the board, forcing not just SOEs but all urban enterprises to improve their performance.[24] Third, TVEs have been a major source of rural tax revenue, reducing the fiscal burden on peasants. Since taxes and levies have been a primary source of peasant grievances, they thereby

---

23 Wing Thye Woo, "The Real Reasons for China's Growth," *The China Journal*, 41 (1999), pp. 129–37; Boudewijn R.A. Bouckaert, "Bureaupreneurs in China: We Did it our Way — A Comparative Study of the Explanation of the Economic Successes of Town–Village Enterprises in China," paper presented at the EALE Conference, Ljubljana, September 2005; Martin Hart-Landsberg and Paul Burkett, "China and Socialism: Market Reform and Class Struggle," *Monthly Review*, 56, 3 (2004), p. 35; Lin and Yao, "Chinese Rural Industrialization."

24 Cai, Park, and Zhao, "The Chinese Labor Market."

contributed to social stability. Moreover, by taking on many of the taxes and charges that used to be levied on peasants, they have also helped shelter peasants from predatory local governments.[25] Fourth, and in key respects most important, by reinvesting profits and rents locally, TVEs have expanded the size of the domestic market and created the conditions for new rounds of investment, job creation, and division of labor.[26]

As Gillian Hart has noted in summing up the developmental advantages of China in comparison with South Africa—where the African peasantry has long been dispossessed of the means of production without a corresponding creation of the demand conditions for its absorption in wage employment—much of Chinese economic growth can be traced to the contribution that TVEs have made to the reinvestment and redistribution of industrial profits within local circuits, and to their use in schools, clinics, and other forms of collective consumption. Moreover, in TVEs with a relatively egalitarian distribution of land among households—like the ones she visited in 1992 in Sichuan and Hunan provinces—residents could procure their livelihood through a combination of intensive cultivation of tiny plots with industrial and other forms of non-agricultural work. Indeed, "a key force propelling [TVEs] growth is that, unlike their urban counterparts, they do not have to provide housing, health, retirement, and other benefits to workers. In effect, much of the cost of reproduction of labor has been deflected from the enterprise—but, at least in some instances, is being supported through redistributive mechanisms." This pattern, Hart goes on to suggest, could be observed not just in China but in Taiwan as well.

> What is distinctive about China and Taiwan—and dramatically different from South Africa—are the redistributive land reforms beginning in the late 1940s that effectively broke the power of the landlord class. The political forces that drove agrarian reforms in China and Taiwan were closely linked and precisely opposite. Yet in both socialist and post-socialist China, and in "capitalist" Taiwan, the redistributive reforms that defined agrarian transformations were marked by rapid, decentralized industrial accumulation *without* dispossession from the land. . . . That some of the

---

25 Wang, "Going Beyond Township and Village Enterprises," pp. 177–8; Thomas P. Bernstein and Xiaobo Lu, *Taxation without Representation in Contemporary Rural China* (New York, Cambridge University Press, 2003).

26 Lin and Yao, "Chinese Rural Industrialization."

most spectacular instances of industrial production in the second half of the twentieth century have taken place without dispossession of the peasant-workers from the land not only sheds light on the distinctively "non-Western" forms of accumulation that underpin global competition . . . [It should also compel us to] revise the teleological assumptions about "primitive accumulation" through which dispossession is seen as a natural concomitant of capitalist development.[27]

From the perspective developed in this book, Hart's plea for a revision of assumptions about primitive accumulation may be reformulated as follows. The separation of agricultural producers from the means of production has been more a consequence of capitalism's creative destruction than one of its preconditions. The most persistent and crucial form of primitive accumulation—or, as Harvey has renamed the process, of accumulation by dispossession—has been the use of military force by Western states to provide the endless accumulation of power and capital with spatial fixes of increasing scale and scope. However, US attempts to bring about the ultimate spatial fix by turning itself into a world state backfired. Instead of creating a world state, it created a world market of unprecedented volume and density in which the region endowed with the largest supplies of low-price, high-quality labor has a decisive competitive advantage. It is no historical accident that this region is East Asia—the heir of a tradition of market economy which, more than any other, mobilized human rather than non-human resources and protected rather than destroyed the economic independence and welfare of agricultural producers.

This is yet another reformulation of Sugihara's thesis of the continuing significance of the East Asian Industrious Revolution. Hart's observation that in the TVEs the intensive cultivation of small plots of land is combined with industrial and other forms of non-agricultural work, and with investments in the improvement of the quality of labor, confirms the validity of the thesis. But so does the frequent observation that, even in urban areas, the chief competitive advantage of Chinese producers is not low wages as such but the use of techniques that use inexpensive educated labor instead of expensive machines and managers. A good illustration is Wanfeng automotive factory near Shanghai, where "there is not a single robot in sight." As in many other Chinese factories, the assembly lines are occupied by

---

27 Gillian Hart, *Disabling Globalization: Places of Power in Post-Apartheid South Africa* (Berkeley, CA, University of California Press, 2002), pp. 199–201.

scores of young men, newly arrived from China's expanding technical schools, working with little more than large electric drills, wrenches, and rubber mallets.

> Engines and body panels that would, in a Western, Korean or Japanese factory, move from station to station on automatic conveyors are hauled by hand and hand truck. This is why Wanfeng can sell its handmade luxury Jeep Tributes in the Middle East for $8,000 to $10,000. The company isn't spending money on multimillion-dollar machines to build cars; instead, it's using highly capable workers [whose] yearly pay . . . is less than the monthly pay of new hires in Detroit.[28]

Generally speaking, as a report in the *Wall Street Journal* points out, accounting statements that show the payroll of a finished product to be only 10 percent of its costs are misleading, because they exclude the full payroll cost of the purchased components and company overheads. When these costs are added in, total labor costs are more in the order of 40 to 60 percent of the final product cost, and in China those labor costs are lower across the board. Indeed, for the most part, the main competitive advantage of China is not that its production workers typically cost 5 percent of their US counterparts but that its engineers and plant managers cost 35 percent or less. Similarly, statistics showing US workers in capital-intensive factories to be several times more productive than their Chinese counterparts ignore the fact that the higher productivity of US workers is due to the replacement of many factory workers with complex flexible-automation and material-handling systems, which reduces labor costs but raises the costs of capital and support systems. By saving on capital and reintroducing a greater role for labor, Chinese factories reverse this process. The design of parts to be made, handled, and assembled manually, for example, reduces the total capital required by as much as one-third.[29]

Moreover, as one would expect from Sugihara's thesis, Chinese businesses substitute inexpensive educated labor, not just for expensive machinery, but for expensive managers as well. Vindicating

28 Fishman, *China, INC*, pp. 205–6. For other illustrations of substitution of low-cost labor for expensive equipment, see George Stalk and David Young, "Globalization Cost Advantage," *Washington Times*, August 24, 2004.

29 T. Hout and J. Lebretton, "The Real Contest Between America and China," *Wall Street Journal Online*, September 16, 2003.

Smith's poor opinion of corporate bureaucratic management, a self-managed labor force "keeps management costs down too."

> Despite the enormous numbers of workers in Chinese factories, the ranks of managers who supervise them are remarkably thin by Western standards. Depending on the work, you might see 15 managers for 5,000 workers, an indication of how incredibly well self-managed they are.[30]

As previously noted, government policies in the field of education have endowed China with a pool of human resources which, along with a huge supply of literate and industrious laborers, includes a large and rapidly expanding supply of engineers, scientists, and technicians. This expanding supply of knowledge-workers facilitates, not only the substitution of inexpensive educated labor for expensive machines and managers, but also—as Smith advocated—the upgrading of the social division of labor towards knowledge-intensive production and innovations. Suffice it to mention that in 2003, while spending nearly five times what China did on research and development, the United States had less than double the number of researchers (1.3 million to 743,000). Moreover, over the past dozen years, China's R&D spending has grown at an annual rate of 17 percent, against the 4–5 percent reported for the United States, Japan, and the European Union.[31]

Social Origins of the Chinese Ascent

The close fit between the ongoing transformation of the Chinese political economy and Smith's conception of market-based development does not mean that Deng's reforms were in any way inspired by Smith's texts. As previously noted, the practices of the eighteenth-century official Chen Hongmou anticipated what Smith later theorized in *The Wealth of Nations*. Those practices originated, not in theory, but in a pragmatic approach, inspired by Chinese traditions, to problems of governance in mid-Qing China. Whether or not Deng ever read Smith's texts, his reforms

---

30 Ted C. Fishman, "The Chinese Century," *New York Times Magazine*, July 4, 2004.

31 Ibid.; G. Naik, "China's Spending for Research Outpaces the U.S.," *Wall Street Journal Online*, September 29, 2006.

originated in an equally pragmatic approach to problems of governance in post-Mao China.

Thus, Wang Hui of Tsinghua University has recently traced the origins of the reforms to a reaction—widely approved inside and outside the CCP—against "the factional struggles and chaotic character of politics during the latter years of the Cultural Revolution." While thoroughly repudiating the Cultural Revolution, the CCP nonetheless "did not repudiate either the Chinese Revolution or socialist values, nor the summation of Mao Zedong thought." Two effects ensued.

> First, the socialist tradition has functioned to a certain extent as an internal restraint on state reforms. Every time the state-party system made a major policy shift, it had to be conducted in dialogue with this tradition. . . . Secondly, the socialist tradition gave workers, peasants and other social collectivities some legitimate means to contest or negotiate the state's corrupt or inegalitarian marketization procedures. Thus, within the historical process of the negation of the Cultural Revolution, a reactivation of China's legacy also provides an opening for the development of a future politics.[32]

For what concerns the relation between the reforms and China's socialist tradition, there are at least two good reasons why the CCP under Deng repudiated the Cultural Revolution but not the tradition established by the Chinese Revolution. First, the factional struggles and political chaos of the latter years of the Cultural Revolution completed, but at the same time threatened to destroy, the achievements of the Chinese Revolution. And second, the onslaught of the Cultural Revolution did not spare the CCP, seriously undermining the bureaucratic foundations of the power and privileges of its cadres and officials. Deng's reforms thus had a double appeal: to party cadres and officials as a means of reconstituting on new foundations their power and privileges; and to the citizenry at large as a means of consolidating the achievements of the Chinese Revolution which the Cultural Revolution had jeopardized.

On the first appeal, the reforms created myriad opportunities for the reorientation of entrepreneurial energies from the political to the economic sphere, which party cadres and officials eagerly seized upon

---

32 Hui Wang, "Depoliticized Politics, From East to West," *New Left Review*, II/41 (2006), pp. 34, 44–5.

to enrich and empower themselves in alliance with government officials and managers of SOEs—often influential party members themselves. In the process, various forms of accumulation by dispossession—including appropriations of public property, embezzlement of state funds, and sales of land-use rights—became the basis of huge fortunes.[33] It nonetheless remains unclear whether this enrichment and empowerment has led to the formation of a capitalist class and, more important, whether such a class, if it has come into existence, has succeeded in seizing control of the commanding heights of Chinese economy and society. Under Jiang Zemin (1989–2002), a positive answer to both questions seemed quite plausible. But under Hu Jintao and Wen Jiabao—despite the shorter time span for assessing their orientation—a reversal seems to be occurring which makes such an answer, especially to the second question, far less plausible.[34]

As for the appeal of Deng's reforms to the citizenry at large, we must first acknowledge the considerable extent to which the success of the reforms has been based on prior achievements of the Chinese Revolution. When Western and Japanese observers praise the education, willingness to learn, and discipline of China's labor, including rural migrants, in comparison to India's, notes Au Loong-

---

33 Yingyi Qian, "Enterprise Reforms in China: Agency Problems and Political Control," *Economics of Transition*, 4, 2 (1996); X.L. Ding, "The Illicit Asset Stripping of Chinese State Firms," *The China Journal*, 43 (2000); Lee and Selden, "Durable Inequality." These and other forms of accumulation by dispossession occurred in conjunction with the accumulation without dispossession emphasized by Hart. It is of course very hard to tell which tendency prevailed at different times in a country of the size and complexity of China, and even more which tendency is more likely to prevail in the future. The position advanced in the text below is that under Jiang Zemin accumulation by dispossession was on the rise and, were it not for the change in policies under Hu Jintao prompted by the escalation of social unrest, it might have eventually prevailed.

34 The reversal has been signaled, not just by the change of policies and the greater preoccupation of the new leadership with social issues, but also in the use of an ongoing anti-corruption campaign to purge the party apparatus of Jiang's followers and to bolster the capacity of the CCP and the central government to effectively implement the change in policies. See J. Kahn, "China's Anti-Graft Bid Bolsters Top Leaders," *International Herald Tribune*, October 4, 2006; R. McGregor, "Push to Bring the Provinces into Line," *Financial Times*, December 12, 2006. Whether the reforms have strengthened or weakened the capacity of the top leadership of the CCP and of the central government to enforce policies effectively at the provincial and local level remains a disputed fact. For opposite views on this issue, see Maria Edin, "State Capacity and Local Agent Control in China: CCP Cadre Management from a Township Perspective," *The China Quarterly*, 173 (2003) and Ho-fung Hung, "Rise of China and the Global Overaccumulation Crisis," paper presented at the Society for the Study of Social Problems Annual Meeting, Montreal, August 2006.

yu, "it never occurs to them that one of the contributing factors to this achievement is the great transformation in land reform earlier, and the collective provision of rural infrastructure and education that followed, not anything related to the market reform later."[35] The boom in agricultural production of 1978–84 did have something to do with the reforms, but only because they built on the legacy of the Mao era. Between 1952 and 1978, the communes had more than doubled China's irrigated farmland and disseminated improved technology, such as greater use of fertilizers and high-yielding semi-dwarf rice, which by 1977 occupied 80 percent of China's rice land. "It was the combination of the productive base built during [the] Mao era along with the incentives provided by the household responsibility system that created the boom in agricultural production."[36]

As Figures 12.1 and 12.2 show, China's greatest advances in per capita income (shown by upward movements of the curves) have occurred since 1980. But the greatest advances in adult life expectancy, and to a lesser extent in adult literacy, that is, in basic welfare (shown by rightward movements of the curves), occurred before 1980. This pattern strongly supports the claim that China's economic success was built on the extraordinary social achievements of the Mao era. In a report published in 1981, even the World Bank recognized the significance of these achievements.

China's most remarkable achievement during the past three decades has been to make the low-income groups far better off in terms of basic needs than their counterparts in most other poor countries. They all have work; their food supply is guaranteed through a mixture of state rationing and collective self-insurance; most of their children are not only at school but are also comparatively well taught; and the great majority have access to basic health care and family planning services. Life expectancy—whose dependence on many other economic and social variables makes it

---

35 Au, "The Post MFA Era," pp. 10–13. By the time Deng's reforms took off, China had already moved well ahead of India in all human development indicators: literacy rate, daily calorie intake, death rate, infant mortality rate, life expectancy, and so on. See Peter Nolan, *Transforming China: Globalization, Transition and Development* (London, Anthem Press, 2004) p. 118.

36 Agarwala, *The Rise of China*, pp. 95–6. On irrigation projects, road and rail expansion, and planting of hybrid rice in the Mao era as bases for reform-era growth, see also Chris Bramall, *Sources of Chinese Economic Growth, 1978–1996* (New York, Oxford University Press, 2000), pp. 95–6, 137–8, 153, 248.

probably the best single indicator of the extent of real poverty in a
country—is outstandingly high for a country at China's per capita
income level.[37]

Whether Deng's reforms have consolidated or undermined these
achievements is a controversial issue which will not be entertained
here except for two observations. First, the indicators of basic welfare
of China's population (adult life expectancy and literacy rate) had
improved so much before the reforms that there was little room for
further major improvements. And yet, by the indicators shown in
Figures 12.1 and 12.2, in the reform era there was further improvement, especially in adult literacy. From this standpoint, therefore, the
reforms appear to have consolidated, rather than undermined, the
prior achievements of the Chinese Revolution.

Second, the importance of China's advances in per capita income in
the reform era should not be belittled, even if they did not involve a
proportional improvement in basic welfare. In a capitalist world, as
we have repeatedly underscored, national wealth, as measured by per

Figure 12.1   Per capita income and adult life expectancy, 1960–2000.

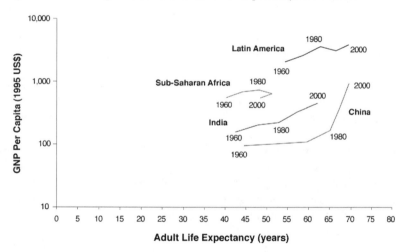

Source: calculations based on GNP, adult life expectancy, and population from World
Bank—World Development Indicators 2004 and 2001.

37 Quoted in Yuyu Li, "The Impact of Rural Migration on Village Development: A Comparative Study in Three Chinese Villages," PhD diss., Department of
Sociology, The Johns Hopkins University. See also Agarwala, *The Rise of China*, p.
55.

Figure 12.2   Per capita income and adult literacy, 1970–2000.

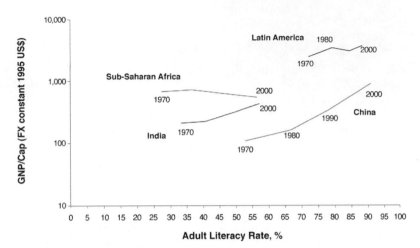

Source: calculations based on GNP and population from World Bank—World
Development Indicators 2004 and 2001; adult literacy rates from United Nations
Population Division 2005.

capita income, is the primary source of national power. Even if the
purpose of the pursuit of national power is the transformation of the
world in a socialist direction, the CCP had little choice but to play the
game of world politics by the extant capitalist rules, as Mao himself
always understood very well. Once impending defeat in Vietnam
forced the United States to readmit China to normal commercial and
diplomatic intercourse with the rest of East Asia and the world at
large, it made perfect sense for Communist China to seize on the
opportunities offered by that intercourse to boost its national wealth
and power. Even before the US invasion of Iraq added new momentum to the Chinese ascent, Richard Bernstein and Ross Munro
crudely but perceptively identified the true political significance of
China's switch to a market economy.

> The irony in Sino-American relations is that when China was in
> the grip of ideological Maoism and displayed such ideological
> ferocity that Americans believed it to be dangerous and menacing,
> it was actually a paper tiger, weak and virtually without global
> influence. Now that China has shed the trappings of Maoism and
> embarked on a pragmatic course of economic development and
> global trade, it appears less threatening but it is in fact acquiring

the wherewithal to back its global ambitions and interests with real power.[38]

A more accurate version of this assessment is that, as long as China was cut off from global trade by US Cold War policies and felt threatened militarily by the USSR, the CCP was driven to use ideology as the main weapon in the struggle to consolidate its power nationally and internationally. But when, in the latter years of the Cultural Revolution, the ideological weapon began to backfire, at about the same time that the United States sought an alliance with China in the Cold War with the USSR, the stage was set for a pragmatic use of the market as an instrument of empowerment of the CCP nationally, and of the PRC internationally. While on the empowerment of the CCP the jury is still out—since it is not clear whether its hold on Chinese state and society has been strengthened or weakened—on the empowerment of the PRC, the verdict is that the economic reforms have been a resounding success.

Why then change course, as the CCP has been doing under its new leadership? What has prompted the change, and in which direction can it be expected to lead China's economy and society? Wang Hui's observations concerning the relation between Deng's reforms and the tradition of the Chinese Revolution provide us with a clue to answering these questions. The foundation of that tradition has been a distinct Chinese brand of Marxism-Leninism, which first emerged with the formation of the Red Army in the late 1920s but developed fully only after Japan took over China's coastal regions in the late 1930s. This ideological innovation had two main components.

First, while the Leninist principle of the vanguard party was retained, the insurrectional thrust of Leninist theory was abandoned. In the deeply fragmented statal structure of warlord–GMD China, there was no "Winter Palace" to be stormed or, rather, there were too many such palaces for any insurrectionary strategy to have any chance of success. The insurrectional aspects of Leninist theory were thus replaced by what Mao later theorized as the "mass line"—the idea that the vanguard party ought to be not just the teacher but also the pupil of the masses. "This from-the-masses-to-the-masses concept"—notes Fairbank—"was indeed a sort of democracy suited to Chinese tradition, where the upper-class official had governed

---

38 Richard Bernstein and Ross H. Munro, "The Coming Conflict with America," *Foreign Affairs*, 76, 2 (1997), p. 22.

best when he had the true interests of the local people at heart and so governed on their behalf."[39]

Second, in seeking a social base the CCP gave priority to the peasantry rather than to the urban proletariat—Marx's and Lenin's revolutionary class. As the 1927 GMD's massacre of Communist-led workers in Shanghai had demonstrated, the coastal regions where the bulk of the urban proletariat was concentrated were far too treacherous a ground from which to challenge foreign domination and the GMD's hegemony over the Chinese bourgeoisie. Driven ever farther from the seats of capitalist expansion by the Western trained and equipped GMD armies, the CCP and the Red Army had no choice but to thrust their roots among the peasantry of poor and remote areas. The result was, in Mark Selden's characterization, "a two-way socialization process," whereby the party-army molded the subaltern strata of Chinese rural society into a powerful revolutionary force, and was in turn shaped by the aspirations and values of these strata.[40]

The combination of these two features with the modernist thrust of Marxism-Leninism has been the bedrock of the Chinese revolutionary tradition and helps to explain key aspects of the Chinese developmental path before and after the reforms, as well as the recent change of policies under Hu. It helps in explaining, first of all, why in Mao's China, in sharp contrast to Stalin's USSR, modernization was pursued, not through the destruction, but through the economic and educational uplifting of the peasantry. Second, it helps in explaining why, before and after the reforms, Chinese modernization has been based, not merely on the internalization of the Western Industrial Revolution, but on the revival of features of the indigenous, rural-based, Industrious Revolution. Third, it helps in explaining why under Mao the tendency towards the emergence of an urban bourgeoisie of state-party officials and intellectuals was fought through their "re-education" in rural areas. Finally, it helps in explaining why Deng's reforms were launched first in agriculture, and why Hu's new course focuses on the expansion of health, education and welfare benefits in rural areas under the banner of a "new socialist countryside."

At the roots of this tradition lies the fundamental problem of how to govern and develop a country with a *rural* population larger than the *entire* population of Africa, or Latin America, or Europe. No other country, except India, ever had a remotely comparable

---

39 John K. Fairbank, *China: A New History* (Cambridge, MA, The Belknap Press, 1992), p. 319.

40 Mark Selden, "Yan'an Communism Reconsidered," *Modern China*, 2, 1 (1995), pp. 37–8.

problem.[41] From this standpoint, however painful an experience for urban officials and intellectuals, the Cultural Revolution consolidated the rural foundations of the Chinese Revolution and laid the ground-work for the success of the economic reforms. Suffice it to mention that, partly as a result of policies and partly as a result of the disruption of urban industries by factional fights, the products of rural enterprises were in great demand, leading to a major expansion of the commune and brigade enterprises out of which many of the TVEs later emerged.[42]

At the same time, the Cultural Revolution jeopardized, not just the power of state-party officials and the social and political achieve-ments of the Chinese Revolution, as previously noted, but also the entire modernist component of the revolutionary tradition. Its re-pudiation in favor of economic reforms was thus presented and perceived as essential to a revival of that component. Over time, however, the very success of the revival swung the pendulum in the opposite direction, seriously undermining the revolutionary tradition by the mid to late 1990s. Two developments in particular signaled this tendency: a huge increase in income inequality and growing popular discontent with the procedures and outcomes of the reforms.

Social Contradictions of Economic Success

The huge increase in income inequality within and between urban and rural areas, as well as among different classes, social strata, and provinces is one of the best-established facts about China's switch to a market economy.[43] As long as this trend could be credibly presented

41 As the Chinese scholar Pei Minxin has noted, counting periods where the central government has lost control of large swaths of territory, China has experi-enced 1,000 years of internal chaos. Quoted in M. Naim, "Only a Miracle Can Save China from Itself," *Financial Times*, September 15, 2003.

42 Lin and Yao, "Chinese Rural Industrialization"; Louis Putterman, "On the Past and Future of China's Township and Village-Owned Enterprises," *World Development*, 25, 10 (1997).

43 See, among others, Yehua D. Wei, *Regional Development in China: States, Globalization and Inequality* (New York, Routledge, 2000); Carl Riskin, Renwei Zhao, and Shih Li, eds, *Retreat from Equality: Essays on the Changing Distribution of Income in China, 1988–1995* (Armonk, NY, M.E. Sharpe, 2001); Andrew Walder, "Markets and Income Inequality in Rural China: Political Advantage in an Ex-panding Economy," *American Sociological Review*, 67, 2 (2002); Hui Wang, *China's New Order: Society, Politics and Economy in Transition* (Cambridge, MA, Harvard University Press, 2003); Ximing Wu and Jeffrey M. Perloff, "China's Income Distribution over Time: Reasons for Rising Inequality," KUDARE Working Paper 977, University of California at Berkeley; Yi Li, *The Structure and Evolution of Chinese Social Stratification* (Lanham, MD, University Press of America, 2005).

as the result of a strategy of unbalanced development that created opportunities of advancement for most, resistance to increasing inequality was limited and could be easily neutralized or repressed. Over time, however, increasing inequality has clashed with the revolutionary tradition seriously undermining social stability.[44]

The traditions of the "mass line" and of the "two-way socialization process" apparently played a role in the reforms themselves.[45] Nevertheless, the more local and provincial party cadres and officials redirected their entrepreneurial energies to the economic sphere and engaged in acts of accumulation by dispossession, the more the tradition of the "mass line" became a fiction, and the "two-way socialization process" between the party-state and the subaltern strata of Chinese society was displaced by a similar process between the party-state and the emerging bourgeoisie. And yet, as Samir Amin claims in a passage quoted in Chapter 1, the revolutionary tradition had endowed China's subaltern strata with a self-confidence and combativeness with few parallels elsewhere in the global South and, we may add, in the global North as well. And as Wang Hui points out, the continuing official adherence of the party-state to that tradition has given some legitimacy to this self-confidence and combativeness.

---

44 In explaining why the huge increase in income inequality did not become a socially destabilizing factor until recently, three considerations should be borne in mind. First, as previously noted, basic welfare continued to improve during the reforms. The greater relative deprivation entailed by increasing inequality was thus accompanied by less absolute deprivation. Second, in China the increase in inequality—as measured by synthetic indicators like the Gini—has been largely due to an improvement (rather than a deterioration) in the position of middle-income groups. See, especially, Wu and Perloff, "China's Income Distribution over Time," figures 2 and 3. Finally, according to Research Group for Social Structure in Contemporary China, *Social Mobility in Contemporary China* (Montreal, America Quantum Media, 2005) p. ch. 4, increasing inequality during the reform period was accompanied by an *increase* in the inter-generational (parents occupation/children occupation) and intra-generational (first occupation/current occupation) mobility. Individuals in the lower-income occupations had thus greater chances than in the pre-reform period to turn the income gap between occupations into a personal gain by moving to a higher-income occupation, and the greater the gap, the greater the gain.

45 In his dealings with Chinese policy makers, for example, Agarwala "found senior leaders demonstrate greater interest in interaction with various levels of society than in more democratically organized societies such as India's" *The rise of China*, p. 90). In a similar vein, Stiglitz has noted that "George Bush has shown the dangers of excessive secrecy and confining decision-making to a narrow circle of sycophants. Most people outside China do not fully appreciate the extent to which its leaders, by contrast, have engaged in extensive deliberations and consultations as they strive to solve the enormous problems they face" ("Development in Defiance of the Washington Consensus." See also Rawski, "Reforming China's Economy," p. 142.

The result has been a proliferation of social struggles in urban and rural areas alike. Officially reported cases of "public order disruptions"—a reference to protests, riots, and other forms of social unrest—escalated from about 10,000 in 1993 to 50,000 in 2002, 58,000 in 2003, 74,000 in 2004, and 87,000 in 2005, declining only slightly in the first six months of 2006. In rural areas, until about 2000 the main grievances prompting mass action were taxes, levies, fees, and various other "burdens." More recently, diversion of land from farming to industrial, real estate, and infrastructural development, environmental degradation, and the corruption of local party and government officials have become the most incendiary issues. Episodes like the 2005 Dongyang riot over pollution from a pesticide factory, in which more than 10,000 residents routed the police leading to the suspension of operations at the plant, have "entered Chinese folklore as proof that determined citizens acting en masse can force the authorities to reverse course and address their needs."[46]

In the urban areas, the "old" working class of the SOEs has since the late 1990s responded to mass lay-offs with a wave of protests that often appealed to standards of justice of the socialist tradition and to the "iron rice bowl" social contract between the working class and the state that prevailed throughout the first four decades of the PRC. For the most part, a combination of repression and concessions easily contained this wave of protest. More recently, however, an unprecedented series of walkouts has heralded the spread of unrest to the "new" working class of mostly young migrants, who constitute the backbone of China's export industries. Combined with growing unrest among urban workers in the service sectors, these two waves are putting to rest the notion common in the West that "there is no labor movement in China": "you can go to almost any city in the country now"—notes Robin Munro of *China Labour Bulletin*—"and there will be several major collective worker protests going on at the same time." It is a spontaneous and relatively inchoate labor move-

---

46 H.W. French, "Protesters in China Get Angrier and Bolder," *International Herald Tribune*, July 20, 2005; T. Friedman, "How to Look at China," *International Herald Tribune*, November 10, 2005; H.W. French, "20 Reported Killed as Chinese Unrest Escalates," *New York Times*, December 9, 2005; J. Muldavin, "In Rural China, a Time Bomb Is Ticking," *International Herald Tribune*, January 1, 2006; C. Ni, "Wave of Social Unrest Continues across China," *Los Angeles Times*, August 10, 2006; M. Magnier, "As China's Spews Pollution, Villagers Rise Up," *Los Angeles Times*, September 3, 2006; M. Magnier, "China Says It's Calmed Down," *Los Angeles Times*, November 8, 2006; Lee and Selden, "Durable Inequality."

ment; but so was the US labor movement during its golden age of the 1930s.[47]

As noted in Chapter 1, this enormous upsurge of social unrest in rural and urban areas has posed an entirely new challenge to the leadership of the CCP and has prompted it to change rhetoric and policies in the pursuit of a more balanced development between rural and urban areas, between regions, and between economy and society, and, most recently, to introduce new labor legislation aimed at expanding workers' rights. Whether the change will actually rescue the socialist tradition and redirect development in a more egalitarian direction is still anybody's guess. What concerns us here, however, is not so much the fate of the socialist tradition in China, as the broader implications of the Chinese ascent for inter-civilizational relations in the world at large. It is to these implications that we now turn.

---

47 B. Smith, J. Brecher, and T. Costello, "China's Emerging Labor Movement," *ZNet* http://www.zmag.org, October 9, 2006. On the earlier wave of unrest, see Ching Kwan Lee, "From the Specter of Mao to the Spirit of the Law: Labor Insurgency in China," *Theory and Society* 31, 2 (2002) and Lee and Selden, "Durable Inequality." On the contrast between the two waves, see Beverly J. Silver, "Labor Upsurges: From Detroit to Ulsan and Beyond," *Critical Sociology*, 31, 3 (2005), pp. 445–7, and *Forces of Labor: Workers' Movements and Globalization since 1870* (Cambridge, Cambridge University Press, 2003), pp. 64–6.

EPILOGUE

The central question from which we began is whether, and under what conditions, the Chinese ascent, with all its shortcomings and likely future setbacks, can be taken as the harbinger of that greater equality and mutual respect among peoples of European and non-European descent that Smith foresaw and advocated 230 years ago. The analysis developed in this book points towards a positive answer but with some major qualifications.

As we have seen in Chapters 7 and 9, the emergence of China as the true winner of the United States' War on Terror has resulted in a reversal of the two countries' influence in East Asia and in the world at large. One expression of this reversal has been what Joshua Cooper Ramo has called the Beijing Consensus—the China-led emergence of "a path for other nations around the world" not simply to develop but also "to fit into the international order in a way that allows them to be truly independent, to protect their way of life and political choices." Ramo points to two features of the new Consensus that are especially appealing to the nations of the global South. One is "localization"—the recognition of the importance of tailoring development to local needs, which necessarily differ from one location to another—in sharp contrast to the one-size-fits-all prescriptions of the increasingly discredited Washington Consensus; and the other is "multilateralism"—the recognition of the importance of interstate cooperation in constructing a new global order based on economic interdependence but respectful of political and cultural differences—in sharp contrast to the unilateralism of US policies. As Arif Dirlik has pointed out, these features of the Beijing Consensus may lead the world in radically different directions. They may lead to the formation of a new Bandung—i.e., a new version of the Third World alliance of the 1950s and 1960s—aimed, like the old, at countering economic and political subordination but suited to an age of unprecedented global economic integration. Or they may lead in the direction of a co-optation of Southern states in North–South alliances aimed at containing the China-led subversion of the global hierarchy of wealth.[1]

The more "realistic" alternatives to the failed neo-conservative strategy aimed at containing China discussed in Chapter 10 point to three different kinds of North–South alliance. Each alternative strategy, we argued, has problems of its own, which have resulted in incoherent US policies towards China. As long as the United States is bogged down militarily in West Asia, the incoherence will probably persist regardless of who rules the roost in Washington. But whether pursued coherently or not, all three strategies have the potential to derail the formation of a new Southern alliance capable of countering Northern domination.

The most disastrous derailment would be the one implicit in Pinkerton's "happy-third" strategy, which advocates a rerun of the first half of the twentieth century—when the US grew rich and powerful by financing and provisioning European states at war with one another—with the difference that the states at war would now be Asian rather than European. The least disastrous derailment would be the one implicit in Kissinger's strategy—which envisages the co-optation of China into a reformed US-centered world order—because, if successful, it would preserve Northern dominance but at least it would not plunge Asia and the global South into the chaos and wars that would ensue from the success of the happy-third strategy. The costs and risks for the South of Kaplan's strategy of encircling China with a US-led military alliance—which advocates a rerun of the Cold War but centered on Asia instead of Europe—would fall somewhere in between. It would provoke deep divisions among Asian and Southern countries and risk the nuclear holocaust that the old Cold War managed to avoid, but it would force the United States to treat with some respect and make concessions to its Southern allies and to be cautious in provoking wars that would involve the US directly. There are, of course, other possibilities, some of which are already being practiced; but they are all variants or

1 Joshua Cooper Ramo, *The Beijing Consensus: Notes on the New Physics of Chinese Power* (London, Foreign Affairs Policy Centre, 2004), pp. 3–4; Arif Dirlik, "Beijing Consensus: Beijing 'Gongshi': Who Recognizes Whom and to What End?" *Globalization and Autonomy Online Compendium*, available at http://www.globalautonomy.ca/global1/position.jsp?index=PP_Dirlik_Beijing Consensus.xml.

combinations of the "third-happy," "co-optation" and "cold-war" strategies.[2]

We should not underestimate the temptation for China to settle for co-optation in a US- or Northern-dominated world order and for other Southern countries to seek or accept US support for their mutual jealousies. But neither should we overestimate the power of the United States, even in collusion with Europe, to succeed in the pursuit of these strategies. Not only has the Iraqi debacle confirmed the limits of coercive means in enforcing the Northern will against Southern resistance; more important in a capitalist world, the financial underpinnings of US and Northern dominance rest on increasingly shaky grounds.

A crucial turning point in this respect has been the Asian financial crisis of 1997–98. Wade and Veneroso have claimed that this crisis confirmed the validity of the dictum, attributed to Andrew Mellon, that "in a depression assets return to their rightful owners."

The combination of massive devaluations, IMF-pushed financial liberalization, and IMF-facilitated recovery may have precipitated the biggest peacetime transfer of assets from domestic to foreign owners in the past fifty years anywhere in the world, dwarfing the transfers from domestic to US owners in Latin America in the 1980s or in Mexico after 1994.[3]

Correct in identifying the immediate effects of the crisis, the diagnosis missed entirely its longer-term effects on North–South relations and on the capacity of the IMF to further facilitate the transfer of Southern assets to Northern owners. As Figure 7.1 shows, the

---

2 These strategies, of course, may be directed not just against China but against other states or against South–South links in general. Thus, the US offer of cooperation in dual-use nuclear and space technologies with India apparently had the immediate objective of blocking the Iran–Pakistan–India gas pipeline so as to isolate Iran and simultaneously break up a South–South connection of great symbolic and material value. See R. Palat, "India Suborned: The Global South and the Geopolitics of India's Vote against Iran," *Japan Focus*, October 24, 2005. Similarly, the US and EU co-optation of India and Brazil into an informal grouping known as the Five Interested Parties (FIPS), consisting of the four of them and Australia, was aimed at turning these two countries from leaders of an emerging Southern alliance into partners of a North–South alliance at the upcoming 2005 Hong Kong meeting of the WTO. Focus on the Global South, "The End of an Illusion. WTO Reform, Global Civil Society and the Road to Hong Kong," *Focus on Trade*, no. 108, April 2005.

3 Robert Wade and Frank Veneroso, "The Asian Crisis: The High Debt Model versus the Wall Street—Treasury—IMF Complex," *New Left Review*, I/228 (1998).

1997–98 crisis marks the beginning of a huge bifurcation between the Northern deficit and the rest-of-the world's surplus in the current-accounts of their respective balances of payments. The bifurcation reflects the fact that there are less and less goods and services that the North, especially the United States, can produce at lower prices than the rest of the world. Much of the rest of the world's surplus still flows to the US financial entrepôt, both to finance the escalating US deficit and to be reinvested around the world, including the global South. But a significant and growing portion of that surplus is bypassing the US entrepôt, both to build up currency reserves and to flow directly to other Southern destinations, thereby relaxing the hold of the IMF and other Northern-controlled financial institutions on Southern countries.[4]

Flush with cash and eager to regain control over their economic policies, Southern countries have bought back their debts reducing the IMF's loan portfolio to the lowest level since the 1980s. A shrinking loan portfolio, notes the *Wall Street Journal*, "greatly diminishes the IMF's influence over global economic policy;" forces it to switch from "arm-twisting" to "persuasion;" and reduces its interest income and cash reserves. "In an irony that has provoked tittering among many [Southern] finance ministers, the agency that has long preached belt-tightening now must practice it itself."[5]

In spite of its massive purchases of US Treasury bonds, China has played a leading role both in rerouting the Southern surplus to Southern destinations and in providing neighboring and distant Southern countries with attractive alternatives to the trade, invest-ment, and assistance of Northern countries and financial institutions. "Here comes a very large new player on the block that has the potential of changing the landscape of overseas development assis-

---

4 The ravages of past financial crises contributed decisively to the build-up of currency reserves in low- and middle-income countries. For most of these countries, "these reserves are simply insurance against financial disaster. A long list of devel-oping countries have experienced devastating crises in the last 15 years: Mexico in 1994; Thailand, Indonesia and other Asian countries in 1997; Russia in 1998; Brazil in 1999; and Argentina in 2002. . . . As the dust settled over the ruins of many former 'emerging' economies, a new creed took hold among policy makers in the developing world: Pile up as much foreign-exchange as possible" (E. Porter, "Are Poor Nations Wasting their Money on Dollars?" *New York Times*, April 30, 2006); "Another Drink? Sure. China Is Paying," *New York Times*, June 5, 2005; F. Kempe, "Why Economists Worry about Who Holds Foreign Currency Reserves," *Wall Street Journal*, May 9, 2006.

5 M. Moffett and B. Davis, "Booming Economy Leaves the IMF Groping for Mission," *Wall Street Journal*, April 21, 2006.

tance," noted the director for the Philippines at the Asian Development Bank (ADB) shortly after China announced an extraordinary package of $2 billion in loans to the Philippines each year for three years, which made the $200 million offered by the World Bank and the ADB look puny; easily outstripped a $1 billion loan under negotiation with Japan; and sheltered the Philippines from Washington's disfavor after President Arroyo pulled the country's troops out of Iraq. This was just one of a large and growing number of similar deals in which China has been out-competing Northern agencies by offering Southern countries more generous terms for access to their natural resources; larger loans with fewer political strings attached and without expensive consultant fees; and big and complicated infrastructure projects in distant areas at as little as half the cost of Northern competitors.[6]

Supplementing and complementing Chinese initiatives, oil-rich countries have also redirected their surpluses to the South. Of great political and symbolic significance has been Venezuela's use of windfall proceeds from high oil prices to free Latin American countries from subordination to Northern interests.

> When Argentina needed loans so that it could say goodbye to the International Monetary Fund, Venezuela committed $2.4 billion. Venezuela bought $300 million in bonds from Ecuador. Washington has historically had enormous influence over economic policy in Latin America through its control over the major sources of credit, including the IMF, the World Bank and the Inter-American Development Bank. Venezuela's role as a new "lender of last resort" has reduced that influence.[7]

Equally important, and potentially more disruptive of Northern financial dominance, has been the interest that Saudi Arabia and other West Asian countries have recently shown in rerouting at least part of their surpluses from the United States and Europe to East and South Asia. According to Western bankers, "We're definitely seeing a big jump in terms of deal flow between the Middle East and Asia, and Southeast Asia and China in particular." Although, for the time

---

6 J. Perlez, "China Competes with West in Aid to its Neighbors," *New York Times*, September 18, 2006; V. Mallet, "Hunt for Resources in the Developing World," *Financial Times*, December 12, 2006.

7 M. Weisbrot, "The Failure of Hugo-Bashing," *Los Angeles Times*, March 9, 2006. See also N. Chomsky, "Latin America and Asia Are Breaking Free of Washington's Grip," *Japan Focus*, March 15, 2006.

being, West Asian investors are not withdrawing money from the United States, "a lot of new money from higher oil prices is not going to North America." The reasons are partly political: the unpopularity of the war in Iraq and things like the backlash in the US that forced Dubai's port company to sell off American holdings after it bought the British port operator P&O. But the most compelling reason is strictly economic: China and all fast growing Asian economies want West Asian oil, and the West Asian capital and liquidity generated by that oil are searching for investments with higher returns than US Treasury bonds.[8]

When, in May 2006, India's prime minister, Manmohan Singh, urged Asian nations at the annual meeting of the ADB to redirect Asian surpluses towards Asian development projects, one US observer found the speech "stunning"—"the harbinger of the end of the dollar and of American hegemony."[9] My argument in Chapter 7 points in a somewhat different direction: US hegemony, as opposed to sheer domination, in all likelihood has already ended; but, just as the pound sterling continued to be used as an international currency three to four decades after the end of British hegemony, so may the dollar. The really important issue here, however, is not whether Asian and other Southern countries will continue to use US dollars as a means of exchange—which, to an unknown extent, they probably will for a long time to come. Rather, it is whether they will continue to put the surpluses of their balances of payments at the disposal of US-controlled agencies, to be turned into instruments of Northern domination; or will instead use them as instruments of Southern emancipation. From this standpoint, there is nothing stunning about Singh's statement, which merely lends support to a practice that is already in place. What is truly stunning is the lack of awareness—in the South no less than in the North—of the extent to which the monetarist counterrevolution of the early 1980s has backfired, creating conditions more favorable than ever before for a new Bandung to bring into existence the commonwealth of civilizations that Smith envisioned long ago.

For a new Bandung can do what the old could not: it can mobilize and use the global market as an instrument of equalization of South–North power relations. The foundations of the old Bandung were

---

8 H. Timmons, "Asia Finding Rich Partner in Mideast," *New York Times*, December 1, 2006.

9 A. Giridharadas, "Singh Urges Asian Self-Reliance," *International Herald Tribune*, May 5, 2006.

strictly political-ideological and, as such, were easily destroyed by the monetarist counterrevolution. The foundations of the Bandung that may be emerging now, in contrast, are primarily economic and, as such, far more solid. As Yashwant Sinha, a former Indian foreign minister put it in a 2003 speech: "In the past, India's engagement with much of Asia, including Southeast and East Asia, was built on an idealistic conception of Asian brotherhood, based on shared experiences of colonialism and of cultural ties. . . . The rhythm of the region today is determined, however, as much by trade, investment and production as by history and culture."[10]

Under these circumstances, Northern resistance to the subversion of the global hierarchy of wealth and power can only succeed with widespread Southern collaboration. Crucial in this respect is what China and India—which by themselves account for more than one-third of the world population—will choose to do. Commenting in the *International Herald Tribune* on news of huge investments by China and India in each other's economies, Howard French aptly asked: "If one places any stock in the notion of creative destruction, what could be more disruptive to the global status quo?"

> With more than 2.3 billion people between them, agreement between India and China on almost any standard makes that item an instant contender for global standard status. What does this mean in practical terms? That the successor to a ubiquitous product like Microsoft Office could very well be Chinese. . . . It could mean that the mobile phone standards of the future are decided jointly in Asia, and not in Europe or the United States. . . . What it clearly means already is that the day when a cozy club of the rich—the United States, the strongest economies of Western Europe and Japan—sets the pace for the rest of world, passing out instructions and assigning grades, is fast drawing to a close.[11]

Yes, it does mean that but on condition that the ruling groups of the global South in general, and of China and India in particular, open up a path capable of emancipating not just their nations but the entire world from the social and ecological devastations entailed in Western

---

10 Quoted in A. Giridharadas, "India Starts Flexing Economic Muscle," *International Herald Tribune*, May 12, 2005.

11 H.W. French, "The Cross-Pollination of India and China," *International Herald Tribune*, November 10, 2005.

capitalist development. An innovation of such world-historical significance requires some awareness of the impossibility of bringing the
benefits of modernization to the majority of the world's population
unless—to paraphrase Sugihara—the Western developmental path
converges with the East Asian path, not the other way round. This is
no new discovery. Almost eighty years ago, in December 1928,
Mohandas Gandhi wrote:

> God forbid that India should ever take to industrialization after the
> manner of the West. The economic imperialism of a single tiny
> island kingdom [England] is today keeping the world in chains. If
> an entire nation of 300 million [India's population at the time] took
> to similar economic exploitation, it would strip the world like
> locusts.[12]

Gandhi already knew then what many leaders of Southern emancipation have yet to learn or have forgotten: Western success along the
extroverted, Industrial Revolution path was based upon the exclusion
of the vast majority of the world's population from access to the
natural and human resources needed to benefit rather than bear the
costs of global industrialization. As such, it never was an option for
that majority. Elvin's considerations concerning the developmental
advantages and disadvantages of China's huge national market in the
eighteenth century demonstrate the absurdity of the contrary view,
still dominant among historians and social scientists across the
ideological spectrum. The huge size of China's market created
opportunities for the social division of labor that were not available
in smaller markets, but it also ruled out innovations that were feasible
in a smaller economy. Between 1741 and the early 1770s, for example,
the introduction of machine-spinning tripled Britain's consumption of
raw cotton.

> To accomplish this tripling for China in a similar space of thirty-
> odd years would have been beyond the cotton-production re-
> sources of the entire eighteenth-century world. Between 1785
> and 1833, the single province of Kwang-tung imported on average
> from India each year six times as much cotton as all Britain used
> annually at the time of Arkwright's first water-frame. Again, an
> expansion of Chinese exports of cotton cloth comparable to

---

12 Quoted in Ramachandra Guha, *Environmentalism: A Global History* (New
York, Longman, 2000), p. 22.

eighteenth-century Britain's both in its speed and in its relative size to the domestic market would have been too great for the available purchasing power of the world at that time.[13]

The economic success of Britain's Industrial Revolution, in other words, was dependent both on the relative and absolute small size of the British economy. A small absolute size meant that a given increase in the import of raw cotton and in the export of cotton manufactures translated into a much higher rate of growth of the economy than it would have in an economy of China's size. And a small size relative to the global economy meant that the rest of the world could supply the natural resources and purchase the products necessary to sustain a high rate of growth to an extent that was inconceivable for China. Had the rulers of Qing China been so insane as to follow in the footsteps of Britain's extroverted Industrial Revolution path, they would have been brought back to their senses by escalating import prices, collapsing export prices, and unbearable social tensions at home, long before they had a chance to "strip the world like locusts."

Two hundred years later China and India face the same problem with a vengeance. The displacement of the tiny UK island by the continental US island as the leader of the Industrial Revolution path has resulted in a further massive increase in the natural-resource intensity, not just of production, but of consumption as well. This massive increase was possible because the vast majority of world population was excluded from the production and consumption standards established by the United States. But as soon as a small minority of the Chinese population (and an even smaller one of the Indian population) gained partial access to those standards, the validity of Gandhi's contention has become obvious to all but the most obtuse defenders of the American way of life. "The world, as it turns out, cannot afford two countries [with a large population] behaving like the United States. It lacks the atmosphere . . . and it also may lack the resources." Bill McKibben calls this a "tragedy" because

China is actually accomplishing some measurable good with its growth. People are enjoying some meat, sending their [children] to school, heating their huts. Whereas we're burning nine times as

---

13 Mark Elvin, *The Pattern of the Chinese Past* (Stanford, CA, Stanford University Press, 1973), pp. 313–14.

much energy per capita so that we can: air-condition game rooms and mow half-acre lots, drive SUVs on every errand, eat tomatoes flown in from Chile. . . . Which is why it seems intuitively obvious when you're in China that the goal of the twenty-first century must somehow be to simultaneously develop the economies of the poorest parts of the world and *undevelop* those of the rich . . . with us using less energy so that they can use more, and eating less meat so that they can eat more. . . . But try to imagine the political possibilities in America . . . of acknowledging that there isn't room for two of us to behave in this way, and that we don't own the rights to our lifestyle simply because we got there first. The current president's father [George Bush Senior] announced, on his way to the parley in Rio that gave rise to the Kyoto treaty, that "the American way of life is not up for negotiation." That's what defines a tragedy.[14]

As it turns out, the latest act of the tragedy, played out in Iraq, has shown that the United States does not have the power to impose coercively upon the world its right to an extravagant way of life and must therefore pay an increasing price for the preservation of that right.[15] But the fact remains that not even a quarter of China's and India's population can adopt the American way of producing and consuming without choking themselves and everybody else to death. Also in this respect, the PRC's new leadership has shown greater awareness than its predecessors of the environmental problems of energy-intensive economic growth. "Model cities" focusing specifically on environmental protection have been established; forests are replanted; the Five Year Plan for 2006–10 has set the ambitious objective of a 20 percent reduction in the energy intensity of the economy and, to this end, a far-reaching industrial policy, banning 399 industrial sub-sectors and restricting another 190 has been announced. It nonetheless remains unclear how these and other measures can restore a seriously compromised ecological balance if, as expected, over the next fifteen years 300 million rural residents

---

14 Bill McKibben, "The Great Leap: Scenes from China's Industrial Revolution," *Harper's Magazine* (December 2005), p. 52.

15 In avidly supporting the war against Iraq, newspaper baron Rupert Murdoch observed that a reduction of the price of oil from $30 to $20 a barrel would have been a good thing for the US economy: D. Kirkpatrick, "Mr. Murdoch's War," *New York Times*, April 7, 2003. The fact that four years into the war the price of oil has instead doubled provides a good measure of the failure of the US attempt to coercively impose its right to extravagant energy consumption.

or more will move into cities where growing fleets of motor vehicles are crowding bicycles out.[16]

In short, by relying too heavily on the energy-consuming Western path, China's rapid economic growth has not yet opened up for itself and the world an ecologically sustainable developmental path. This reliance does not just threaten to bring the "economic miracle" to a premature end, because of pressure on scarce resources (including clean air and water). More important, it is both a result and a cause of the widening cleavage between those who have been in a position to appropriate the benefits of rapid economic growth and those who had to bear its costs. As we have seen in Chapter 12, this cleavage has resulted in a major wave of popular unrest, in which ecological grievances loomed large and which has prompted a major reorientation of Chinese policies towards a more balanced development between rural and urban areas, between regions, and between economy and society. All we need to add to bring our study to a close is that the eventual outcome of this reorientation is of crucial importance for the future not just of Chinese society but of world society as well.

If the reorientation succeeds in reviving and consolidating China's traditions of self-centered market-based development, accumulation *without* dispossession, mobilization of human rather than non-human resources, and government through mass participation in shaping policies, then the chances are that China will be in a position to contribute decisively to the emergence of a commonwealth of civilizations truly respectful of cultural differences. But, if the reorientation fails, China may well turn into a new epicenter of social and political chaos that will facilitate Northern attempts to re-establish a crumbling global dominance or, to paraphrase once again Schumpeter, help humanity burn up in the horrors (or glories) of the escalating violence that has accompanied the liquidation of the Cold War world order.

---

16 Lester R. Brown, "A New World Order," *Guardian*, January 25, 2006; *Quarterly Update*, World Bank Office, Beijing, February 2006, pp. 13–16; K. Bradsher, "China Set to Act on Fuel Economy," *New York Times*, November 18, 2003; J. Kynge, "New Agenda for a New Generation," *Financial Times*, December 16, 2003; A. Lorenz, "China's Environmental Suicide: A Government Minister Speaks," *openDemocracy*, April 5, 2005.

BIBLIOGRAPHY

Note: Newspaper and magazine articles quoted in the footnotes are not included here.

Abu-Lughod, Janet. 1989. *Before European Hegemony: The World System A.D. 1250–1350*. New York: Oxford University Press.

Adas, Michael. 1989. *Machines as Measure of Men. Science, Technology and Ideologies of Western Dominance*. Ithaca, NY: Cornell University Press.

Agarwala, Ramgopal. 2002. *The Rise of China: Threat or Opportunity?* New Delhi: Bookwell.

Aglietta, Michel. 1979. *A Theory of Capitalist Regulation: The US Experience*. London: New Left Books.

Agnew, John. 1987. *The United States in the World-Economy: A Regional Geography*. Cambridge: Cambridge University Press.

Aguilar, Alonso. 1968. *Pan-Americanism from Monroe to the Present: A View from the Other Side*. New York: Monthly Review Press.

Akamatsu, K. 1961. "A Theory of Unbalanced Growth in the World Economy." *Weltwirtschaftliches Archiv*, 86 (1): 196–217.

Amin, Samir. 1976. *Unequal Development*. New York: Monthly Review Press.

————. 2005. "China, Market Socialism, and U.S. Hegemony." *Review* (Fernand Braudel Center), 28 (3): 259–79.

Amsden, Alice. 2001. *The Rise of "The Rest."* New York: Oxford University Press.

————. 2003. "Good-bye Dependency Theory, Hello Dependency Theory." *Studies in Comparative International Development*, 38 (1): 32–8.

Anderson, Perry. 1979. *Lineages of the Absolutist State*. London: New Left Books.

Appiah, K. Anthony, et al. 2004. "The Election and America's Future." *New York Review*, November 4: 6–17.

Arendt, Hannah. 1966. *The Origins of Totalitarianism*. New York: Harcourt, Brace & World.

Armstrong, Philip, and Andrew Glyn. 1986. *Accumulation, Profits, State Spending: Data for Advanced Capitalist Countries 1952–1983*. Oxford: Oxford Institute of Economics and Statistics.

Armstrong, Philip, Andrew Glyn, and John Harrison. 1984. *Capitalism since World War II. The Making and Breakup of the Great Boom*. London: Fontana.

Arrighi, Giovanni. 1983. *The Geometry of Imperialism*. Revised edition. London: Verso.

————. 1994. *The Long Twentieth Century: Money, Power and the Origins of our Times*. London: Verso.

————. 1996. "The Rise of East Asia: World Systemic and Regional Aspects," *International Journal of Sociology and Social Policy*, 16 (7): 6–44.

————. 2002. "The African Crisis: World-Systemic and Regional Aspects." *New Left Review*, II/15: 5–36.

Arrighi, Giovanni, Terence K. Hopkins, and Immanuel Wallerstein. 1989. *Antisystemic Movements*. London: Verso.

Arrighi, Giovanni, Po-keung Hui, Ho-fung Hung, and Mark Selden. 2003. "Historical Capitalism, East and West." In G. Arrighi, T. Hamashita, and M. Selden, eds, *The Resurgence of East Asia. 500, 150 and 50 Year Perspectives*, pp. 259–333. London and New York: Routledge.

Arrighi, Giovanni, Satoshi Ikeda, and Alex Irwan. 1993. "The Rise of East Asia: One Miracle or Many?" In R.A. Palat, ed., *Pacific Asia and the Future of the World-Economy*, pp, 42–65. Westport, CT: Greenwood Press.

Arrighi, Giovanni, and Beverly J. Silver. 1984. "Labor Movements and Capital Migration: The US and Western Europe in World-Historical Perspective." In Charles Bergquist ed., *Labor in the Capitalist World-Economy*, pp. 183–216. Beverly Hills, CA: Sage.

————. 1999. *Chaos and Governance in the Modern World System*. Minneapolis, MN: University of Minnesota Press.

————. 2001. "Capitalism and World (Dis)Order." *Review of International Studies*, 27: 257–79.

Arrighi, Giovanni, Beverly J. Silver, and Benjamin D. Brewer. 2003. "Industrial Convergence and the Persistence of the North–South Divide." *Studies in Comparative International Development*, 38 (1): 3–31.

————. 2003. "A Reply to Alice Amsden." *Studies in Comparative International Development*, 38 (1).

————. 2005. "Industrial Convergence and the Persistence of the North–South Divide: A Rejoinder to Firebaugh." *Studies in Comparative International Development*, 40 (1): 83–8.

Atwell, William S. 1986. "Some Observations on the 'Seventeenth-Century Crisis' in China and Japan." *Journal of Asian Studies*, XLV: 223–44.

————. 1998. "Ming China and the Emerging World Economy, *c.* 1470–1650," in Denis Twitchett and Frederick Mote, eds, *The Cambridge History of China, Vol. 8 (2), The Ming Dynasty*, pp. 376–416. Cambridge: Cambridge University Press.

Au, Loong-yu. 2005. "The Post MFA Era and the Rise of China." *Asian Labour Update*, 56, Fall. Available at http://www.globalmon.org.hk/eng/Post-MFA-era.pdf.

Bacevich, Andrew. 2004. "A Modern Major General." *New Left Review*, II/29: 123–34.

Bagchi, Amiya Kumar. 1982. *The Political Economy of Underdevelopment*. Cambridge: Cambridge University Press.

————. 2005. *Perilous Passage. Mankind and the Global Ascendancy of Capital*. Lantham, MD: Rowman & Littlefield.

Baker, Christopher. 1981. "Economic Reorganization and the Slump in Southeast Asia." *Comparative Studies in Society and History*, 23 (3): 325–49.

Balakrishnan, Gopal, ed. 2003. *Debating Empire*. London: Verso.

Barbour, Violet. 1950. *Capitalism in Amsterdam in the Seventeenth Century*. Baltimore, MD: Johns Hopkins University Press.

Barraclough, Geoffrey. 1967. *An Introduction to Contemporary History*. Harmondsworth: Penguin.

Barrat Brown, Michael. 1963. *After Imperialism*. London: Heinemann.
————. 1974. *The Economics of Imperialism*. Harmondsworth: Penguin.
Barrow, Clyde W. 2004. "God, Money, and the State. The Spirits of American Empire." Forschungsgruppe Europäische Gemeinschaften (FEG), Arbeitspapier 22. Universität Marburg, Marburg.
Bartlett, Beatrice S. 1991. *Monarchs and Ministers: The Grand Council in Mid-Ch'ing China, 1723–1820*. Berkeley, CA: University of California Press.
Becattini, Giacomo. 1990. "The Marshallian Industrial District as a Socio-Economic Notion." In F. Pyke, G. Becattini, and W. Sengenberger, eds, *Industrial Districts and Inter-Firm Cooperation in Italy*, pp. 37–51. Geneva: International Institute for Labor Studies.
Benjamin, Daniel, and Steven Simon. 2005. *The Next Attack: The Failure of the War on Terror and a Strategy for Getting it Right*. New York: Times Books.
Bergesen, Albert, and Ronald Schoenberg. 1980. "Long Waves of Colonial Expansion and Contraction, 1415–1969." In A. Bergesen, ed., *Studies of the Modern World-System*. New York: Academic Press.
Bernstein, Richard, and Ross H. Munro. 1997. "The Coming Conflict with America." *Foreign Affairs*, 76 (2): 18–32.
Bernstein, Thomas P., and Xiaobo Lu. 2003. *Taxation without Representation in Contemporary Rural China*. New York: Cambridge University Press.
Blackburn, Robin. 2002. *Banking on Death: Or, Investing in Life. The History and Future of Pensions*. London: Verso.
Block, Fred. 1977. *The Origins of International Economic Disorder: A Study of the United States International Monetary Policy from World War II to the Present*. Berkeley, CA: University of California Press.
Bond, Brian, ed. 1967. *Victorian Military Campaigns*. London: Hutchinson.
Bouckaert, Boudewijn R.A. 2005."Bureaupreneurs in China: We Did it our Way– A Comparative Study of the Explanation of the Economic Successes of Town–Village Enterprises in China." Paper presented at the EALE Conference. Ljubljana, September.
Boxer, Charles R. 1965. *The Dutch Seaborne Empire 1600–1800*. New York: Knopf.
Bramall, Chris. 2000. *Sources of Chinese Economic Growth, 1978–1996*. New York: Oxford University Press.
Braudel, Fernand. 1977. *Afterthoughts on Material Civilization and Capitalism*. Baltimore, MD: Johns Hopkins University Press.
————. 1982. *Civilization and Capitalism, 15th–18th Century, Volume II: The Wheels of Commerce*. New York: Harper & Row.
————. 1984. *Civilization and Capitalism, 15th–18th Century, Volume III: The Perspective of the World*. New York: Harper & Row.
Braverman, Harry. 1974. *Labor and Monopoly Capital: The Degradation of Work in the Twentieth Century*. New York: Monthly Review Press.
Bray, Francesca. 1986. *The Rice Economies: Technology and Development in Asian Societies*. Berkeley, CA: University of California Press.
Brenner, Robert. 1977. "The Origins of Capitalist Development: A Critique of Neo-Smithian Marxism." *New Left Review*, I/104: 25–92.
————. 1981. "World System Theory and the Transition to Capitalism: Historical and Theoretical Perspectives." Unpublished English version of a paper published in Jochen Blaschke, ed., *Perspectiven des Weltsystems*. Frankfurt: Campus Verlag, 1983.

————. 1998. "The Economics of Global Turbulence: A Special Report on the World Economy, 1950–1998." *New Left Review*, I/229: 1–264.

————. 2002. *The Boom and the Bubble: The U.S. in the World Economy*. London: Verso.

————. 2006. *The Economics of Global Turbulence. The Advanced Capitalist Economies from Long Boom to Long Downturn, 1945–2005*. London: Verso.

Brenner, Robert, and Christopher Isett. 2002. "England's Divergence from China's Yangzi Delta: Property Relations, Microeconomics, and Patterns of Development." *The Journal of Asian Studies*, 61 (2): 609–62.

Brooks, Timothy. 1998. *The Confusions of Pleasure. Commerce and Culture in Ming China*. Berkeley, CA: University of California Press.

Brusco, Sebastiano. 1986. "Small Firms and Industrial Districts: The Experience of Italy." In D. Keeble and F. Weaver, eds, *New Firms and Regional Development*, pp. 184–202. London: Croom Helm.

Brzezinski, Zbigniew, and John J. Mearsheimer. 2005. "Clash of the Titans." *Foreign Policy*, January/February. Available at http://www.foreignpolicy.com.

Burawoy, Michael. 1982. *Manufacturing Consent: Changes in the Labor Process under Monopoly Capitalism*. Chicago: University of Chicago Press.

Burley, Ann-Marie. 1993. "Regulating the World: Multilateralism, International Law, and the Projection of the New Deal Regulatory State." In J.G. Ruggie, ed., *Multilateralism Matters: The Theory and Praxis of an Institutional Form*, pp. 125–56. New York: Columbia University Press.

Cai, Fang, Albert Park, and Yaohui Zhao. 2004. "The Chinese Labor Market." Paper presented at the Second Conference on China's Economic Transition: Origins, Mechanisms, and Consequences. University of Pittsburgh, Pittsburgh, November 5–7.

Cain, P.J., and A.G. Hopkins. 1980. "The Political Economy of British Expansion Overseas, 1750–1914." *Economic History Review*, 2nd series, 33 (4): 463–90.

Cairncross, A.K. 1953. *Home and Foreign Investment, 1870–1913*. Cambridge: Cambridge University Press.

Calleo, David P. 1970. *The Atlantic Fantasy*. Baltimore, MD: Johns Hopkins University Press.

————. 1982. *The Imperious Economy*. Cambridge, MA: Harvard University Press.

————. 1987. *Beyond American Hegemony: The Future of the Western Alliance*. New York: Basic Books.

Castells, Manuel, and Alejandro Portes. 1989. "World Underneath: The Origins, Dynamics, and Effects of the Informal Economy." In A. Portes, M. Castells, and L.A. Benton, eds, *The Informal Economy. Studies in Advanced and Less Developed Countries*, pp. 11–39. Baltimore, MD: Johns Hopkins University Press.

Chan, Anita. 2000. "Globalization, China's Free (Read Bounded) Labor Market, and the Trade Union." *Asia Pacific Business Review*, 6 (3–4): 260–79.

Chandler, Alfred. 1977. *The Visible Hand: The Managerial Revolution in American Business*. Cambridge, MA: The Belknap Press.

————. 1990. *Scale and Scope: The Dynamics of Industrial Capitalism*. Cambridge, MA: The Belknap Press.

Chapman, Stanley D. 1992. *Merchant Enterprise in Britain: From the Industrial Revolution to World War I*. New York: Cambridge University Press.

Chase-Dunn, Christopher, and Thomas Hall. 1997. *Rise and Demise: Comparing World-Systems*. Boulder, CO: Westview Press.

Chaudhuri, K.N. 1990, *Asia before Europe. Economy and Civilization of the Indian Ocean from the Rise of Islam to 1750*. Cambridge: Cambridge University Press.

Chen, Ciyu. 1984. "On the Foreign Trade of China in the 19th Century and the China–India–Britain Triangular Trade." In *Essays in Chinese Maritime History*, pp. 131–73. Taipei: Sun Yat-sen Institute for Social Sciences and Philosophy, Academia Sinica.

Cipolla, Carlo. 1976. *Before the Industrial Revolution. European Society and Economy, 1000–1700*. New York: Norton.

Clancy, Tom, with Anthony Zinni and Tony Koltz. 2004. *Battle Ready*. New York: Putnam.

Clarke, Richard. 2004. *Against All Enemies: Inside America's War on Terror*. New York: Free Press.

Cohen, Benjamin. 1996, "Phoenix Risen. The Resurrection of Global Finance." *World Politics*, 48: 268–96.

Cohen, Jerome B. 1958. *Japan's Postwar Economy*. Bloomington, IN: Indiana University Press.

Coyett, Frederick. 1903 [1675]. *Verwaerloosde Formosa*. In William Campbell, ed., *Formosa under the Dutch: Described from Contemporary Records*, pp. 383–538. London: Kegan Paul, Trench & Trubner.

Crotty, James. 1999. "Review of *Turbulence in the World Economy* by Robert Brenner." *Challenge*, 42 (3): 108–30.

Cumings, Bruce. 1987. "The Origins and Development of the Northeast Asian Political Economy: Industrial Sectors, Product Cycles, and Political Consequences." In F.C. Deyo, ed., *The Political Economy of the New Asian Industrialism*, pp. 44–83. Ithaca, NY: Cornell University Press.

————. 1993. "The Political Economy of the Pacific Rim." In R.A. Palat, ed., *Pacific-Asia and the Future of the World-System*, pp. 21–37. Westport, CT: Greenwood Press.

————. 1993. "Global Realm with No Limit, Global Realm with No Name." *Radical History Review*, 57: 47–8.

————. 1997. "Japan and Northeast Asia into the Twenty-First Century." In P.J. Katzenstein and T. Shiraishi, eds, *Network Power. Japan and Asia*, pp. 136–68. Ithaca, NY: Cornell University Press.

Curtin, Philip D. 2000. *The World and the West: The European Challenge and the Overseas Response in the Age of Empire*. Cambridge: Cambridge University Press.

Cushman, Jennifer Wayne. 1993. *Fields from the Sea. Chinese Junk Trade with Siam during the Late Eighteenth and Early Nineteenth Centuries*. Studies on Southeast Asia, Southeast Asia Program, Cornell University, Ithaca, NY.

Davis, Mike. 2001. *Late Victorian Holocausts: El Niño Famines and the Making of the Third World*. London: Verso.

Davis, Ralph. 1966. "The Rise of Protection in England, 1689–1786." *Economic History Review*, 2nd series, 19: 306–17.

————. 1969. "English Foreign Trade, 1700–1774." In W.E. Minchinton, ed., *The Growth of English Overseas Trade in the Seventeenth and Eighteenth Centuries*, pp. 99–120. London: Methuen.

————. 1979. *The Industrial Revolution and British Overseas Trade*. Leicester: Leicester University Press.

de Cecco, Marcello. 1982. "Inflation and Structural Change in the Euro–Dollar Market." *EUI Working Papers*, 23. Florence: European University Institute.

————. 1984. *The International Gold Standard: Money and Empire*. 2nd edn. New York: St. Martin's Press.

Dehio, Ludwig. 1962. *The Precarious Balance: Four Centuries of the European Power Struggle*. New York: Vintage.

de Vries, Jan. 1994. "The Industrial Revolution and the Industrious Revolution." *Journal of Economic History*, 54 (2): 249–70.

Ding, X.L. 2000. "The Illicit Asset Stripping of Chinese State Firms." *The China Journal*, 43: 1–28.

Dirlik, Arif. n.d. "Beijing Consensus: Beijing 'Gongshi.' Who Recognizes Whom and to What End?" *Globalization and Autonomy Online Compendium*. Available at http://www.globalautonomy.ca/global1/position.jsp?index=PP_-Dirlik_BeijingConsensus.xml.

Drucker, Peter. 1969. *The Age of Discontinuity*. New York: Harper & Row.

Duara, Prasenjit. 1997. "Nationalists among Transnationals: Overseas Chinese and the Idea of China, 1900–1911." In A. Ong and D.M. Nonini, eds, *Ungrounded Empires: The Cultural Politics of Modern Chinese Transnationalism*, pp. 39–59. New York: Routledge.

Duus, Peter. 1984. "Economic Dimensions of Meiji Imperialism: The Case of Korea, 1895–1910." In R.H. Myers and M.R. Peattie, eds, *The Japanese Colonial Empire, 1895–1945*, pp. 128–71. Princeton, NJ: Princeton University Press.

Edin, Maria. 2003. "State Capacity and Local Agent Control in China: CCP Cadre Management from a Township Perspective." *The China Quarterly*, 173: 35–52.

Edwards, Richard. 1979. *Contested Terrain*. New York: Basic Books.

Eichengreen, Barry, and Richard Portes. 1986. "Debt and Default in the 1930s: Causes and Consequences." *European Economic Review*, (30): 599–640.

Elisonas, Jurgis. 1991. "The Inseparable Trinity: Japan's Relations with China and Korea." In John Hall, ed., *The Cambridge History of Japan, Vol. 4, Early Modern Japan*, pp. 235–300. Cambridge: Cambridge University Press.

Elliott, John E. 1980. "Marx and Schumpeter on Capitalism's Creative Destruction: A Comparative Restatement." *The Quarterly Journal of Economics*, XCV (1): 45–68.

Elliott, J.H. 1970. *The Old World and the New 1492–1650*. Cambridge: Cambridge University Press.

Elliott, William Y., ed. 1955. *The Political Economy of American Foreign Policy: Its Concepts, Strategy, and Limits*. New York: Henry Holt.

Elvin, Mark. 1973. *The Pattern of the Chinese Past*. Stanford, CA: Stanford University Press.

Esherick, Joseph. 1972. "Harvard on China: The Apologetics of Imperialism." *Bulletin of Concerned Asian Scholars*, IV (4): 9–16.

Fairbank, John K., ed. 1968. *The Chinese World Order*. Cambridge, MA: Harvard University Press.

Fairbank, John K. 1983. *The United States and China*. Cambridge, MA: Harvard University Press.

————. 1989. "Keeping Up with the New China." *New York Review*, March 16: 17–20.

————. 1992. *China. A New History*. Cambridge, MA: The Belknap Press.

Feis, Herbert. 1965. *Europe: The World's Banker, 1870–1914*. New York: Norton.

Ferguson, Niall. 2004. *Colossus: The Price of America's Empire*. New York: Penguin.

Feuerwerker, Albert. 1958. *China's Early Industrialization: Sheng Hsuan-Huai 1844–1916 and Mandarin Enterprise*. Cambridge, MA: Harvard University Press.

————. 1970. "Handicraft and Manufactured Cotton Textiles in China, 1871–1910." *Journal of Economic History*, 30 (2): 338–78.

Fishman, Ted C. 2005. *China, INC. How the Rise of the Next Superpower Challenges America and the World*. New York: Scribner.

Flynn, Dennis O., Lionel Frost, and A.J.H. Latham, eds. 1999. *Pacific Centuries. Pacific and Pacific Rim History since the Sixteenth Century*. London: Routledge.

Flynn, Dennis O., and Arturo Giraldez. 1995. "Born with 'Silver Spoon': The Origin of World Trade in 1571." *Journal of World History*, 6 (2): 201–11.

————. 1999. "Spanish Profitability in the Pacific: The Philippines in the Sixteenth and Seventeenth Centuries." In Dennis O. Flynn, Lionel Frost, and A.J.H. Latham, eds, *Pacific Centuries: Pacific and Pacific Rim History since the Sixteenth Century*. London: Routledge.

Frank, Andre Gunder. 1969. *Capitalism and Underdevelopment in Latin America*. New York: Monthly Review Press.

————. 1974. "On the Roots of Development and Underdevelopment in the New World: Smith and Marx vs the Weberians." *International Review of Sociology*, 2nd series, 10 (2–3): 109–55.

————. 1978. "Multilateral Merchandise Trade Imbalances and Uneven Economic Development." *Journal of European Economic History*, 5 (2): 407–38.

————. 1998. *ReOrient: Global Economy in the Asian Age*. Berkeley, CA: University of California Press.

————. 2005. "Meet Uncle Sam—Without Clothes—Parading around China and the World." Available at www.rrojasdatabank.info/agfrank/no-clothes.htm.

Frank, Thomas. 2005. *What's the Matter with Kansas? How Conservatives Won the Heart of America*. New York: Owl Books.

Freeman-Grenville, G.S.P. 2002. *Historical Atlas of Islam*. New York: Continuum.

Friedman, Thomas L. 2005. *The World Is Flat. A Brief History of the Twenty-First Century*. New York: Farrar, Straus & Giroux.

Fukasaku, Kichiro, and David Wall. 1994. *China's Long March to an Open Economy*. Paris: OECD.

Gamble, Andrew. 1985. *Britain in Decline*. London: Macmillan.

Gao, Weinong. 1993. *Zou xiang jinshi de Zhongguo yu "chaogong" guo guanxi*. (The Relation between China and its Tributary States in Modern Times.) Guangdong: Guangdong gaodeng jiaoyu chubanshe.

Gernet, Jaques. 1982. *A History of Chinese Civilization*. New York: Cambridge University Press.

Giddens, Anthony. 1987. *The Nation-State and Violence*. Berkeley, CA: University of California Press.

Gilpin, Robert. 1987. *The Political Economy of International Relations*. Princeton, NJ: Princeton University Press.

Goldstein, Joshua S., and David P. Rapkin. 1991. "After Insularity. Hegemony and the Future World Order." *Futures*, 23: 935–59.

Gordon, David, Richard Edwards, and Michael Reich. 1982. *Segmented Work,*

Divided Workers: The Historical Transformation of Labor in the United States. New York: Cambridge University Press.

Gramsci, Antonio. 1971. *Selections from the Prison Notebooks*. New York: International Publishers.

Greenberg, Michael. 1951. *British Trade and the Opening of China 1800–1842*. Cambridge: Cambridge University Press.

Guan, Luquan. 1994. *Songdai Guangzhou de haiwai maoyi*. (The Guangzhou Sea Trade in the Song Dynasty.) Guangzhou: Guangdong renmin chubanshe.

Guha, Ramachandra. 2000. *Environmentalism: A Global History*. New York: Longman.

Guha, Ranajit. 1992. "Dominance without Hegemony and its Historiography." In R. Gupta, ed., *Subaltern Studies IV*: 210–305. New York: Oxford University Press.

Guo, Yugui. 2005. *Asia's Educational Edge: Current Achievements in Japan, Korea, Taiwan, China, and India*. Oxford: Lexington.

Haakonssen, Knud. 1981. *The Science of a Legislator. The Natural Jurisprudence of David Hume and Adam Smith*. Cambridge: Cambridge University Press.

Hamashita, Takeshi. 1988. "The Tribute Trade System of Modern Asia." *The Memoirs of the Toyo Bunko*, XLVI: 7–25.

————. 1993. "Tribute and Emigration: Japan and the Chinese Administration of Foreign Affairs." *Senri Ethnological Studies*, XXV: 69–86.

————. 1994. "The Tribute Trade System and Modern Asia." In A.J.H. Latham and H. Kawakatsu, eds, *Japanese Industrialization and the Asian Economy*, pp. 91–107. London and New York: Routledge.

————. 1997. "The Intra-Regional System in East Asia in Modern Times." In Peter J., Katzenstein and T. Shiraishi, eds, *Network Power. Japan and Asia*, pp. 113–35. Ithaca, NY: Cornell University Press.

Hamilton, Gary G. and Wei-an Chang. 2003. "The Importance of Commerce in the Organization of China's Late Imperial Economy." In G. Arrighi, T. Hamashita, and M. Selden, eds, *The Resurgence of East Asia. 500, 150 and 50 Year Perspectives*, pp. 173–213. London and New York: Routledge.

Hao, Yen-p'ing. 1986. *The Commercial Revolution in Nineteenth-Century China*. Berkeley, CA: California University Press.

Hardt, Michael, and Antonio Negri. 2000. *Empire*. Cambridge, MA: Harvard University Press.

Harrison, Bennett. 1994. *Lean and Mean: The Changing Landscape of Corporate Power in the Age of Flexibility*. New York: Basic Books.

Hart, Gillian. 2002. *Disabling Globalization: Places of Power in Post-Apartheid South Africa*. Berkeley, CA: University of California Press.

Hart-Landsberg, Martin, and Paul Burkett. 2004. "China and Socialism: Market Reform and Class Struggle." *Monthly Review*, 56 (3): 7–123.

Harvey, David. 1982. *Limits to Capital*. Oxford: Basil Blackwell.

————. 1995. "Globalization in Question." *Rethinking Marxism*, VIII (4): 1–17.

————. 2000. *Spaces of Hope*. Berkeley, CA: University of California Press.

————. 2001. *Spaces of Capital: Towards a Critical Geography*. New York: Routledge.

————. 2003. *The New Imperialism*. New York: Oxford University Press.

————. 2005. *A Brief History of Neoliberalism*. New York: Oxford University Press.

Headrick, Daniel R. 1988. *The Tentacles of Progress: Technology Transfer in the Age of Imperialism, 1850–1940*. London: Oxford University Press.

Hegel, G.W.F. 1967. *The Philosophy of Right*. New York: Oxford University Press.

Heilbroner, Robert. 1991. "Economic Predictions." *The New Yorker*, July 8: 70–7.

Held, David, Anthony McGrew, David Goldblatt, and Jonathan Perraton. 1999. *Global Transformations*. Stanford, CA: Stanford University Press.

Hersh, Seymour M. 2003. "The Stovepipe." *The New Yorker*, October 27: 77–87.

————. 2004. *Chain of Command: The Road from 9/11 to Abu Ghraib*. New York: HarperCollins.

Hirschman, Albert O. 1977. *The Passions and the Interests. Political Arguments for Capitalism before its Triumph*. Princeton, NJ: Princeton University Press.

Ho, Chumei. 1994. "The Ceramic Trade in Asia, 1602–82." In A.J.H. Latham and H. Kawakatsu, eds, *Japanese Industrialization and the Asian Economy*. London and New York: Routledge.

Hobbes, Thomas. 1968. *Leviathan*. Edited by C.B. Macpherson. Harmondsworth: Penguin.

Hobsbawm, Eric J. 1968. *Industry and Empire: An Economic History of Britain since 1750*. London: Weidenfeld & Nicolson.

————. 1979. *The Age of Capital 1848–1875*. New York: New American Library.

————. 1991. *Nations and Nationalism since 1780: Programme, Myth, Reality*. Cambridge: Cambridge University Press.

————. 1994. *The Age of Extremes: A History of the World, 1914–1991*. New York: Vintage.

Hofstadter, R. 1996. *The Paranoid Style in American Politics and Other Essays*. Cambridge, MA: Harvard University Press.

Huang, Philip C.C. 1985. *The Peasant Economy and Social Change in North China*. Stanford, CA: Stanford University Press.

————. 1990. *The Peasant Family and Rural Development in the Yangzi Delta, 1350–1988*. Stanford, CA: Stanford University Press.

————. 2002. "Development or Involution in Eighteenth-Century Britain and China? A Review of Kenneth Pomeranz's *The Great Divergence: China, Europe, and the Making of the Modern World Economy*." *The Journal of Asian Studies*, 61 (2): 501–38.

Huang, Ray. 1969. "Fiscal Administration during the Ming Dynasty." In Charles O. Hucker, ed., *Chinese Government in Ming Times*, pp. 73–128. New York: Columbia University Press.

Hugill, Peter J. 1993. *World Trade since 1431. Geography, Technology, and Capitalism*. Baltimore, MD: Johns Hopkins University Press.

Hui, Po-keung. 1995. "Overseas Chinese Business Networks: East Asian Economic Development in Historical Perspective." PhD diss., Department of Sociology, State University of New York at Binghamton.

Hung, Ho-fung. 2001. "Imperial China and Capitalist Europe in the Eighteenth-Century Global Economy." *Review* (Fernand Braudel Center), 24 (4): 473–513.

————. 2001. "Maritime Capitalism in Seventeenth-Century China: The Rise and Fall of Koxinga in Comparative Perspective." Unpublished manuscript. Department of Sociology, The Johns Hopkins University.

————. 2003. "Orientalist Knowledge and Social Theories: China and

European Conceptions of East–West Differences from 1600 to 1900." *Sociological Theory*, 21 (3): 254–80.

————. 2004. "Early Modernities and Contentious Politics in Mid-Qing China, *c.* 1740–1839." *International Sociology*, 19 (4): 478–503.

————. 2006. "Rise of China and the Global Overaccumulation Crisis." Paper presented at the Society for the Study of Social Problems Annual Meeting, Montreal, August.

Hymer, Stephen. 1972. "The Multinational Corporation and the Law of Uneven Development." In J.N. Bhagwati, ed., *Economics and World Order*, pp. 113–40. New York: Macmillan.

Ikeda, Satoshi. 1996, "World Production." In T.K. Hopkins, I. Wallerstein et al., eds, *The Age of Transition: Trajectory of the World-System 1945–2025*, pp. 38–86. London, Zed Books.

————. 1996. "The History of the Capitalist World-System vs. The History of East-Southeast Asia." *Review* (Fernand Braudel Center), 19 (1): 49–76.

International Monetary Fund (various years). *International Financial Statistics Yearbook*. Washington, DC: International Monetary Fund.

Iriye, Akira. 1970. "Imperialism in East Asia." In J. Crowley, ed., *Modern East Asia*, pp. 122–50. New York: Harcourt.

Irwan, Alex. 1995. "Japanese and Ethnic Chinese Business Networks in Indonesia and Malaysia." PhD diss., Department of Sociology, State University of New York at Binghamton.

Israel, Jonathan. 1989. *Dutch Primacy in World Trade, 1585–1740*. Oxford: Clarendon Press.

Itoh, Makoto. 1990. *The World Economic Crisis and Japanese Capitalism*. New York: St Martin's Press.

Jenks, Leland H. 1938. *The Migration of British Capital to 1875*. New York and London: Knopf.

Jing, Junjian. 1982. "Hierarchy in the Qing Dynasty." *Social Science in China: A Quarterly Journal*, 3 (1): 156–92.

Johnson, Chalmers. 2004. "Why I Intend to Vote for John Kerry." *The History News Network*, June 14. Available at http://hnn.us/.

————. 2004. *The Sorrows of Empire: Militarism, Secrecy, and the End of the Republic*. New York: Metropolitan Books.

————. "No Longer the 'Lone' Superpower: Coming to Terms with China." Japan Policy Research Institute. Available at http://www.jpri.org.

Johnson, Linda Cooke. 1993. "Shanghai: An Emerging Jiangnan Port, 1638–1840". In Linda Cooke Johnson, ed., *Cities of Jiangnan in Late Imperial China*, pp. 151–82. Albany: State University of New York Press.

Johnson, Russell. 2003. "'Pre-Conditioning' for Industry: Civil War Military Service and the Making of an American Working Class." Paper presented at the 25th Annual North American Labor History Conference, Wayne State University, Detroit, October 16–18.

Judt, Tony. 2005. "Europe vs. America." *New York Review*, February 10: 37–41.

Kaplan, Robert D. 2005. "How We Would Fight China." *Atlantic Monthly*, June: 49–64.

Kasaba, Resat. 1993. "Treaties and Friendships: British Imperialism, the Ottoman Empire, and China in the Nineteenth Century." *Journal of World History*, 4 (2): 213–41.

Kawakatsu, Heita. 1994. "Historical Background." In A.J.H. Latham and H. Kawakatsu, eds, *Japanese Industrialization and the Asian Economy*, pp. 4–8. London and New York: Routledge.

Kennedy, Paul. 1976. *The Rise and Fall of British Naval Mastery*. London: Scribner.

——————. 1987. *The Rise and Fall of the Great Powers: Economic Change and Military Conflict from 1500 to 2000*. New York: Random House.

——————. 2004. "Mission Impossible?" *New York Review*, June 10: 16–19.

Kissinger, Henry. 1964. *A World Restored: Europe after Napoleon. The Politics of Conservatism in a Revolutionary Age*. New York: Grosset & Dunlap.

Kojima, K. 2000. "The 'Flying Geese' Model of Asian Economic Development: Origin, Theoretical Extensions, and Regional Policy Implications." *Journal of Asian Economics*, 11: 375–401.

Kojima, K., and Terutomo Ozawa. 1985. "Toward a Theory of Industrial Restructuring and Dynamic Comparative Advantage." *Hitotsubashi Journal of Economics*, 26 (2): 135–45.

Kraar, Louis. 1993. "The New Power in Asia." *Fortune*, October 31: 38–44.

Krasner, Stephen. 1988. "A Trade Strategy for the United States." *Ethics and International Affairs*, 2: 17–35.

Kreisler, Harry. 2002. "Through the Realist Lens." *Conversations with History: Conversation with John Mearsheimer*. Institute of International Studies, UC Berkeley, April 8. Available at http://globetrotter.berkeley.edu/.

Kriedte, Peter. 1983. *Peasants, Landlords, and Merchant Capitalists: Europe and the World Economy, 1500–1800*. Cambridge: Cambridge University Press.

Krippner, Greta R. 2005. "The Financialization of the American Economy." *Socio-Economic Review*, 3: 173–208.

Krugman, Paul. 1994. "The Myth of Asia's Miracle." *Foreign Affairs*, 73 (6): 62–78.

Kwong, Peter. 2006. "China and the US Are Joined at the Hip. The Chinese Face of Neoliberalism." *Counterpunch*, weekend edition, October 7/8.

Kynge, James. 2006. *China Shakes the World*. Boston, MA: Houghton Mifflin.

Landes, David S. 1969. *The Unbound Prometheus: Technological Change and Industrial Development in Western Europe from 1750 to the Present*. Cambridge: Cambridge University Press.

Lardy, Nicholas R. 1992. *Foreign Trade and Economic Reform in China, 1978–1990*. Cambridge: Cambridge University Press.

Lee, Ching Kwan. 2002. "From the Specter of Mao to the Spirit of the Law: Labor Insurgency in China." *Theory and Society*, 31 (2): 189–228.

Lee, Ching Kwan, and Mark Selden. 2007. "Durable Inequality: The Legacies of China's Revolutions and the Pitfalls of Reforms." In J. Foran, D. Lane, and A. Zivkovic, eds, *Revolution in the Making of the Modern World: Social Identities, Globalization, and Modernity*. London: Routledge.

Lee, John. 1999. "Trade and Economy in Preindustrial East Asia, *c*. 1500–*c*. 1800: East Asia in the Age of Global Integration." *The Journal of Asian Studies*, 58 (1): 2–26.

Lefebvre, Henri. 1976. *The Survival of Capitalism: Reproduction of the Relations of Production*. New York: St Martin's Press.

Leibenstein, Harvey. 1963. *Economic Backwardness and Economic Growth*. New York: Wiley.

Lewis, Archibald. 1970. *The Islamic World and the West, A.D. 622–1492*. New York: Wiley.

Li, Yi. 2005. *The Structure and Evolution of Chinese Social Stratification.* Lanham, MD: University Press of America.

Li, Yuyu. 2006. "The Impact of Rural Migration on Village Development: A Comparative Study in Three Chinese Villages." PhD diss., Department of Sociology, The Johns Hopkins University, Baltimore, MD.

Lin, Justin Yifu, and Yang Yao. n.d. "Chinese Rural Industrialization in the Context of the East Asian Miracle." China Center for Economic Research, Beijing University. Available at http://www.esocialsciences.com/articles/displayArticles.asp?Article_ID=647.

Lin, Manhong. 1991. "The Silver Drain of China and the Reduction in World Silver and Gold Production (1814–1850)." In *Essays in Chinese Maritime History IV*, pp. 1–44. Taipei: Sun Yat-sen Institute for Social Sciences and Philosophy, Academia Sinica.

Lin, Nan. 1995. "Local Market Socialism: Local Corporatism in Action in Rural China." *Theory and Society*, 24: 301–54.

Liu Binyan, and Perry Link. 1998. "A Great Leap Backward?" *New York Review*, October 8: 19–23.

Lo, Jung-pang. 1969. "Maritime Commerce and its Relation to the Sung Navy." *Journal of the Economic and Social History of the Orient*, XII: 57–101.

Lynn, Barry. 2006. "The Case for Breaking Up Wal-Mart." *Harper's Magazine*, July 24.

McCormick, Thomas J. 1989. *America's Half Century: United States Foreign Policy in the Cold War*. Baltimore, MD: Johns Hopkins University Press.

McElwee, William L. 1974. *The Art of War, Waterloo to Mons*. London: Weidenfeld & Nicolson.

McKibben, Bill. 2005. "The Great Leap. Scenes from China's Industrial Revolution." *Harper's Magazine*, December: 42–52.

Mackie, Jamie. 1992. "Changing Patterns of Chinese Big Business." In R. McVey, ed., *Southeast Asian Capitalists*. Southeast Asian Program, Cornell University, Ithaca, NY.

————. 1998. "Business Success among Southeast Asian Chinese—The Role of Culture, Values, and Social Structures." In R.W. Hefner, ed., *Market Cultures. Society and Morality in the New Asian Capitalism*. Boulder, CO: Westview Press.

McNamara, Robert. 1970. "The True Dimension of the Task." *International Development Review*, 1: 1–7.

McNeill, William. 1982. *The Pursuit of Power: Technology, Armed Force, and Society since A.D. 1000*. Chicago: University of Chicago Press.

————. 1998. "World History and the Rise and Fall of the West." *Journal of World History*, 9 (2): 215–37.

Maddison, Angus. 2007. *Contours of the World Economy, 1–2030 AD*. New York: Oxford University Press.

Magdoff, Harry, and John Bellamy Foster. 2004. "China and Socialism: Market Reform and Class Struggle. Editors' Foreword." *Monthly Review*, 56 (3): 2–6.

Mamdani, Mahmood. 2004. *Good Muslim, Bad Muslim: America, the Cold War, and the Roots of Terror*. New York: Pantheon.

Mann, Michael. 2003. *Incoherent Empire*. London: Verso.

Mann, Susan. 1992. "Household Handicrafts and State Policy in Qing Times." In J.K. Leonard and J. Watt, eds, *To Achieve Security and Wealth: The Qing State and the Economy*, pp. 75–96. Ithaca, NY: Cornell University Press.

Marks, Robert B. 2007. *The Origins of the Modern World. A Global and Ecological Narrative from the Fifteenth to the Twenty-First Century*. Lantham, MD: Rowman & Littlefield.

Marshall, Alfred. 1919. *Industry and Trade*. London: Macmillan.

Marx, Karl. 1959. *Capital*. Vol. I. Moscow: Foreign Languages Publishing House.

————. 1962. *Capital*. Vol. III. Moscow: Foreign Languages Publishing House.

————. 1973. *Grundrisse. Foundations of the Critique of Political Economy*. New York: Vintage.

————. 1978. "Crisis Theory (from *Theories of Surplus Value*)." In R.C. Tucker, ed., *The Marx–Engels Reader*. New York: Norton.

Marx, Karl, and Frederick Engels. 1967. *The Communist Manifesto*. Harmondsworth: Penguin.

Mathias, Peter. 1969. *The First Industrial Nation: An Economic History of Britain 1700–1914*. London: Methuen.

Mayer, Arno J. 2003. "Beyond the Drumbeat: Iraq, Preventive War, 'Old Europe.'"*Monthly Review*, 54 (10) March.

Mearsheimer, John J. 2001. *The Tragedy of Great Power Politics*. New York: W.W. Norton.

Minchinton, W.E., ed. 1969. *The Growth of English Overseas Trade in the Seventeenth and Eighteenth Centuries*. London: Methuen.

Moffitt, Michael. 1983. *The World's Money. International Banking from Bretton Woods to the Brink of Insolvency*. New York: Simon & Schuster.

Muller, Jerry Z. 1993. *Adam Smith in his Time and Ours: Designing the Decent Society*. New York: Free Press.

Nakamura, Takafusa. 1981. *The Postwar Japanese Economy*. Tokyo: Tokyo University Press.

Nathan, Andrew J. 1972. "Imperialism's Effects on China." *Bulletin of Concerned Asian Scholars*, 4 (4): 3–8.

Nelson, Richard. 1956. "A Theory of the Low-Level Equilibrium Trap in Underdeveloped Economies." *The American Economic Review*, 46 (4): 894–908.

Nolan, Peter. 2004. *Transforming China. Globalization, Transition and Development*. London: Anthem Press.

Northup, David. 1995. *Indentured Labor in the Age of Imperialism, 1834–1922*. Cambridge: Cambridge University Press.

Nye, Joseph S. 1990. *Bound to Lead: The Changing Nature of American Power*. New York: Basic Books.

O'Brien, Patrick. 2001. "Metanarratives in Global Histories of Material Progress." *The International History Review*, 23 (2): 345–67.

O'Connor, James. 1973. *The Fiscal Crisis of the State*. New York: St Martin's Press.

Oi, Jean. 1999. *Rural China Takes Off: Institutional Foundations of Economic Reform*. Berkeley, CA: University of California Press.

Okimoto, Daniel I., and Thomas P. Rohlen. 1988. *Inside the Japanese System: Readings on Contemporary Society and Political Economy*. Stanford, CA: Stanford University Press.

Ong, Aihwa, and Donald M. Nonini, eds. 1997. *Ungrounded Empires: The Cultural Politics of Modern Chinese Transnationalism*. New York: Routledge.

Owen, D.E. 1934. *British Opium Policy in China and India*. New Haven, CT: Yale University Press.

Ozawa, Terutomo. 1979. *Multinationalism, Japanese Style: The Political Economy of Outward Dependency*. Princeton, NJ: Princeton University Press.

————. 1993. "Foreign Direct Investment and Structural Transformation: Japan as a Recycler of Market and Industry." *Business and the Contemporary World*, 5 (2): 129–50.

————. 2003. "Pax Americana-Led Macro-Clustering and Flying-Geese-Style Catch-Up in East Asia: Mechanisms of Regionalized Endogenous Growth." *Journal of Asian Economics*, 13: 699–713.

Palat, Ravi A. 1995. "Historical Transformations in Agrarian Systems Based on Wet-Rice Cultivation: Toward an Alternative Model of Social Change." In P. McMichael, ed., *Food and Agrarian Orders in the World-Economy*, pp. 55–77. Westport, CT: Praeger.

Panich, Leo, and Sam Gindin. 2003. "Global Capitalism and American Empire." In L. Panich and C. Leys, eds, *The New Imperial Challenge*. London: Merlin Press.

Parboni, Riccardo. 1981. *The Dollar and its Rivals*. London: Verso.

Parker, Geoffrey. 1989. "Taking Up the Gun." *MHQ: The Quarterly Journal of Military History*, 1 (4): 88–101.

Parsons, Talcott. 1960. *Structure and Process in Modern Societies*. New York: Free Press.

————. 1964. "Some Reflections on the Place of Force in Social Process." In H. Eckstein, ed. *Internal War*, pp. 33–70. Glencoe, IL: Free Press.

Peattie, Mark. 1984. "Introduction," to Ramon Myers and Mark Peattie, *The Japanese Colonial Empire, 1895–1945*, pp. 3–26. Princeton, NJ: Princeton University Press.

Perdue, Peter C. 1987. *Exhausting the Earth: State and Peasant in Hunan, 1500–1850*. Cambridge, MA: Harvard University Press.

————. 2003. "A Frontier View of Chineseness." In G. Arrighi, T. Hamashita, and M. Selden, eds, *The Resurgence of East Asia. 500, 150 and 50 Year Perspectives*, pp. 51–77. London and New York: Routledge.

Phelps Brown, E.H. 1975. "A Non-Monetarist View of the Pay Explosion." *Three Banks Review*, 105: 3–24.

Pinkerton, James P. 2005. "Superpower Showdown." *The American Conservative,* November 7. Available at http://www.amconmag.com.

Piore, Michael J., and Charles F. Sabel. 1984. *The Second Industrial Divide: Possibilities for Prosperity*. New York: Basic Books.

Polanyi, Karl. 1957. *The Great Transformation: The Political and Economic Origins of our Time*. Boston, MA: Beacon Press.

Pomeranz, Kenneth. 2000. *The Great Divergence: Europe, China, and the Making of the Modern World Economy*. Princeton, NJ: Princeton University Press.

Prestowitz, Clyde. 2005. *Three Billion New Capitalists. The Great Shift of Wealth and Power to the East*. New York: Basic Books.

Putterman, Louis. 1997. "On the Past and Future of China's Township and Village-Owned Enterprises." *World Development*, 25 (10): 1639–55.

Qian, Yingyi. 1996. "Enterprise Reforms in China: Agency Problems and Political Control." *Economics of Transition*, 4 (2): 427–47.

Quesnay, François. 1969. "From *Despotism in China*." In F. Schurmann and O. Schell, eds, *Imperial China*, pp. 115–20. New York: Vintage.

Ramo, Joshua Cooper. 2004. *The Beijing Consensus: Notes on the New Physics of Chinese Power*. London: Foreign Affairs Policy Centre.

Rawski, Thomas G. 1999. "Reforming China's Economy: What Have We Learned?" *The China Journal*, 41: 139–56.

Research Group for Social Structure in Contemporary China, Chinese Academy of Social Sciences. 2005. *Social Mobility in Contemporary China*. Montreal: America Quantum Media.

Riskin, Carl, Renwei Zhao, and Shih Li, eds. 2001. *Retreat from Equality: Essays on the Changing Distribution of Income in China, 1988–1995*. Armonk, NY: M.E. Sharpe.

Rosenberg, Nathan. 1965. "Adam Smith on the Division of Labour: Two Views or One?" *Economica*, 32 (127): 127–39.

Rowe, William. 1990. "Modern Chinese Social History in Comparative Perspective." In P.S. Ropp, ed., *Heritage of China: Contemporary Perspectives on Chinese Civilization*, pp. 242–62. Berkeley, CA: University of California Press.

————. 2001. *Saving the World. Chen Hongmou and Elite Consciousness in Eighteenth-Century China*. Stanford, CA: Stanford University Press.

Rozman, Gilbert. 1991. *The East Asian Region: Confucian Heritage and its Modern Adaptation*. Princeton, NJ: Princeton University Press.

Saul, S.B. 1969. *The Myth of the Great Depression, 1873–1896*. London: Macmillan.

Schlesinger, Arthur Jr. 2004. "The Making of a Mess." *New York Review*, September 22: 40–3.

Schumpeter, Joseph. 1954. *History of Economic Analysis*. New York: Oxford University Press.

————. 1954. *Capitalism, Socialism, and Democracy*. London: George Allen & Unwin.

————. 1961. *The Theory of Economic Development*. New York: Oxford University Press.

————. 1964. *Business Cycles: A Theoretical, Historical, and Statistical Analysis of the Capitalist Process*. New York: McGraw Hill.

Schurmann, Franz. 1974. *The Logic of World Power: An Inquiry into the Origins, Currents, and Contradictions of World Politics*. New York: Pantheon.

Segal, Adam. 2004. "Is America Losing its Edge?" *Foreign Affairs*, November–December. Available at http://www.foreignaffairs.org.

Selden, Mark. 1995. "Yan'an Communism Reconsidered." *Modern China*, 21 (1): 8–44.

————. 1997. "China, Japan and the Regional Political Economy of East Asia, 1945–1995." In P. Katzenstein and T. Shiraishi, eds, *Network Power. Japan and Asia*, pp. 306–40. Ithaca, NY: Cornell University Press.

Semmel, Bernard. 1970. *The Rise of Free Trade Imperialism*. Cambridge: Cambridge University Press.

Shaikh, Anwar. 1999. "Explaining the Global Economic Crisis." *Historical Materialism*, 5: 103–44.

Shambaugh, David. 2004. "China and Europe: The Emerging Axis." *Current History*, 103 (674): 243–8.

Shenkar, Oded. 2006. *The Chinese Century*. Upper Saddle River, NJ: Wharton School Publishing.

Shiba, Yoshinobu. 1983. "Sung Foreign Trade: Its Scope and Organization." In M. Rossabi, ed., *China among Equals: The Middle Kingdom and its Neighbors, 10th–14th Centuries*, pp. 89–115. Berkeley, CA: University of California Press.

Silver, Beverly J. 2003. *Forces of Labor: Workers' Movements and Globalization since 1870*. Cambridge: Cambridge University Press.

————. 2005. "Labor Upsurges: From Detroit to Ulsan and Beyond." *Critical Sociology*, 31 (3): 439–51.

Silver, Beverly J., and Giovanni Arrighi. 2003. "Polanyi's 'Double Movement': The *Belle Époques* of British and U.S. Hegemony Compared." *Politics and Society*, 31 (2): 325–55.

Skinner, W.G. 1985. "The Structure of Chinese History." *Journal of Asian Studies*, 44 (2): 271–92.

Sklar, Martin J. 1988. *The Corporate Reconstruction of American Capitalism, 1890–1916. The Market, the Law, and Politics*. Cambridge: Cambridge University Press.

Smith, Adam. 1961. *An Inquiry into the Nature and Causes of the Wealth of Nations*. 2 vols. London: Methuen.

Smith, Neil. 1984. *Uneven Development. Nature, Capital and the Production of Space*. Oxford: Basil Blackwell.

So, Alvin Y. 1986. *The South China Silk District*. Albany: State University of New York Press.

So, Alvin Y., and Stephen W.K. Chiu. 1995. *East Asia and the World-Economy*. Newbury Park, CA: Sage.

Soros, George. 2004. *The Bubble of American Supremacy: Correcting the Misuse of American Power*. New York: Public Affairs.

Stedman Jones, Gareth. 1972. "The History of US Imperialism." In R. Blackburn, ed., *Ideology in Social Science*, pp. 207–37. New York: Vintage.

Stiglitz, Joseph. 2002. *Globalization and its Discontents*. New York: Norton.

Stinchcombe, Arthur L. 1968. *Constructing Social Theories*. New York: Harcourt, Brace & World.

Stopford, John M., and John H. Dunning. 1983. *Multinationals: Company Performance and Global Trends*. London: Macmillan.

Strange, Susan. 1986. *Casino Capitalism*. Oxford: Basil Blackwell.

Sugihara, Kaoru. 1996. "The European Miracle and the East Asian Miracle. Towards a New Global Economic History." *Sangyo to keizai*, XI (12): 27–48.

————. 2003. "The East Asian Path of Economic Development: A Long-Term Perspective." In G. Arrighi, T. Hamashita, and M. Selden, eds, *The Resurgence of East Asia. 500, 150 and 50 Year Perspectives*, pp. 78–123. London and New York: Routledge.

————. 2004. "The State and the Industrious Revolution in Japan." Working paper no. 02/04, Global Economic History Network, Department of Economic History, London School of Economics, London.

Summers, Lawrence H. 2004. "America Overdrawn." *Foreign Policy*, 143: 46–9.

Suskind, Ron. 2004. *The Price of Loyalty: George W. Bush, the White House, and the Education of Paul O'Neill*. New York: Simon & Schuster.

Sweezy, Paul. 1946. *The Theory of Capitalist Development*. London: Dobson.

Sylos-Labini, Paolo. 1976. "Competition: The Product Markets." In T. Wilson and A.S. Skinner, eds, *The Market and the State: Essays in Honor of Adam Smith*, pp. 200–32. Oxford: Clarendon Press.

Tang, Jun. 2003–04. "Selection from Report on Poverty and Anti-Poverty in Urban China." *Chinese Sociology and Anthropology*, 36 (2–3).

Taylor, Peter. 1994. "Ten Years that Shook the World? The United Provinces as First Hegemonic State." *Sociological Perspectives*, 37 (1): 25–46.

Therborn, Göran. 1995. *European Modernity and Beyond: The Trajectory of European Societies, 1945–2000*. London: Sage Publications.

Thornton, Edward. 1835. *India, its State and Prospects*. London: Parbury, Allen & Co.

Tilly, Charles. 1985. "War Making and State Making as Organized Crime." In P.B. Evans, D. Rueschemeyer, and T. Skocpol, eds, *Bringing the State Back In*, pp.169–91. Cambridge: Cambridge University Press.

Tomlinson, B.R. 1975. "India and the British Empire, 1880–1935." *The Indian Economic and Social History Review*, 12 (4): 337–80.

Tong, W. James. 1991. *Disorder under Heaven: Collective Violence in the Ming Dynasty*. Stanford, CA: Stanford University Press.

Tronti, Mario. 1971. *Operai e capitale*. Turin: Einaudi.

Tsai, Jung-fang. 1993. *Hong Kong in Chinese History: Community and Social Unrest in the British Colony, 1842–1913*. New York: Columbia University Press.

Tsai, Kellee S. 2004. "Off Balance: The Unintended Consequences of Fiscal Federalism in China." *Journal of Chinese Political Science*, 9 (2): 7–26.

Tsiang, Ting-fu. 1967. "The English and the Opium Trade." In F. Schurmann and O. Schell, eds, *Imperial China*, pp. 132–45. New York: Vintage.

Unger, Jonathan. 2002. *The Transformation of Rural China*. Armonk, NY: M.E. Sharpe.

Urquhart, Brian. 2004. "The Good General." *New York Review*, September 23: 28–33.

Veblen, Thorstein. 1978. *The Theory of Business Enterprise*. New Brunswick, NJ: Transaction Books.

Vernon, Raymond. 1966. "International Investment and International Trade in the Product Cycle". *Quarterly Journal of Economics*, 80 (2): 190–207.

Versluysen, Eugène L. 1981. *The Political Economy of International Finance*. New York: St Martin's Press.

Wade, Robert. 1992. "East Asian Economic Success: Conflicting Perspectives, Partial Insights, Shaky Evidence." *World Politics*, 44: 270–320.

————. 2004. "Is Globalization Reducing Poverty and Inequality?" *World Development*, 32 (4): 567–89.

Wade, Robert, and Frank Veneroso. 1998. "The Asian Crisis: The High Debt Model versus the Wall Street–Treasury–IMF Complex." *New Left Review*, I/ 228: 3–22.

Wakeman, Frederic. 1985. *The Great Enterprise: The Manchu Reconstruction of Imperial Order in Seventeenth-Century China*. Berkeley, CA: University of California Press.

Walder, Andrew. 1995. "Local Governments as Industrial Firms: An Organizational Analysis of China's Transitional Economy." *American Journal of Sociology*, 101 (2): 263–301.

Walder, Andrew. 2002. "Markets and Income Inequality in Rural China: Political Advantage in an Expanding Economy." *American Sociological Review*, 67 (2): 231–53.

Waldinger, Roger, Chris Erickson, Ruth Milkman, Daniel J.B. Mitchell, Abel Valenzuela, Kent Wong, and Maurice Zeitlin. 1998. "Helots No More: A Case Study of the Justice for Janitors Campaign in Los Angeles." In K. Bronfenbrenner, S. Friedman, R.W. Hurd, R.A. Oswald, and R.L. Seeber, eds, *Organizing to Win*, pp. 102–19. Ithaca, NY: Cornell University Press.

Waley, Arthur. 1958. *The Opium War through Chinese Eyes*. London, Allen & Unwin.

Walter, Andrew. 1991. *World Power and World Money*. New York: St Martin's Press.

Wang, Gungwu. 1991. *China and the Chinese Overseas*. Singapore: Times Academic Press.

————. 1998. "Ming Foreign Relations: Southeast Asia." In Denis Twitchett and Frederick Mote, eds, *The Cambridge History of China Vol. 8 (2), The Ming Dynasty*, pp. 301–32. Cambridge: Cambridge University Press.

Wang, Hui. 2003. *China's New Order: Society, Politics and Economy in Transition*. Cambridge, MA: Harvard University Press.

————. 2006. "Depoliticized Politics, from East to West." *New Left Review*, II/41: 29–45.

Wang, Juan. 2005. "Going Beyond Township and Village Enterprises in Rural China." *Journal of Contemporary China*, 14 (42):177–87.

Wang, Yeh-chien. 1973. *Land Taxation in Imperial China, 1750–1911*. Cambridge, MA: Harvard University Press.

Washbrook, David. 1990. "South Asia, the World System, and World Capitalism." *The Journal of Asian Studies*, (49) 3: 479–508.

Weber, Max. 1961. *General Economic History*. New York: Collier.

————. 1978. *Economy and Society*. Berkeley, CA: University of California Press.

Wei, Yehua D. 2000. *Regional Development in China. States, Globalization and Inequality*. New York: Routledge.

Weigall, David. 1987. *Britain and the World, 1815–1986: A Dictionary of International Relations*. New York: Batsford.

Werhane, Patricia. 1991. *Adam Smith and his Legacy for Modern Capitalism*. New York: Oxford University Press.

West, E.G. 1964. "Adam Smith's Two Views on the Division of Labour." *Economica*, 31 (122): 23–32.

Whiting, Susan H. 2001. *Power and Wealth in Rural China: The Political Economy of Institutional Change*. Cambridge: Cambridge University Press.

Wilkins, Mira. 1970. *The Emergence of Multinational Enterprise*. Cambridge: Cambridge University Press.

Will, Pierre-Etienne, and R. Bin Wong. 1991. *Nourish the People: The State Civilian Granary System in China, 1650–1850*. Ann Arbor: University of Michigan Press.

Wills, John E. Jr. 1979. "Maritime China from Wang Chih to Shih Lang: Themes in Peripheral History." In Jonathan D. Spence and John E. Wills Jr., eds, *Conquest, Region, and Continuity in Seventeenth Century China*, pp. 203–38. New Haven, CT, and London: Yale University Press.

————. 1998. "Relations with Maritime Europeans." In Denis Twitchett and Frederick Mote, eds, *The Cambridge History of China Vol. 8 (2), The Ming Dynasty*, pp. 333–75. Cambridge: Cambridge University Press.

Winch, Donald. 1978. *Adam Smith's Politics. An Essay in Historiographic Revision*. Cambridge: Cambridge University Press.

————. 1983. "Science of the Legislator: Adam Smith and After." *The Economic Journal*, 93: 501–20.

Wolf, Eric. 1982. *Europe and the People Without History*. Berkeley, CA: University California Press.

Wong, R. Bin. 1997. *China Transformed. Historical Change and the Limits of European Experience*. Ithaca, NY: Cornell University Press.

————. 2004. "The Role of the Chinese State in Long-Distance Commerce." Working Paper no. 05/04, Global Economic History Network, Department of Economic History, London School of Economics.

Wong, Siu-lun. 1988. *Emigrant Entrepreneurs*. Hong Kong: Oxford University Press.

Wong, Young-tsu. 1983. "Security and Warfare on the China Coast: The Taiwan Question in the Seventeenth Century." *Monumenta Serica*, XXXV: 111–96.

Woo, Wing Thye. 1999. "The Real Reasons for China's Growth." *The China Journal*, 41: 115–37.

World Bank. 1984. *World Tables*. Vols. 1 and 2. Washington DC: World Bank.

—————. Various years. *World Development Indicators*. CD ROM. Washington DC: World Bank.

Wright, Steve. 2002. *Storming Heaven: Class Composition and Class Struggle in Italian Autonomist Marxism*. London: Pluto.

—————. 2004. "Children of a Lesser Marxism?" *Historical Materialism*, 12 (1): 261–76.

Wrigley, E.A. 1988. *Continuity, Chance and Change: The Character of the Industrial Revolution in England*. Cambridge: Cambridge University Press.

—————. 1989. "The Limits to Growth: Malthus and the Classical Economists." In M. S. Teitebaum and J.M. Winter, eds, *Population and Resources in Western Intellectual Traditions*. Cambridge: Cambridge University Press.

Wu, Ximing, and Jeffrey M. Perloff, 2004. "China's Income Distribution over Time: Reasons for Rising Inequality." KUDARE Working Paper 977, University of California at Berkeley. Available at SSRN: http://ssrn.com/abstract=506462.

Wu, Yuan-li, and Chun-hsi Wu. 1980. *Economic Development in Southeast Asia. The Chinese Dimension*. Stanford, CA: Hoover Institution Press.

Yang, Lien-sheng. 1952. *Money and Credit in China. A Short History*. Cambridge, MA: Harvard University Press.

Yen, Zhongping et al. 1957. *Zhongguo jindai jingjishi tongji* (Collections of Statistical Data of Modern Chinese Economic History). Beijing: Scientific Publishers.

Zhang, Binchuan. 1991. "Mingqing haishang maoyi zhengce: biguanzishou?" (The Sea Trade Policy of Ming and Qing: Closed Door and Conservative?) *Selected Essays in Chinese Maritime History* IV, pp. 45–59. Taipei: Academia Sinica.

Zolberg, Aristide R. 1995. "Response: Working-Class Dissolution." *International Labor and Working-Class History*, 47: 28–38.

INDEX